ENDORSEMENTS.

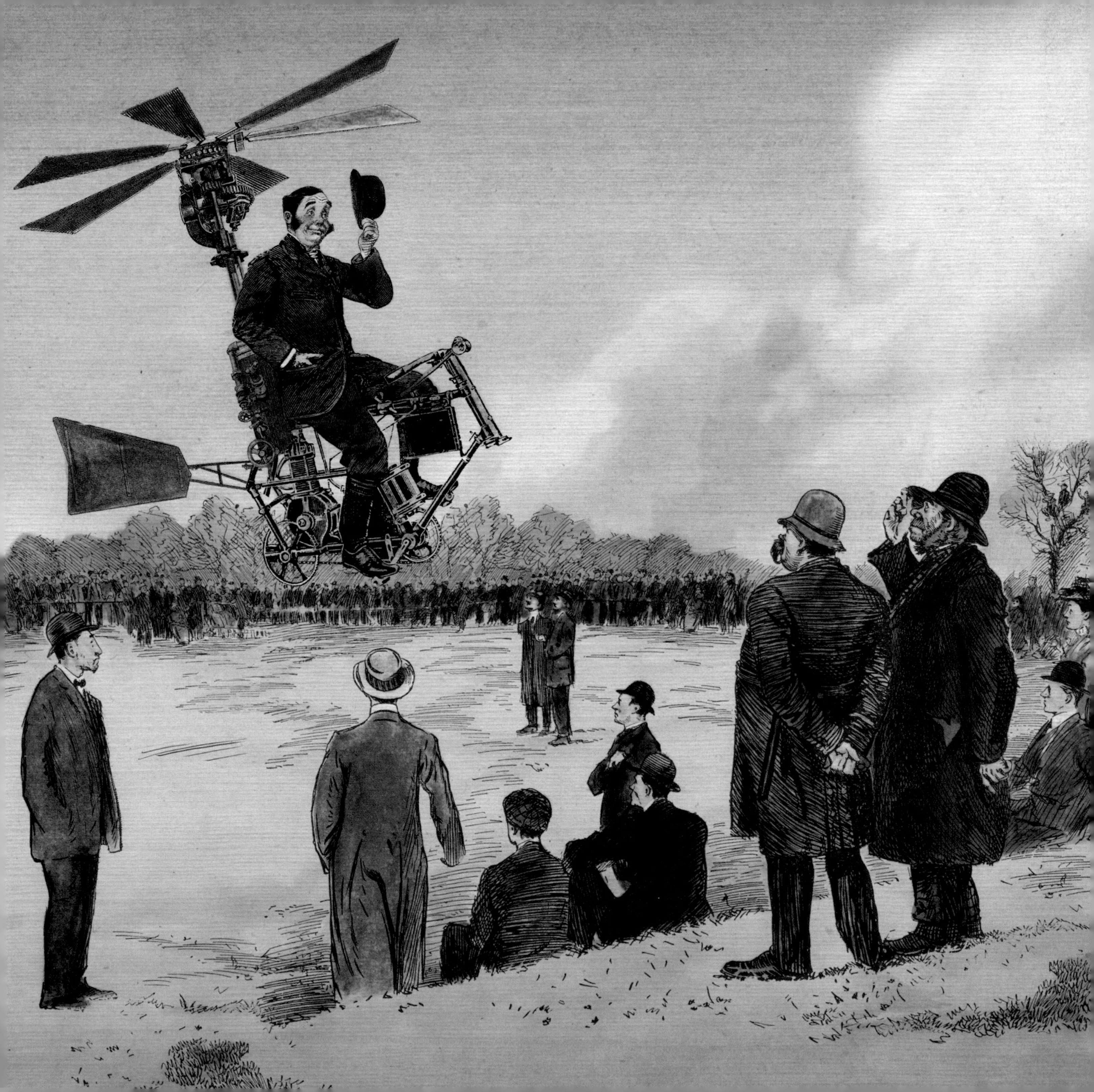

EXTRA LARGE POST CARD

Place Postage Stamp Here.

With signature only:
Domestic, 1c.
Foreign, 2c.

With message:
Domestic, 2c.
Foreign, 5c.

ON SECOND THOUGHT YOU HAD PROBABLY BETTER PUT THIS IN AN ENVELOPE.

Dapper Caps & Pedal-Copters

[Entered at the Central Post Office as Third Class Humor.]

A JOCULAR JOURNAL OF PROGRESS, INVENTIVENESS, AND DIVERSION.

WONDERMARK ENTERPRISES, Editors & Proprietors.

PUBLISHED BY
DARK HORSE BOOKS, MILWAUKIE, OREGON.

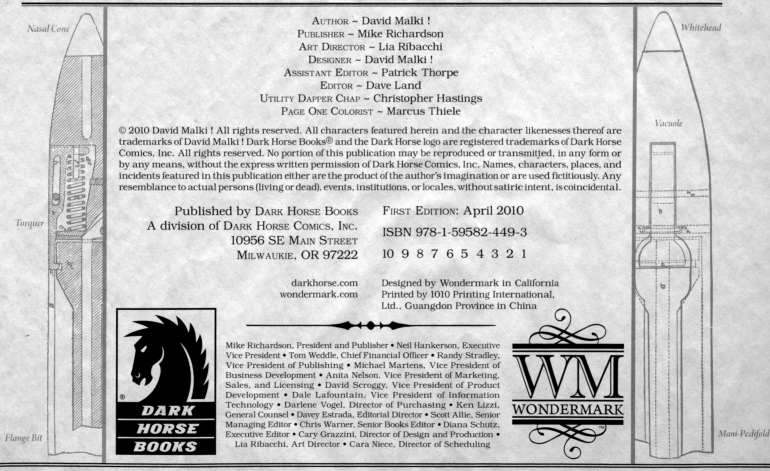

Nasal Cone

Torquer

Flange Bit

Whitehead

Vacuole

Mani-Pedifold

AUTHOR ~ David Malki !
PUBLISHER ~ Mike Richardson
ART DIRECTOR ~ Lia Ribacchi
DESIGNER ~ David Malki !
ASSISTANT EDITOR ~ Patrick Thorpe
EDITOR ~ Dave Land
UTILITY DAPPER CHAP ~ Christopher Hastings
PAGE ONE COLORIST ~ Marcus Thiele

Published by DARK HORSE BOOKS
A division of DARK HORSE COMICS, INC.
10956 SE MAIN STREET
MILWAUKIE, OR 97222

darkhorse.com
wondermark.com

FIRST EDITION: April 2010

ISBN 978-1-59582-449-3

10 9 8 7 6 5 4 3 2 1

Designed by Wondermark in California
Printed by 1010 Printing International,
Ltd., Guangdon Province in China

Dr. Pastornak continually lectures and writes for children on the subjects of science education and career guidance.

Advertisements.

Letter press, each insertion --- 75 cents an inch.
Engravings, each insertion --- $1.00 an inch.

(About eight inchlets to an inch.)

Advertisements must be received ready for printing, free of errors, spurious claims, factually inaccurate statements and medically unlikely assertions. For 25¢ more, also receive this publisher's unqualified endorsement.

KEMP'S HUMANURE CATCHER,

RESERVOIR,

and CART COMBINED.

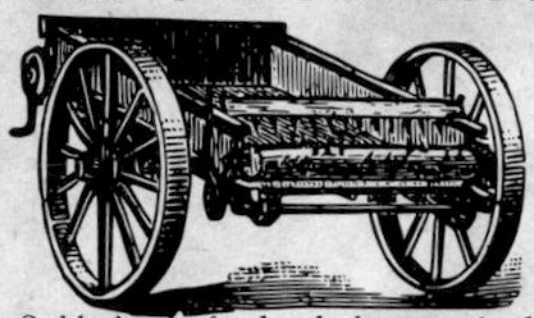

Greatest Hygienic invention of the age. Saves cleaning chamber-pots or digging outhouse trench. Fresh waste accumulates on cart, which when full is simply set ablaze and tumbled over any cliff.

Sold singly for bachelors, or in dozens for family use.

KEMP & BURPEE M'F'G CO., Syracuse, Onondago Co., N. Y.

MALLEABLE METALS AND ALLOYS FOR CASTING FEVERISH FIGURES OF FANTASIES WHATEVER YOUR TWISTED NOGGIN CONTRIVES OF

THOMAS DEVLIN & CO.

WE CAN HOLD OUR NOSE AND MAKE IT.

H. W. JOHNS' ASBESTOS DRESSINGS.

TRADE MARK

FOR SAFETY IN THE WORKSHOP, FACTORY, OUTDOORS, EVENINGS OUT, ETC.

STRICTLY FIREPROOF.

This miracle material has been formed into functional and fashionable shirts, trousers, capes, vests, over-coats and hosiery. *Never must you go without protection.*

H. W. JOHNS M'F'G CO.,

87 Maiden Lane, New York.

Sole Manufacturers of H. W. Johns' Genuine

ASBESTOS SUITS, BALL-GOWNS, TUXEDOES & SOCIETY-WEAR.

Special prices at the hundredweight. Send for sample.

EUREKA SAFETY POWER !

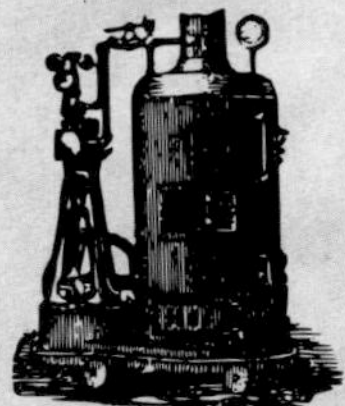

Probably **impossible to explode.** Tested to 9 lbs. pressure per square inch. Beyond that we mustn't venture, but bold machinists should "go nuts." *Guaranteed for the life of the product.* Should it fail, its life is over and our guarantee void. Still, send for circular.

B. W. PAYNE & SONS,

Corning, N. Y.

HATMAKERS.

Before buying plaster forms, see our catalog of fresh-boiled man-skulls. PAUPERS' AFTER-LIFE Ltd., Waltham, Mass.

MACHINERY

of every description. All kinds of crazy crap. We don't know what half this junk is. GEORGE'S METALLIC PILE.

The "DEVICE."

A NEW LIFTING AND NON-LIFTING MECHANISM.

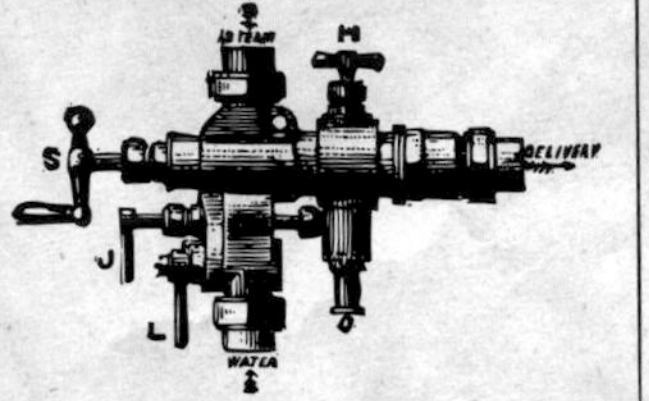

H
S
DELIVERY
J
L
WATER

Best in the World at Lifting and Non-Lifting. It lifts and then it Non-Lifts; non-lifts and, yes, lifts. Does both with dispatch.

Also Patented:

APPLIANCE

OR

Water Apparatus,

For Doing Something With Liquid.

Things and Contraptions, &c.

NATHAN & DREYFUS;

Many Uses for All These. **92 & 94 Liberty St., New York.**

LIGHT GRAY IRON DENTURES to order promptly, Plain, Bronzed, or Galvanized.

Each set coated with rust-proof paint.

LIVINGSTON D.D.S., Iron Founders, Pittsburgh, Pa.

BAIRD'S BOOKS

FOR PRACTICAL MEN.

NEW TITLES.

Brown.—*Five Hundred and Seven Metals I Invented In A Dream.* By Henry T. Brown..............................**$2.00**

Phelps.—*Dynamic Mechanical Physics, In Words Of One Syllable.* By J. C. Phelps. Illustrated...............**$1.25**

Retlock.—*The American Cottage Cheese Connoisseur.* By John Retlock. 75 engravings............................**$1.00**

Smith.—*The Fundamentals of Architecture As Expressed In Dance.* By Elwood Smith. 250 engravings........**$1.75**

Terror.—*Practical Rules for the Proportions of Modern Engines and Boilers for Use In International Villainy.* By Gen. Xavier Terror (USN Ret.)........................**$3.50**

FULL CATALOG AVAILABLE. Baird's, 613 Broadway, N. Y.

FOOT BREAKERS AND TOE CRUSHERS.

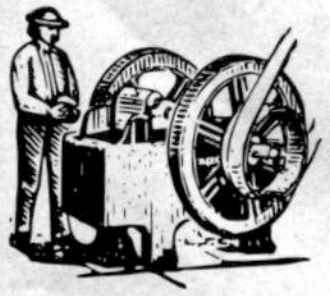

We manufacture and supply at short notice and lowest rates. Foot and Toe Crushers containing the invention described in Letters Patent, issued to Mr. S. L. Marsden, July 20th. 1880. All Crushers supplied by us are constructed under the superintendence of Mr. Marsden, who, for the past fifteen years, has been connected with the manufacture of Face Crushers in this country and England. Our devices are the strongest and most devastating commercially available outside of China. Bones will be reduced to powder; no level of healing is physically possible. Circulars sent free with inquiry.

FARREL FOUNDRY AND MACHINE CO., Manufrs., Ansonia, Conn.
COPELAND & BACON, Agents, New York.

STEMWINDING PERMUTATION LOCKS.

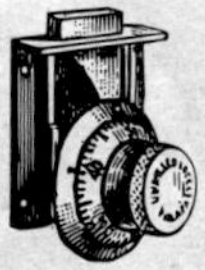

These are *keyless*, dial Locks, for *drawers, breeches, trousers, privy clothes, corsets, girdles, hosiery, nightclothes, etc.* Owner may set them on *any* 1, 2, 3, or 4 of 50 numbers. *Millions* of possible changes. Very *simple*, easily fitted. May be used upon a child of nine years; will thoroughly prevent any manner of *exploration.* Or, for use upon *bachelor daughters, comely wives traveling alone, spinster housemaids, etc.* A very great step *in advance of the best* keyed locks for security and convenience. For illustrated price list, send stamp to the manufacturers.

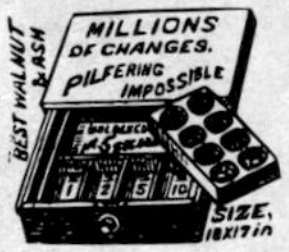

MILLIONS OF CHANGES.
PILFERING IMPOSSIBLE
BEST WALNUT & ASH
SIZE,

D. K. MILLER CHASTITY LOCK COMPANY, PHILADELPHIA, PA.

GLADWIN IMPROVED PEN OR PENCIL

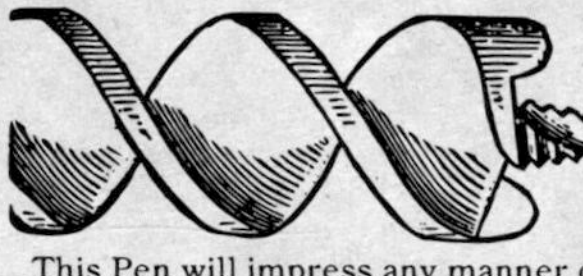

This Pen will impress any manner of permanent marks on all surfaces. Glass; gummy or knotty wood; soft metal; livestock—*the marks are indelible and sharp.* Send for catalogue. GARDNER & CHANDLER, 1321 Washington St., Boston.

CELEBRATED

HUMAN FABRICATION MACHINES

GOLEMS,

HOMUNCULUS, LICHES, &c

DR. V. FRANKENSTEIN III, ESQ.

CORRESPOND WITH US. 925 MARKET ST. PHILADELPHIA, PA. U.S.A.

AVAIL YOURSELF OF OUR LARGE STOCK.

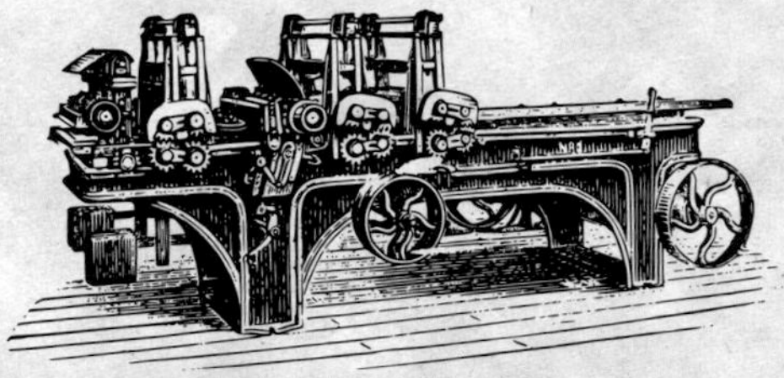

CALDER'S IMPROVED BED.

For Slumber, Marital Relations, Etc.

NEW device for gentleman of means; just patented. Oiled rollers reduce nocturnal friction 90 per cent.; prevents wear; no chafing. Optional pincers for mechanical massage after long day of Decision-making. For circulars;

WILLIAM CROWE, 409 Harrison Ave., Boston, Mass.

USED MACHINERY WIPES.

Smear oil and dirt all over anything you desire. *Guaranteed* to be filthy, nasty, & soiled—just how you *like* it, you *beast.*

BROWN M'F'G CO., 33 Central St., Providence, R. I.

Address all these things in your letter. You know yourself best. Godspeed to you.

Contents.

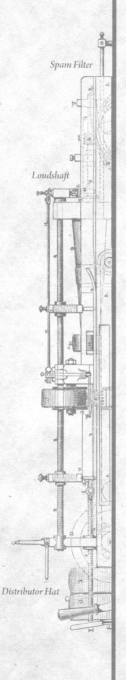

Spam Filter
Loudshaft
Distributor Hat

Tax Bracket
Rose Axle
K'Nex
Ignition Dingus

along the way. There will be tensions, and rivalries, and companies will try to buy you out, or bury your discoveries.

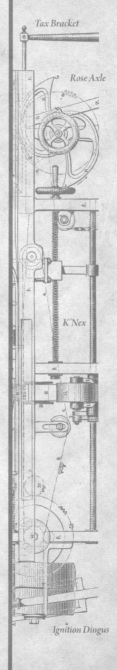

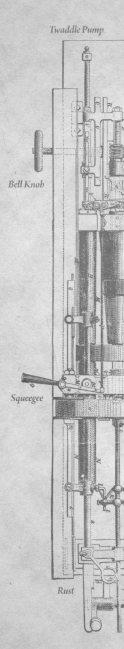

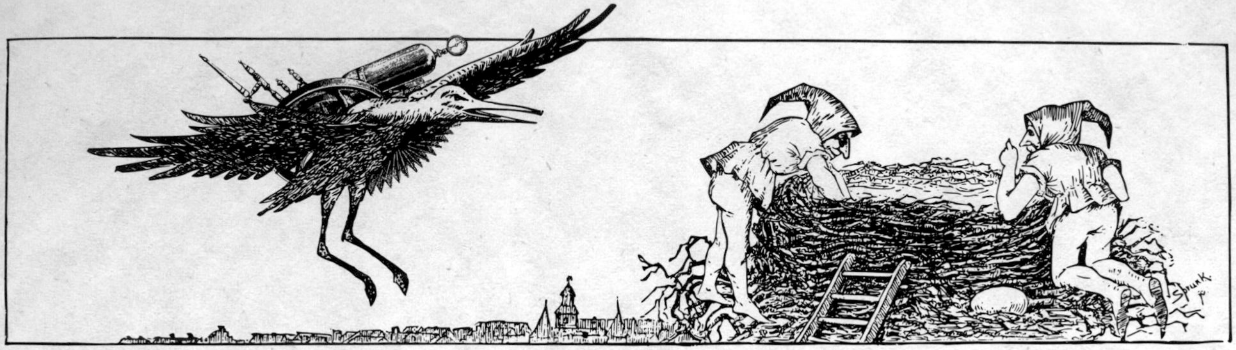

Twaddle Pump
Bell Knob
Squeegee
Rust

Preface.

A BRIEF EXPLANATION OF THE WHY AND HOW.

During the last few years we have seen an incredible gain in humanity's progress over the mean, once-untamable world. Throngs of birds that once plagued our cities are being systematically exterminated by the addition of window-laden sky-scrapers. Greater and greater engines are being built to take advantage of Cruel Aunt Earth's inexhaustible and bothersomely-abundant resource: coal. In one college in St. Louis, the students are turning up to classes with coal in their jacket-pockets; it had fallen from their walls in the night. The clever professors have turned the bother into an exercise in engineering, challenging the students to design a furnace to dispose of all this excess at minimal cost to the school. The result is a monstrous behemoth that runs day and night, producing no useful output save for handily eliminating the problem of the surplus material. Some have suggested that the engine be used to generate electricity for the lamps, which are now required at all hours to penetrate the cloud-cover exhausted by the engine, but these few cranks have wisely been shouted down by the mass.

Truly we have wrought ourselves an age of plenty. Science rules the roost; all queries now raised are subject immediately to rational examination by the best minds on the topic, and answers are commonplace. We have taken a legacy left to us by backwards ancestors fumbling in firelight, run it through a press, set it to type, distributed it to all corners of the globe by wire, radio, steam-train, and gossip, set the population of the globe on its improvement, and finally produced a million units of Future in our up-to-date factories. We have seized Apollo, milled him in steel and brass, and called him Edison; we have conquered Zeus, stomped on his crown, fashioned him a toga of the American Constitution in linotype, and paraded him through our streets to be mocked. Enjoy this collection of comic strips!

strongly enough: in order for this to have *any* chance of success, YOU ALL MUST DO THIS. There will be mistakes

OUR READERS ARE no doubt familiar with the much-praised Sandoval Method of rapid reading, which looks to be a great improvement on the current ("tortoisonal") method and which we have every confidence will soon be widely used in every office and schoolhouse in the land. We have prepared the text below so that our book may easily be read by Sandoval practitioners in the future, and thus be spared the obsolescence that imminently threatens much of the media extant today. ♛

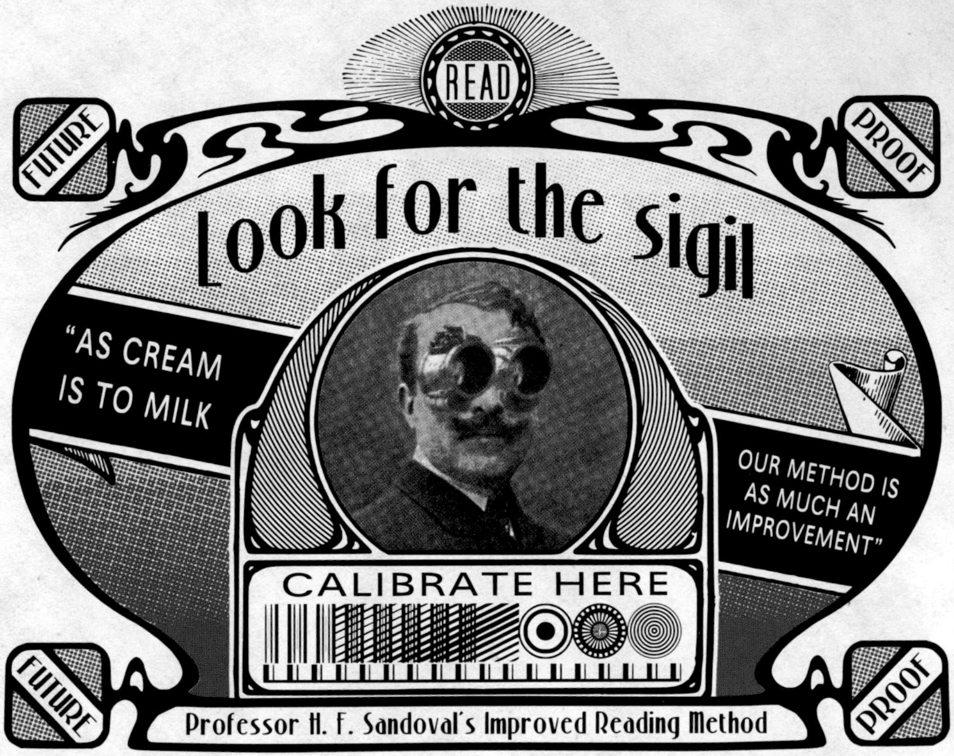
READ
FUTURE
PROOF
Look for the sigil
"AS CREAM IS TO MILK
OUR METHOD IS AS MUCH AN IMPROVEMENT"
CALIBRATE HERE
FUTURE
PROOF
Professor H. F. Sandoval's Improved Reading Method

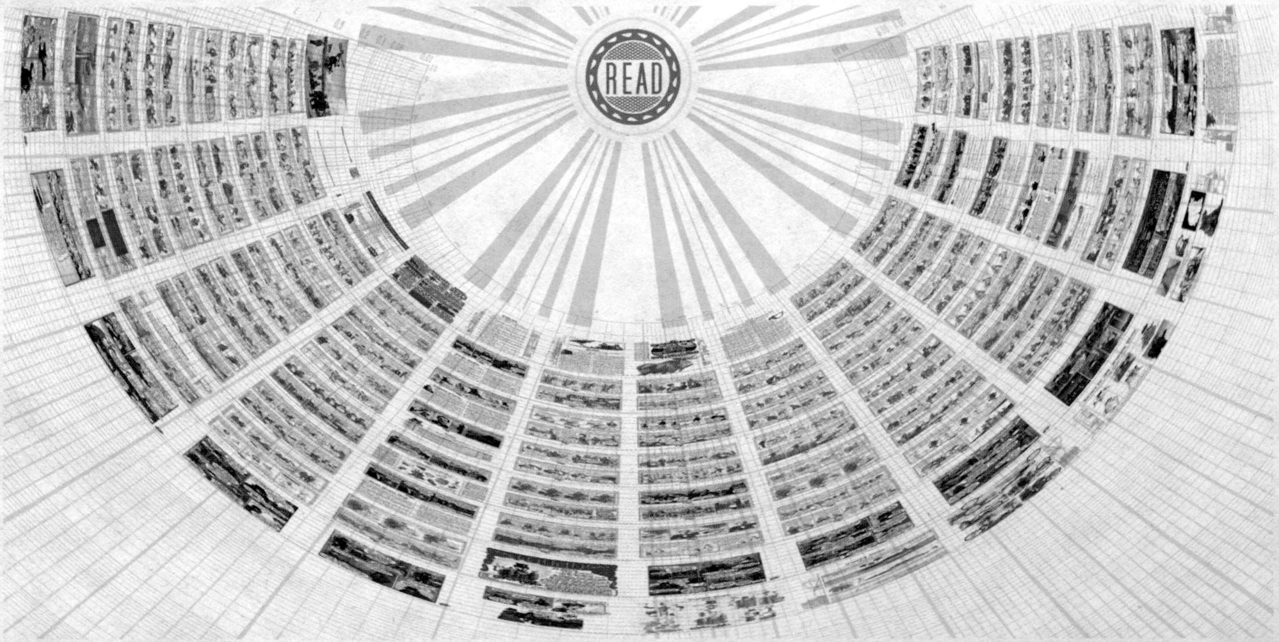
READ

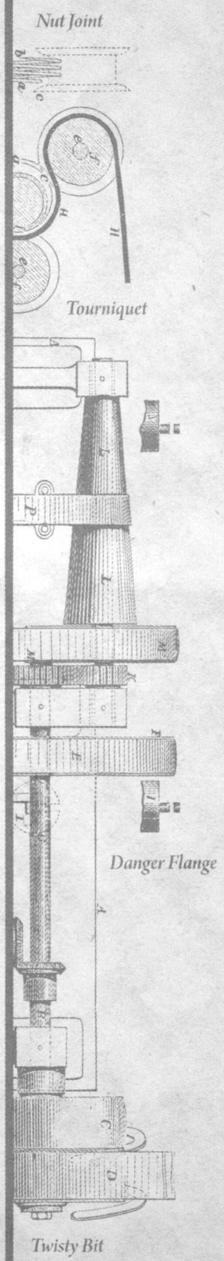
Nut Joint
Tourniquet
Danger Flange
Twisty Bit

ter is coming up. If only a few of you children heed my words, I fear it will not be sufficient. I cannot emphasize this

OFFICIAL.

INDEX OF TOPICAL REFERENCES

FOR WHICH

Contextual Information is Required.

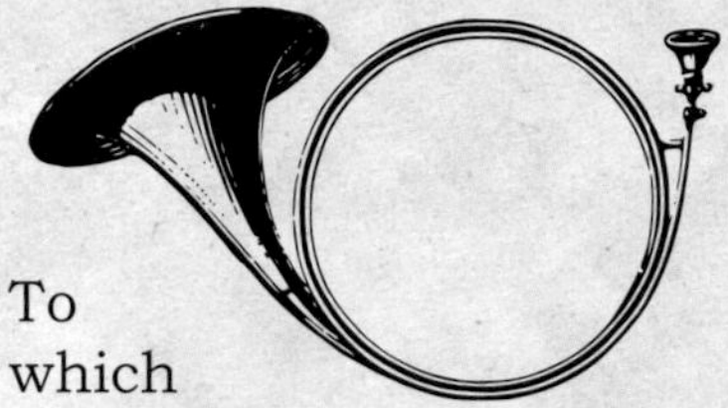

Collections such as these both accentuate the deficiencies of the past and give us a realization of our present advantages. In many cases, the work on the pages to come includes allusions that presuppose a familiarity on the part of the reader with events contemporaneous to the initial publishing—contextual information lost in a volume such as this. To rectify this, we have emblazoned the emblem at right near the comics for which some background information may aid in the reader's full understanding. There is no shame in accepting this aid; it is offered freely and without judgment, and no accusation regarding the reader's ability for comprehension should be inferred.

On the pages to come, a number within the emblem will correspond with the list on this page.

1.—No special information for this comic; just wanted to be sure you're clear on how this system works. Okay, let's go!

2.—This comic originally ran on Columbus Day. Again, not a terribly important detail, but we're still ramping up the system. All right—now the training wheels are off.

3.—The iPhone, with its bevy of apps, was still a gleam in Steve Jobs' Chinese manufacturers' eyes when this comic originally ran. Still waiting on my tire gauge though.

4.—In retrospect, even *I* shouldn't have cared about this.

5.—This begins a series of holiday-themed comics. The comics in this book may well be labeled my "tied to a specific calendar event" period.

6.—My mother assures me that this is exactly what I said.

7.—The very next day the senator resigned in disgrace.

8.—By this point, the Writers Guild strike had left viewers without scripted television programming for several months, and the contractually-mandated return of some shows (even without writers) was greeted with enthusiasm.

9.—For a while, hipsters would carry these everywhere to voice support for the revolution. They were *so serious* too.

10.—This comic ran even before Barack Obama went on to make "change" his campaign rallying cry. Maybe it gave him the idea.

11.—Another day-and-date comic, this one for St. Patrick's Day. Previous themed comics (you may have noticed) referenced Valentine's Day and Martin Luther King Jr. Day.

12.—The Olympics still capture the world's attention every four years, for reasons that are beyond many.

13.—This was before we realized the truth about her face.

14.—All this Obama material is going to age really well. Like "Bloom County" talking about Reagan. I can't wait.

15.—The day you read this, America will still probably be at war in Afghanistan. But in case it isn't, well, it was.

16.—It is hard to recall the mood surrounding the very first bailout; it was novel. But now there have been so many.

17.—There came a point when I grew sick of politics.

18.—As you might guess, this comic ran on Election Day.

19.—"Robocalls" was a cute term for a galling practice.

20.—Everybody thought they were changing the world.

member: there will be plenty of time for that once people are living forever. Here—the space for you to write your let-

IN WHICH BILL SUFFERS A SUDDEN ATTACK

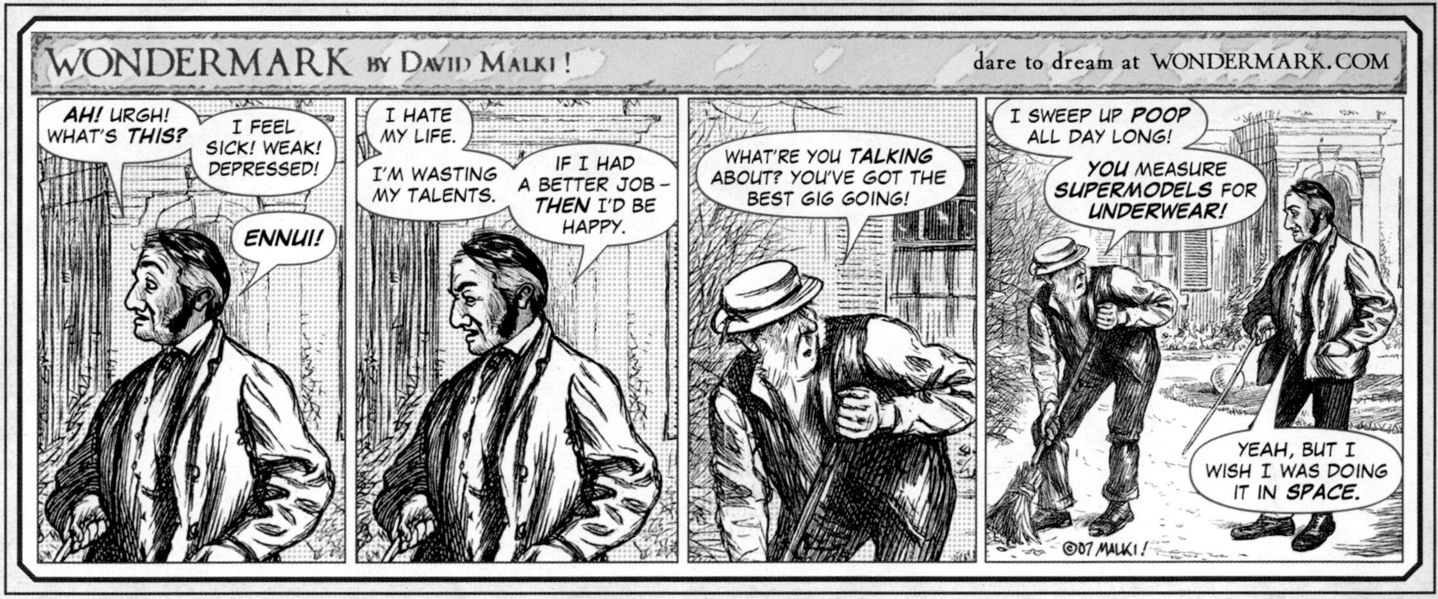
WONDERMARK BY DAVID MALKI !
dare to dream at WONDERMARK.COM
AH! URGH! WHAT'S THIS?
I FEEL SICK! WEAK! DEPRESSED!
ENNUI!
I HATE MY LIFE.
I'M WASTING MY TALENTS.
IF I HAD A BETTER JOB – THEN I'D BE HAPPY.
WHAT'RE YOU TALKING ABOUT? YOU'VE GOT THE BEST GIG GOING!
I SWEEP UP POOP ALL DAY LONG!
YOU MEASURE SUPERMODELS FOR UNDERWEAR!
YEAH, BUT I WISH I WAS DOING IT IN SPACE.
©07 MALKI !

floating around, tape measure curling in zero-G like a wispy line of yellow smoke—THAT's the stuff

IN WHICH RICK HAS HIS SUSPICIONS

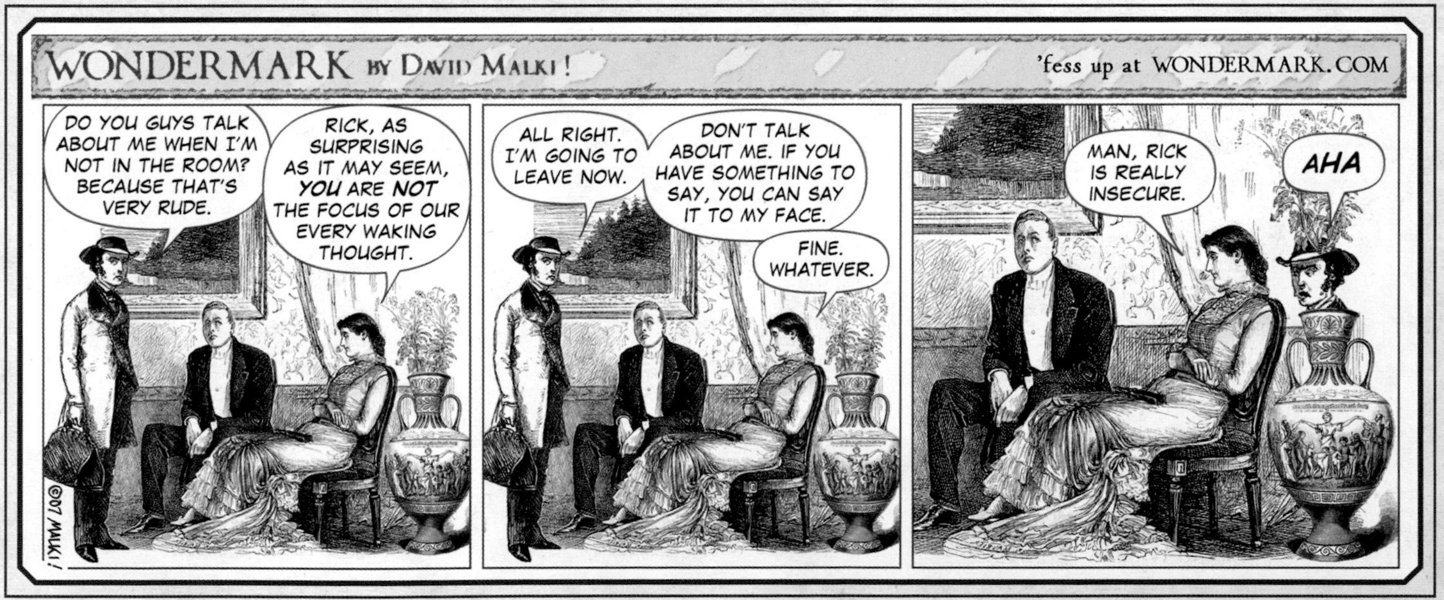
WONDERMARK BY DAVID MALKI !
'fess up at WONDERMARK.COM
DO YOU GUYS TALK ABOUT ME WHEN I'M NOT IN THE ROOM? BECAUSE THAT'S VERY RUDE.
RICK, AS SURPRISING AS IT MAY SEEM, YOU ARE NOT THE FOCUS OF OUR EVERY WAKING THOUGHT.
©07 MALKI !
ALL RIGHT. I'M GOING TO LEAVE NOW.
DON'T TALK ABOUT ME. IF YOU HAVE SOMETHING TO SAY, YOU CAN SAY IT TO MY FACE.
FINE. WHATEVER.
MAN, RICK IS REALLY INSECURE.
AHA

dude in the middle is just gonna stay out of this one

1

start, the easier it will be for you to resist the temptations of the world and its toxic pro-intimacy propaganda. Re-

IN WHICH THE BANQUET GETS AWKWARD

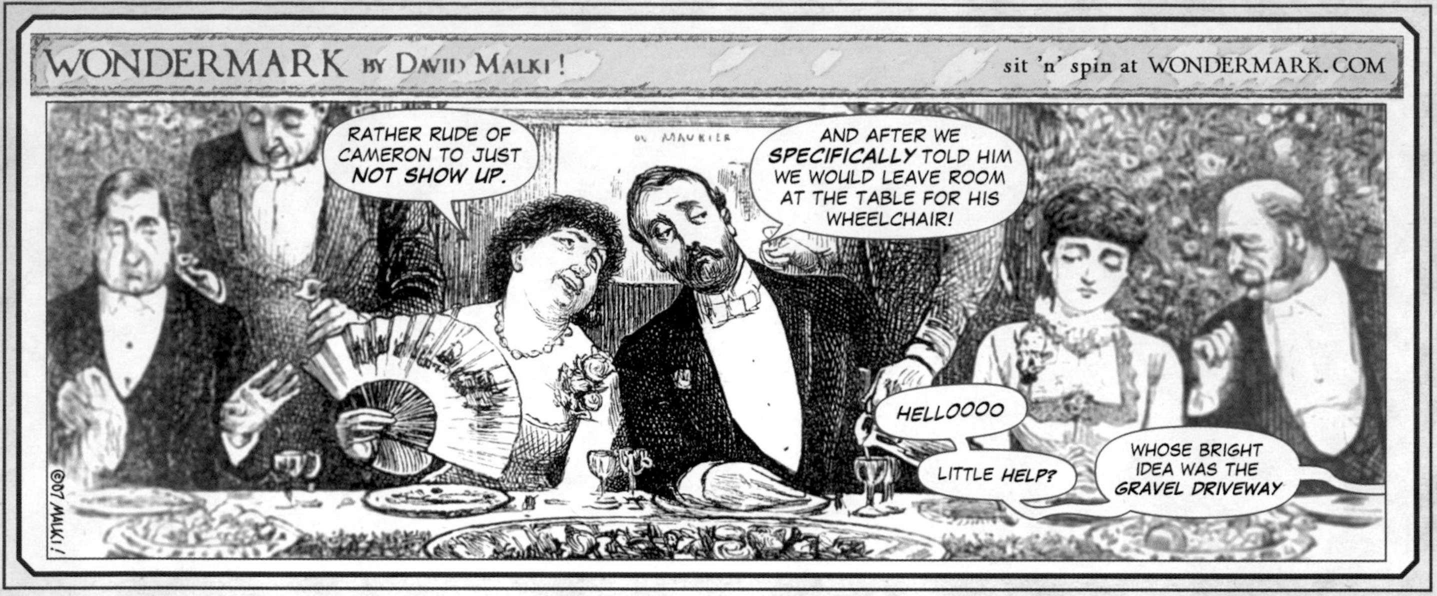
WONDERMARK BY DAVID MALKI !
sit 'n' spin at WONDERMARK.COM
RATHER RUDE OF CAMERON TO JUST NOT SHOW UP.
AND AFTER WE SPECIFICALLY TOLD HIM WE WOULD LEAVE ROOM AT THE TABLE FOR HIS WHEELCHAIR!
HELLOOOO
LITTLE HELP?
WHOSE BRIGHT IDEA WAS THE GRAVEL DRIVEWAY
©07 MALKI !

the man on the far left is declining a refill from a jeweled vial of tears collected from the woman second from right

IN WHICH THE HOLIDAY HERALDS DISSENT

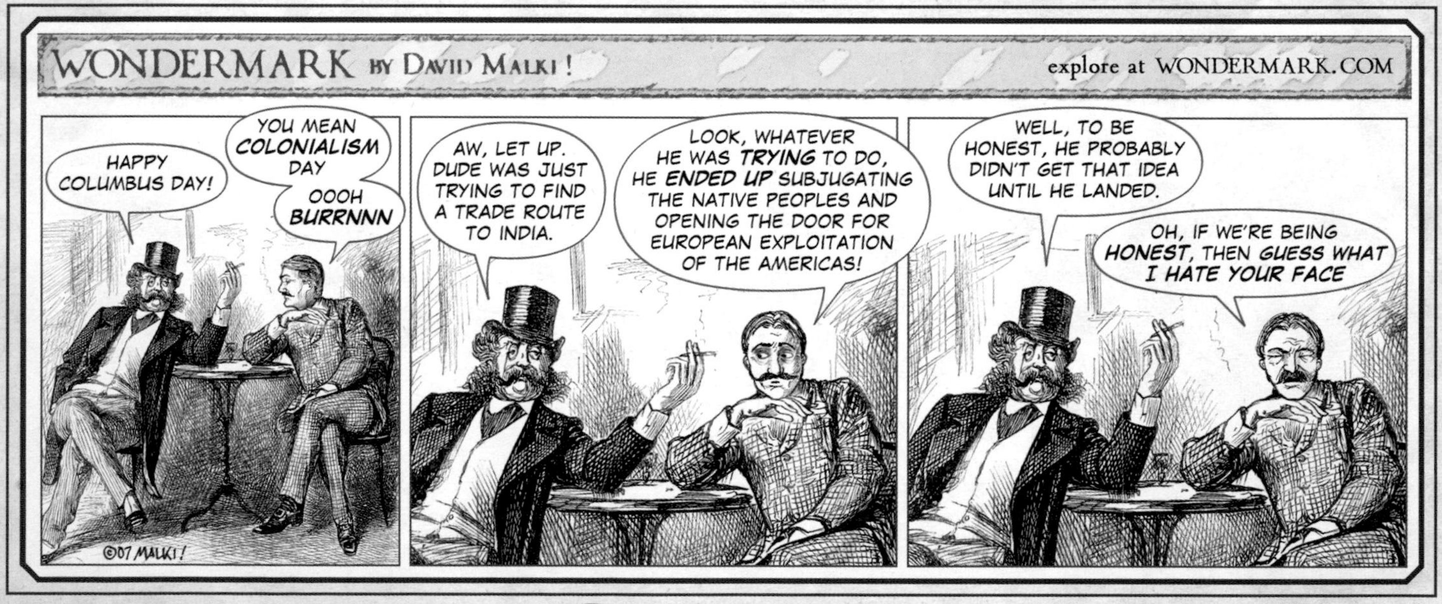
WONDERMARK BY DAVID MALKI !
explore at WONDERMARK.COM
HAPPY COLUMBUS DAY!
YOU MEAN COLONIALISM DAY
OOOH BURRNNN
AW, LET UP. DUDE WAS JUST TRYING TO FIND A TRADE ROUTE TO INDIA.
LOOK, WHATEVER HE WAS TRYING TO DO, HE ENDED UP SUBJUGATING THE NATIVE PEOPLES AND OPENING THE DOOR FOR EUROPEAN EXPLOITATION OF THE AMERICAS!
WELL, TO BE HONEST, HE PROBABLY DIDN'T GET THAT IDEA UNTIL HE LANDED.
OH, IF WE'RE BEING HONEST, THEN GUESS WHAT I HATE YOUR FACE
©07 MALKI !

not my face! the one thing i can never change! (besides my lucky underpants)

of biology, chemistry, pharmacology, and related fields, and to immerse yourself in them utterly—for the earlier you

WONDERMARK BY DAVID MALKI !
beat the crowd at WONDERMARK.COM
TIRED OF NINJA MONKEY ROBOTS FIGHTING ZOMBIE PIRATE JESUS? SO'S EVERYBODY! THAT'S WHY WE'VE COMPILED, FOR HANDY REFERENCE, NEXT YEAR'S MEMES!
GET A HEAD START!
DEEP-SEA DIVERS
BEFUDDLED WIZARDS
TREASURES OF ANTIQUITY
NAUGHTY JESTERS
GENDARMES
SULTANS/ CALIPHS
BEARS IN ILL-FITTING HATS
THIS GUY
©07 MALKI !

Color by Carly Monardo • whirringblender.com

not pictured: WWI-era German officers in pointy helmets, fakirs, stripes-wearing prisoners complete with shackles and iron balls, Larry Flynt

INTERNATIONAL FRATERNAL CORPS OF BEARS IN ILL-FITTING HATS

MEMBERSHIP APPLICATION

1. Name Joseph Gabbeford

2a. Are you a bear? (YES) *NO* *2b. If yes, type of bear* Brown *If no, STOP. Discard this application.*

3a. Do you wear a hat? YES ~~NO~~ *3b. If yes, type of hat* Gold Fa Pamma *If no, STOP. Discard this application.*

4a. Your actual hat size (estimate if unsure) 30? *4b. Size of the hat that you wear* 8¼

5. Subtract 4a from 4b. Result: -21 3/4

2 to -2: STOP. Discard this application.
2⅛ to 5 or -2⅛ to -5: A representative will contact you for further interviewing.
5⅛ and greater, or -5⅛ and smaller: AUTOMATIC APPROVAL.
Please remit your membership dues in the attached envelope.
Payment types accepted: Legal tender; notes of credit; honey.
Due to new postal regulations, BERRIES ARE NO LONGER ACCEPTED.

Also See Pages 94-95

to keep your priorities straight; you can even put it in your letter if you like. Resolve to commit yourself to the studies

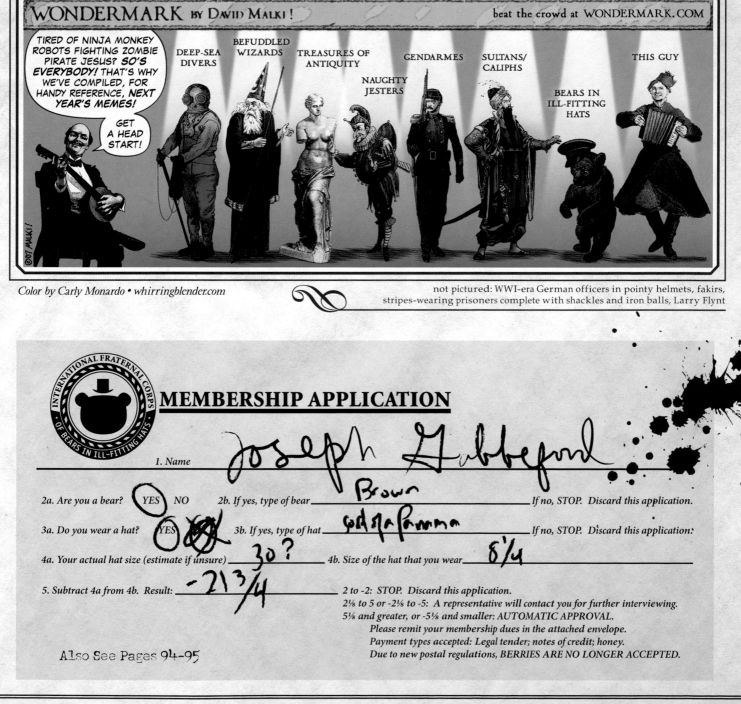

IN WHICH CONCOCTIONS ARE PEDDLED

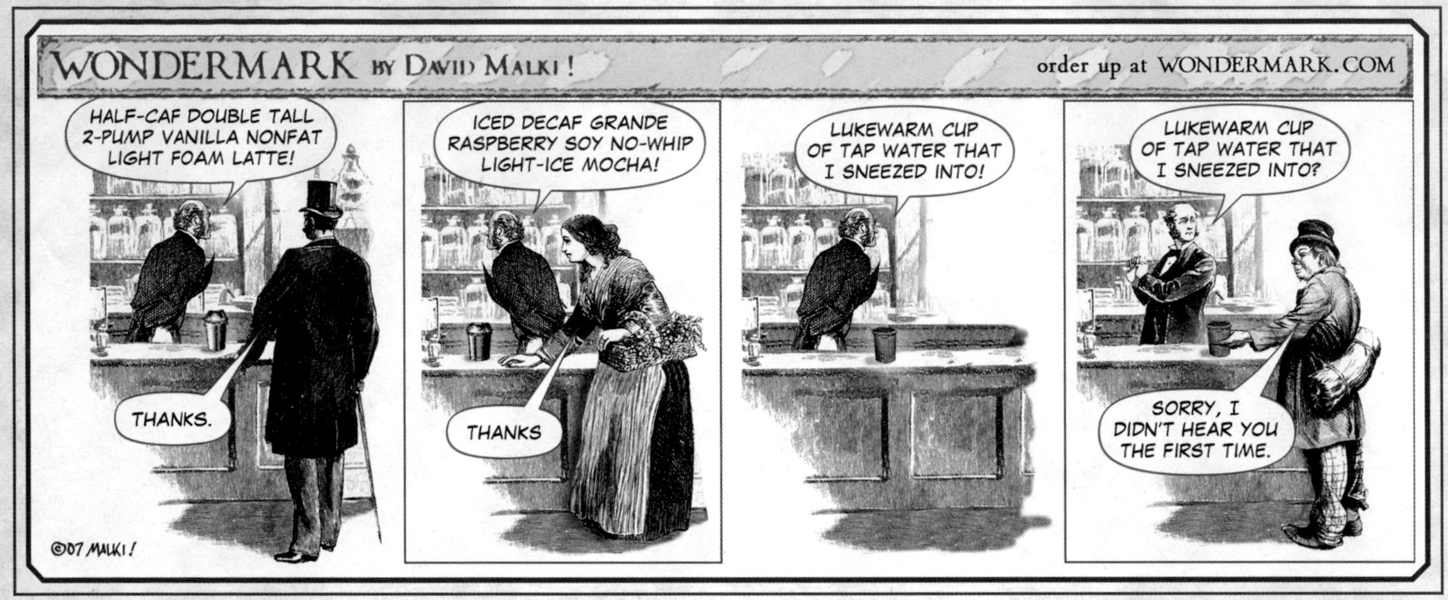
WONDERMARK BY DAVID MALKI !
order up at WONDERMARK.COM
HALF-CAF DOUBLE TALL 2-PUMP VANILLA NONFAT LIGHT FOAM LATTE!
THANKS.
ICED DECAF GRANDE RASPBERRY SOY NO-WHIP LIGHT-ICE MOCHA!
THANKS
LUKEWARM CUP OF TAP WATER THAT I SNEEZED INTO!
LUKEWARM CUP OF TAP WATER THAT I SNEEZED INTO?
SORRY, I DIDN'T HEAR YOU THE FIRST TIME.
©07 MALKI !

it cost $3.85

IN WHICH IT'S WHAT MONTH ALREADY?

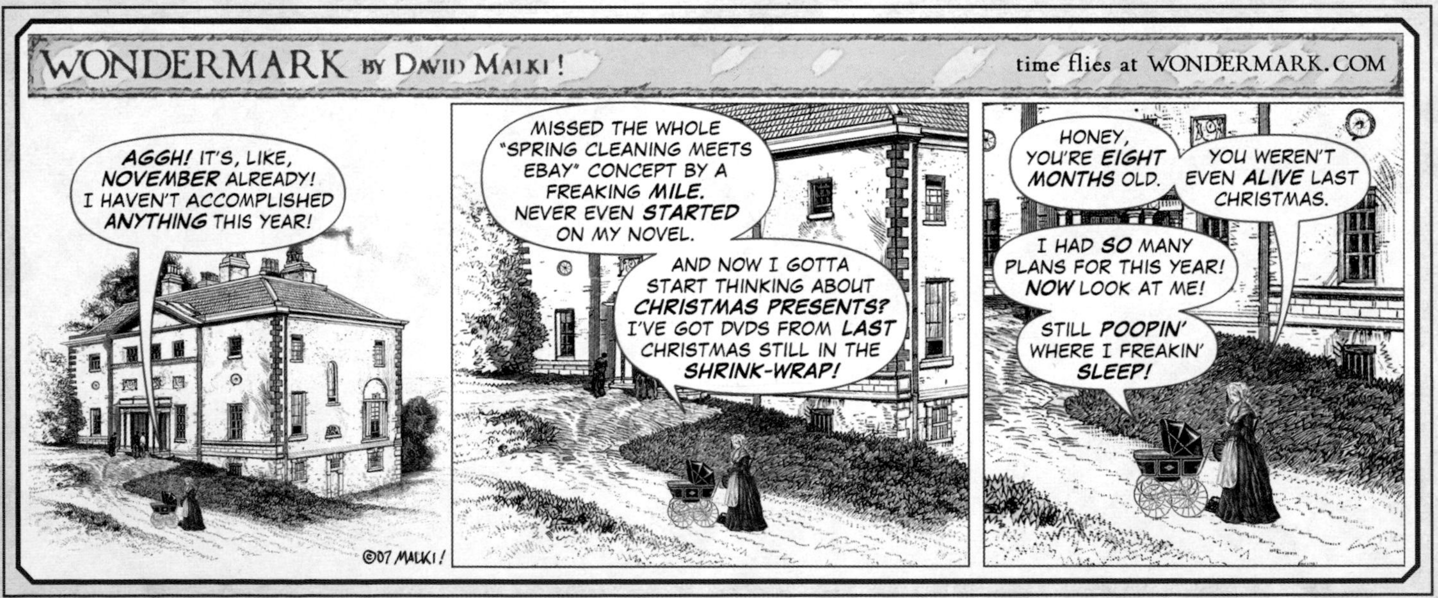
WONDERMARK BY DAVID MALKI !
time flies at WONDERMARK.COM
AGGH! IT'S, LIKE, NOVEMBER ALREADY! I HAVEN'T ACCOMPLISHED ANYTHING THIS YEAR!
MISSED THE WHOLE "SPRING CLEANING MEETS EBAY" CONCEPT BY A FREAKING MILE. NEVER EVEN STARTED ON MY NOVEL.
AND NOW I GOTTA START THINKING ABOUT CHRISTMAS PRESENTS? I'VE GOT DVDS FROM LAST CHRISTMAS STILL IN THE SHRINK-WRAP!
HONEY, YOU'RE EIGHT MONTHS OLD.
YOU WEREN'T EVEN ALIVE LAST CHRISTMAS.
I HAD SO MANY PLANS FOR THIS YEAR! NOW LOOK AT ME!
STILL POOPIN' WHERE I FREAKIN' SLEEP!
©07 MALKI !

seems like i did learn to talk pretty well in that time, though, which in itself is sort of a coup

mous from your discoveries. Fame draws to itself love; the opposite is never true. Remember this whenever you need

IN WHICH THIS IS LIFE, NOW

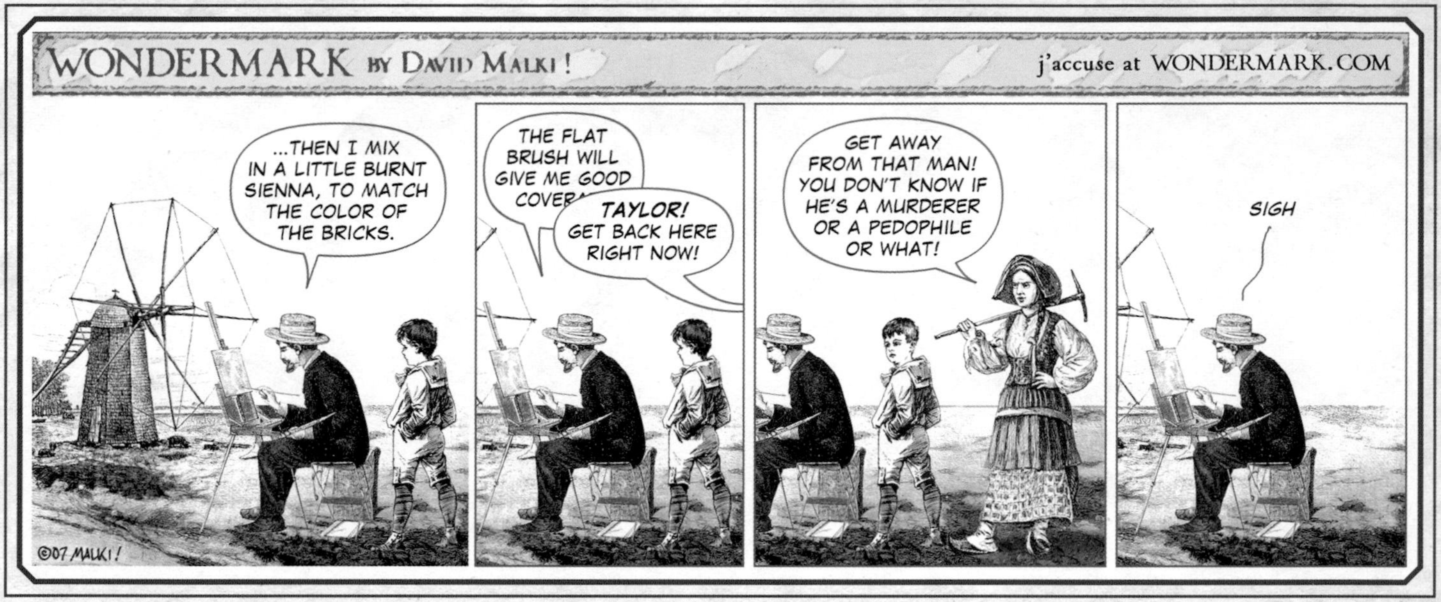
WONDERMARK BY DAVID MALKI !
j'accuse at WONDERMARK.COM
...THEN I MIX IN A LITTLE BURNT SIENNA, TO MATCH THE COLOR OF THE BRICKS.
THE FLAT BRUSH WILL GIVE ME GOOD COVERA
TAYLOR! GET BACK HERE RIGHT NOW!
GET AWAY FROM THAT MAN! YOU DON'T KNOW IF HE'S A MURDERER OR A PEDOPHILE OR WHAT!
SIGH
©07 MALKI!

i suppose it would just be depressing to keep a tally of how often this happens to me

IN WHICH REGINALD ALLAYS VARIOUS CONCERNS

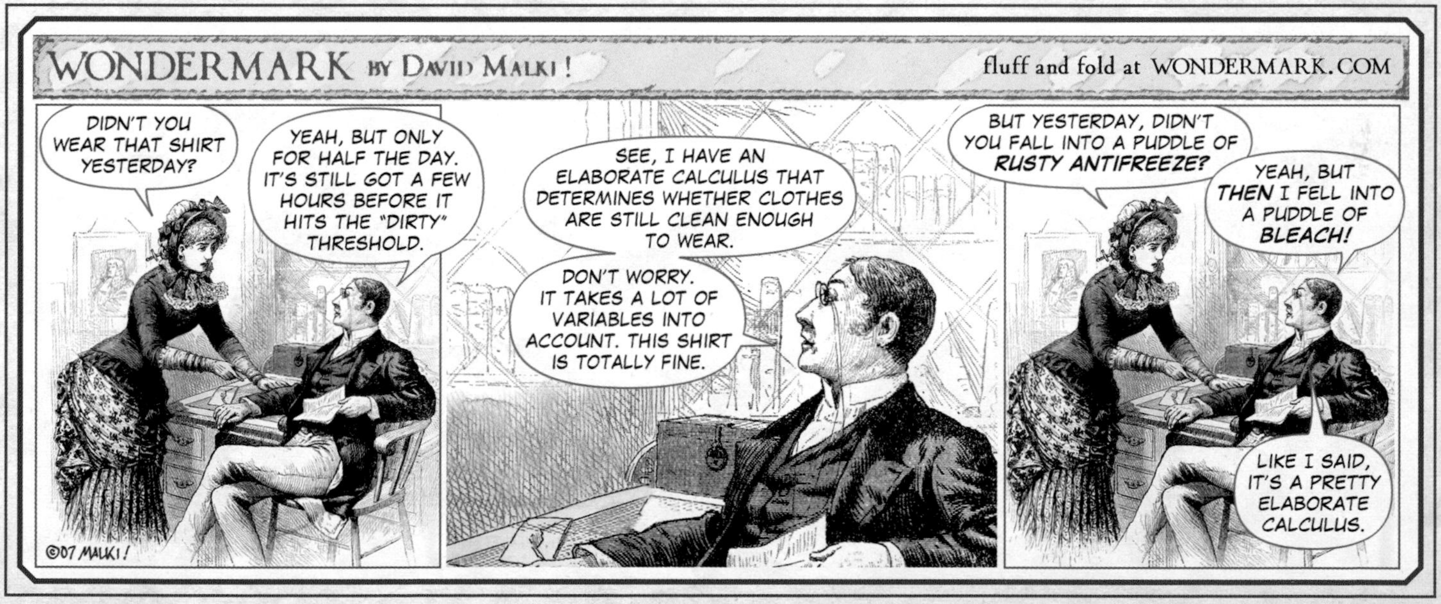
WONDERMARK BY DAVID MALKI !
fluff and fold at WONDERMARK.COM
DIDN'T YOU WEAR THAT SHIRT YESTERDAY?
YEAH, BUT ONLY FOR HALF THE DAY. IT'S STILL GOT A FEW HOURS BEFORE IT HITS THE "DIRTY" THRESHOLD.
SEE, I HAVE AN ELABORATE CALCULUS THAT DETERMINES WHETHER CLOTHES ARE STILL CLEAN ENOUGH TO WEAR.
DON'T WORRY. IT TAKES A LOT OF VARIABLES INTO ACCOUNT. THIS SHIRT IS TOTALLY FINE.
BUT YESTERDAY, DIDN'T YOU FALL INTO A PUDDLE OF **RUSTY ANTIFREEZE?**
YEAH, BUT **THEN** I FELL INTO A PUDDLE OF **BLEACH!**
LIKE I SAID, IT'S A PRETTY ELABORATE CALCULUS.
©07 MALKI!

apparently the word 'calculus' is also the term for dental tartar.
DOUBLE-MEANING COMIC TODAY FOLKS

teenager, with predictable results. *Grow up.* There will be other, better lovers for you in the future, once you are fa-

IN WHICH INNOVATION IS SUDDEN

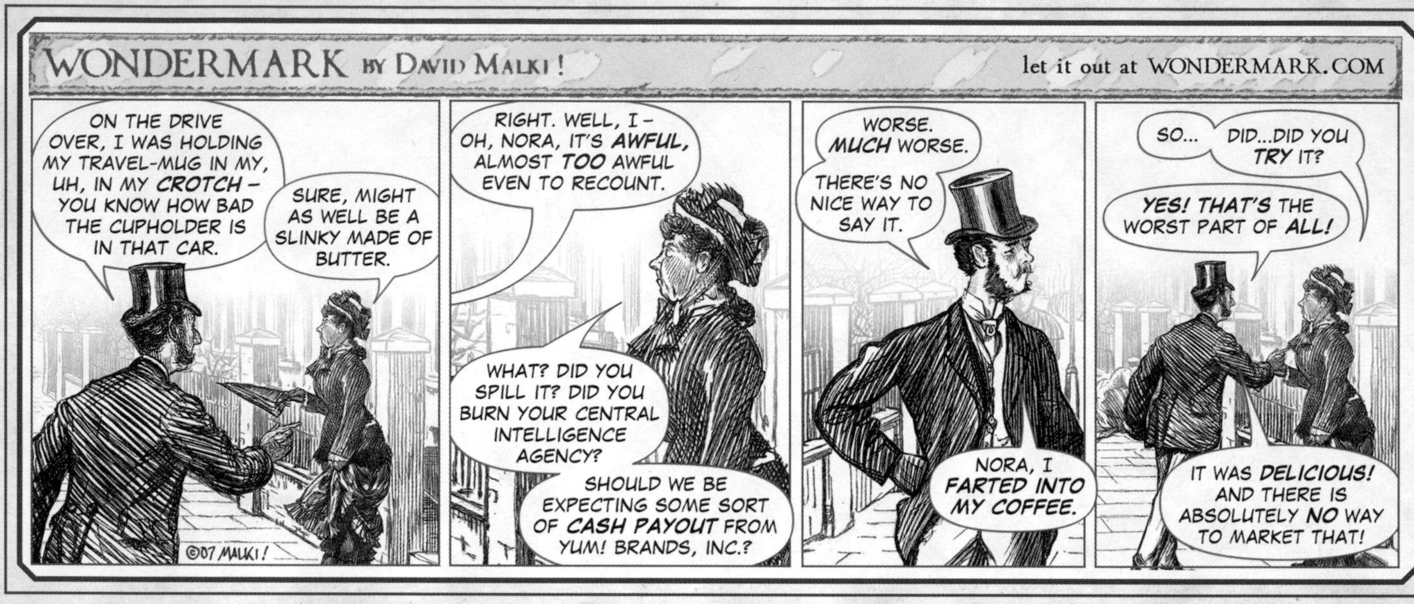
WONDERMARK BY DAVID MALKI !
let it out at WONDERMARK.COM
ON THE DRIVE OVER, I WAS HOLDING MY TRAVEL-MUG IN MY, UH, IN MY **CROTCH** – YOU KNOW HOW BAD THE CUPHOLDER IS IN THAT CAR.
SURE, MIGHT AS WELL BE A SLINKY MADE OF BUTTER.
©07 MALKI!
RIGHT. WELL, I – OH, NORA, IT'S **AWFUL,** ALMOST **TOO** AWFUL EVEN TO RECOUNT.
WHAT? DID YOU SPILL IT? DID YOU BURN YOUR CENTRAL INTELLIGENCE AGENCY?
SHOULD WE BE EXPECTING SOME SORT OF **CASH PAYOUT** FROM YUM! BRANDS, INC.?
WORSE. **MUCH** WORSE.
THERE'S NO NICE WAY TO SAY IT.
NORA, I **FARTED INTO MY COFFEE.**
SO...
DID...DID YOU **TRY** IT?
YES! THAT'S THE WORST PART OF **ALL!**
IT WAS **DELICIOUS!** AND THERE IS ABSOLUTELY **NO** WAY TO MARKET THAT!

i guess with enough blinking banner ads nothing is IMPOSSIBLE to market

IN WHICH MUCH IS LEARNED

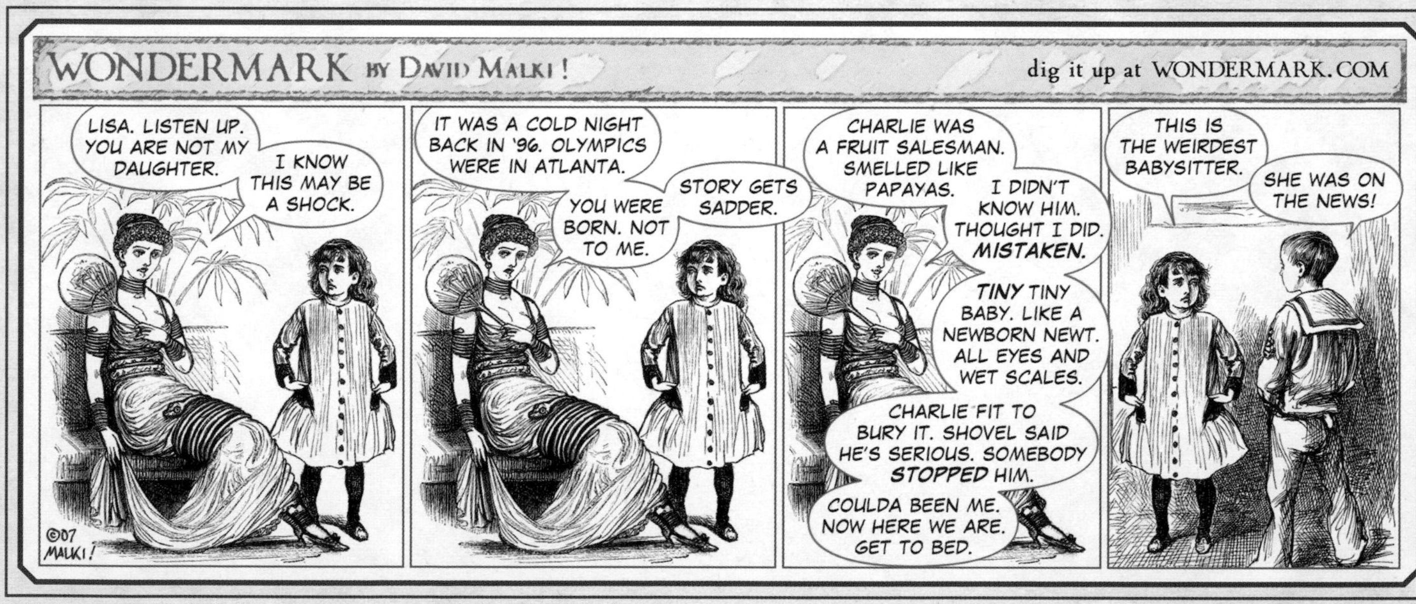
WONDERMARK BY DAVID MALKI !
dig it up at WONDERMARK.COM
LISA. LISTEN UP. YOU ARE NOT MY DAUGHTER.
I KNOW THIS MAY BE A SHOCK.
©07 MALKI!
IT WAS A COLD NIGHT BACK IN '96. OLYMPICS WERE IN ATLANTA.
STORY GETS SADDER.
YOU WERE BORN. NOT TO ME.
CHARLIE WAS A FRUIT SALESMAN. SMELLED LIKE PAPAYAS.
I DIDN'T KNOW HIM. THOUGHT I DID. **MISTAKEN.**
TINY TINY BABY. LIKE A NEWBORN NEWT. ALL EYES AND WET SCALES.
CHARLIE FIT TO BURY IT. SHOVEL SAID HE'S SERIOUS. SOMEBODY **STOPPED** HIM.
COULDA BEEN ME. NOW HERE WE ARE. GET TO BED.
THIS IS THE WEIRDEST BABYSITTER.
SHE WAS ON THE NEWS!

so are we!

put off going to college, and dally around taking odd jobs, and get yourself romantically entangled with some moronic

IN WHICH A TALE IS MADE LAME

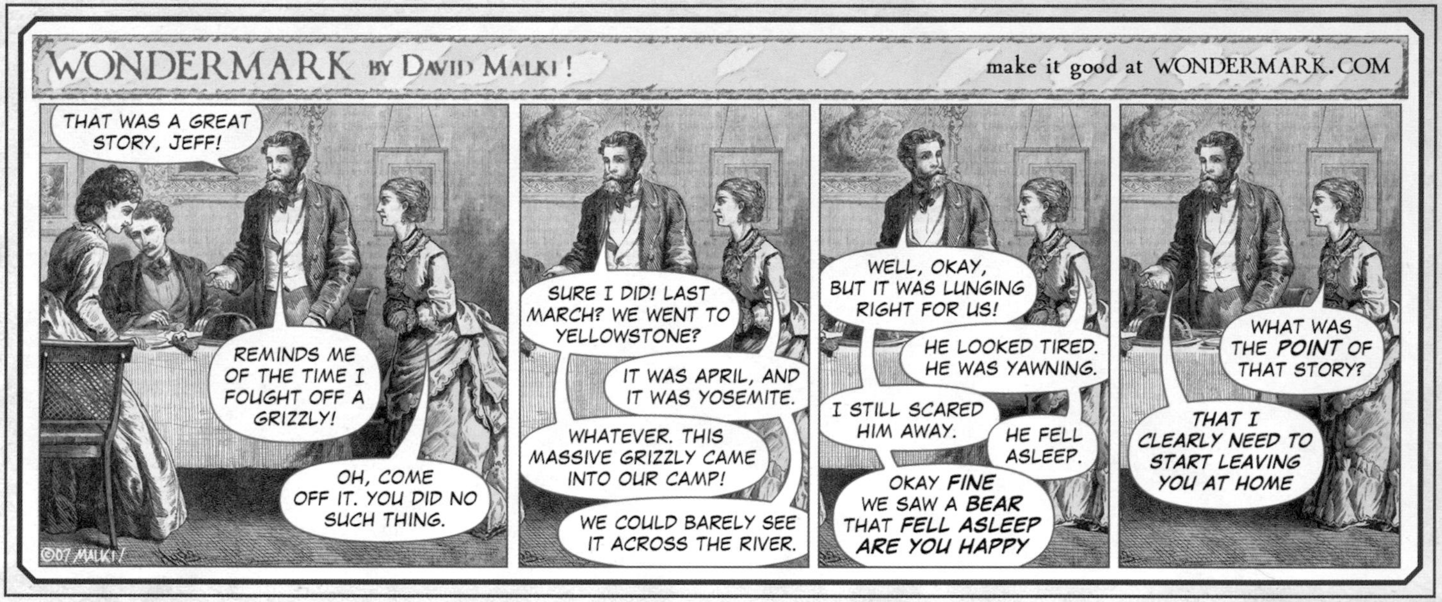
WONDERMARK BY DAVID MALKI !
make it good at WONDERMARK.COM
THAT WAS A GREAT STORY, JEFF!
REMINDS ME OF THE TIME I FOUGHT OFF A GRIZZLY!
OH, COME OFF IT. YOU DID NO SUCH THING.
©07 MALKI !
SURE I DID! LAST MARCH? WE WENT TO YELLOWSTONE?
IT WAS APRIL, AND IT WAS YOSEMITE.
WHATEVER. THIS MASSIVE GRIZZLY CAME INTO OUR CAMP!
WE COULD BARELY SEE IT ACROSS THE RIVER.
WELL, OKAY, BUT IT WAS LUNGING RIGHT FOR US!
HE LOOKED TIRED. HE WAS YAWNING.
I STILL SCARED HIM AWAY.
HE FELL ASLEEP.
OKAY FINE WE SAW A BEAR THAT FELL ASLEEP ARE YOU HAPPY
WHAT WAS THE POINT OF THAT STORY?
THAT I CLEARLY NEED TO START LEAVING YOU AT HOME

jeff's story had not been about bears at all

IN WHICH FEATURE AUTOMATONS

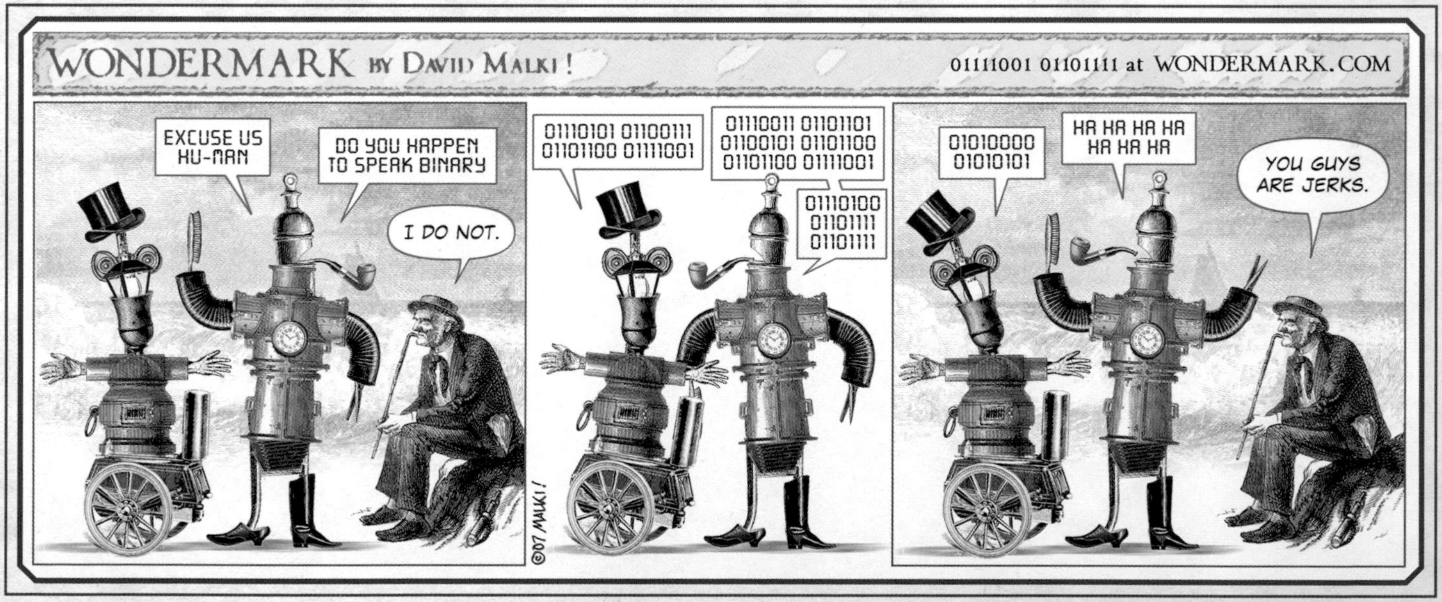
WONDERMARK BY DAVID MALKI !
01111001 01101111 at WONDERMARK.COM
EXCUSE US HU-MAN
DO YOU HAPPEN TO SPEAK BINARY
I DO NOT.
01110101 01100111 01101100 01111001
01110011 01101101 01100101 01101100 01101100 01111001
01110100 01101111 01101111
©07 MALKI !
01010000 01010101
HA HA HA HA HA HA HA
YOU GUYS ARE JERKS.

screw you guys

hurry. There are many adults who are much older than you, and who cannot afford to wait around while you decide to

IN WHICH THIS DUDE MAY NOT BE STRICTLY LICENSED

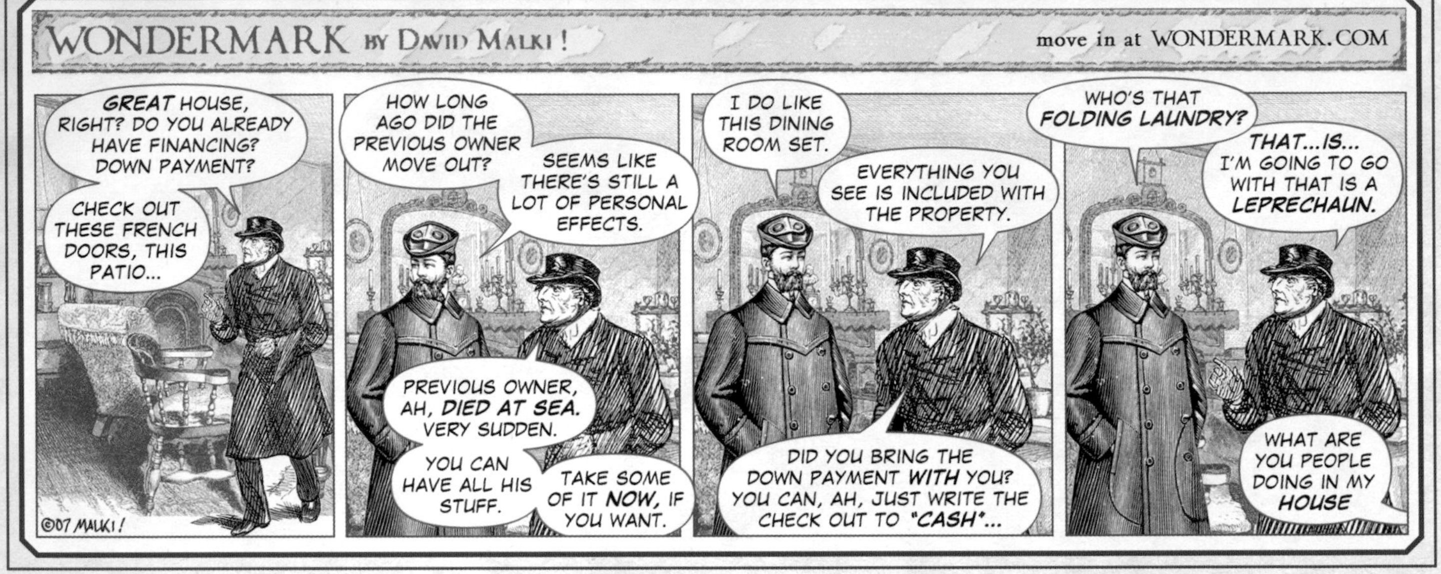
WONDERMARK BY DAVID MALKI !
move in at WONDERMARK.COM
GREAT HOUSE, RIGHT? DO YOU ALREADY HAVE FINANCING? DOWN PAYMENT?
CHECK OUT THESE FRENCH DOORS, THIS PATIO...
©07 MALKI !
HOW LONG AGO DID THE PREVIOUS OWNER MOVE OUT?
SEEMS LIKE THERE'S STILL A LOT OF PERSONAL EFFECTS.
PREVIOUS OWNER, AH, DIED AT SEA. VERY SUDDEN.
YOU CAN HAVE ALL HIS STUFF.
TAKE SOME OF IT NOW, IF YOU WANT.
I DO LIKE THIS DINING ROOM SET.
EVERYTHING YOU SEE IS INCLUDED WITH THE PROPERTY.
DID YOU BRING THE DOWN PAYMENT WITH YOU? YOU CAN, AH, JUST WRITE THE CHECK OUT TO "CASH"...
WHO'S THAT FOLDING LAUNDRY?
THAT...IS... I'M GOING TO GO WITH THAT IS A LEPRECHAUN.
WHAT ARE YOU PEOPLE DOING IN MY HOUSE

he is not even irish

IN WHICH THE WHOLE POINT IS MISSED

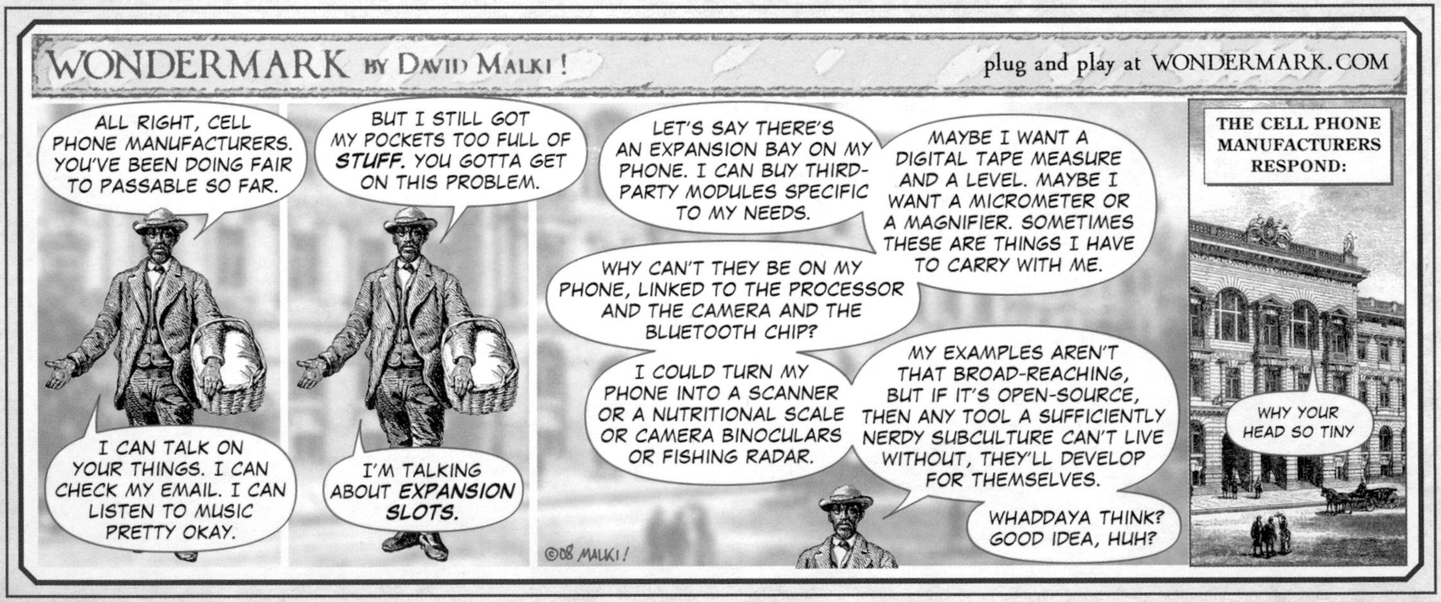
WONDERMARK BY DAVID MALKI !
plug and play at WONDERMARK.COM
ALL RIGHT, CELL PHONE MANUFACTURERS. YOU'VE BEEN DOING FAIR TO PASSABLE SO FAR.
I CAN TALK ON YOUR THINGS. I CAN CHECK MY EMAIL. I CAN LISTEN TO MUSIC PRETTY OKAY.
BUT I STILL GOT MY POCKETS TOO FULL OF STUFF. YOU GOTTA GET ON THIS PROBLEM.
I'M TALKING ABOUT EXPANSION SLOTS.
LET'S SAY THERE'S AN EXPANSION BAY ON MY PHONE. I CAN BUY THIRD-PARTY MODULES SPECIFIC TO MY NEEDS.
MAYBE I WANT A DIGITAL TAPE MEASURE AND A LEVEL. MAYBE I WANT A MICROMETER OR A MAGNIFIER. SOMETIMES THESE ARE THINGS I HAVE TO CARRY WITH ME.
WHY CAN'T THEY BE ON MY PHONE, LINKED TO THE PROCESSOR AND THE CAMERA AND THE BLUETOOTH CHIP?
I COULD TURN MY PHONE INTO A SCANNER OR A NUTRITIONAL SCALE OR CAMERA BINOCULARS OR FISHING RADAR.
MY EXAMPLES AREN'T THAT BROAD-REACHING, BUT IF IT'S OPEN-SOURCE, THEN ANY TOOL A SUFFICIENTLY NERDY SUBCULTURE CAN'T LIVE WITHOUT, THEY'LL DEVELOP FOR THEMSELVES.
WHADDAYA THINK? GOOD IDEA, HUH?
©08 MALKI !
THE CELL PHONE MANUFACTURERS RESPOND:
WHY YOUR HEAD SO TINY

i never have a tire pressure gauge when i need one. but if it were built into my phone? ROAD SAFETY GET ON IT

interests, because you are determined to conquer aging—which will benefit all adults, even you one day! But you must

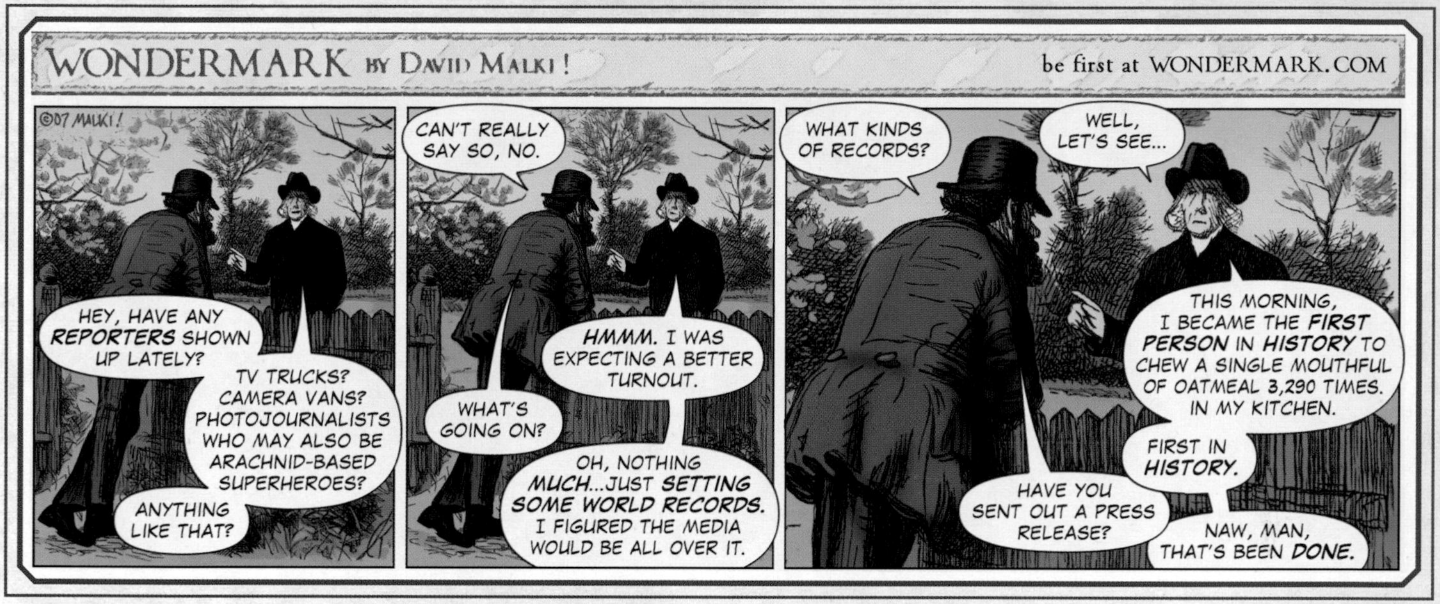
WONDERMARK BY DAVID MALKI !
be first at WONDERMARK.COM
©07 MALKI !
HEY, HAVE ANY REPORTERS SHOWN UP LATELY?
TV TRUCKS? CAMERA VANS? PHOTOJOURNALISTS WHO MAY ALSO BE ARACHNID-BASED SUPERHEROES?
ANYTHING LIKE THAT?
CAN'T REALLY SAY SO, NO.
HMMM. I WAS EXPECTING A BETTER TURNOUT.
WHAT'S GOING ON?
OH, NOTHING MUCH...JUST SETTING SOME WORLD RECORDS. I FIGURED THE MEDIA WOULD BE ALL OVER IT.
WHAT KINDS OF RECORDS?
WELL, LET'S SEE...
THIS MORNING, I BECAME THE FIRST PERSON IN HISTORY TO CHEW A SINGLE MOUTHFUL OF OATMEAL 3,290 TIMES. IN MY KITCHEN.
FIRST IN HISTORY.
HAVE YOU SENT OUT A PRESS RELEASE?
NAW, MAN, THAT'S BEEN DONE.

Color by Carly Monardo • whirringblender.com

Simon would rather the Guinness book be utterly exhaustive. He would gladly read a 58,000-page edition.

Further Records

SET BY THE GENTLEMAN.

GREATEST NUMBER of pistachios discarded for insufficiently gapped shell while watching reruns of *Scarecrow & Mrs. King:* 51

FASTEST TRAVERSAL of the span between the bathroom and the laundry room by a pantsless individual unsure of whether he heard a knock at the door: 6.0 SEC

MOST LENGTHY diatribe on the subject of inappropriate pizza toppings at a child's birthday party delivered to a stranger who did not attend said party: 74 MIN

FARTHEST HORIZONTAL DISTANCE traveled on a rolling office chair across the roof of an apartment building while under the influence of cough syrup: 46 METERS

FARTHEST VERTICAL DISTANCE traveled from the roof of an apartment building to the sidewalk outside the same building without breaking physical contact with a rolling office chair: 65 METERS

SHORTEST HOSPITAL STAY by an individual with forty-three broken bones and a concussion: 8 MIN

MOST EPITHETS hurled at members of the medical profession on the subject of health insurance by an individual with absolutely no conception of how said system works: 90

MOST LANES OF TRAFFIC crossed illegally and under one's own power by an individual with forty-three broken bones and a concussion: 28

MOST DAMAGE CAUSED, measured in dollars, by an individual hobbling across a major highway interchange in a blood-soaked hospital gown: $317,040

LONGEST CONTINUOUS SCREAM uttered by an individual performing self-surgery in his garage with a pair of Vise-Grips® and an office stapler, attempting to correct multiple compound skeletal fractures: 55 MIN 13 SEC

NEW COLORS OBSERVED by said individual in the throes of agonizing pain: YELLORPLE, BLEEN, INDIGILVER

QUICKEST TRANSITION into blaming the whole affair on the Government's destruction of personal liberty: 28 SEC

not serious, and at worst may consider you a bother. It is often useful to explain to them that the letter is in their best

IN WHICH PIRATES MUST PART

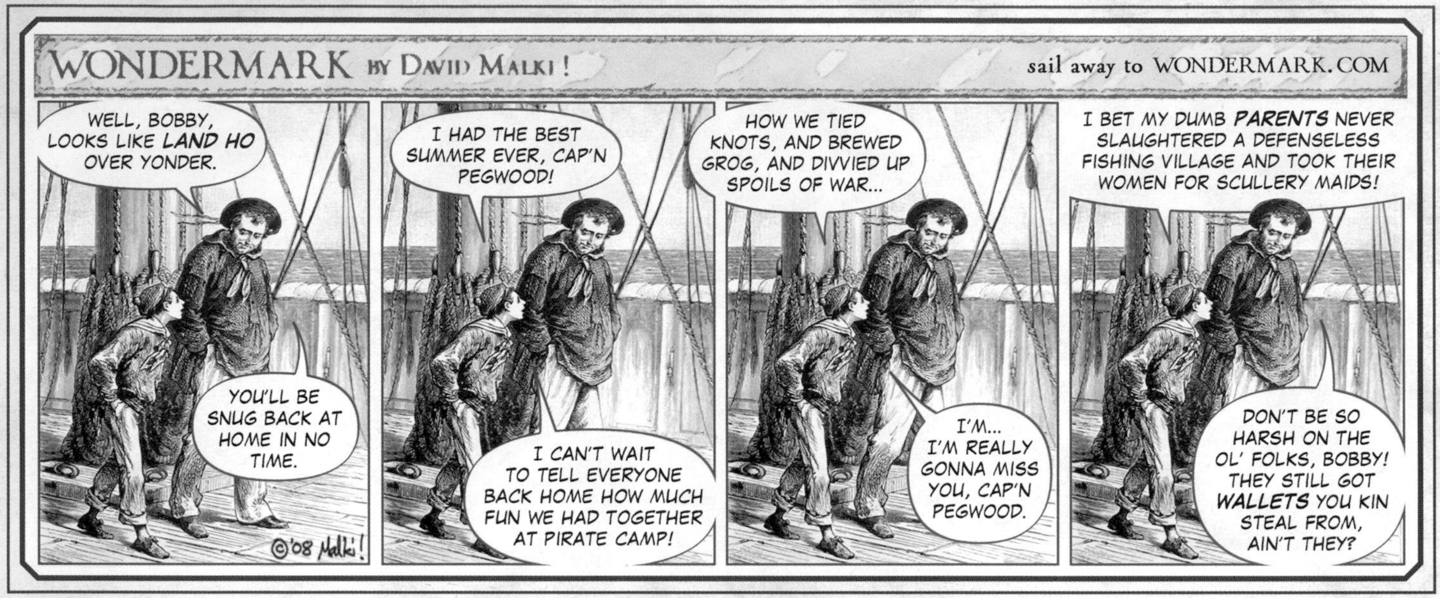
WONDERMARK BY DAVID MALKI !
sail away to WONDERMARK.COM
WELL, BOBBY, LOOKS LIKE LAND HO OVER YONDER.
YOU'LL BE SNUG BACK AT HOME IN NO TIME.
©'08 Malki!
I HAD THE BEST SUMMER EVER, CAP'N PEGWOOD!
I CAN'T WAIT TO TELL EVERYONE BACK HOME HOW MUCH FUN WE HAD TOGETHER AT PIRATE CAMP!
HOW WE TIED KNOTS, AND BREWED GROG, AND DIVVIED UP SPOILS OF WAR...
I'M... I'M REALLY GONNA MISS YOU, CAP'N PEGWOOD.
I BET MY DUMB PARENTS NEVER SLAUGHTERED A DEFENSELESS FISHING VILLAGE AND TOOK THEIR WOMEN FOR SCULLERY MAIDS!
DON'T BE SO HARSH ON THE OL' FOLKS, BOBBY! THEY STILL GOT WALLETS YOU KIN STEAL FROM, AIN'T THEY?

remember to call your mom a wench like I taught ya

IN WHICH DINNER PROVES ELUSIVE

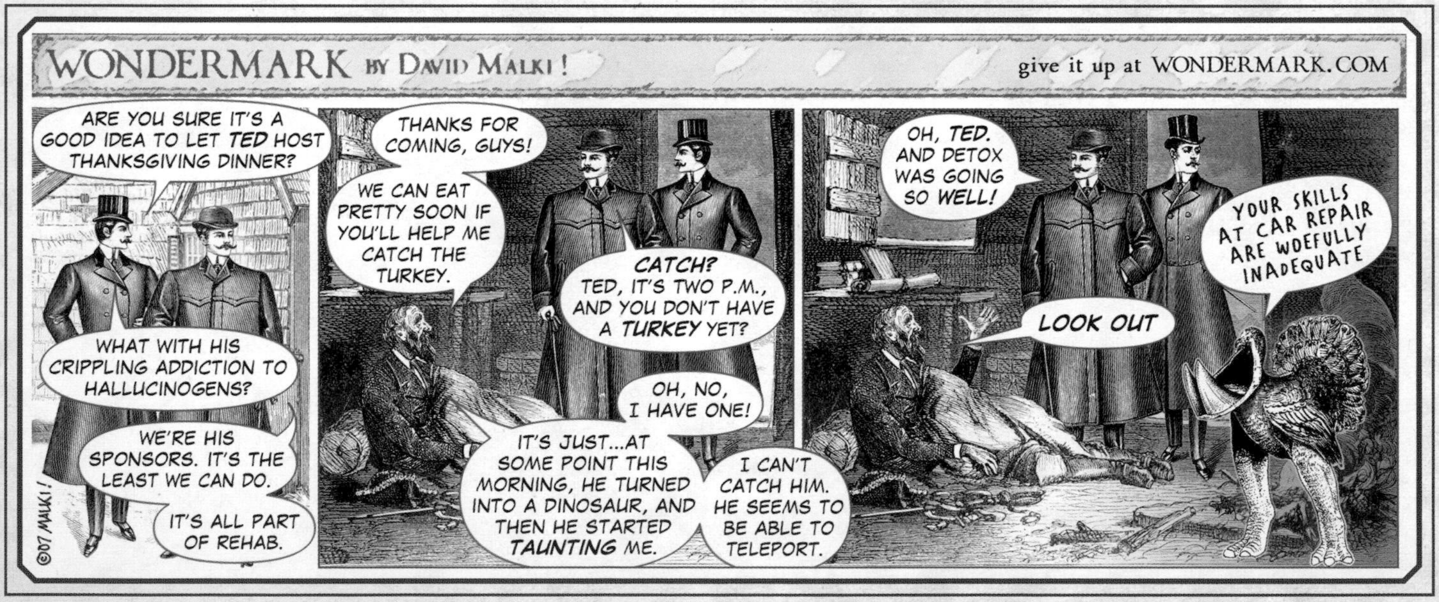
WONDERMARK BY DAVID MALKI !
give it up at WONDERMARK.COM
ARE YOU SURE IT'S A GOOD IDEA TO LET TED HOST THANKSGIVING DINNER?
WHAT WITH HIS CRIPPLING ADDICTION TO HALLUCINOGENS?
WE'RE HIS SPONSORS. IT'S THE LEAST WE CAN DO.
IT'S ALL PART OF REHAB.
©07 MALKI!
THANKS FOR COMING, GUYS!
WE CAN EAT PRETTY SOON IF YOU'LL HELP ME CATCH THE TURKEY.
CATCH? TED, IT'S TWO P.M., AND YOU DON'T HAVE A TURKEY YET?
OH, NO, I HAVE ONE!
IT'S JUST...AT SOME POINT THIS MORNING, HE TURNED INTO A DINOSAUR, AND THEN HE STARTED TAUNTING ME.
I CAN'T CATCH HIM. HE SEEMS TO BE ABLE TO TELEPORT.
OH, TED. AND DETOX WAS GOING SO WELL!
LOOK OUT
YOUR SKILLS AT CAR REPAIR ARE WOEFULLY INADEQUATE

I HAVE TAKEN THE LIBERTY OF DISMANTLING YOUR 1978 DATSUN 280Z

to you when you are older. You will have to try hard to keep a straight face, because they will at best think you are

IN WHICH TRADE SECRETS ARE REVEALED

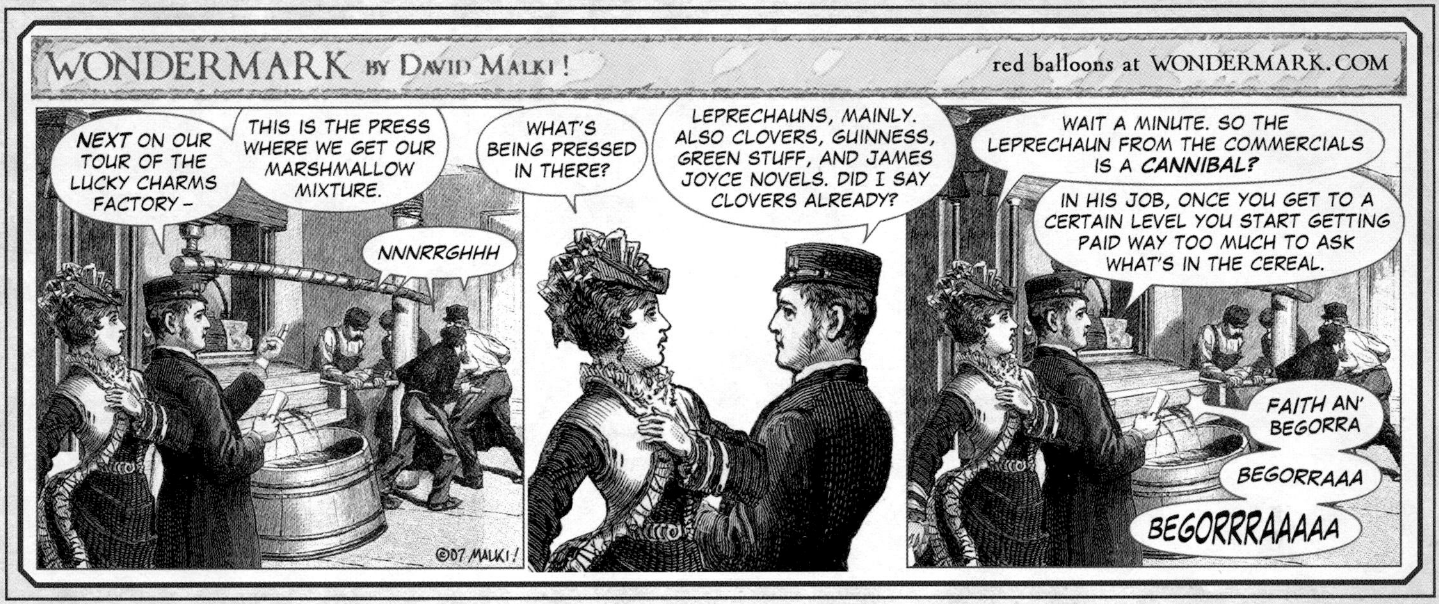
WONDERMARK BY DAVID MALKI !
red balloons at WONDERMARK.COM
NEXT ON OUR TOUR OF THE LUCKY CHARMS FACTORY –
THIS IS THE PRESS WHERE WE GET OUR MARSHMALLOW MIXTURE.
NNNRRGHHH
©07 MALKI !
WHAT'S BEING PRESSED IN THERE?
LEPRECHAUNS, MAINLY. ALSO CLOVERS, GUINNESS, GREEN STUFF, AND JAMES JOYCE NOVELS. DID I SAY CLOVERS ALREADY?
WAIT A MINUTE. SO THE LEPRECHAUN FROM THE COMMERCIALS IS A CANNIBAL?
IN HIS JOB, ONCE YOU GET TO A CERTAIN LEVEL YOU START GETTING PAID WAY TOO MUCH TO ASK WHAT'S IN THE CEREAL.
FAITH AN' BEGORRA
BEGORRAAA
BEGORRRAAAAA

they are not simply 'magically delicious.' as head flavor manager I work 70+ hour work-weeks and I DO NOT APPRECIATE KIDS THINKING IT JUST HAPPENS BY ITSELF

IN WHICH MALL PARKING SUCKS

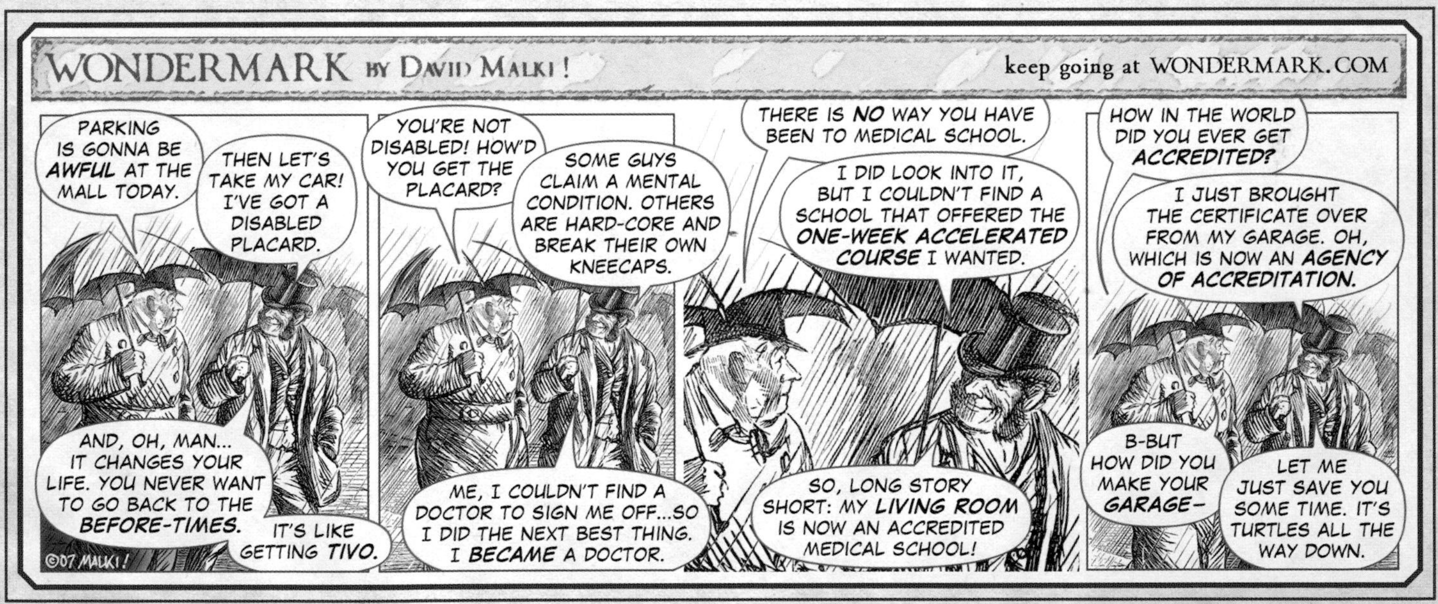
WONDERMARK BY DAVID MALKI !
keep going at WONDERMARK.COM
PARKING IS GONNA BE AWFUL AT THE MALL TODAY.
THEN LET'S TAKE MY CAR! I'VE GOT A DISABLED PLACARD.
AND, OH, MAN... IT CHANGES YOUR LIFE. YOU NEVER WANT TO GO BACK TO THE BEFORE-TIMES.
IT'S LIKE GETTING TIVO.
©07 MALKI !
YOU'RE NOT DISABLED! HOW'D YOU GET THE PLACARD?
SOME GUYS CLAIM A MENTAL CONDITION. OTHERS ARE HARD-CORE AND BREAK THEIR OWN KNEECAPS.
ME, I COULDN'T FIND A DOCTOR TO SIGN ME OFF...SO I DID THE NEXT BEST THING. I BECAME A DOCTOR.
THERE IS NO WAY YOU HAVE BEEN TO MEDICAL SCHOOL.
I DID LOOK INTO IT, BUT I COULDN'T FIND A SCHOOL THAT OFFERED THE ONE-WEEK ACCELERATED COURSE I WANTED.
SO, LONG STORY SHORT: MY LIVING ROOM IS NOW AN ACCREDITED MEDICAL SCHOOL!
HOW IN THE WORLD DID YOU EVER GET ACCREDITED?
I JUST BROUGHT THE CERTIFICATE OVER FROM MY GARAGE. OH, WHICH IS NOW AN AGENCY OF ACCREDITATION.
B-BUT HOW DID YOU MAKE YOUR GARAGE–
LET ME JUST SAVE YOU SOME TIME. IT'S TURTLES ALL THE WAY DOWN.

Parking is an important issue to some.

older self of the idealism you once had! When you are finished, ask a parent or teacher to keep the letter and mail it

IN WHICH IT'S TIME TO GET UP

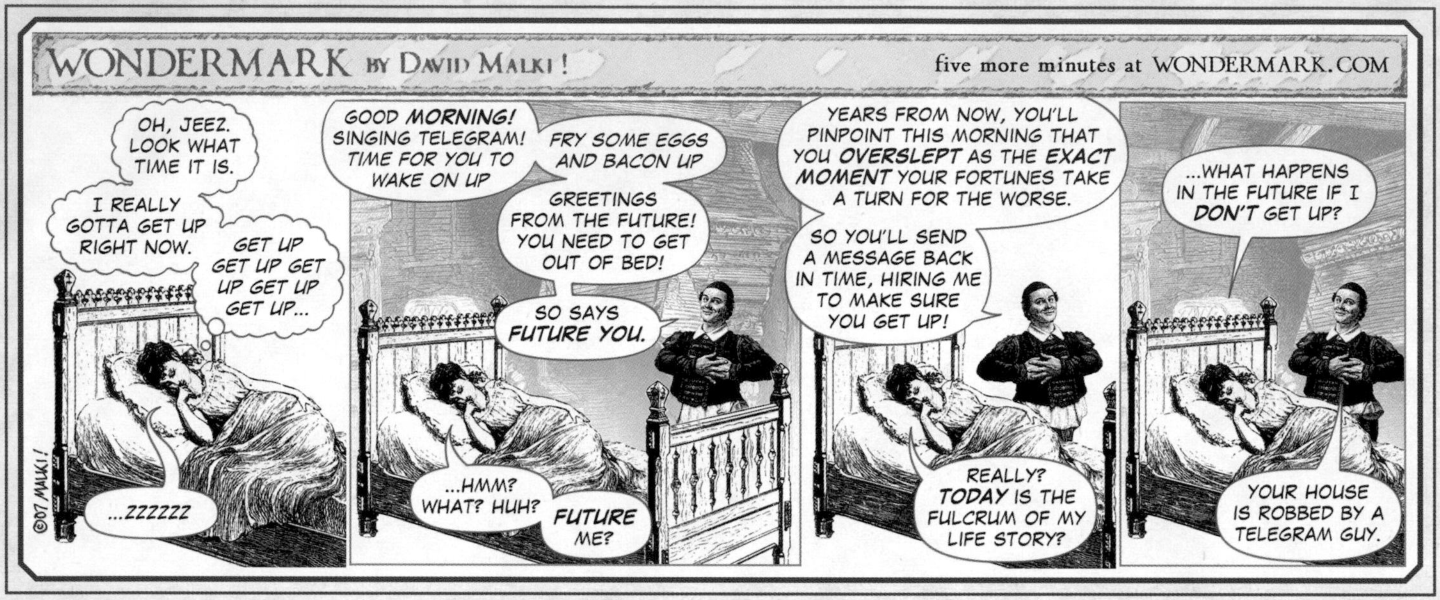
WONDERMARK BY DAVID MALKI !
five more minutes at WONDERMARK.COM
OH, JEEZ. LOOK WHAT TIME IT IS.
I REALLY GOTTA GET UP RIGHT NOW.
GET UP GET UP GET UP GET UP GET UP...
...ZZZZZZ
©07 MALKI!
GOOD MORNING! SINGING TELEGRAM! TIME FOR YOU TO WAKE ON UP
FRY SOME EGGS AND BACON UP
GREETINGS FROM THE FUTURE! YOU NEED TO GET OUT OF BED!
SO SAYS FUTURE YOU.
...HMM? WHAT? HUH?
FUTURE ME?
YEARS FROM NOW, YOU'LL PINPOINT THIS MORNING THAT YOU OVERSLEPT AS THE EXACT MOMENT YOUR FORTUNES TAKE A TURN FOR THE WORSE.
SO YOU'LL SEND A MESSAGE BACK IN TIME, HIRING ME TO MAKE SURE YOU GET UP!
REALLY? TODAY IS THE FULCRUM OF MY LIFE STORY?
...WHAT HAPPENS IN THE FUTURE IF I DON'T GET UP?
YOUR HOUSE IS ROBBED BY A TELEGRAM GUY.

every day is the fulcrum of your life story

IN WHICH CARDS ARE LICKED

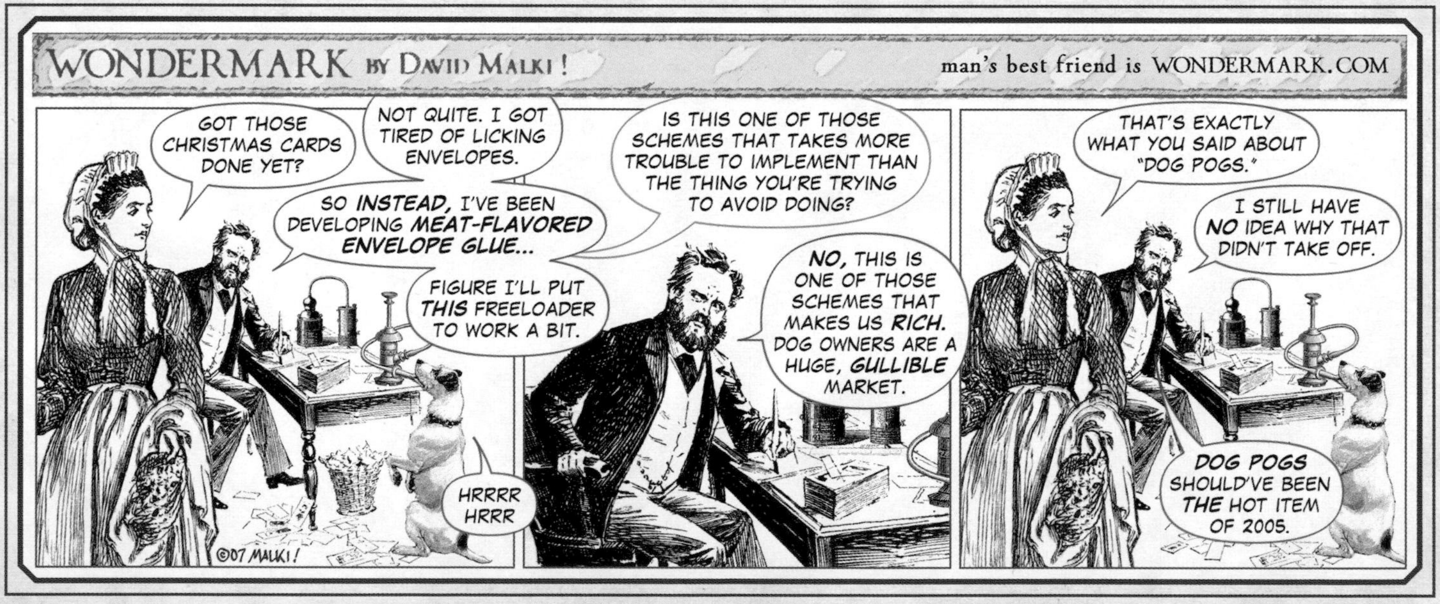
WONDERMARK BY DAVID MALKI !
man's best friend is WONDERMARK.COM
GOT THOSE CHRISTMAS CARDS DONE YET?
NOT QUITE. I GOT TIRED OF LICKING ENVELOPES.
SO INSTEAD, I'VE BEEN DEVELOPING MEAT-FLAVORED ENVELOPE GLUE...
FIGURE I'LL PUT THIS FREELOADER TO WORK A BIT.
HRRRR HRRR
©07 MALKI!
IS THIS ONE OF THOSE SCHEMES THAT TAKES MORE TROUBLE TO IMPLEMENT THAN THE THING YOU'RE TRYING TO AVOID DOING?
NO, THIS IS ONE OF THOSE SCHEMES THAT MAKES US RICH. DOG OWNERS ARE A HUGE, GULLIBLE MARKET.
THAT'S EXACTLY WHAT YOU SAID ABOUT "DOG POGS."
I STILL HAVE NO IDEA WHY THAT DIDN'T TAKE OFF.
DOG POGS SHOULD'VE BEEN THE HOT ITEM OF 2005.

there must be a gentleman's agreement between envelope manufacturers to make their glues taste uniformly like ass

all the wonderful ideas you have—now, while you are young and not yet jaded. Consider this letter a reminder to your

IN WHICH JOY IS MANDATED

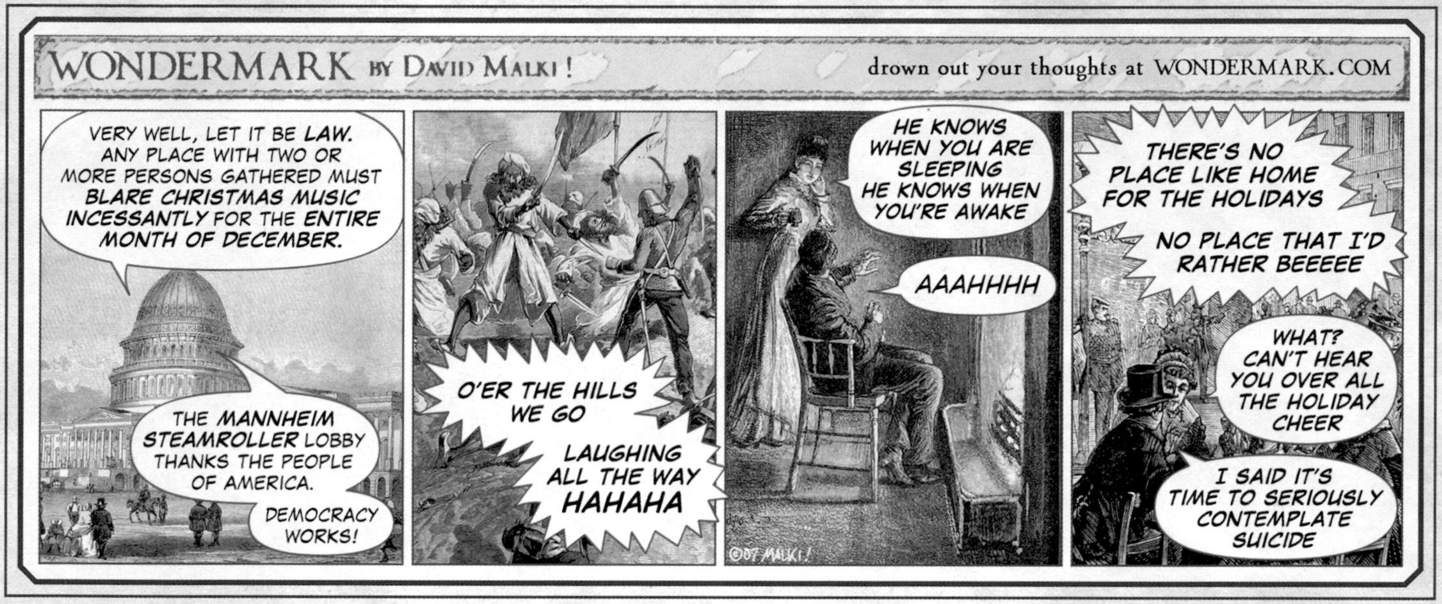
WONDERMARK BY DAVID MALKI !
drown out your thoughts at WONDERMARK.COM
VERY WELL, LET IT BE LAW. ANY PLACE WITH TWO OR MORE PERSONS GATHERED MUST BLARE CHRISTMAS MUSIC INCESSANTLY FOR THE ENTIRE MONTH OF DECEMBER.
THE MANNHEIM STEAMROLLER LOBBY THANKS THE PEOPLE OF AMERICA.
DEMOCRACY WORKS!
O'ER THE HILLS WE GO
LAUGHING ALL THE WAY HAHAHA
HE KNOWS WHEN YOU ARE SLEEPING HE KNOWS WHEN YOU'RE AWAKE
AAAHHHH
©07 MALKI!
THERE'S NO PLACE LIKE HOME FOR THE HOLIDAYS
NO PLACE THAT I'D RATHER BEEEEE
WHAT? CAN'T HEAR YOU OVER ALL THE HOLIDAY CHEER
I SAID IT'S TIME TO SERIOUSLY CONTEMPLATE SUICIDE

'tis the season!

IN WHICH A DOG MAKES A PROMISE

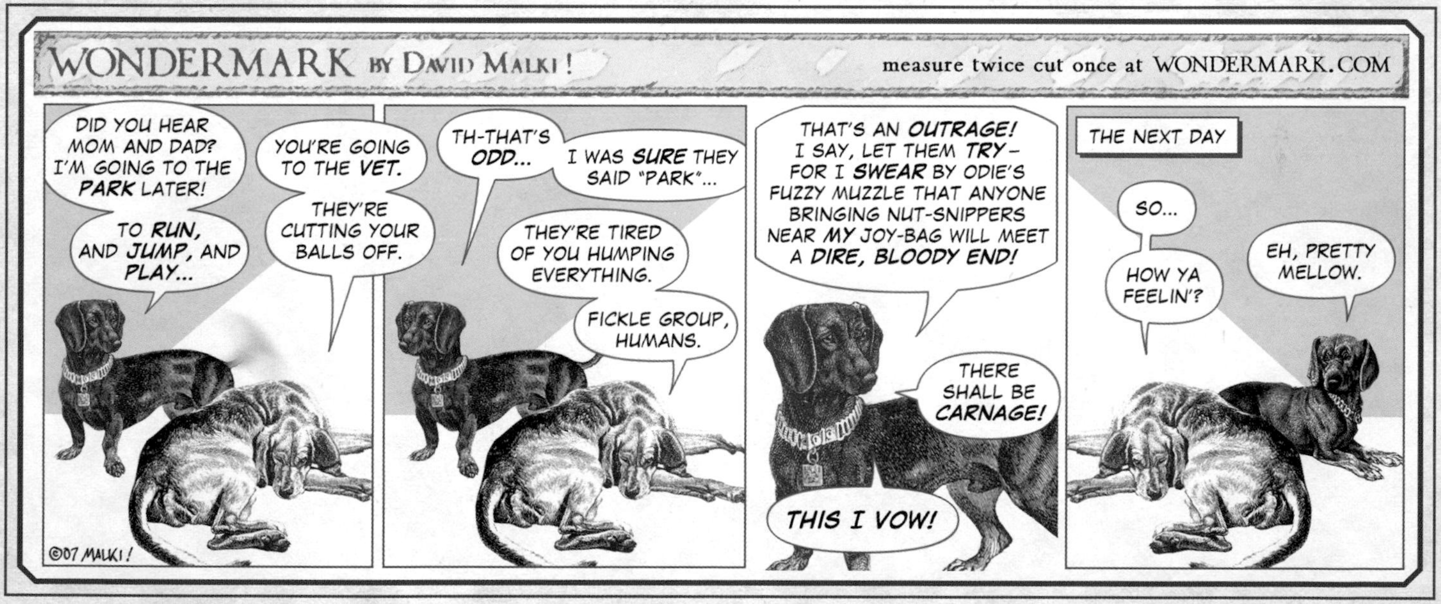
WONDERMARK BY DAVID MALKI !
measure twice cut once at WONDERMARK.COM
DID YOU HEAR MOM AND DAD? I'M GOING TO THE PARK LATER!
TO RUN, AND JUMP, AND PLAY...
YOU'RE GOING TO THE VET.
THEY'RE CUTTING YOUR BALLS OFF.
©07 MALKI!
TH-THAT'S ODD...
I WAS SURE THEY SAID "PARK"...
THEY'RE TIRED OF YOU HUMPING EVERYTHING.
FICKLE GROUP, HUMANS.
THAT'S AN OUTRAGE! I SAY, LET THEM TRY— FOR I SWEAR BY ODIE'S FUZZY MUZZLE THAT ANYONE BRINGING NUT-SNIPPERS NEAR MY JOY-BAG WILL MEET A DIRE, BLOODY END!
THERE SHALL BE CARNAGE!
THIS I VOW!
THE NEXT DAY
SO...
HOW YA FEELIN'?
EH, PRETTY MELLOW.

you know how I used to be all gaga over that poodle down the block? well, funny thing—now when I look at her all I can think is HIGH MAINTENANCE

discoveries you might like to make, and in the following space, write a letter to an older version of yourself, describing

THE TRUE MEANING OF CHRISTMAS

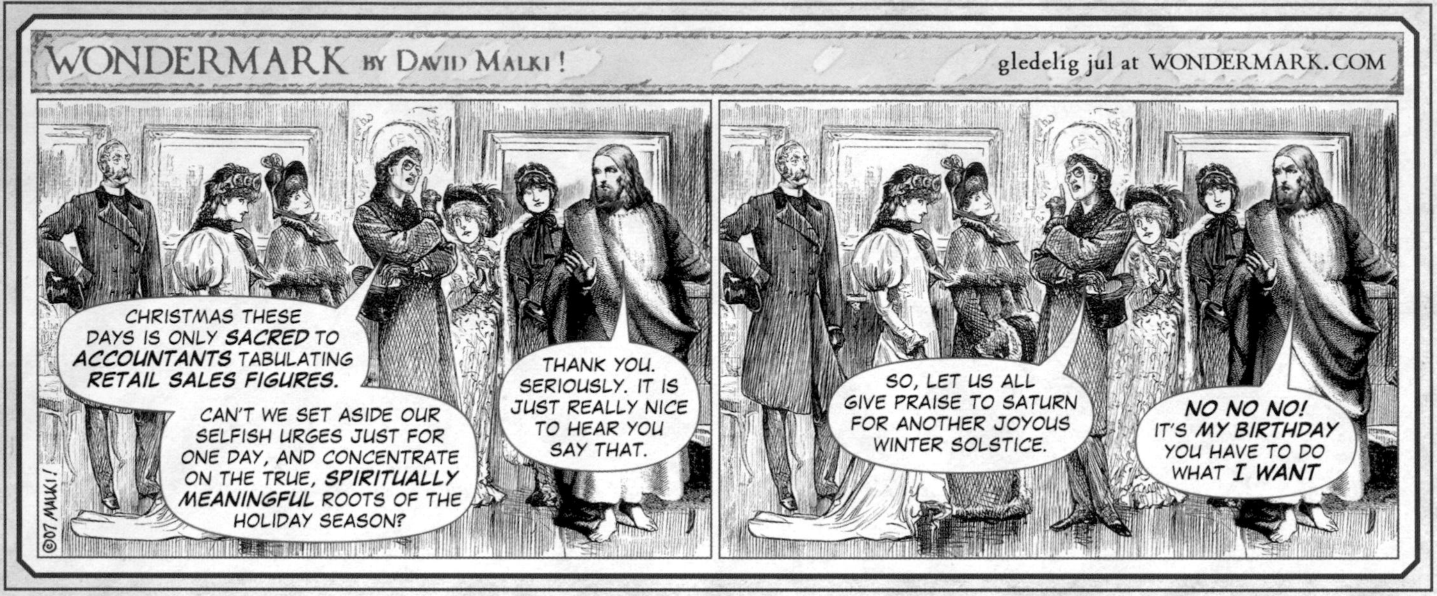
WONDERMARK BY DAVID MALKI !
gledelig jul at WONDERMARK.COM
CHRISTMAS THESE DAYS IS ONLY SACRED TO ACCOUNTANTS TABULATING RETAIL SALES FIGURES.
CAN'T WE SET ASIDE OUR SELFISH URGES JUST FOR ONE DAY, AND CONCENTRATE ON THE TRUE, SPIRITUALLY MEANINGFUL ROOTS OF THE HOLIDAY SEASON?
THANK YOU. SERIOUSLY. IT IS JUST REALLY NICE TO HEAR YOU SAY THAT.
SO, LET US ALL GIVE PRAISE TO SATURN FOR ANOTHER JOYOUS WINTER SOLSTICE.
NO NO NO! IT'S MY BIRTHDAY YOU HAVE TO DO WHAT I WANT
©07 MALKI !

technically the roman saturnalia and the pagan solstice festival were separate and both co-opted by Christianity centuries apart but WHATEVER, HISTORICAL ACCURACY

IN WHICH MARK FACES DENIAL

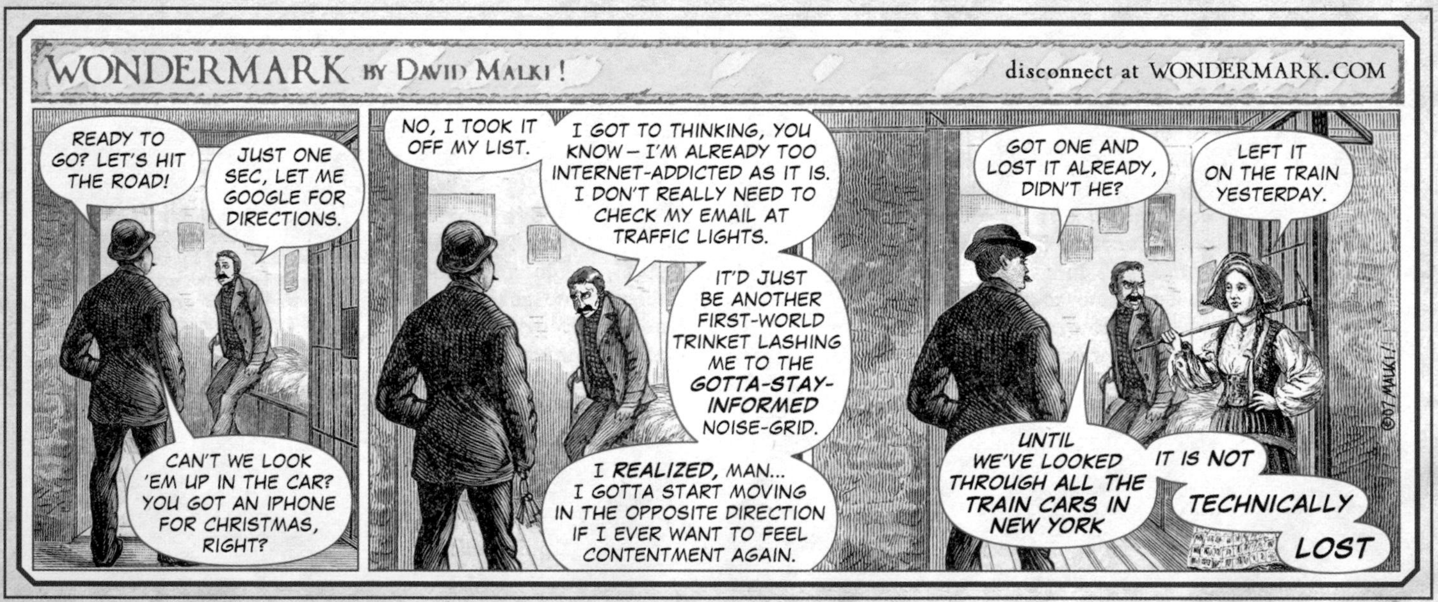
WONDERMARK BY DAVID MALKI !
disconnect at WONDERMARK.COM
READY TO GO? LET'S HIT THE ROAD!
JUST ONE SEC, LET ME GOOGLE FOR DIRECTIONS.
CAN'T WE LOOK 'EM UP IN THE CAR? YOU GOT AN IPHONE FOR CHRISTMAS, RIGHT?
NO, I TOOK IT OFF MY LIST.
I GOT TO THINKING, YOU KNOW – I'M ALREADY TOO INTERNET-ADDICTED AS IT IS. I DON'T REALLY NEED TO CHECK MY EMAIL AT TRAFFIC LIGHTS.
IT'D JUST BE ANOTHER FIRST-WORLD TRINKET LASHING ME TO THE GOTTA-STAY-INFORMED NOISE-GRID.
I REALIZED, MAN... I GOTTA START MOVING IN THE OPPOSITE DIRECTION IF I EVER WANT TO FEEL CONTENTMENT AGAIN.
GOT ONE AND LOST IT ALREADY, DIDN'T HE?
LEFT IT ON THE TRAIN YESTERDAY.
UNTIL WE'VE LOOKED THROUGH ALL THE TRAIN CARS IN NEW YORK
IT IS NOT TECHNICALLY LOST
©07 MALKI !

only 6,399 left to search!

And now that you have learned a little about inventing, and gotten yourself into a creative mind-set, think about any

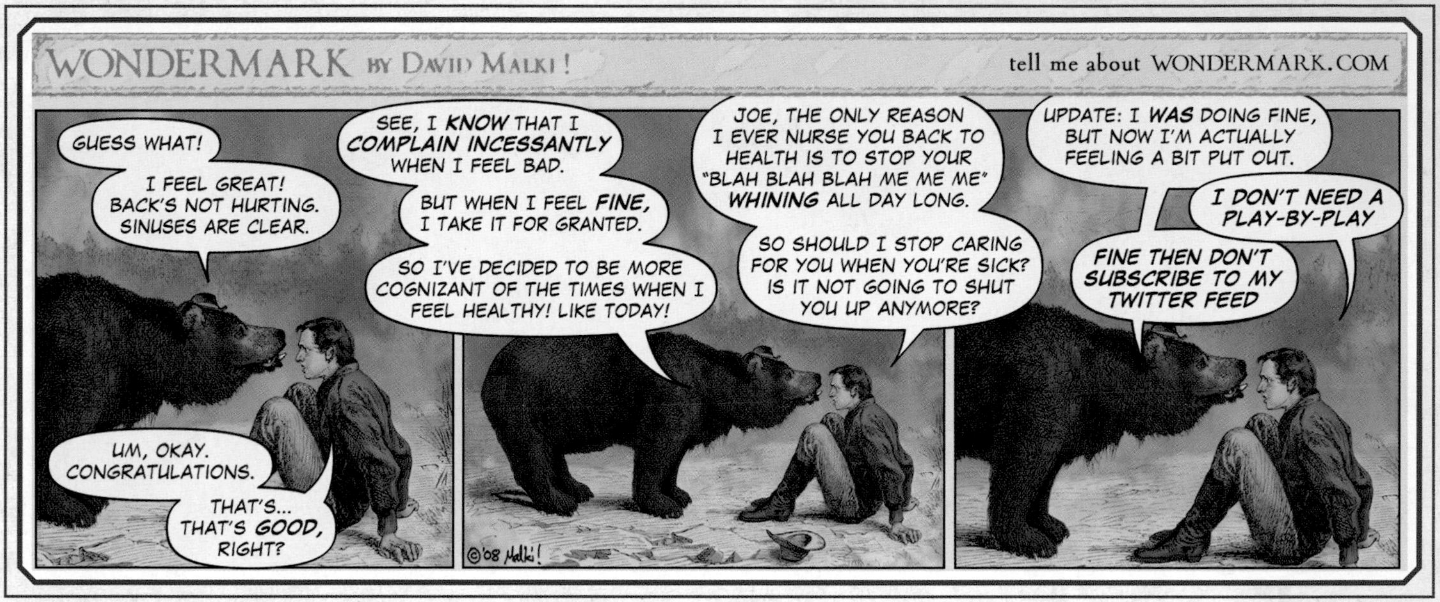
WONDERMARK BY DAVID MALKI !
tell me about WONDERMARK.COM
GUESS WHAT!
I FEEL GREAT! BACK'S NOT HURTING. SINUSES ARE CLEAR.
UM, OKAY. CONGRATULATIONS.
THAT'S... THAT'S GOOD, RIGHT?
SEE, I KNOW THAT I COMPLAIN INCESSANTLY WHEN I FEEL BAD.
BUT WHEN I FEEL FINE, I TAKE IT FOR GRANTED.
SO I'VE DECIDED TO BE MORE COGNIZANT OF THE TIMES WHEN I FEEL HEALTHY! LIKE TODAY!
©08 Malki!
JOE, THE ONLY REASON I EVER NURSE YOU BACK TO HEALTH IS TO STOP YOUR "BLAH BLAH BLAH ME ME ME" WHINING ALL DAY LONG.
SO SHOULD I STOP CARING FOR YOU WHEN YOU'RE SICK? IS IT NOT GOING TO SHUT YOU UP ANYMORE?
UPDATE: I WAS DOING FINE, BUT NOW I'M ACTUALLY FEELING A BIT PUT OUT.
I DON'T NEED A PLAY-BY-PLAY
FINE THEN DON'T SUBSCRIBE TO MY TWITTER FEED

Color by Marcus Thiele • themonkeymind.livejournal.com

that hat doesn't look like it fits joe very well!

twitter

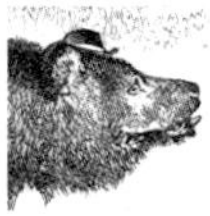

illfittinghat

Feet are sore from walking, but less than I expected considering the condition of the soil. Can't really complain!
10:20 PM May 16th from forest

Saw some squirrels coughing this afternoon. I hope there's not some bug going around.
7:41 PM May 18th from forest

Well obviously there are BUGS around. I mean sicknesses. Didn't mean to offend any bugs - many of them are perfectly nice.
7:42 PM May 18th from forest

I went to brush a twig off my ear but it was a bee!
5:09 AM May 28th from forest

Small ants that I can't see are no problem. Big ants freak me out a little. I know it's not PC, but it's honest.
3:35 AM Jun 29th from txt

"Bear boxes" at campsites are, despite the name, surprisingly hard for bears to use. It's like, who designed this? Did they even ASK a bear?
2:19 PM Jul 6th from forest

This stupid badger thinks justz 'cause I handed him a berry that we're best freaking friends. SO ANNOYING
2:48 PM Aug 2nd, 2008 from forest

I literally just farted out a bumblebee.
10:01 PM Sep 4th from forest

Bluejay called me fat. I called him an ugly son of an empty-skulled maggot-ridden nincompigeon. Now we both feel bad.
7:26 PM Feb 10th from TwitPine

Oh jeez I just realized my nose has been wet for like the last year solid. IS MY NOSE SUPPOSED TO BE WET
9:08 PM Apr 2nd from TwitPine

ents live longer, and stay healthy into old age. What greater discovery could there be than the power over death itself!

IN WHICH BABIES SHOULD JUST SHUT UP ALREADY

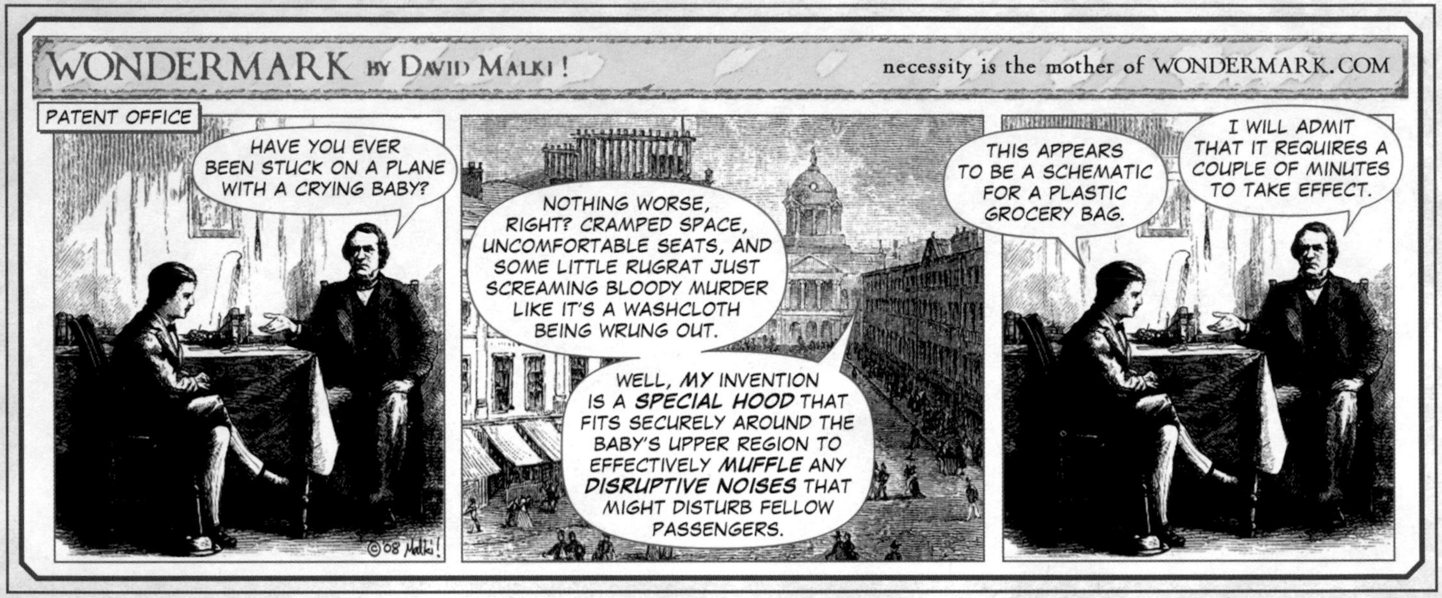
WONDERMARK BY DAVID MALKI !
necessity is the mother of WONDERMARK.COM
PATENT OFFICE
HAVE YOU EVER BEEN STUCK ON A PLANE WITH A CRYING BABY?
NOTHING WORSE, RIGHT? CRAMPED SPACE, UNCOMFORTABLE SEATS, AND SOME LITTLE RUGRAT JUST SCREAMING BLOODY MURDER LIKE IT'S A WASHCLOTH BEING WRUNG OUT.
WELL, *MY* INVENTION IS A *SPECIAL HOOD* THAT FITS SECURELY AROUND THE BABY'S UPPER REGION TO EFFECTIVELY *MUFFLE* ANY *DISRUPTIVE NOISES* THAT MIGHT DISTURB FELLOW PASSENGERS.
THIS APPEARS TO BE A SCHEMATIC FOR A PLASTIC GROCERY BAG.
I WILL ADMIT THAT IT REQUIRES A COUPLE OF MINUTES TO TAKE EFFECT.
©'08 Malki!

a sorely needed addition to those little travel kits
with the eye-masks and the mini-socks

FACEBOOK, DISTILLED.

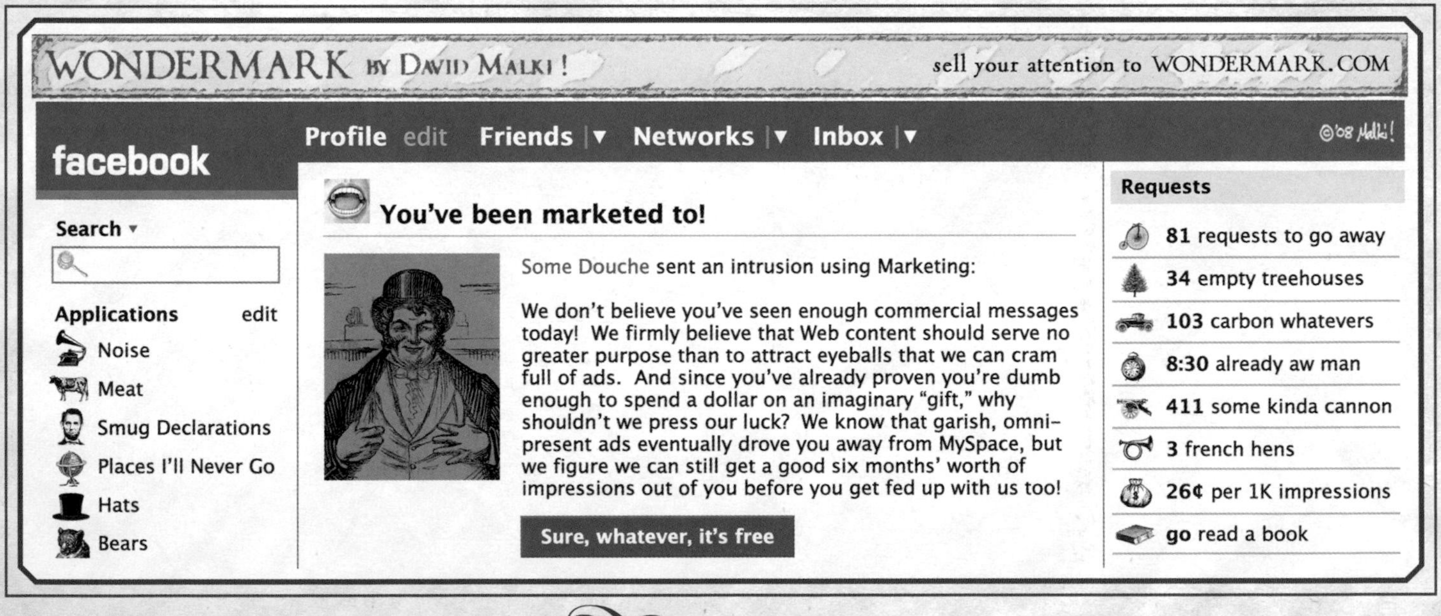
WONDERMARK BY DAVID MALKI !
sell your attention to WONDERMARK.COM
facebook
Profile edit Friends Networks Inbox
©'08 Malki!
Search
Applications edit
Noise
Meat
Smug Declarations
Places I'll Never Go
Hats
Bears
You've been marketed to!
Some Douche sent an intrusion using Marketing:
We don't believe you've seen enough commercial messages today! We firmly believe that Web content should serve no greater purpose than to attract eyeballs that we can cram full of ads. And since you've already proven you're dumb enough to spend a dollar on an imaginary "gift," why shouldn't we press our luck? We know that garish, omni-present ads eventually drove you away from MySpace, but we figure we can still get a good six months' worth of impressions out of you before you get fed up with us too!
Sure, whatever, it's free
Requests
81 requests to go away
34 empty treehouses
103 carbon whatevers
8:30 already aw man
411 some kinda cannon
3 french hens
26¢ per 1K impressions
go read a book

now everyone join the wondermark facebook group

like yourselves to *make* all those new discoveries—*medical* discoveries perhaps, to help your parents and grandpar-

IN WHICH LIFE'S SOLE ENERGY-SOURCE IS RENEWED

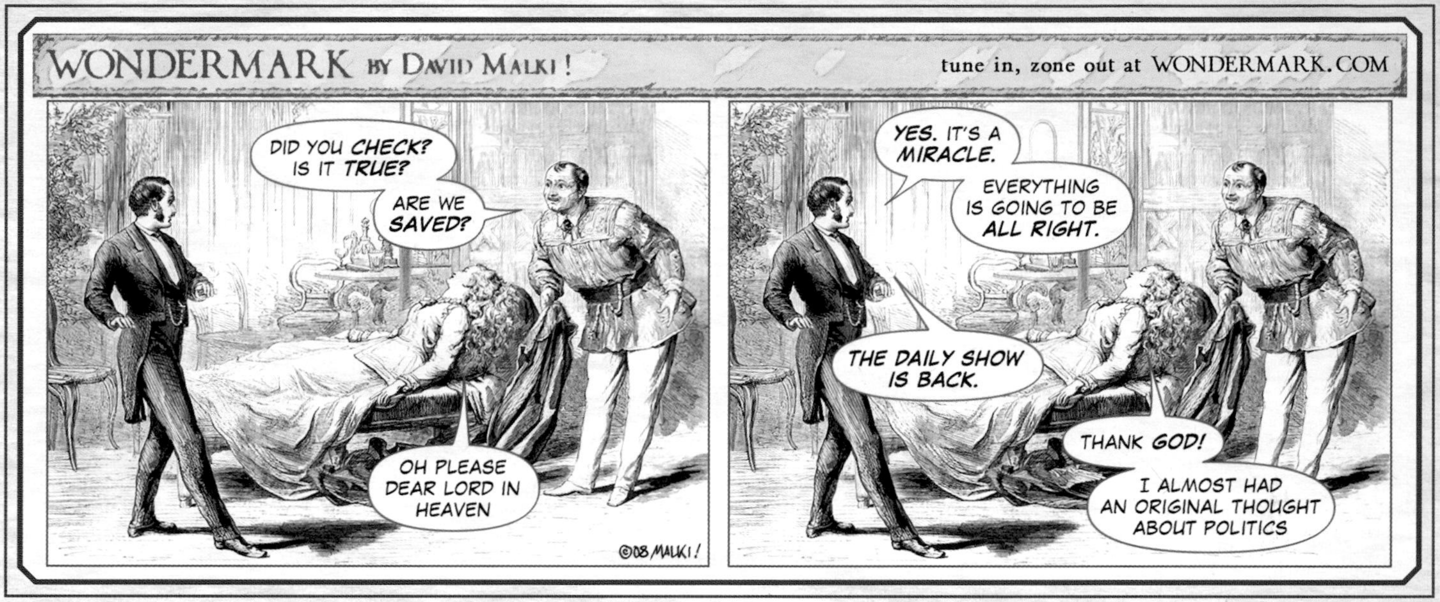
WONDERMARK BY DAVID MALKI !
tune in, zone out at WONDERMARK.COM
DID YOU CHECK? IS IT TRUE?
ARE WE SAVED?
OH PLEASE DEAR LORD IN HEAVEN
©08 MALKI !
YES. IT'S A MIRACLE.
EVERYTHING IS GOING TO BE ALL RIGHT.
THE DAILY SHOW IS BACK.
THANK GOD!
I ALMOST HAD AN ORIGINAL THOUGHT ABOUT POLITICS

8

I like *The Daily Show* a lot, but nobody seems to listen to Jon when he insists (truthfully) that it's a comedy show, not a factual news show.

IN WHICH EXCUSES ARE FORMULATED

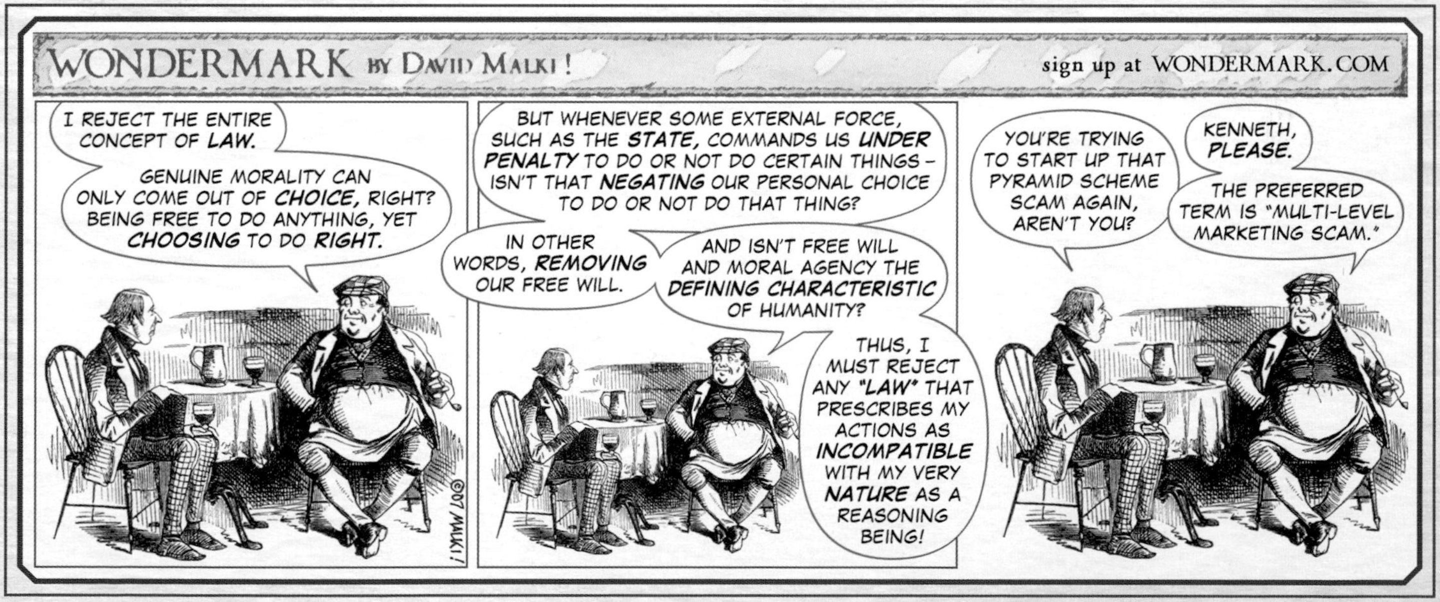
WONDERMARK BY DAVID MALKI !
sign up at WONDERMARK.COM
I REJECT THE ENTIRE CONCEPT OF LAW.
GENUINE MORALITY CAN ONLY COME OUT OF CHOICE, RIGHT? BEING FREE TO DO ANYTHING, YET CHOOSING TO DO RIGHT.
©07 MALKI !
BUT WHENEVER SOME EXTERNAL FORCE, SUCH AS THE STATE, COMMANDS US UNDER PENALTY TO DO OR NOT DO CERTAIN THINGS – ISN'T THAT NEGATING OUR PERSONAL CHOICE TO DO OR NOT DO THAT THING?
IN OTHER WORDS, REMOVING OUR FREE WILL.
AND ISN'T FREE WILL AND MORAL AGENCY THE DEFINING CHARACTERISTIC OF HUMANITY?
THUS, I MUST REJECT ANY "LAW" THAT PRESCRIBES MY ACTIONS AS INCOMPATIBLE WITH MY VERY NATURE AS A REASONING BEING!
YOU'RE TRYING TO START UP THAT PYRAMID SCHEME SCAM AGAIN, AREN'T YOU?
KENNETH, PLEASE.
THE PREFERRED TERM IS "MULTI-LEVEL MARKETING SCAM."

kenneth this is the opportunity of a lifetime

advanced science by a great deal, further than we can scarcely imagine. But it will take fine young men and women

IN WHICH DESTINY IS HERALDED

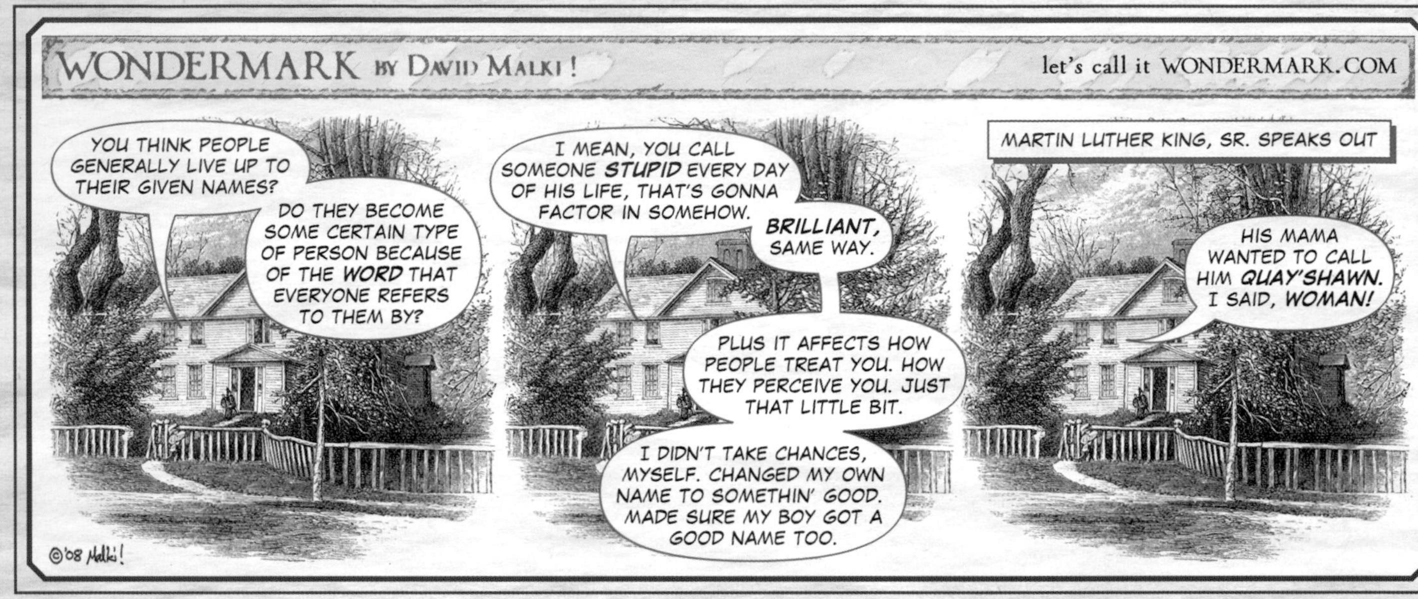
WONDERMARK BY DAVID MALKI !
let's call it WONDERMARK.COM
YOU THINK PEOPLE GENERALLY LIVE UP TO THEIR GIVEN NAMES?
DO THEY BECOME SOME CERTAIN TYPE OF PERSON BECAUSE OF THE WORD THAT EVERYONE REFERS TO THEM BY?
I MEAN, YOU CALL SOMEONE STUPID EVERY DAY OF HIS LIFE, THAT'S GONNA FACTOR IN SOMEHOW.
BRILLIANT, SAME WAY.
PLUS IT AFFECTS HOW PEOPLE TREAT YOU. HOW THEY PERCEIVE YOU. JUST THAT LITTLE BIT.
I DIDN'T TAKE CHANCES, MYSELF. CHANGED MY OWN NAME TO SOMETHIN' GOOD. MADE SURE MY BOY GOT A GOOD NAME TOO.
MARTIN LUTHER KING, SR. SPEAKS OUT
HIS MAMA WANTED TO CALL HIM QUAY'SHAWN. I SAID, WOMAN!
©'08 Malki!

sir that is very interesting but i actually just called to try to trick you into giving out your credit card number over the phone

IN WHICH JOUSTING'S FUTURE LOOKS GRIM

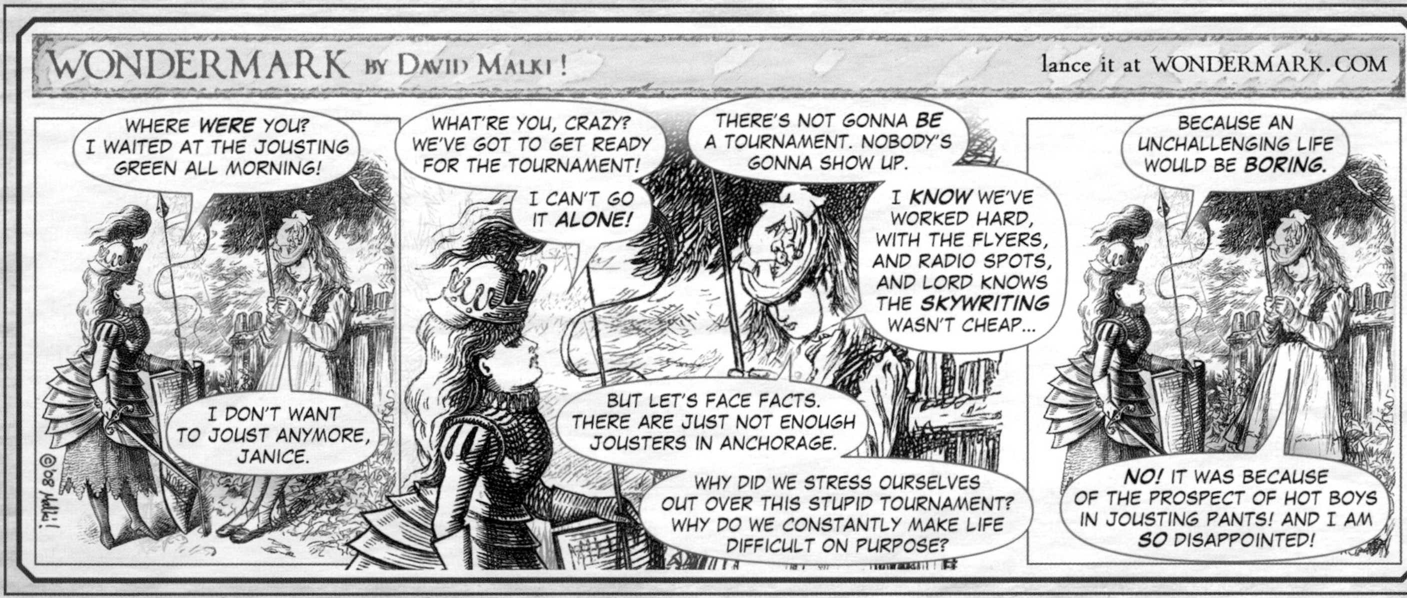
WONDERMARK BY DAVID MALKI !
lance it at WONDERMARK.COM
WHERE WERE YOU? I WAITED AT THE JOUSTING GREEN ALL MORNING!
I DON'T WANT TO JOUST ANYMORE, JANICE.
WHAT'RE YOU, CRAZY? WE'VE GOT TO GET READY FOR THE TOURNAMENT!
I CAN'T GO IT ALONE!
THERE'S NOT GONNA BE A TOURNAMENT. NOBODY'S GONNA SHOW UP.
I KNOW WE'VE WORKED HARD, WITH THE FLYERS, AND RADIO SPOTS, AND LORD KNOWS THE SKYWRITING WASN'T CHEAP...
BUT LET'S FACE FACTS. THERE ARE JUST NOT ENOUGH JOUSTERS IN ANCHORAGE.
WHY DID WE STRESS OURSELVES OUT OVER THIS STUPID TOURNAMENT? WHY DO WE CONSTANTLY MAKE LIFE DIFFICULT ON PURPOSE?
BECAUSE AN UNCHALLENGING LIFE WOULD BE BORING.
NO! IT WAS BECAUSE OF THE PROSPECT OF HOT BOYS IN JOUSTING PANTS! AND I AM SO DISAPPOINTED!

are boys ever hotter than when clad in fine, form-fitting jousting pants?

Children! Do you know what will happen in the future? I am sure we will have made many discoveries and

IN WHICH DAN WEIGHS HIS OPTIONS

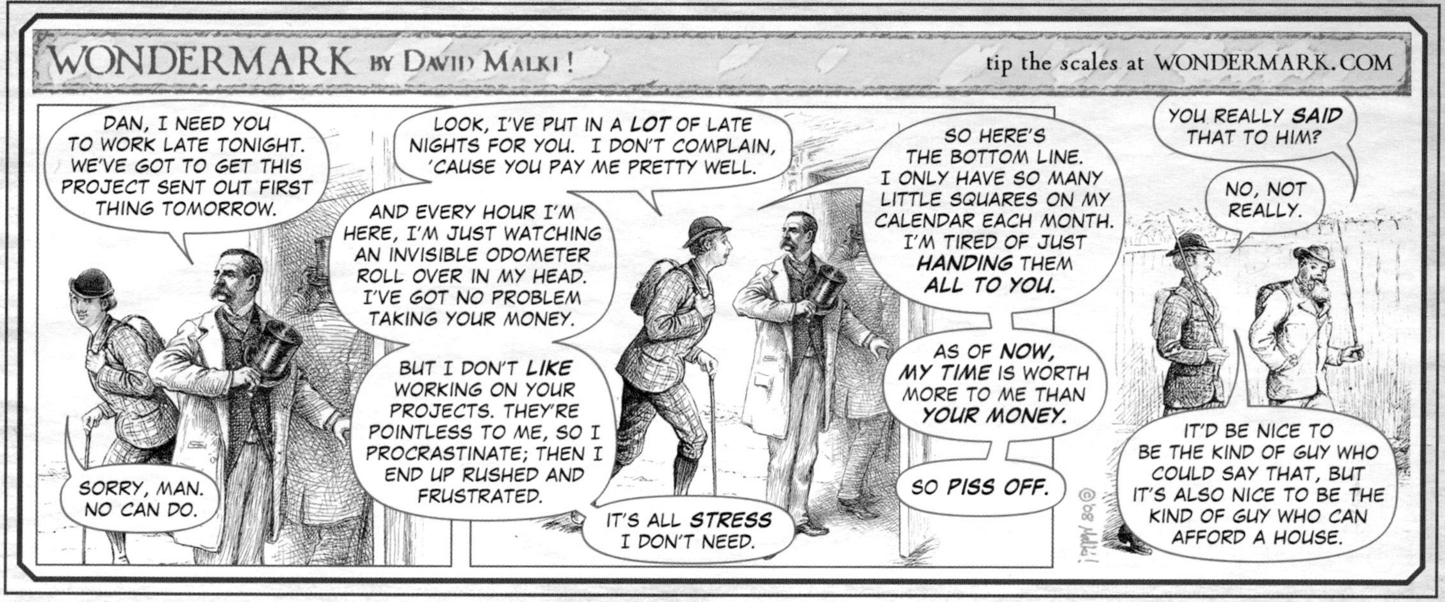
WONDERMARK BY DAVID MALKI !
tip the scales at WONDERMARK.COM
DAN, I NEED YOU TO WORK LATE TONIGHT. WE'VE GOT TO GET THIS PROJECT SENT OUT FIRST THING TOMORROW.
SORRY, MAN. NO CAN DO.
LOOK, I'VE PUT IN A *LOT* OF LATE NIGHTS FOR YOU. I DON'T COMPLAIN, 'CAUSE YOU PAY ME PRETTY WELL.
AND EVERY HOUR I'M HERE, I'M JUST WATCHING AN INVISIBLE ODOMETER ROLL OVER IN MY HEAD. I'VE GOT NO PROBLEM TAKING YOUR MONEY.
BUT I DON'T *LIKE* WORKING ON YOUR PROJECTS. THEY'RE POINTLESS TO ME, SO I PROCRASTINATE; THEN I END UP RUSHED AND FRUSTRATED.
IT'S ALL *STRESS* I DON'T NEED.
SO HERE'S THE BOTTOM LINE. I ONLY HAVE SO MANY LITTLE SQUARES ON MY CALENDAR EACH MONTH. I'M TIRED OF JUST *HANDING* THEM *ALL TO YOU.*
AS OF *NOW, MY TIME* IS WORTH MORE TO ME THAN *YOUR MONEY.*
SO *PISS OFF.*
©'08 Malki!
YOU REALLY *SAID* THAT TO HIM?
NO, NOT REALLY.
IT'D BE NICE TO BE THE KIND OF GUY WHO COULD SAY THAT, BUT IT'S ALSO NICE TO BE THE KIND OF GUY WHO CAN AFFORD A HOUSE.

the project was to taste-test delicious new flavors of ice cream!
IMAGINARY DAN MISSED OUT

IN WHICH EVENTS END POORLY

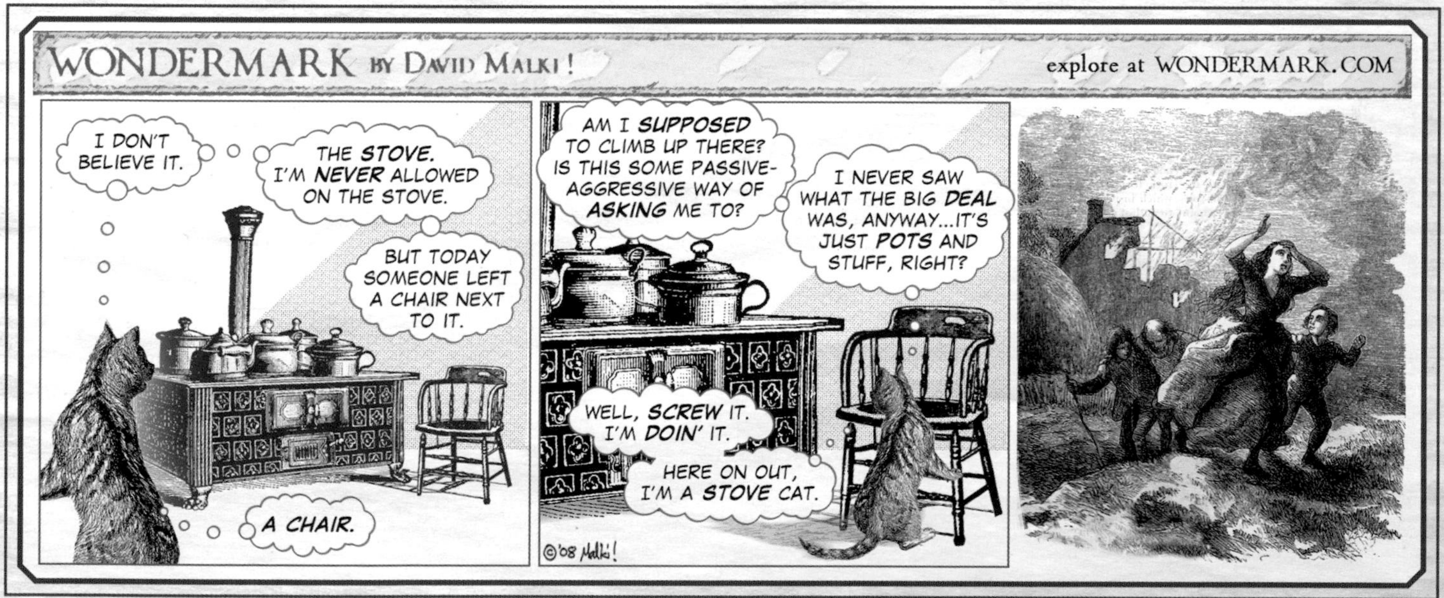
WONDERMARK BY DAVID MALKI !
explore at WONDERMARK.COM
I DON'T BELIEVE IT.
THE *STOVE.* I'M *NEVER* ALLOWED ON THE STOVE.
BUT TODAY SOMEONE LEFT A CHAIR NEXT TO IT.
A CHAIR.
AM I *SUPPOSED* TO CLIMB UP THERE? IS THIS SOME PASSIVE-AGGRESSIVE WAY OF *ASKING* ME TO?
I NEVER SAW WHAT THE BIG *DEAL* WAS, ANYWAY...IT'S JUST *POTS* AND STUFF, RIGHT?
WELL, *SCREW* IT. I'M *DOIN'* IT.
HERE ON OUT, I'M A *STOVE* CAT.
©'08 Malki!

YOU FAILED THE TEST MITTENS

IN WHICH MINDY REBUFFS AN ENTREATY

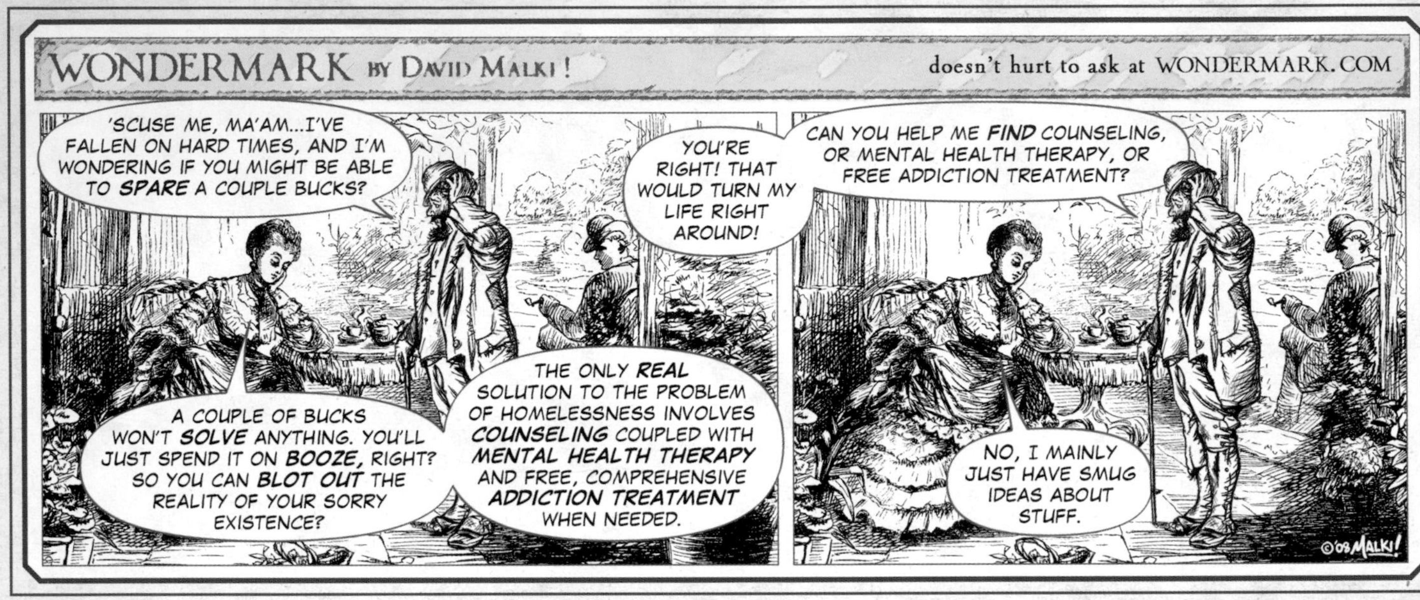
WONDERMARK BY DAVID MALKI !
doesn't hurt to ask at WONDERMARK.COM
'SCUSE ME, MA'AM...I'VE FALLEN ON HARD TIMES, AND I'M WONDERING IF YOU MIGHT BE ABLE TO SPARE A COUPLE BUCKS?
A COUPLE OF BUCKS WON'T SOLVE ANYTHING. YOU'LL JUST SPEND IT ON BOOZE, RIGHT? SO YOU CAN BLOT OUT THE REALITY OF YOUR SORRY EXISTENCE?
THE ONLY REAL SOLUTION TO THE PROBLEM OF HOMELESSNESS INVOLVES COUNSELING COUPLED WITH MENTAL HEALTH THERAPY AND FREE, COMPREHENSIVE ADDICTION TREATMENT WHEN NEEDED.
YOU'RE RIGHT! THAT WOULD TURN MY LIFE RIGHT AROUND!
CAN YOU HELP ME FIND COUNSELING, OR MENTAL HEALTH THERAPY, OR FREE ADDICTION TREATMENT?
NO, I MAINLY JUST HAVE SMUG IDEAS ABOUT STUFF.
©08 MALKI!

now get out of here before I call the cops

IN WHICH THE EVENING DOES NOT END WITH A KISS

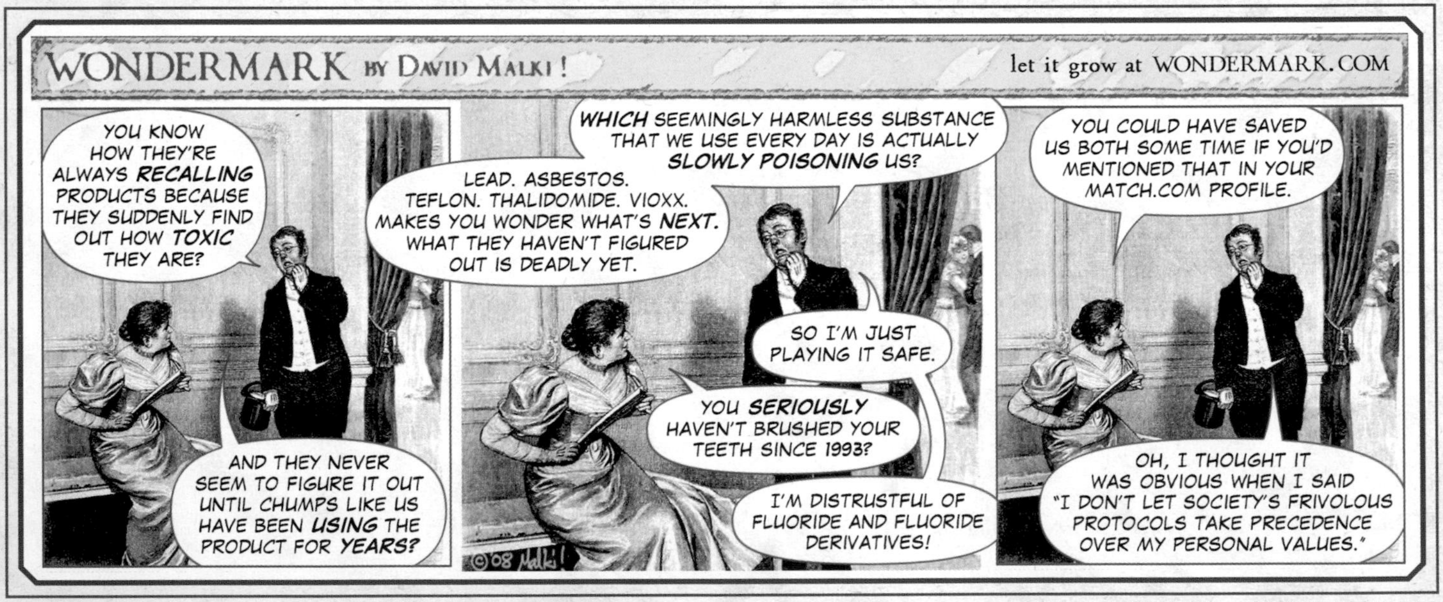
WONDERMARK BY DAVID MALKI !
let it grow at WONDERMARK.COM
YOU KNOW HOW THEY'RE ALWAYS RECALLING PRODUCTS BECAUSE THEY SUDDENLY FIND OUT HOW TOXIC THEY ARE?
AND THEY NEVER SEEM TO FIGURE IT OUT UNTIL CHUMPS LIKE US HAVE BEEN USING THE PRODUCT FOR YEARS?
LEAD. ASBESTOS. TEFLON. THALIDOMIDE. VIOXX. MAKES YOU WONDER WHAT'S NEXT. WHAT THEY HAVEN'T FIGURED OUT IS DEADLY YET.
WHICH SEEMINGLY HARMLESS SUBSTANCE THAT WE USE EVERY DAY IS ACTUALLY SLOWLY POISONING US?
SO I'M JUST PLAYING IT SAFE.
YOU SERIOUSLY HAVEN'T BRUSHED YOUR TEETH SINCE 1993?
I'M DISTRUSTFUL OF FLUORIDE AND FLUORIDE DERIVATIVES!
©08 Malki!
YOU COULD HAVE SAVED US BOTH SOME TIME IF YOU'D MENTIONED THAT IN YOUR MATCH.COM PROFILE.
OH, I THOUGHT IT WAS OBVIOUS WHEN I SAID "I DON'T LET SOCIETY'S FRIVOLOUS PROTOCOLS TAKE PRECEDENCE OVER MY PERSONAL VALUES."

you have to RESPECT my PERSONAL VALUES
especially ones I got from a WEBSITE

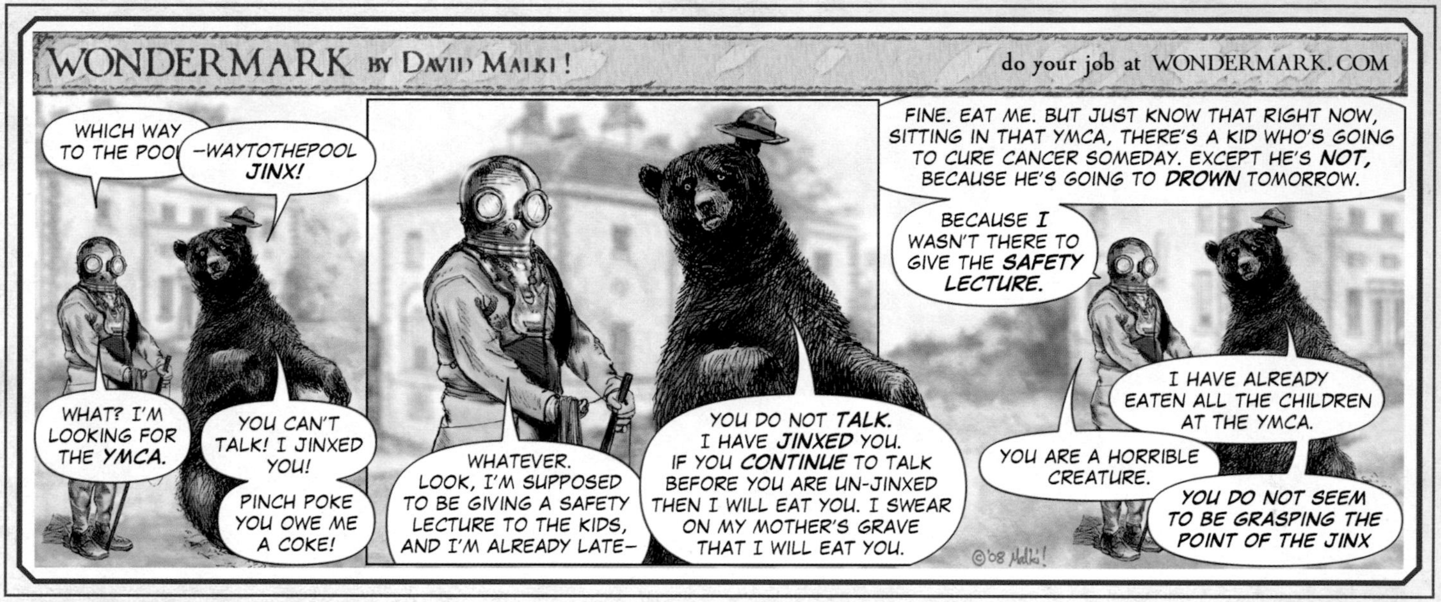
WONDERMARK BY DAVID MALKI !
do your job at WONDERMARK.COM
WHICH WAY TO THE POO[
-WAYTOTHEPOOL JINX!
WHAT? I'M LOOKING FOR THE YMCA.
YOU CAN'T TALK! I JINXED YOU!
PINCH POKE YOU OWE ME A COKE!
WHATEVER. LOOK, I'M SUPPOSED TO BE GIVING A SAFETY LECTURE TO THE KIDS, AND I'M ALREADY LATE–
YOU DO NOT TALK. I HAVE JINXED YOU. IF YOU CONTINUE TO TALK BEFORE YOU ARE UN-JINXED THEN I WILL EAT YOU. I SWEAR ON MY MOTHER'S GRAVE THAT I WILL EAT YOU.
FINE. EAT ME. BUT JUST KNOW THAT RIGHT NOW, SITTING IN THAT YMCA, THERE'S A KID WHO'S GOING TO CURE CANCER SOMEDAY. EXCEPT HE'S NOT, BECAUSE HE'S GOING TO DROWN TOMORROW.
BECAUSE I WASN'T THERE TO GIVE THE SAFETY LECTURE.
I HAVE ALREADY EATEN ALL THE CHILDREN AT THE YMCA.
YOU ARE A HORRIBLE CREATURE.
YOU DO NOT SEEM TO BE GRASPING THE POINT OF THE JINX
©'08 Malki!

Color by Philip R. Obermarck • philobermarck.com

Like so many of us, convincing himself that his job is Critically Important To The World is the only thing that gets Herve out of bed and into that stanky diving gear every morning.

Dramatic Review

NORBERT'S LATEST TRIUMPH.

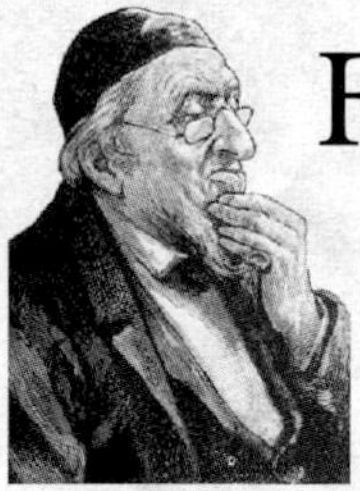

Followers of the theatre are by now well-versed in the talent and stagecraft of Norbert the Elephant. The pachyderm actor has never less than astounded his critics—and rarely has such a lauded talent ever *surpassed* every prior achievement. Yet that precisely is what Mr. the Elephant has done with his latest drama.

We have already had occasion to recommend very cordially the previous works of Mr. the Elephant's *oeuvre*, both in their conception and in the manner by which they are executed. His works are not merely nor mainly important in a *theatrical* mien—the sentiments to which he bears such earnest witness will be as new and as universal in the ages to come as today; the vigor of his thought and style will lose nothing to the lapse of time.

And thus comes his latest triumph, a dramatic reversal of all we have come to know and expect from Norbert. He is nearly invisible in a new role as Guido the Murderous Bear, although to those studied in Norbert's manners, enough of the elephant protrudes through the character to make evident his studied mastery. The performance hammers into permanence the rarely-challenged notion that as a delineator of character, without exaggeration, without sarcasm or lamentation, we think Norbert the Elephant has no superior, if he has any equal; and *In Which Children Suffer* gains what merit it has entirely from him.

It is a testament to Norbert's skill that the work is enjoyable at all. This tale of a certain Herve the Diver's (a pedestrian Brian Swanson)'s encounter with said bear (as portrayed by Mr. the Elephant) is near the antipodes of social relevance, being yet another trivial expression of the vulgar Bears In Ill-Fitting Hats movement so popular in the school-yards and penny-papers where fashions rise and die inexplicably—and inevitably without consequence.

Yet Norbert, in guise of the bear, stands firm as the piece's riveting center. In this manner he demonstrates to us his absolute command over the stage: we know at once that *every* character is his, that *any* character may yet be his in future, and the only question yet left lingering is: may *we all* actually be others of his performances as well?

SOLUTION: THE PEOPLE IN THE 'AFTER' PHOTO HAVE JUST BEEN LOUDLY AND CRUELLY REMINDED

IN WHICH JAKE DOES HIS BEST

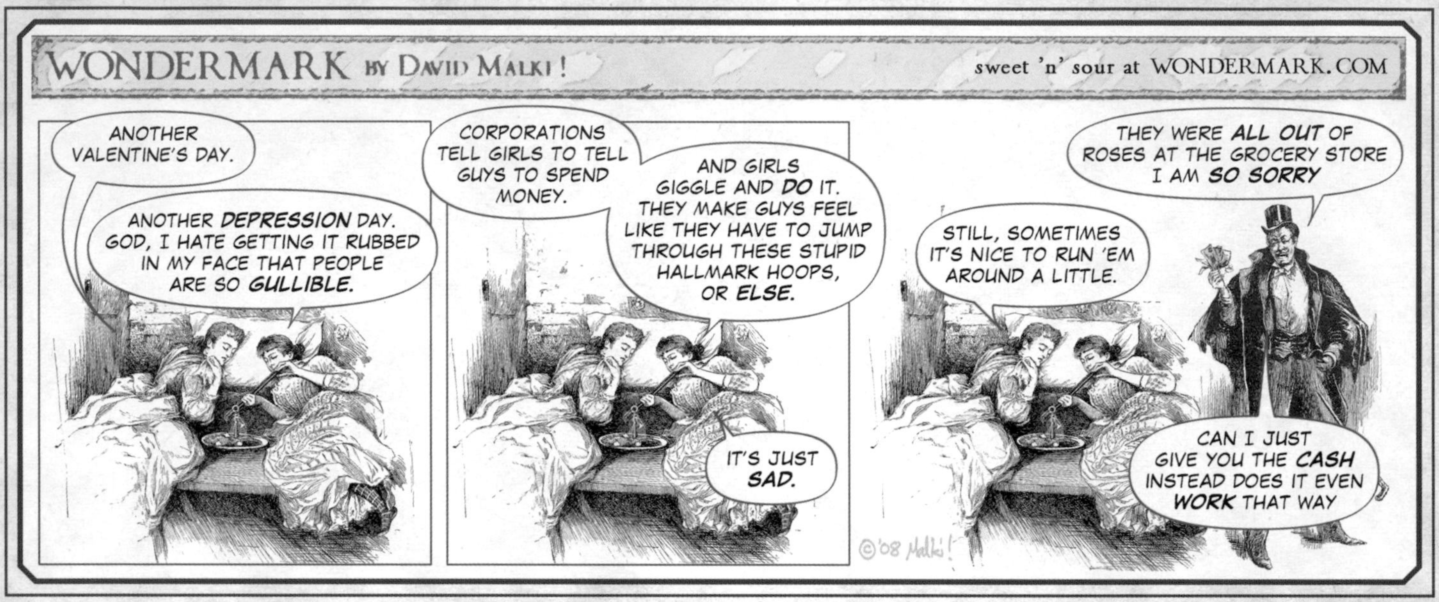
WONDERMARK BY DAVID MALKI !
sweet 'n' sour at WONDERMARK.COM
ANOTHER VALENTINE'S DAY.
ANOTHER DEPRESSION DAY. GOD, I HATE GETTING IT RUBBED IN MY FACE THAT PEOPLE ARE SO GULLIBLE.
CORPORATIONS TELL GIRLS TO TELL GUYS TO SPEND MONEY.
AND GIRLS GIGGLE AND DO IT. THEY MAKE GUYS FEEL LIKE THEY HAVE TO JUMP THROUGH THESE STUPID HALLMARK HOOPS, OR ELSE.
IT'S JUST SAD.
THEY WERE ALL OUT OF ROSES AT THE GROCERY STORE I AM SO SORRY
STILL, SOMETIMES IT'S NICE TO RUN 'EM AROUND A LITTLE.
CAN I JUST GIVE YOU THE CASH INSTEAD DOES IT EVEN WORK THAT WAY
©'08 Malki!

since you INSIST on flaunting your boyfriend everywhere I have no choice but to create my OWN holiday just for lonely people. It shall fall on the third Monday in February. It shall be called Presidents' Day

IN WHICH RICH READS STATISTICS

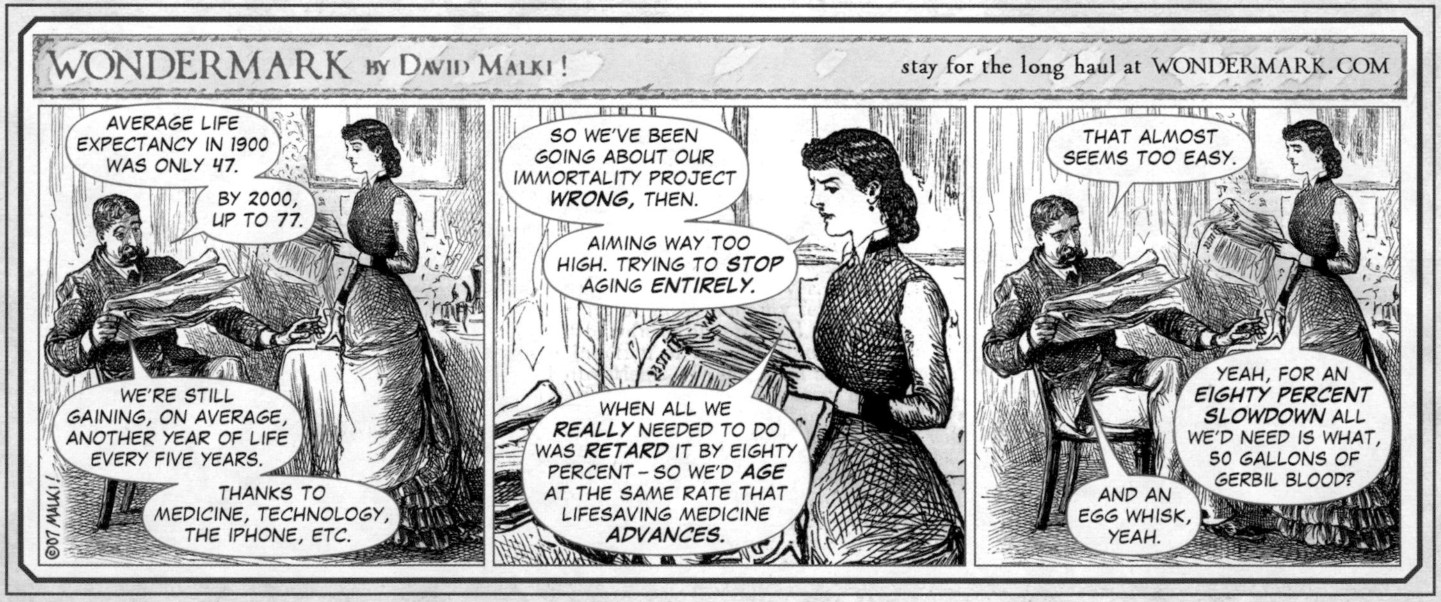
WONDERMARK BY DAVID MALKI !
stay for the long haul at WONDERMARK.COM
AVERAGE LIFE EXPECTANCY IN 1900 WAS ONLY 47.
BY 2000, UP TO 77.
WE'RE STILL GAINING, ON AVERAGE, ANOTHER YEAR OF LIFE EVERY FIVE YEARS.
THANKS TO MEDICINE, TECHNOLOGY, THE IPHONE, ETC.
©07 MALKI!
SO WE'VE BEEN GOING ABOUT OUR IMMORTALITY PROJECT WRONG, THEN.
AIMING WAY TOO HIGH. TRYING TO STOP AGING ENTIRELY.
WHEN ALL WE REALLY NEEDED TO DO WAS RETARD IT BY EIGHTY PERCENT – SO WE'D AGE AT THE SAME RATE THAT LIFESAVING MEDICINE ADVANCES.
THAT ALMOST SEEMS TOO EASY.
YEAH, FOR AN EIGHTY PERCENT SLOWDOWN ALL WE'D NEED IS WHAT, 50 GALLONS OF GERBIL BLOOD?
AND AN EGG WHISK, YEAH.

race you to the pet store

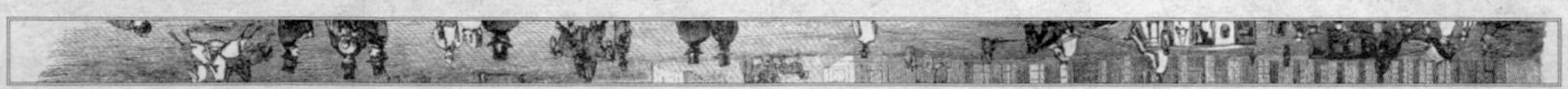

IN WHICH PROGRESS LOOKS LIKELY

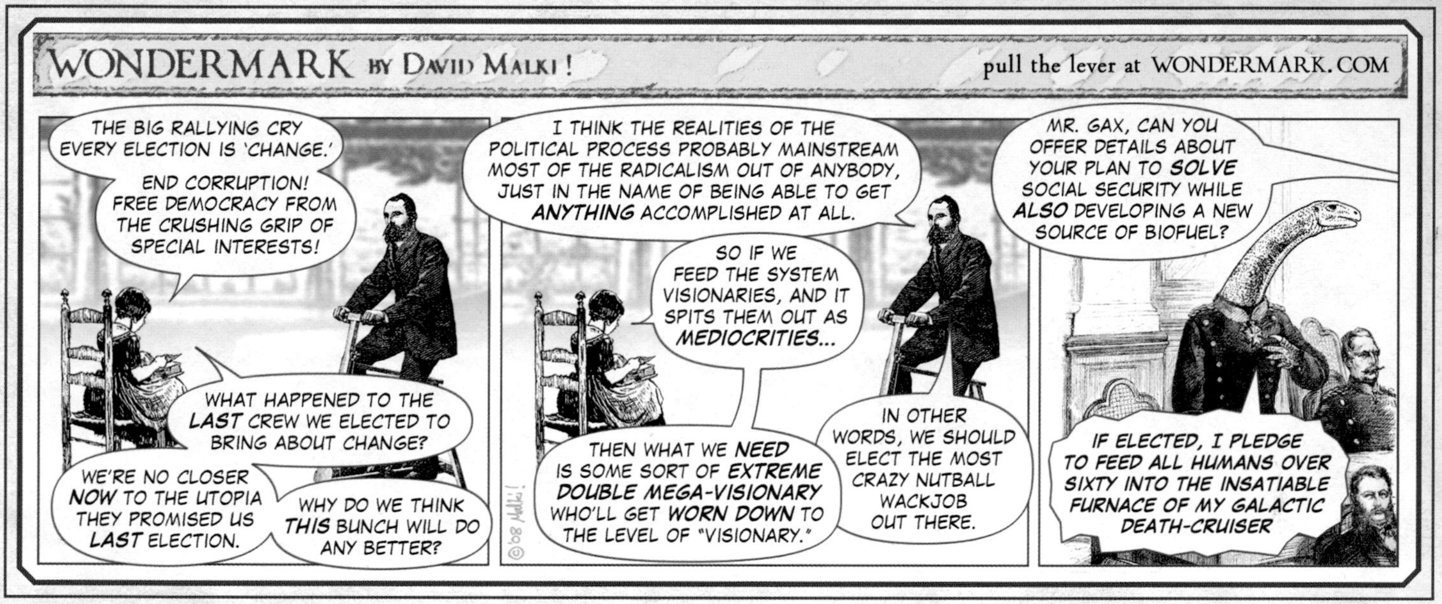
WONDERMARK BY DAVID MALKI !
pull the lever at WONDERMARK.COM
THE BIG RALLYING CRY EVERY ELECTION IS 'CHANGE.'
END CORRUPTION! FREE DEMOCRACY FROM THE CRUSHING GRIP OF SPECIAL INTERESTS!
WHAT HAPPENED TO THE LAST CREW WE ELECTED TO BRING ABOUT CHANGE?
WE'RE NO CLOSER NOW TO THE UTOPIA THEY PROMISED US LAST ELECTION.
WHY DO WE THINK THIS BUNCH WILL DO ANY BETTER?
I THINK THE REALITIES OF THE POLITICAL PROCESS PROBABLY MAINSTREAM MOST OF THE RADICALISM OUT OF ANYBODY, JUST IN THE NAME OF BEING ABLE TO GET ANYTHING ACCOMPLISHED AT ALL.
SO IF WE FEED THE SYSTEM VISIONARIES, AND IT SPITS THEM OUT AS MEDIOCRITIES...
THEN WHAT WE NEED IS SOME SORT OF EXTREME DOUBLE MEGA-VISIONARY WHO'LL GET WORN DOWN TO THE LEVEL OF "VISIONARY."
IN OTHER WORDS, WE SHOULD ELECT THE MOST CRAZY NUTBALL WACKJOB OUT THERE.
©'08 Malki !
MR. GAX, CAN YOU OFFER DETAILS ABOUT YOUR PLAN TO SOLVE SOCIAL SECURITY WHILE ALSO DEVELOPING A NEW SOURCE OF BIOFUEL?
IF ELECTED, I PLEDGE TO FEED ALL HUMANS OVER SIXTY INTO THE INSATIABLE FURNACE OF MY GALACTIC DEATH-CRUISER

10

ALSO I WILL OUTLAW TREE SAP

IN WHICH HAIR VEXES

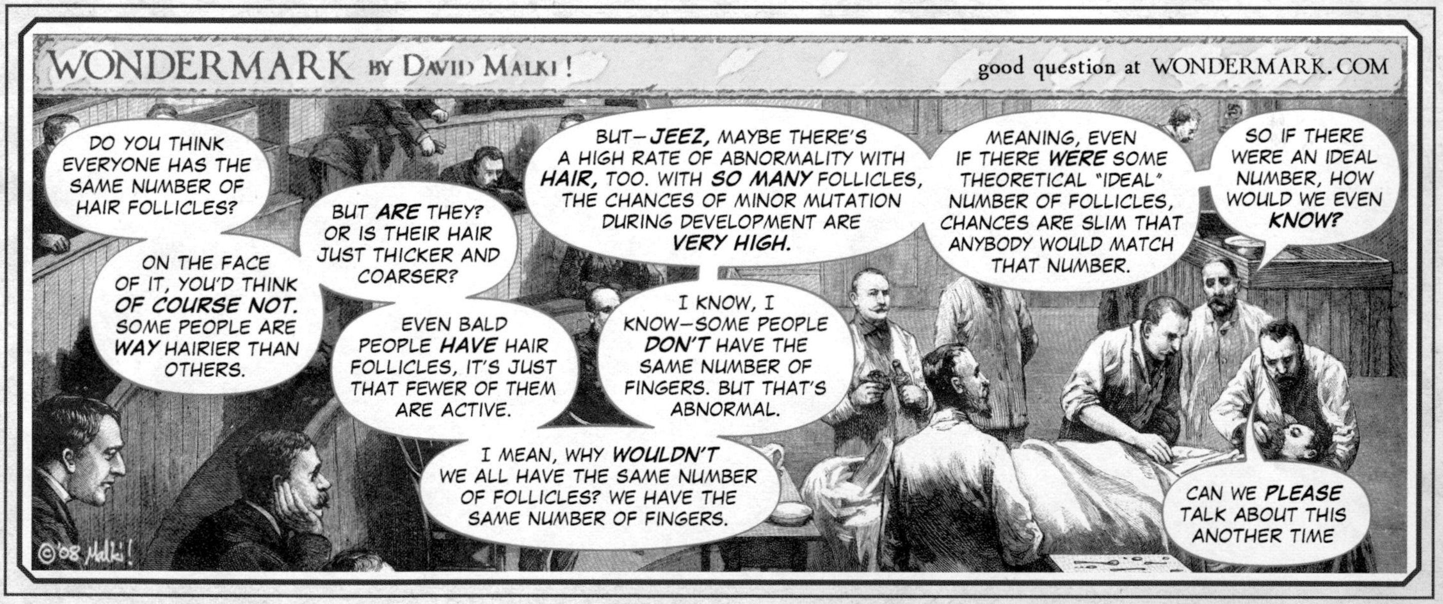
WONDERMARK BY DAVID MALKI !
good question at WONDERMARK.COM
DO YOU THINK EVERYONE HAS THE SAME NUMBER OF HAIR FOLLICLES?
ON THE FACE OF IT, YOU'D THINK OF COURSE NOT. SOME PEOPLE ARE WAY HAIRIER THAN OTHERS.
BUT ARE THEY? OR IS THEIR HAIR JUST THICKER AND COARSER?
EVEN BALD PEOPLE HAVE HAIR FOLLICLES, IT'S JUST THAT FEWER OF THEM ARE ACTIVE.
I MEAN, WHY WOULDN'T WE ALL HAVE THE SAME NUMBER OF FOLLICLES? WE HAVE THE SAME NUMBER OF FINGERS.
I KNOW, I KNOW—SOME PEOPLE DON'T HAVE THE SAME NUMBER OF FINGERS. BUT THAT'S ABNORMAL.
BUT—JEEZ, MAYBE THERE'S A HIGH RATE OF ABNORMALITY WITH HAIR, TOO. WITH SO MANY FOLLICLES, THE CHANCES OF MINOR MUTATION DURING DEVELOPMENT ARE VERY HIGH.
MEANING, EVEN IF THERE WERE SOME THEORETICAL "IDEAL" NUMBER OF FOLLICLES, CHANCES ARE SLIM THAT ANYBODY WOULD MATCH THAT NUMBER.
SO IF THERE WERE AN IDEAL NUMBER, HOW WOULD WE EVEN KNOW?
CAN WE PLEASE TALK ABOUT THIS ANOTHER TIME
©'08 Malki !

no

IN WHICH A FORTUNE IS SOUGHT

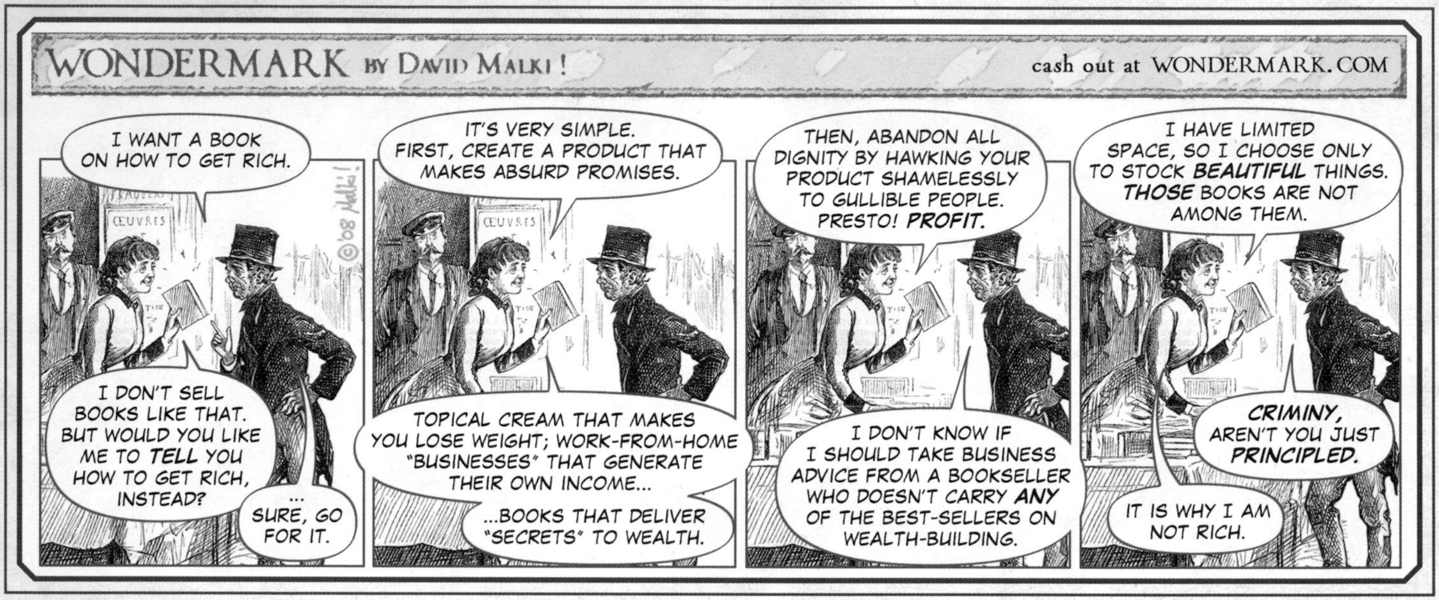
WONDERMARK BY DAVID MALKI !
cash out at WONDERMARK.COM
I WANT A BOOK ON HOW TO GET RICH.
I DON'T SELL BOOKS LIKE THAT. BUT WOULD YOU LIKE ME TO **TELL** YOU HOW TO GET RICH, INSTEAD?
... SURE, GO FOR IT.
IT'S VERY SIMPLE. FIRST, CREATE A PRODUCT THAT MAKES ABSURD PROMISES.
TOPICAL CREAM THAT MAKES YOU LOSE WEIGHT; WORK-FROM-HOME "BUSINESSES" THAT GENERATE THEIR OWN INCOME...
...BOOKS THAT DELIVER "SECRETS" TO WEALTH.
THEN, ABANDON ALL DIGNITY BY HAWKING YOUR PRODUCT SHAMELESSLY TO GULLIBLE PEOPLE. PRESTO! **PROFIT.**
I DON'T KNOW IF I SHOULD TAKE BUSINESS ADVICE FROM A BOOKSELLER WHO DOESN'T CARRY **ANY** OF THE BEST-SELLERS ON WEALTH-BUILDING.
I HAVE LIMITED SPACE, SO I CHOOSE ONLY TO STOCK **BEAUTIFUL** THINGS. **THOSE** BOOKS ARE NOT AMONG THEM.
CRIMINY, AREN'T YOU JUST **PRINCIPLED.**
IT IS WHY I AM NOT RICH.

life could be so easy, you know

IN WHICH ARE TRIED UNCONVENTIONAL METHODS

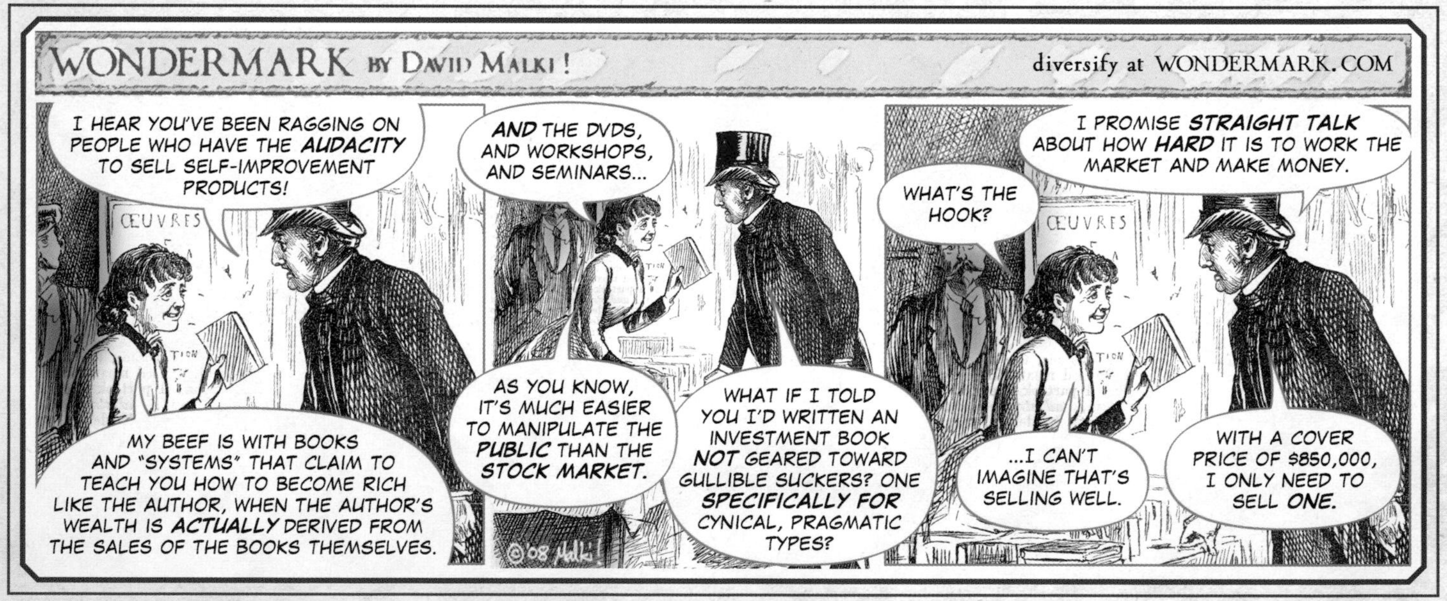
WONDERMARK BY DAVID MALKI !
diversify at WONDERMARK.COM
I HEAR YOU'VE BEEN RAGGING ON PEOPLE WHO HAVE THE **AUDACITY** TO SELL SELF-IMPROVEMENT PRODUCTS!
MY BEEF IS WITH BOOKS AND "SYSTEMS" THAT CLAIM TO TEACH YOU HOW TO BECOME RICH LIKE THE AUTHOR, WHEN THE AUTHOR'S WEALTH IS **ACTUALLY** DERIVED FROM THE SALES OF THE BOOKS THEMSELVES.
AND THE DVDS, AND WORKSHOPS, AND SEMINARS...
AS YOU KNOW, IT'S MUCH EASIER TO MANIPULATE THE **PUBLIC** THAN THE **STOCK MARKET.**
WHAT IF I TOLD YOU I'D WRITTEN AN INVESTMENT BOOK **NOT** GEARED TOWARD GULLIBLE SUCKERS? ONE **SPECIFICALLY FOR** CYNICAL, PRAGMATIC TYPES?
WHAT'S THE HOOK?
I PROMISE **STRAIGHT TALK** ABOUT HOW **HARD** IT IS TO WORK THE MARKET AND MAKE MONEY.
...I CAN'T IMAGINE THAT'S SELLING WELL.
WITH A COVER PRICE OF $850,000, I ONLY NEED TO SELL **ONE.**

i had them printed at kinko's, so, you know, not actually that much of a markup

This stuff doesn't grow on trees, you know. It doesn't grow on damn *trees*.

IN WHICH A HARD ROAD LIES AHEAD

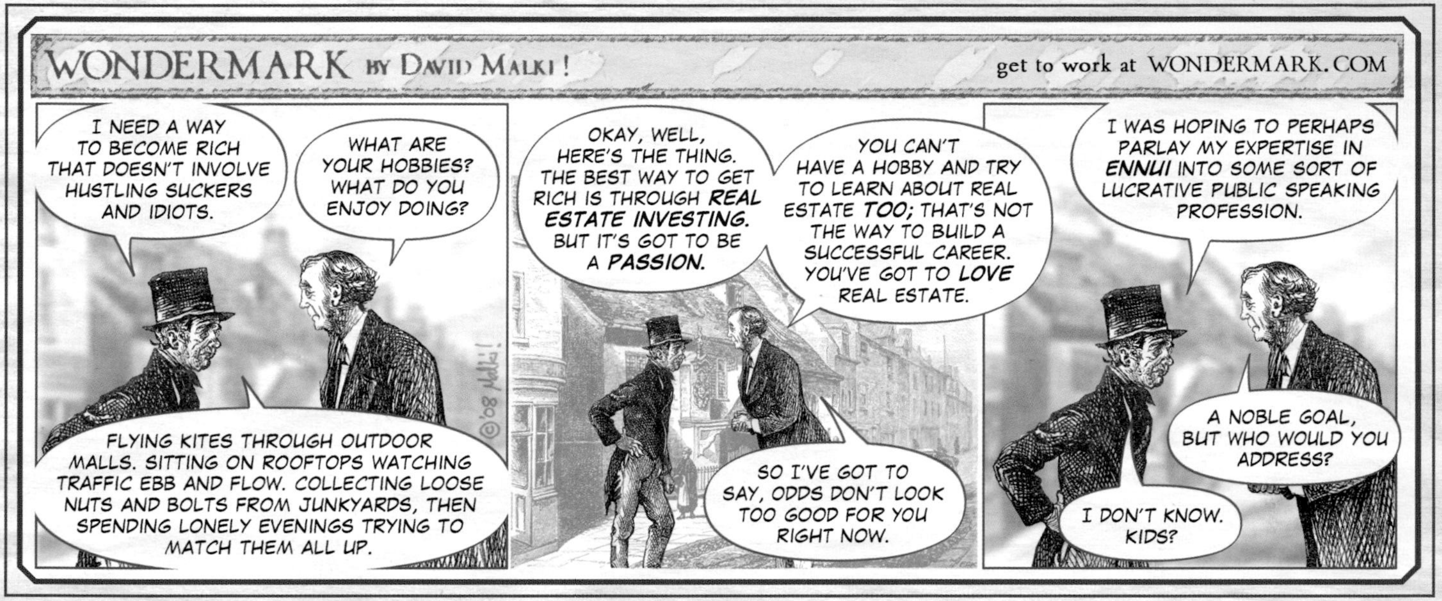
WONDERMARK BY DAVID MALKI !
get to work at WONDERMARK.COM
I NEED A WAY TO BECOME RICH THAT DOESN'T INVOLVE HUSTLING SUCKERS AND IDIOTS.
WHAT ARE YOUR HOBBIES? WHAT DO YOU ENJOY DOING?
FLYING KITES THROUGH OUTDOOR MALLS. SITTING ON ROOFTOPS WATCHING TRAFFIC EBB AND FLOW. COLLECTING LOOSE NUTS AND BOLTS FROM JUNKYARDS, THEN SPENDING LONELY EVENINGS TRYING TO MATCH THEM ALL UP.
©'08 Malki !
OKAY, WELL, HERE'S THE THING. THE BEST WAY TO GET RICH IS THROUGH **REAL ESTATE INVESTING.** BUT IT'S GOT TO BE A **PASSION.**
YOU CAN'T HAVE A HOBBY AND TRY TO LEARN ABOUT REAL ESTATE **TOO;** THAT'S NOT THE WAY TO BUILD A SUCCESSFUL CAREER. YOU'VE GOT TO **LOVE** REAL ESTATE.
SO I'VE GOT TO SAY, ODDS DON'T LOOK TOO GOOD FOR YOU RIGHT NOW.
I WAS HOPING TO PERHAPS PARLAY MY EXPERTISE IN **ENNUI** INTO SOME SORT OF LUCRATIVE PUBLIC SPEAKING PROFESSION.
A NOBLE GOAL, BUT WHO WOULD YOU ADDRESS?
I DON'T KNOW. KIDS?

everyone just trudging out of the assembly staring at their feet

IN WHICH ALL COMES TO NAUGHT

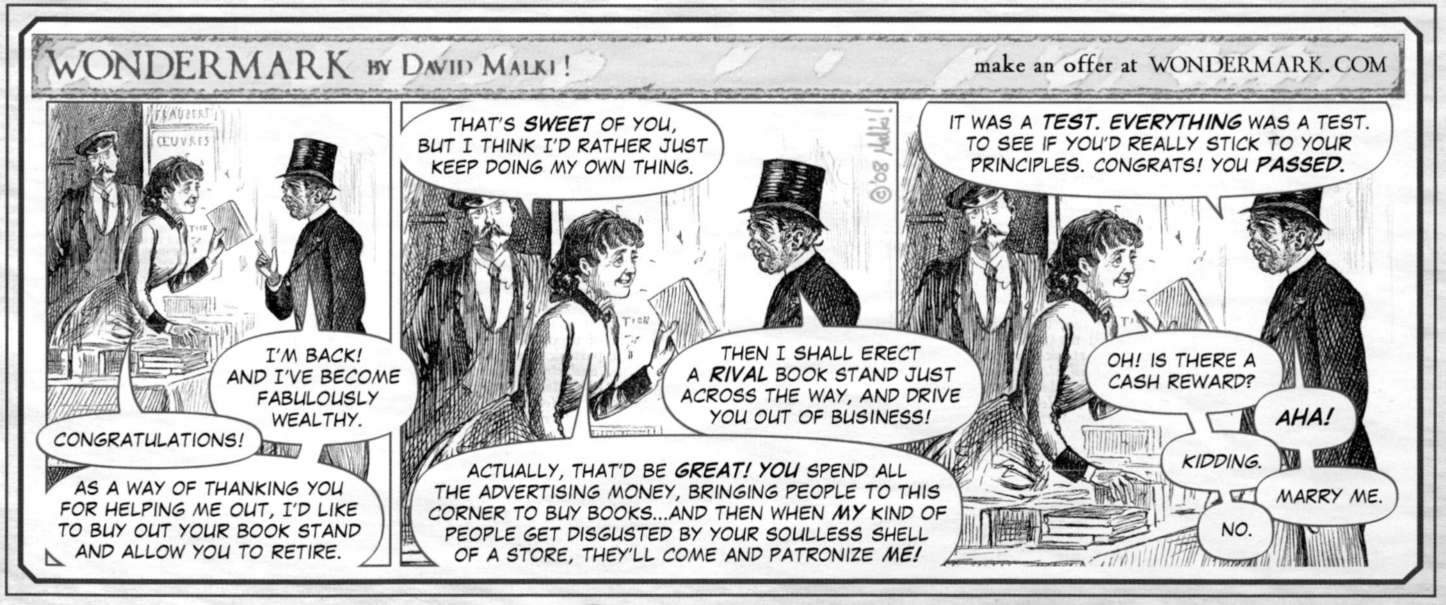
WONDERMARK BY DAVID MALKI !
make an offer at WONDERMARK.COM
I'M BACK! AND I'VE BECOME FABULOUSLY WEALTHY.
CONGRATULATIONS!
AS A WAY OF THANKING YOU FOR HELPING ME OUT, I'D LIKE TO BUY OUT YOUR BOOK STAND AND ALLOW YOU TO RETIRE.
THAT'S **SWEET** OF YOU, BUT I THINK I'D RATHER JUST KEEP DOING MY OWN THING.
©'08 Malki !
THEN I SHALL ERECT A **RIVAL** BOOK STAND JUST ACROSS THE WAY, AND DRIVE YOU OUT OF BUSINESS!
ACTUALLY, THAT'D BE **GREAT! YOU** SPEND ALL THE ADVERTISING MONEY, BRINGING PEOPLE TO THIS CORNER TO BUY BOOKS...AND THEN WHEN **MY** KIND OF PEOPLE GET DISGUSTED BY YOUR SOULLESS SHELL OF A STORE, THEY'LL COME AND PATRONIZE **ME!**
IT WAS A **TEST. EVERYTHING** WAS A TEST. TO SEE IF YOU'D REALLY STICK TO YOUR PRINCIPLES. CONGRATS! YOU **PASSED.**
OH! IS THERE A CASH REWARD?
AHA!
KIDDING.
MARRY ME.
NO.

how 'bout now? how 'bout now? how 'bout...now?

give whoever (or *whatever*) keeps wasting his expensive film a stern talking-to?

IN WHICH SOAP FAILS

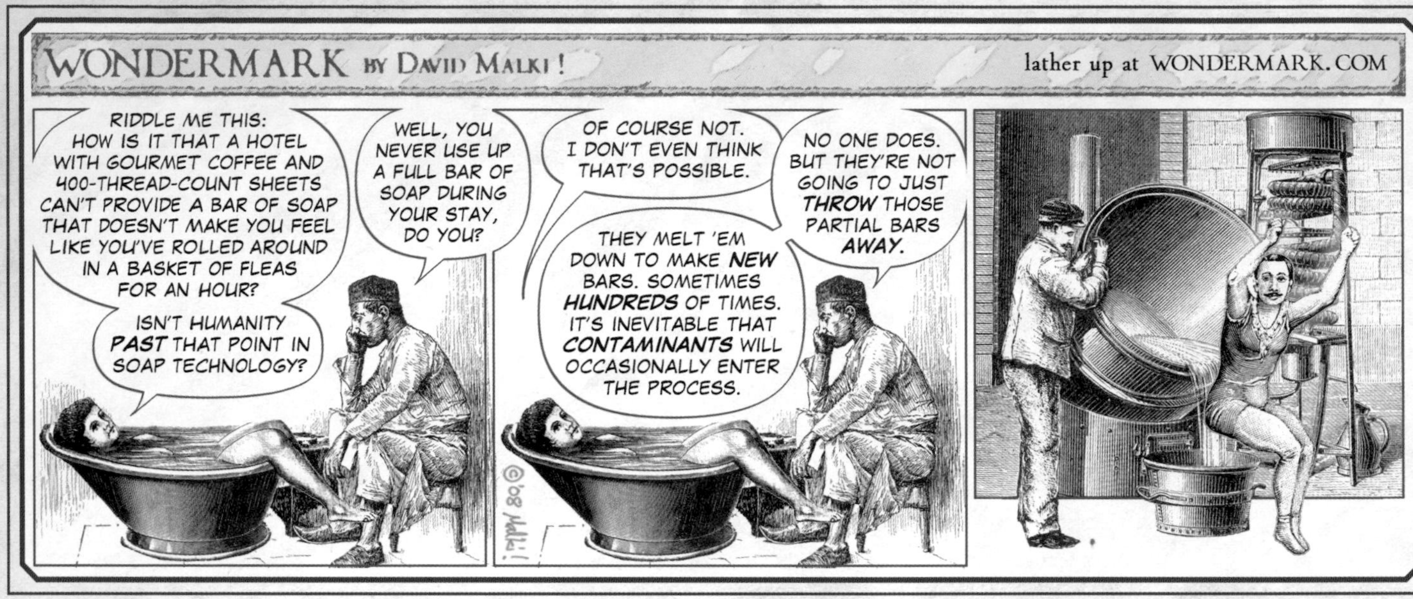
WONDERMARK BY DAVID MALKI !
lather up at WONDERMARK.COM
RIDDLE ME THIS: HOW IS IT THAT A HOTEL WITH GOURMET COFFEE AND 400-THREAD-COUNT SHEETS CAN'T PROVIDE A BAR OF SOAP THAT DOESN'T MAKE YOU FEEL LIKE YOU'VE ROLLED AROUND IN A BASKET OF FLEAS FOR AN HOUR?
ISN'T HUMANITY **PAST** THAT POINT IN SOAP TECHNOLOGY?
WELL, YOU NEVER USE UP A FULL BAR OF SOAP DURING YOUR STAY, DO YOU?
©'08 Malki !
OF COURSE NOT. I DON'T EVEN THINK THAT'S POSSIBLE.
NO ONE DOES. BUT THEY'RE NOT GOING TO JUST **THROW** THOSE PARTIAL BARS **AWAY.**
THEY MELT 'EM DOWN TO MAKE **NEW** BARS. SOMETIMES **HUNDREDS** OF TIMES. IT'S INEVITABLE THAT **CONTAMINANTS** WILL OCCASIONALLY ENTER THE PROCESS.

now we can claim it has 'organic ingredients'

A REASONABLE SOLUTION

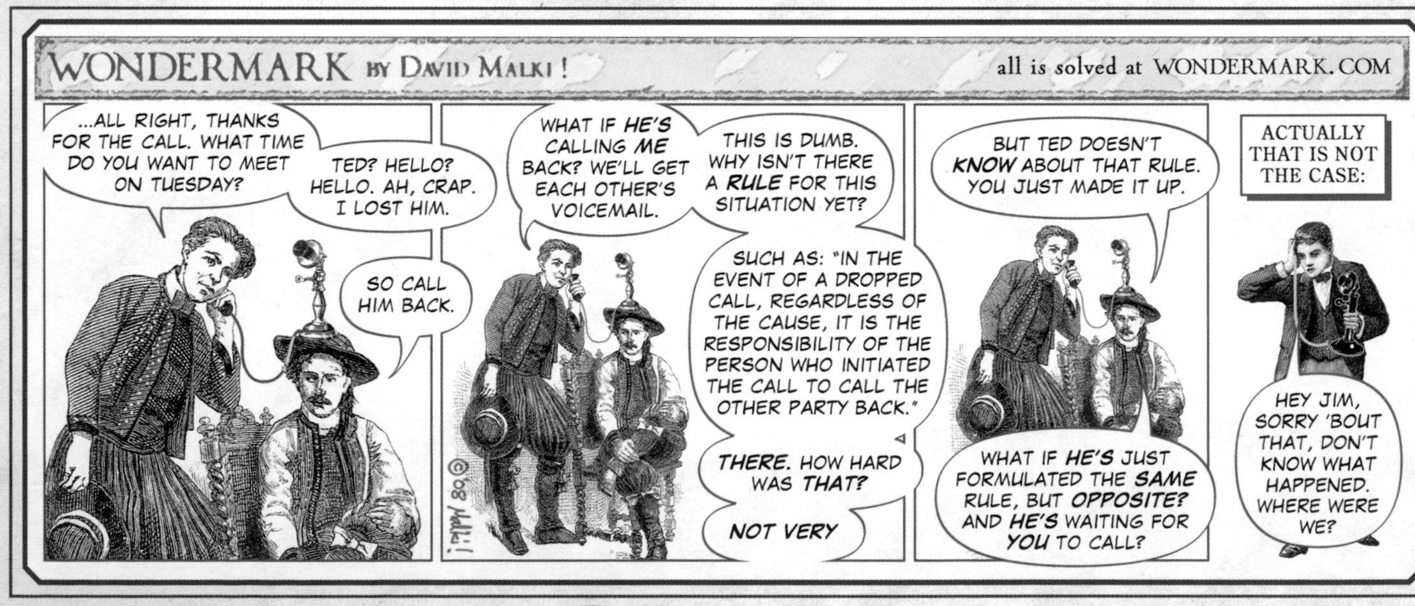
WONDERMARK BY DAVID MALKI !
all is solved at WONDERMARK.COM
...ALL RIGHT, THANKS FOR THE CALL. WHAT TIME DO YOU WANT TO MEET ON TUESDAY?
TED? HELLO? HELLO. AH, CRAP. I LOST HIM.
SO CALL HIM BACK.
WHAT IF **HE'S** CALLING **ME** BACK? WE'LL GET EACH OTHER'S VOICEMAIL.
THIS IS DUMB. WHY ISN'T THERE A **RULE** FOR THIS SITUATION YET?
SUCH AS: "IN THE EVENT OF A DROPPED CALL, REGARDLESS OF THE CAUSE, IT IS THE RESPONSIBILITY OF THE PERSON WHO INITIATED THE CALL TO CALL THE OTHER PARTY BACK."
THERE. HOW HARD WAS **THAT?**
NOT VERY
©'08 Malki !
BUT TED DOESN'T **KNOW** ABOUT THAT RULE. YOU JUST MADE IT UP.
WHAT IF **HE'S** JUST FORMULATED THE **SAME** RULE, BUT **OPPOSITE?** AND **HE'S** WAITING FOR **YOU** TO CALL?
ACTUALLY THAT IS NOT THE CASE:
HEY JIM, SORRY 'BOUT THAT, DON'T KNOW WHAT HAPPENED. WHERE WERE WE?

this is a real rule now okay

the *before* and *after* images and spot what's different about them, so that George can

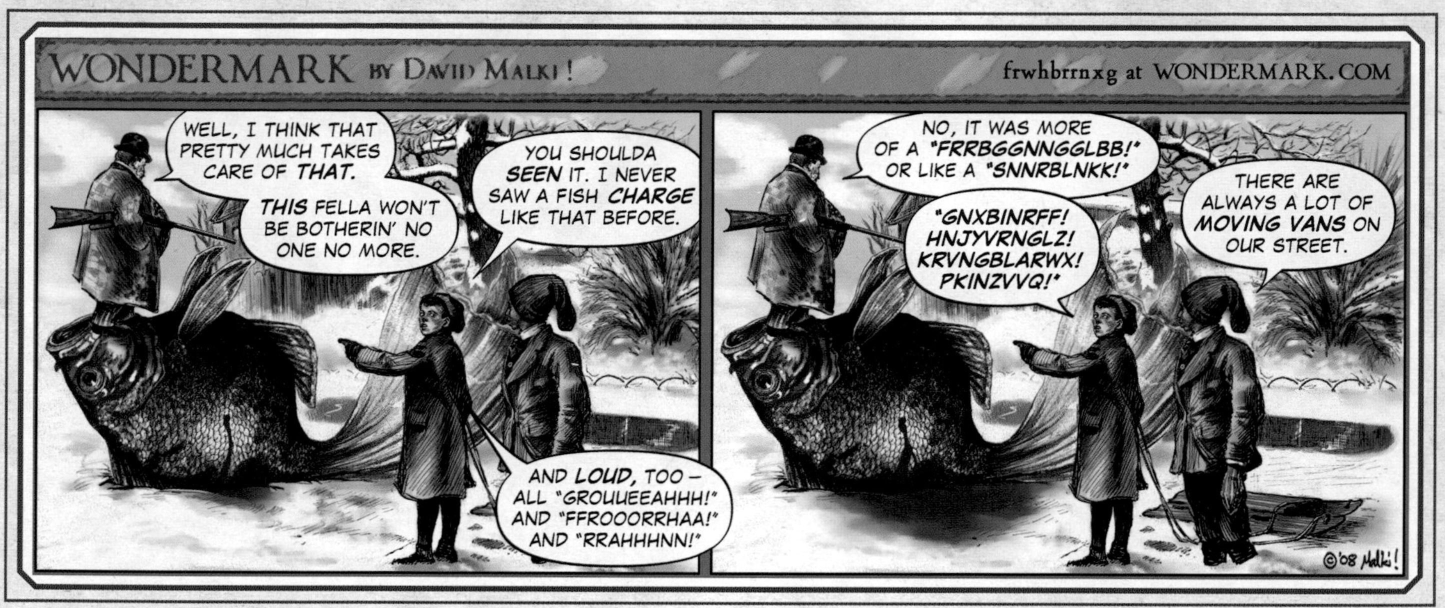
WONDERMARK BY DAVID MALKI !
frwhbrrnxg at WONDERMARK.COM
WELL, I THINK THAT PRETTY MUCH TAKES CARE OF THAT.
THIS FELLA WON'T BE BOTHERIN' NO ONE NO MORE.
YOU SHOULDA SEEN IT. I NEVER SAW A FISH CHARGE LIKE THAT BEFORE.
AND LOUD, TOO — ALL "GROUUEEAHHH!" AND "FFROOORRHAA!" AND "RRAHHHNN!"
NO, IT WAS MORE OF A "FRRBGGNNGGLBB!" OR LIKE A "SNNRBLNKK!"
"GNXBINRFF! HNJYVRNGLZ! KRVNGBLARWX! PKINZVVQ!"
THERE ARE ALWAYS A LOT OF MOVING VANS ON OUR STREET.
©'08 Malki!

Color by Jolly Rotten • jollyrotten.de

probably for unrelated reasons

craigslist > for sale / wanted > organic foods

fresh sushi-grade fish - $8/lb - you cut

Come and get it! All the fresh fish you want. Pick the choicest bits, first come first served. NOT farm-raised fish -- totally wild and native. Eat local!

• it's NOT ok to contact this poster with services or other commercial interests

craigslist > for sale / wanted > farm & garden

fish for compost - $3/lb - you haul away

Great organic material for gardening. I'll provide plastic bags and help you scoop. Come and get it, it's going fast!

• it's NOT ok to contact this poster with services or other commercial interests

craigslist > for sale / wanted > barter

will trade old fish for ???

Looking for an iPod Touch or newer Xbox, but make me your best offer. I've got a lot of this stuff, so I'm happy to do multiple trades for smaller batches.

• it's NOT ok to contact this poster with services or other commercial interests

craigslist > for sale / wanted > free stuff

approx. 700 lbs. of rotting fish

Craft project? Frat prank? Biofuel? I don't know and I don't care. Come and take all you want. Email for pics.

• it's NOT ok to contact this poster with services or other commercial interests

craigslist > gigs > labor gigs

disposal crew for biowaste

Need to haul about 1/2 ton of fish to dump/ocean/wherever it goes. You'll need a truck or at least a station wagon. I'll also pay to clean your vehicle after.

• Compensation: $20.00
• it's NOT ok to contact this poster with services or other commercial interests

craigslist > housing > housing swap

premium suburban 2BR/2BA

Big house, new kitchen. Approx. 30 sq. ft. of yard is unusable. Ideal place for someone without much of a sense of smell. Long-term swaps preferred.

• it's NOT ok to contact this poster with services or other commercial interests

Something is changing in the scene during his exposure. Can you look closely at

IN WHICH A LONG HAUL LIES AHEAD

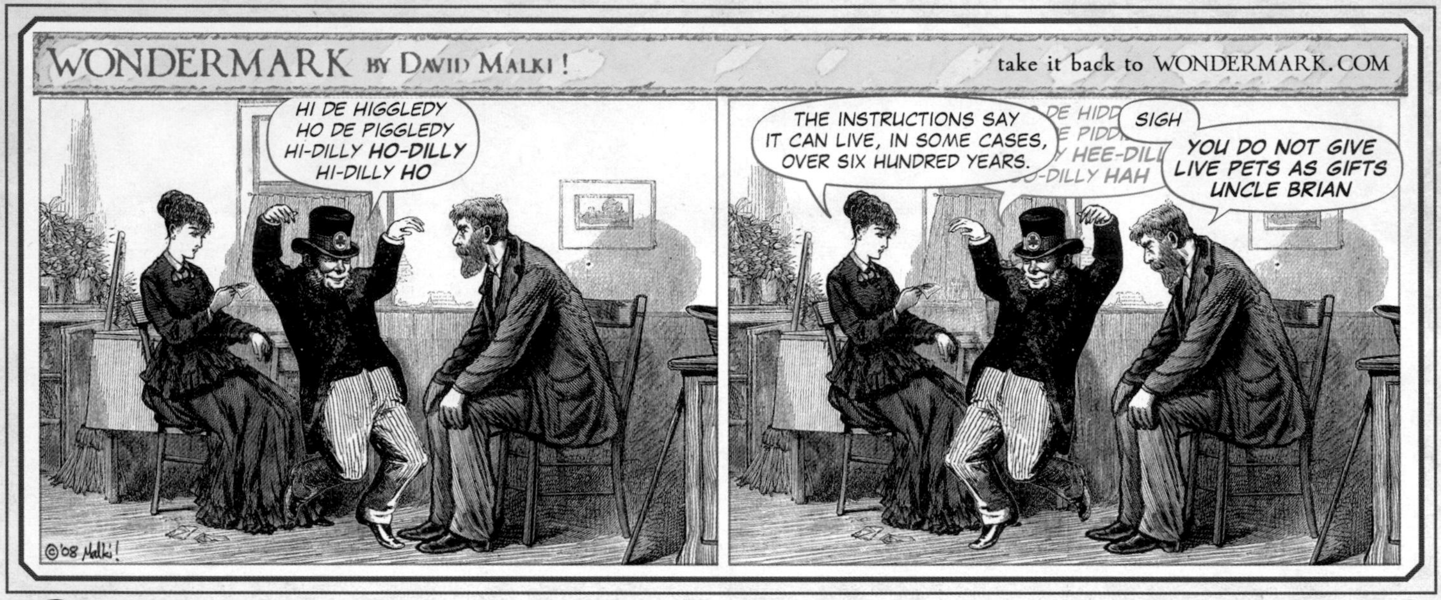
WONDERMARK BY DAVID MALKI !
take it back to WONDERMARK.COM
HI DE HIGGLEDY HO DE PIGGLEDY HI-DILLY HO-DILLY HI-DILLY HO
©'08 Malki!
THE INSTRUCTIONS SAY IT CAN LIVE, IN SOME CASES, OVER SIX HUNDRED YEARS.
SIGH
YOU DO NOT GIVE LIVE PETS AS GIFTS UNCLE BRIAN

11

sure the baby minotaur was cute but FOR HOW LONG

IN WHICH THINGS GROW DARK

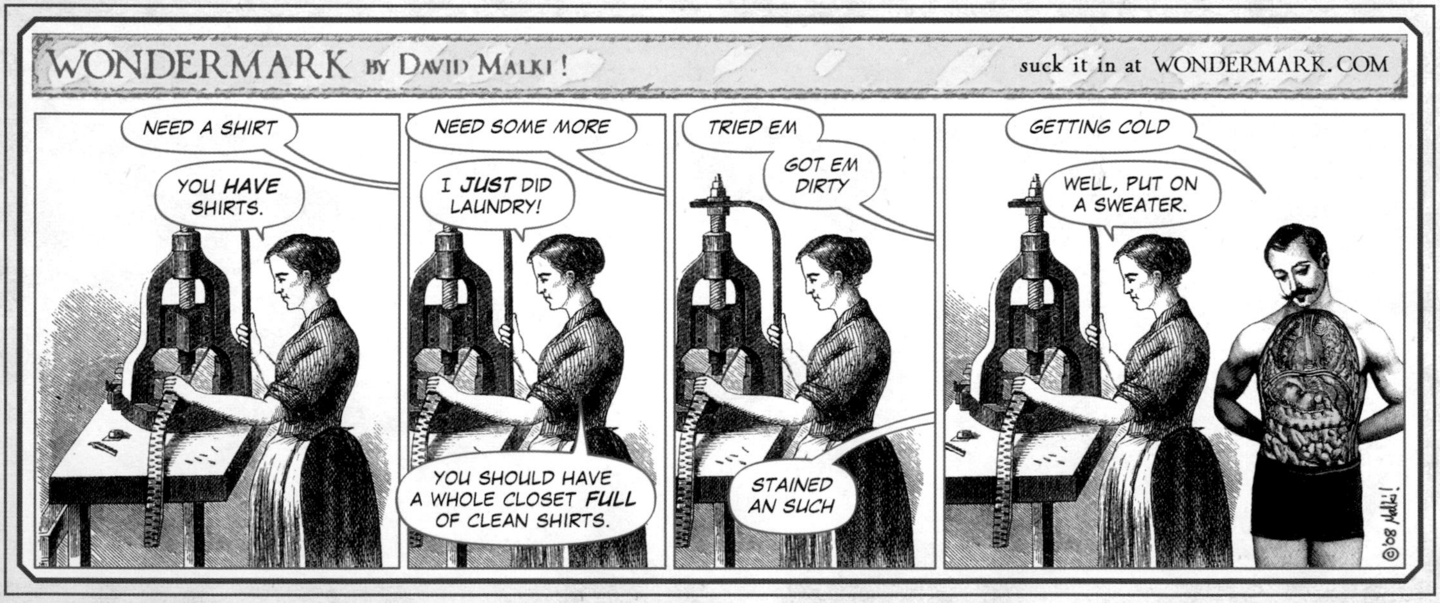
WONDERMARK BY DAVID MALKI !
suck it in at WONDERMARK.COM
NEED A SHIRT
YOU HAVE SHIRTS.
NEED SOME MORE
I JUST DID LAUNDRY!
YOU SHOULD HAVE A WHOLE CLOSET FULL OF CLEAN SHIRTS.
TRIED EM
GOT EM DIRTY
STAINED AN SUCH
GETTING COLD
WELL, PUT ON A SWEATER.
©'08 Malki!

not one of the good ones though

George Eastman is trying to take photographs, but they keep turning out blurry!

IN WHICH BAGGAGE IS EMBLAZONED

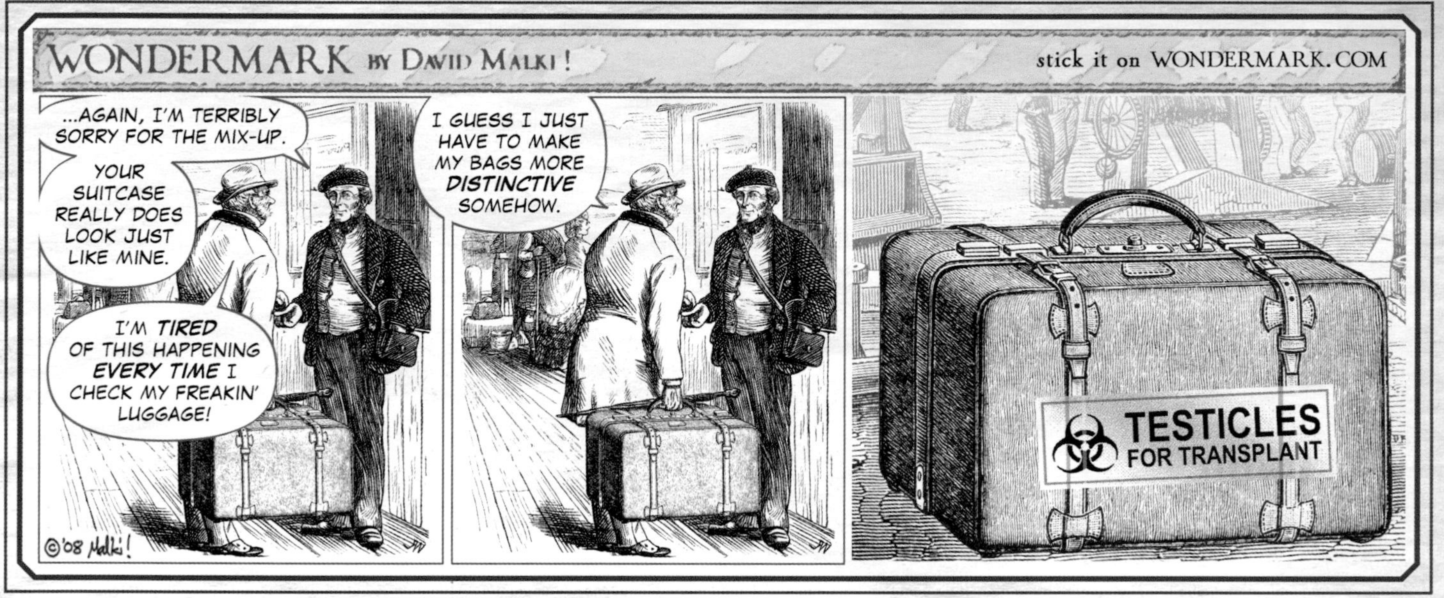
WONDERMARK BY DAVID MALKI !
stick it on WONDERMARK.COM
...AGAIN, I'M TERRIBLY SORRY FOR THE MIX-UP.
YOUR SUITCASE REALLY DOES LOOK JUST LIKE MINE.
I'M TIRED OF THIS HAPPENING EVERY TIME I CHECK MY FREAKIN' LUGGAGE!
I GUESS I JUST HAVE TO MAKE MY BAGS MORE DISTINCTIVE SOMEHOW.
TESTICLES FOR TRANSPLANT
©'08 Malki!

this should prevent any more mishaps

IN WHICH THINGS GET WORSE

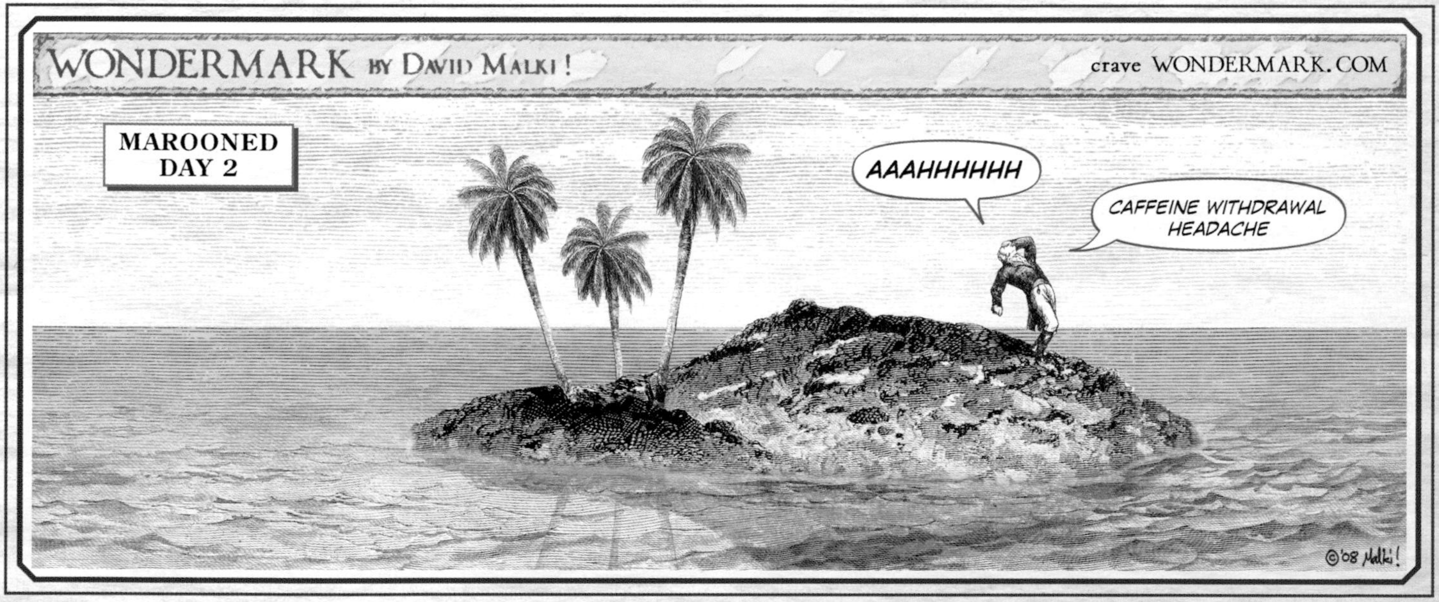
WONDERMARK BY DAVID MALKI !
crave WONDERMARK.COM
MAROONED DAY 2
AAAHHHHHH
CAFFEINE WITHDRAWAL HEADACHE
©'08 Malki!

day 3: somehow sleep 'til three p.m.

SOLUTION

A PUSHY ANTEATER SEES A HELPMATE VIOLATE THIS
BLUNT, FIT COED. - GROW LIVER HILT

IN WHICH TRADE SECRETS ARE REVEALED

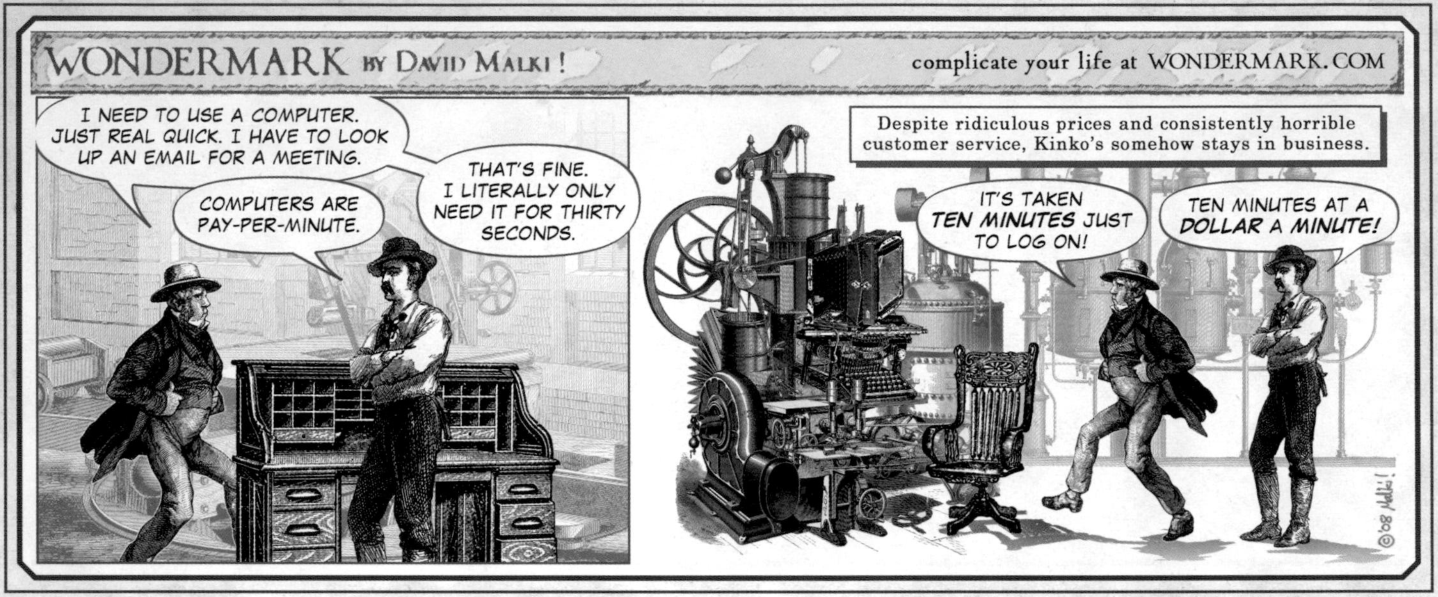
WONDERMARK BY DAVID MALKI !
complicate your life at WONDERMARK.COM
I NEED TO USE A COMPUTER. JUST REAL QUICK. I HAVE TO LOOK UP AN EMAIL FOR A MEETING.
COMPUTERS ARE PAY-PER-MINUTE.
THAT'S FINE. I LITERALLY ONLY NEED IT FOR THIRTY SECONDS.
Despite ridiculous prices and consistently horrible customer service, Kinko's somehow stays in business.
IT'S TAKEN TEN MINUTES JUST TO LOG ON!
TEN MINUTES AT A DOLLAR A MINUTE!
©'08 Malki !

The man is checking his email for the steps to a dance that will forcibly repel ants from his trousers. He has a chronic condition.

IN WHICH AMERICA IS SUPER-SIZED

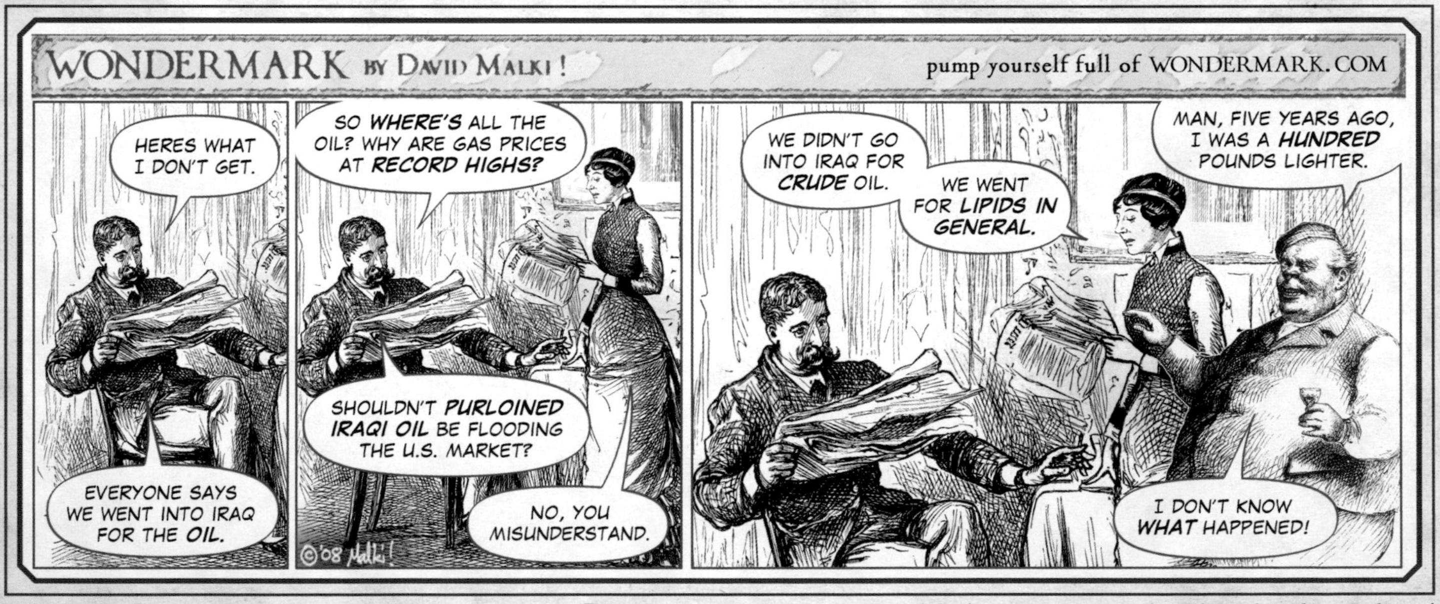
WONDERMARK BY DAVID MALKI !
pump yourself full of WONDERMARK.COM
HERES WHAT I DON'T GET.
EVERYONE SAYS WE WENT INTO IRAQ FOR THE OIL.
SO WHERE'S ALL THE OIL? WHY ARE GAS PRICES AT RECORD HIGHS?
SHOULDN'T PURLOINED IRAQI OIL BE FLOODING THE U.S. MARKET?
NO, YOU MISUNDERSTAND.
©'08 Malki !
WE DIDN'T GO INTO IRAQ FOR CRUDE OIL.
WE WENT FOR LIPIDS IN GENERAL.
MAN, FIVE YEARS AGO, I WAS A HUNDRED POUNDS LIGHTER.
I DON'T KNOW WHAT HAPPENED!

granted the foreign situation can't easily explain the waistline of everyone in the country, but it could be a pretty handy scapegoat

EHT RIPAALEN YSTSA PU EBUCESA TI SOTEN'D EAVH
HET MITE OT AFLL. - LEOIRVL HGWIRT

IN WHICH THE MOMENT IS FLEETING

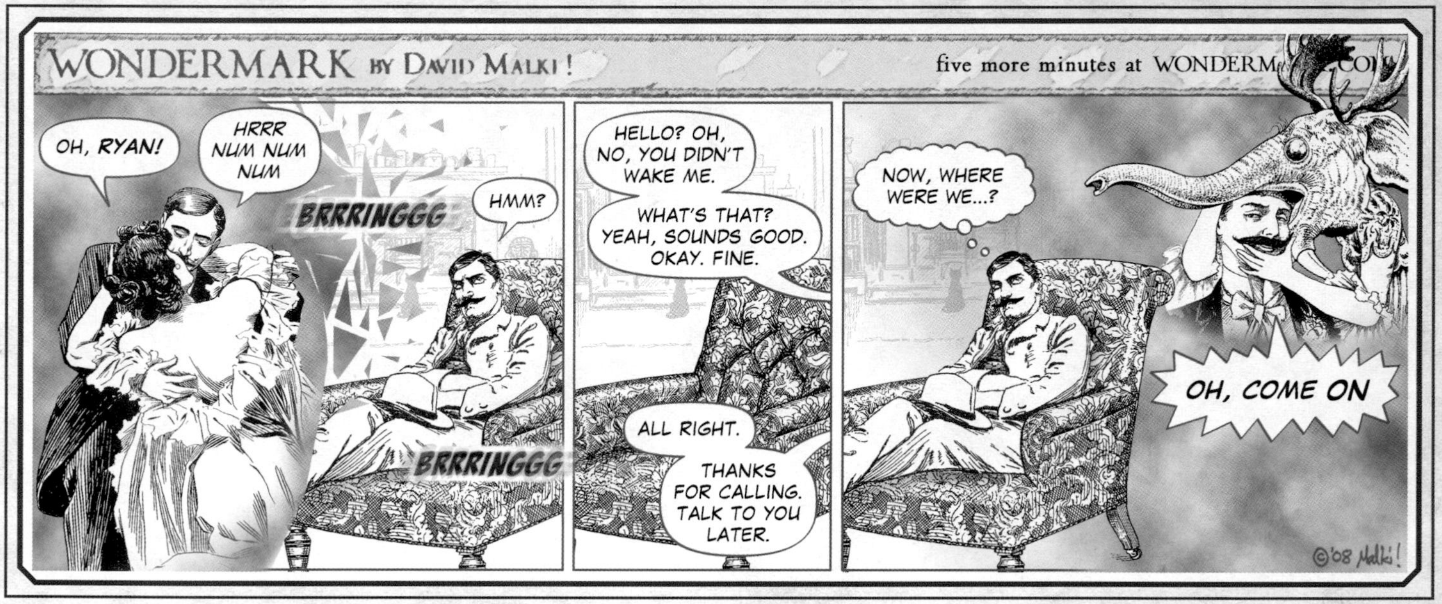
WONDERMARK BY DAVID MALKI !
five more minutes at WONDERM
OH, RYAN!
HRRR NUM NUM NUM
BRRRINGGG
HMM?
BRRRINGGG
HELLO? OH, NO, YOU DIDN'T WAKE ME.
WHAT'S THAT? YEAH, SOUNDS GOOD. OKAY. FINE.
ALL RIGHT.
THANKS FOR CALLING. TALK TO YOU LATER.
NOW, WHERE WERE WE...?
OH, COME ON
©'08 Malki!

isn't that always the way

IN WHICH IT'S FRIKKIN BRIGHT

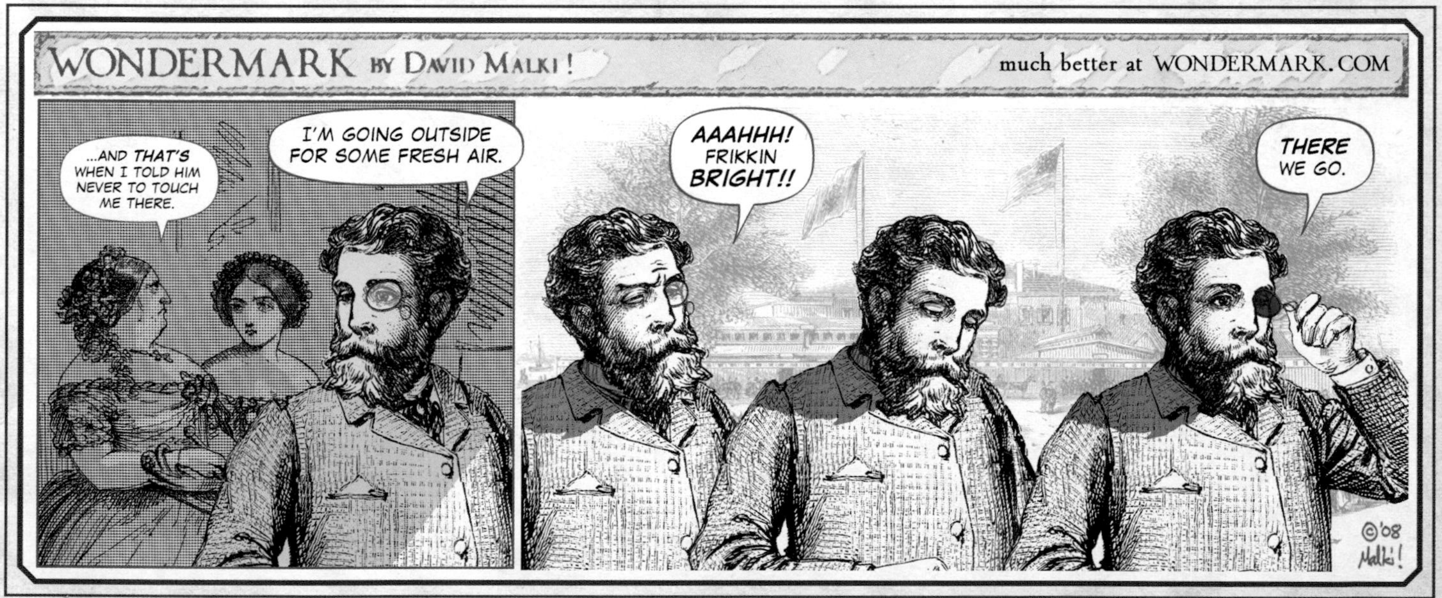
WONDERMARK BY DAVID MALKI !
much better at WONDERMARK.COM
...AND THAT'S WHEN I TOLD HIM NEVER TO TOUCH ME THERE.
I'M GOING OUTSIDE FOR SOME FRESH AIR.
AAAHHH! FRIKKIN BRIGHT!!
THERE WE GO.
©'08 Malki!

Don't you wish YOU had a sunglass monocle?

Babbage *hates* anagrams. He doesn't know why, they've just always bugged him.

IN WHICH CUSTOMERS ARE SERVED ONLY GRUDGINGLY

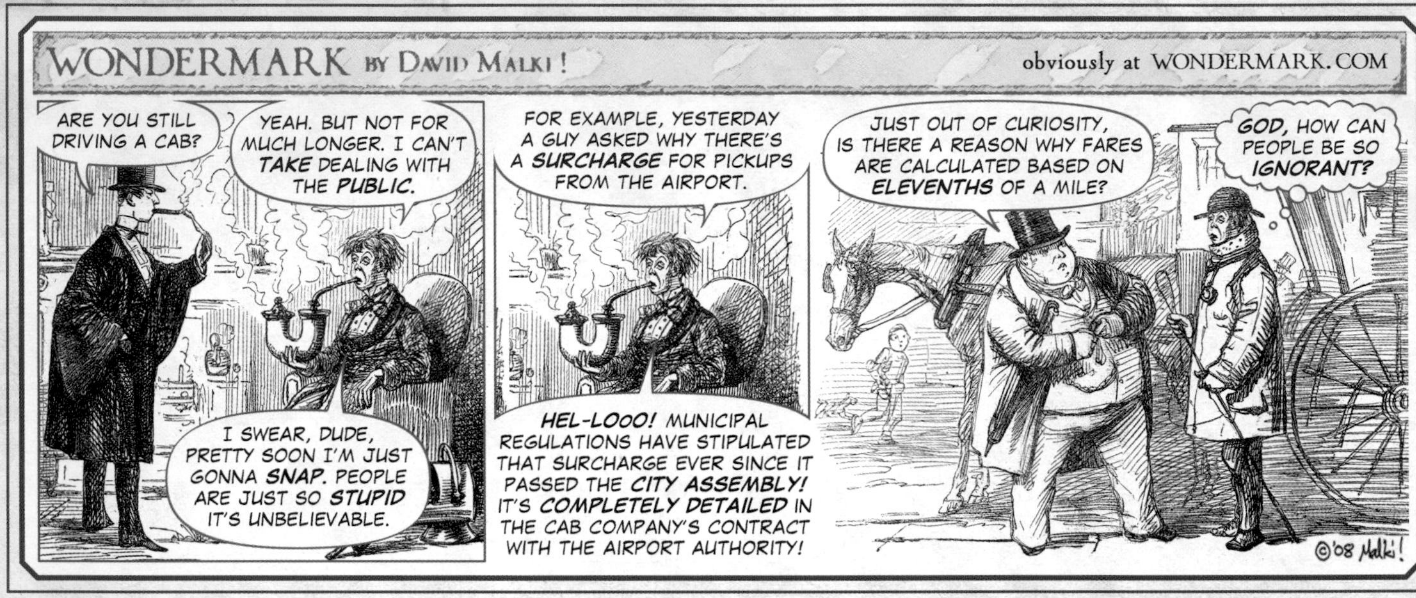
WONDERMARK BY DAVID MALKI !
obviously at WONDERMARK.COM
ARE YOU STILL DRIVING A CAB?
YEAH. BUT NOT FOR MUCH LONGER. I CAN'T TAKE DEALING WITH THE PUBLIC.
I SWEAR, DUDE, PRETTY SOON I'M JUST GONNA SNAP. PEOPLE ARE JUST SO STUPID IT'S UNBELIEVABLE.
FOR EXAMPLE, YESTERDAY A GUY ASKED WHY THERE'S A SURCHARGE FOR PICKUPS FROM THE AIRPORT.
HEL-LOOO! MUNICIPAL REGULATIONS HAVE STIPULATED THAT SURCHARGE EVER SINCE IT PASSED THE CITY ASSEMBLY! IT'S COMPLETELY DETAILED IN THE CAB COMPANY'S CONTRACT WITH THE AIRPORT AUTHORITY!
JUST OUT OF CURIOSITY, IS THERE A REASON WHY FARES ARE CALCULATED BASED ON ELEVENTHS OF A MILE?
GOD, HOW CAN PEOPLE BE SO IGNORANT?
©'08 Malki!

because charging by twelfths of a mile would be ridiculous

A FINE SPRING DAY

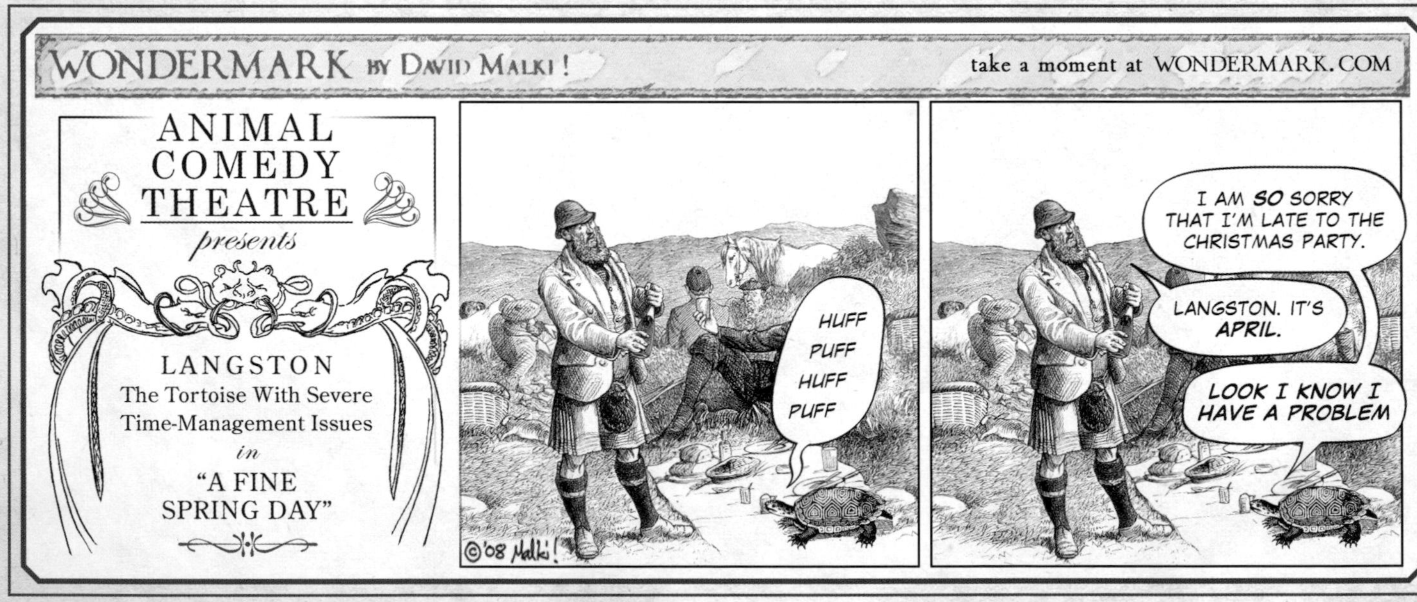
WONDERMARK BY DAVID MALKI !
take a moment at WONDERMARK.COM
ANIMAL COMEDY THEATRE
presents
LANGSTON
The Tortoise With Severe Time-Management Issues
in
"A FINE SPRING DAY"
HUFF PUFF HUFF PUFF
©'08 Malki!
I AM SO SORRY THAT I'M LATE TO THE CHRISTMAS PARTY.
LANGSTON. IT'S APRIL.
LOOK I KNOW I HAVE A PROBLEM

don't we all

To get back at Babbage, Ada Lovelace has scrambled several words into anagrams!

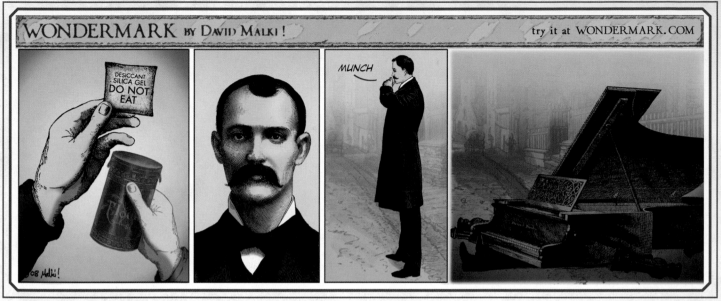

WONDERMARK BY DAVID MALKI !
try it at WONDERMARK.COM
DESICCANT SILICA GEL DO NOT EAT
MUNCH
'08 Malki!

Color by Carly Monardo • whirringblender.com

it really is pretty straightforward

JIFFY DROP
Heavy Lift & Release Specialists
Boca Raton, FL

Invoice

2459

Customer A&D Flour Co. - Enforcement Division Date 28 Mar 20 08
(413) CU 2-8672 ATTN: J.R.

CODE	DESCRIPTION	RATE
SR-15	Crane lift of piano (80 ft.)	$600.00
313-U	Subject tracking/targeting -- 4 hrs. @ $28.00	$112.00
B19	Drop	$ 5.00
7PRX	Cleanup -- 3.25 hrs @ $19.00	$ 61.75
	PLEASE PAY	$778.75

NO RETURNS ON SPECIAL ORDERS • ALL ESTIMATES MUST BE APPROVED IN WRITING
ALL MUNICIPAL PAPERWORK MUST BE FILED BEFORE WORK BEGINS

SOLUTION

THE VALUE OF AN IDEA LIES IN THE USING OF IT.
- THOMAS EDISON

IN WHICH ELMER IS ALWAYS IRATE

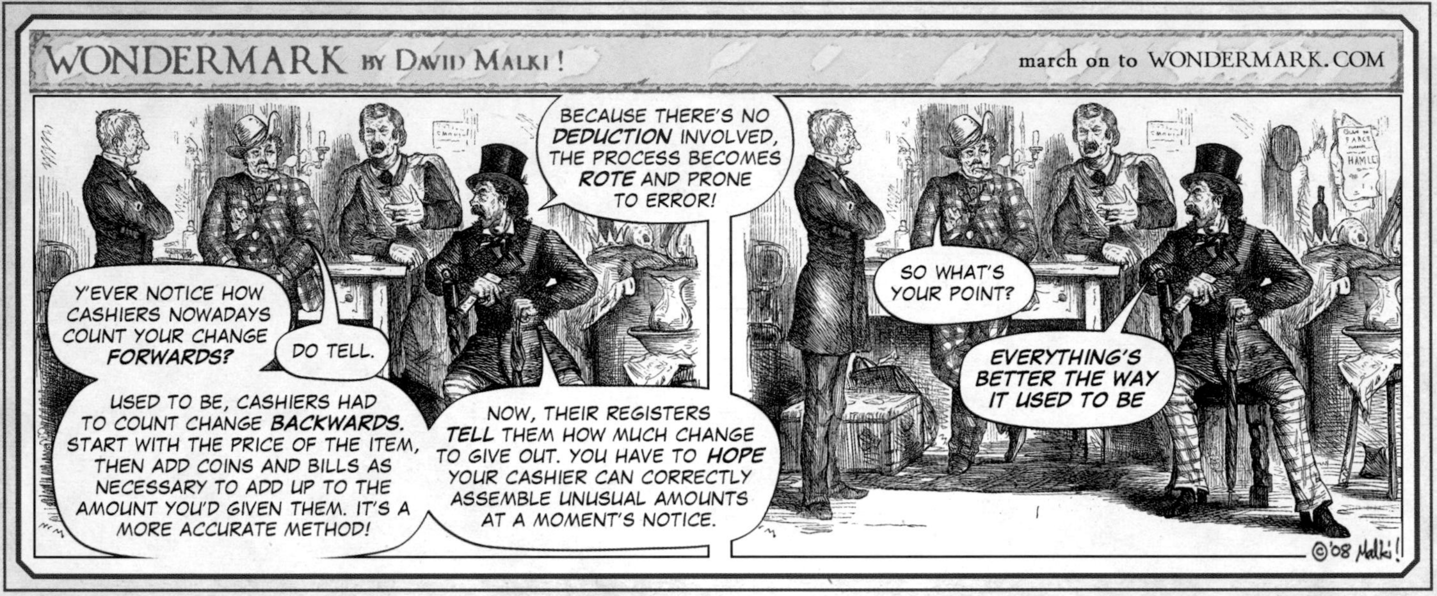
WONDERMARK BY DAVID MALKI !
march on to WONDERMARK.COM
Y'EVER NOTICE HOW CASHIERS NOWADAYS COUNT YOUR CHANGE FORWARDS?
DO TELL.
USED TO BE, CASHIERS HAD TO COUNT CHANGE BACKWARDS. START WITH THE PRICE OF THE ITEM, THEN ADD COINS AND BILLS AS NECESSARY TO ADD UP TO THE AMOUNT YOU'D GIVEN THEM. IT'S A MORE ACCURATE METHOD!
NOW, THEIR REGISTERS TELL THEM HOW MUCH CHANGE TO GIVE OUT. YOU HAVE TO HOPE YOUR CASHIER CAN CORRECTLY ASSEMBLE UNUSUAL AMOUNTS AT A MOMENT'S NOTICE.
BECAUSE THERE'S NO DEDUCTION INVOLVED, THE PROCESS BECOMES ROTE AND PRONE TO ERROR!
SO WHAT'S YOUR POINT?
EVERYTHING'S BETTER THE WAY IT USED TO BE
©'08 Malki !

kids these days! so selfish! they're supposed to care about ME!

IN WHICH A LEON FILMS A COMMERCIAL

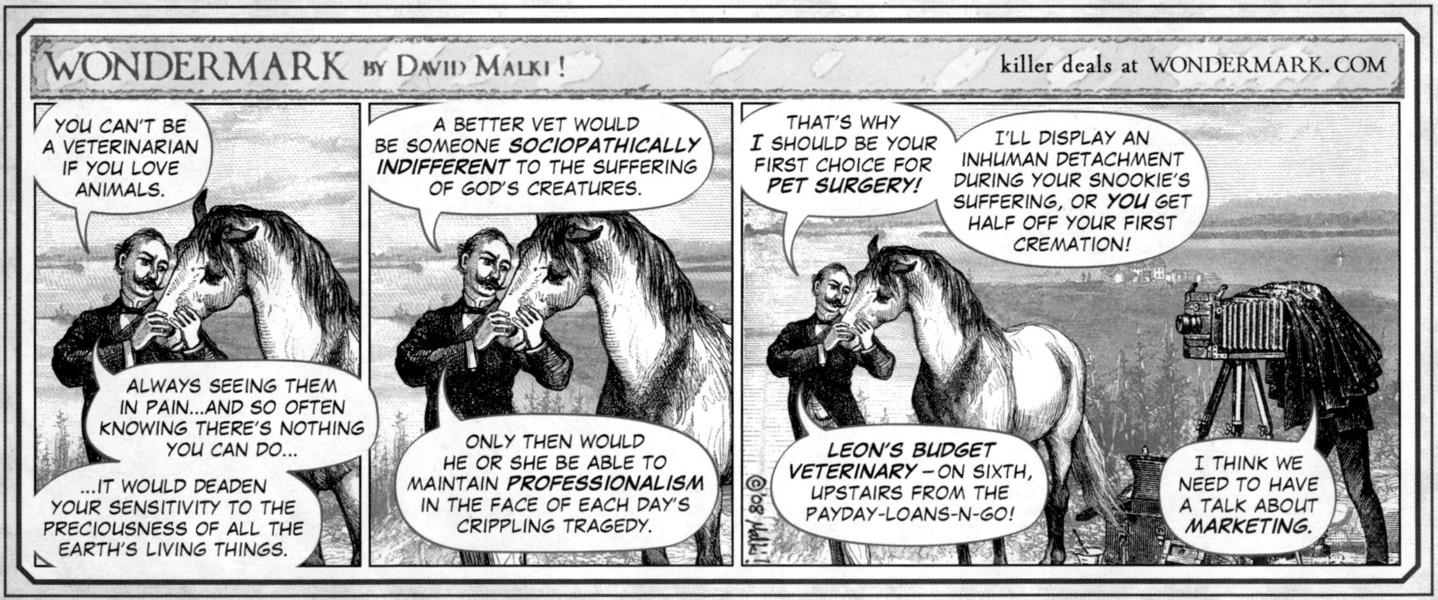
WONDERMARK BY DAVID MALKI !
killer deals at WONDERMARK.COM
YOU CAN'T BE A VETERINARIAN IF YOU LOVE ANIMALS.
ALWAYS SEEING THEM IN PAIN...AND SO OFTEN KNOWING THERE'S NOTHING YOU CAN DO...
...IT WOULD DEADEN YOUR SENSITIVITY TO THE PRECIOUSNESS OF ALL THE EARTH'S LIVING THINGS.
A BETTER VET WOULD BE SOMEONE SOCIOPATHICALLY INDIFFERENT TO THE SUFFERING OF GOD'S CREATURES.
ONLY THEN WOULD HE OR SHE BE ABLE TO MAINTAIN PROFESSIONALISM IN THE FACE OF EACH DAY'S CRIPPLING TRAGEDY.
THAT'S WHY I SHOULD BE YOUR FIRST CHOICE FOR PET SURGERY!
I'LL DISPLAY AN INHUMAN DETACHMENT DURING YOUR SNOOKIE'S SUFFERING, OR YOU GET HALF OFF YOUR FIRST CREMATION!
LEON'S BUDGET VETERINARY — ON SIXTH, UPSTAIRS FROM THE PAYDAY-LOANS-N-GO!
I THINK WE NEED TO HAVE A TALK ABOUT MARKETING.
©'08 Malki !

Leon is pretty sure this is how he wants to position his business.

SGD MNSDR HM LW RZED VHKK CHD VHSG LD, XNT CDUHK.
- MHJNKZ SDRKZ

IN WHICH JOHN HAS SOME QUESTIONS

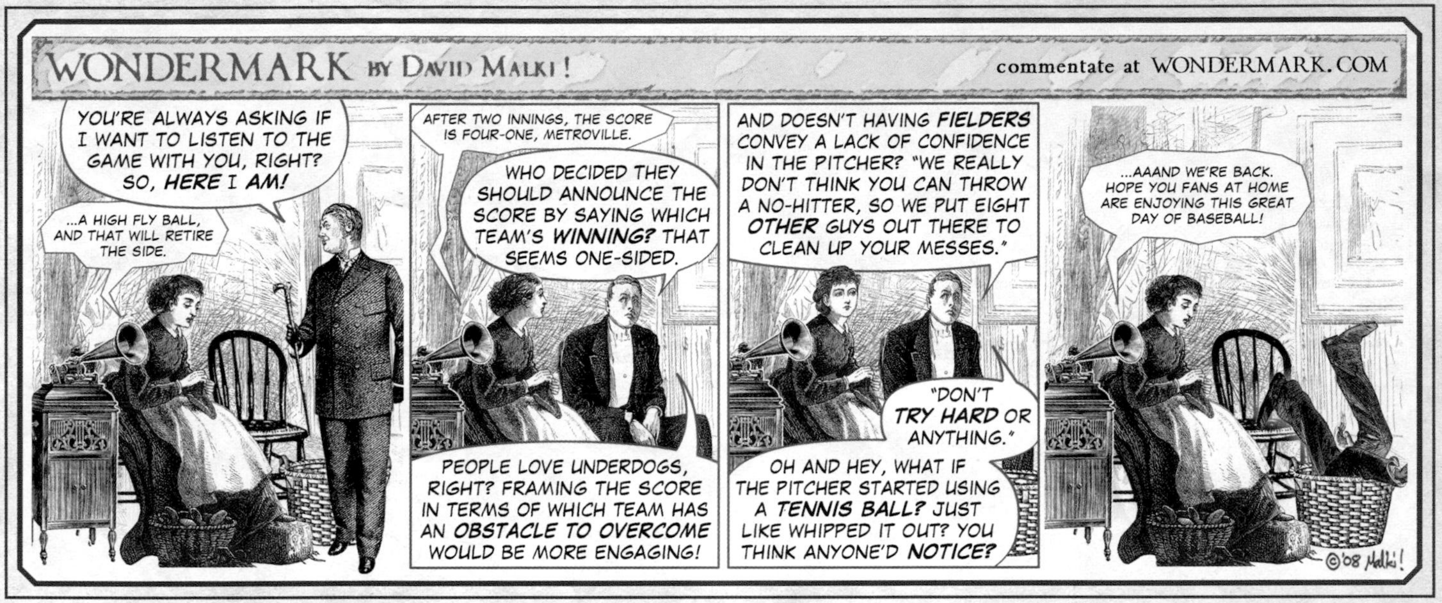
WONDERMARK BY DAVID MALKI !
commentate at WONDERMARK.COM
YOU'RE ALWAYS ASKING IF I WANT TO LISTEN TO THE GAME WITH YOU, RIGHT? SO, HERE I AM!
...A HIGH FLY BALL, AND THAT WILL RETIRE THE SIDE.
AFTER TWO INNINGS, THE SCORE IS FOUR-ONE, METROVILLE.
WHO DECIDED THEY SHOULD ANNOUNCE THE SCORE BY SAYING WHICH TEAM'S WINNING? THAT SEEMS ONE-SIDED.
PEOPLE LOVE UNDERDOGS, RIGHT? FRAMING THE SCORE IN TERMS OF WHICH TEAM HAS AN OBSTACLE TO OVERCOME WOULD BE MORE ENGAGING!
AND DOESN'T HAVING FIELDERS CONVEY A LACK OF CONFIDENCE IN THE PITCHER? "WE REALLY DON'T THINK YOU CAN THROW A NO-HITTER, SO WE PUT EIGHT OTHER GUYS OUT THERE TO CLEAN UP YOUR MESSES."
"DON'T TRY HARD OR ANYTHING."
OH AND HEY, WHAT IF THE PITCHER STARTED USING A TENNIS BALL? JUST LIKE WHIPPED IT OUT? YOU THINK ANYONE'D NOTICE?
...AAAND WE'RE BACK. HOPE YOU FANS AT HOME ARE ENJOYING THIS GREAT DAY OF BASEBALL!
©'08 Malki !

i think someone would probably notice

IN WHICH MARTIN COULD RETHINK HIS PASTIMES

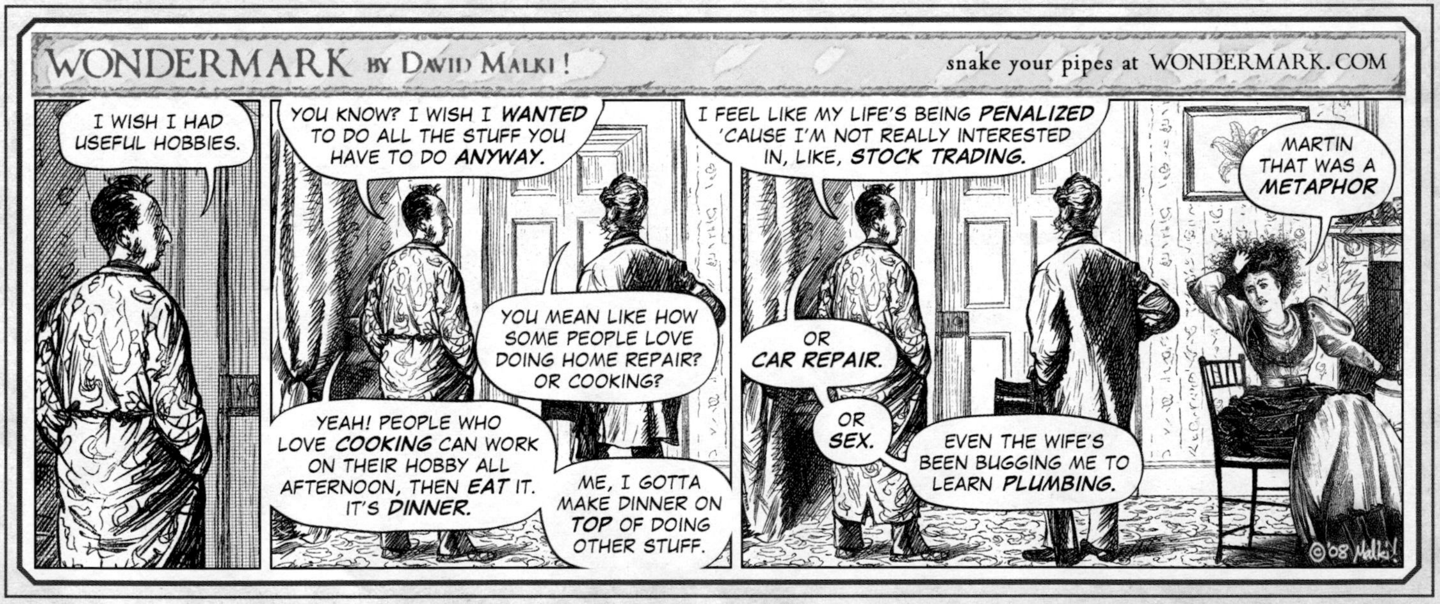
WONDERMARK BY DAVID MALKI !
snake your pipes at WONDERMARK.COM
I WISH I HAD USEFUL HOBBIES.
YOU KNOW? I WISH I WANTED TO DO ALL THE STUFF YOU HAVE TO DO ANYWAY.
YOU MEAN LIKE HOW SOME PEOPLE LOVE DOING HOME REPAIR? OR COOKING?
YEAH! PEOPLE WHO LOVE COOKING CAN WORK ON THEIR HOBBY ALL AFTERNOON, THEN EAT IT. IT'S DINNER.
ME, I GOTTA MAKE DINNER ON TOP OF DOING OTHER STUFF.
I FEEL LIKE MY LIFE'S BEING PENALIZED 'CAUSE I'M NOT REALLY INTERESTED IN, LIKE, STOCK TRADING.
OR CAR REPAIR.
OR SEX.
EVEN THE WIFE'S BEEN BUGGING ME TO LEARN PLUMBING.
MARTIN THAT WAS A METAPHOR
©'08 Malki !

martin's hobbies mostly involve spending long hours imagining, in painstaking detail, what life might be like on a planet where cheetos are legal tender

been replaced with another. HINT: THE FIRST WORD IS "THE".)

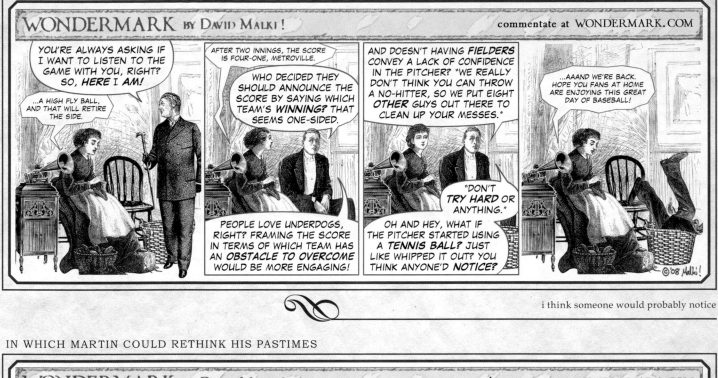

IN WHICH DINNER ELUDES TWO

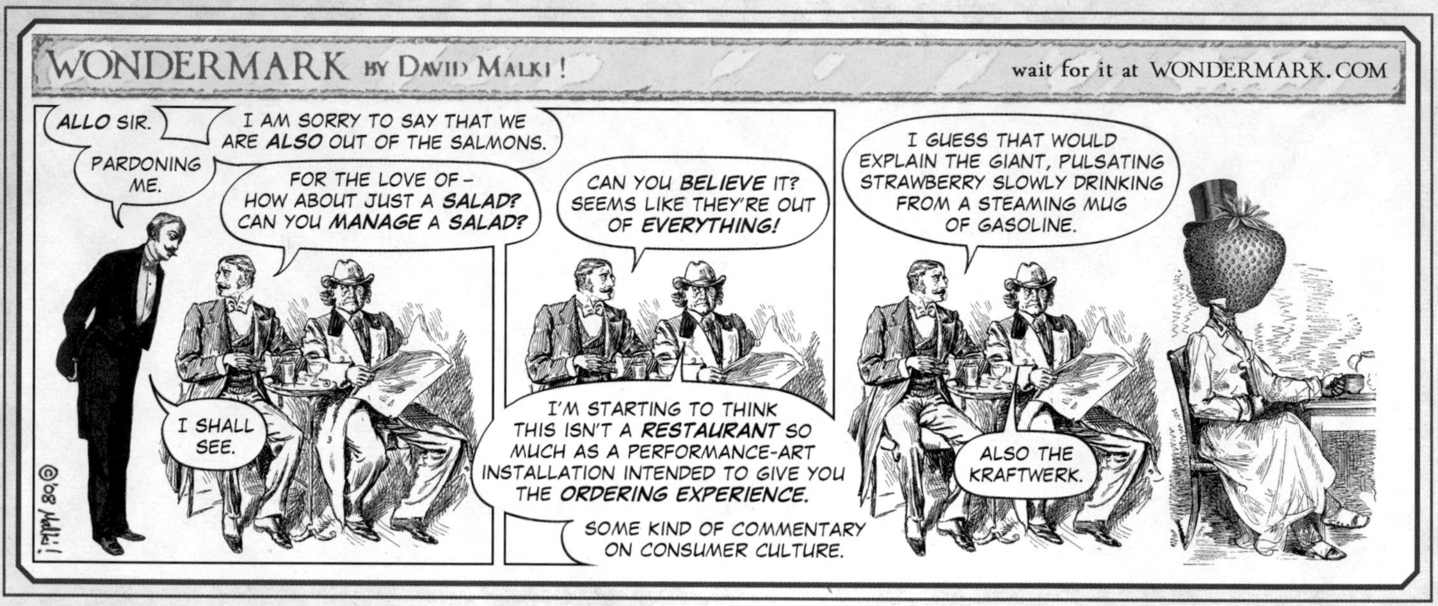
WONDERMARK BY DAVID MALKI !
wait for it at WONDERMARK.COM
ALLO SIR.
PARDONING ME.
I AM SORRY TO SAY THAT WE ARE ALSO OUT OF THE SALMONS.
FOR THE LOVE OF – HOW ABOUT JUST A SALAD? CAN YOU MANAGE A SALAD?
I SHALL SEE.
CAN YOU BELIEVE IT? SEEMS LIKE THEY'RE OUT OF EVERYTHING!
I'M STARTING TO THINK THIS ISN'T A RESTAURANT SO MUCH AS A PERFORMANCE-ART INSTALLATION INTENDED TO GIVE YOU THE ORDERING EXPERIENCE.
SOME KIND OF COMMENTARY ON CONSUMER CULTURE.
I GUESS THAT WOULD EXPLAIN THE GIANT, PULSATING STRAWBERRY SLOWLY DRINKING FROM A STEAMING MUG OF GASOLINE.
ALSO THE KRAFTWERK.

the waiter pronounced it 'sall-mons'

IN WHICH EVERYONE ELSE JUST SITS QUIETLY

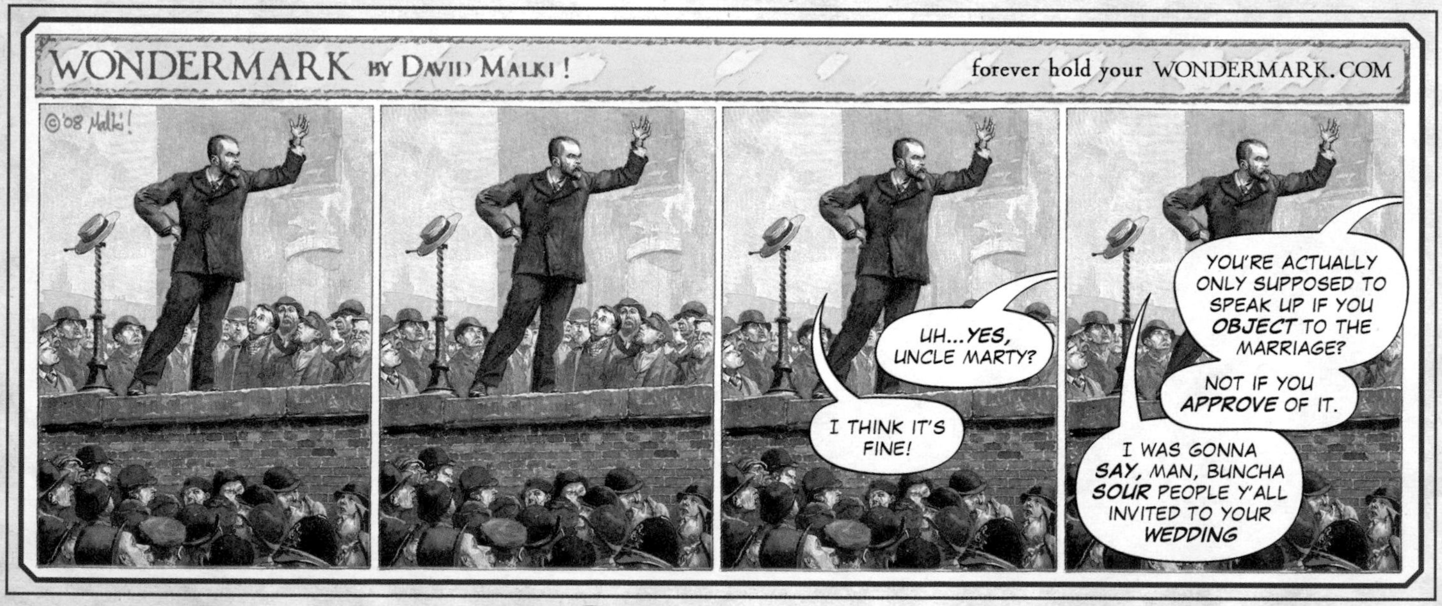
WONDERMARK BY DAVID MALKI !
forever hold your WONDERMARK.COM
©'08 Malki!
UH...YES, UNCLE MARTY?
I THINK IT'S FINE!
YOU'RE ACTUALLY ONLY SUPPOSED TO SPEAK UP IF YOU OBJECT TO THE MARRIAGE?
NOT IF YOU APPROVE OF IT.
I WAS GONNA SAY, MAN, BUNCHA SOUR PEOPLE Y'ALL INVITED TO YOUR WEDDING

Uncle Marty always has to be the center of attention.

inventor! Can you decode it? *(Each letter of the alphabet has systematically and consistently*

IN WHICH PETE IS SET OFF

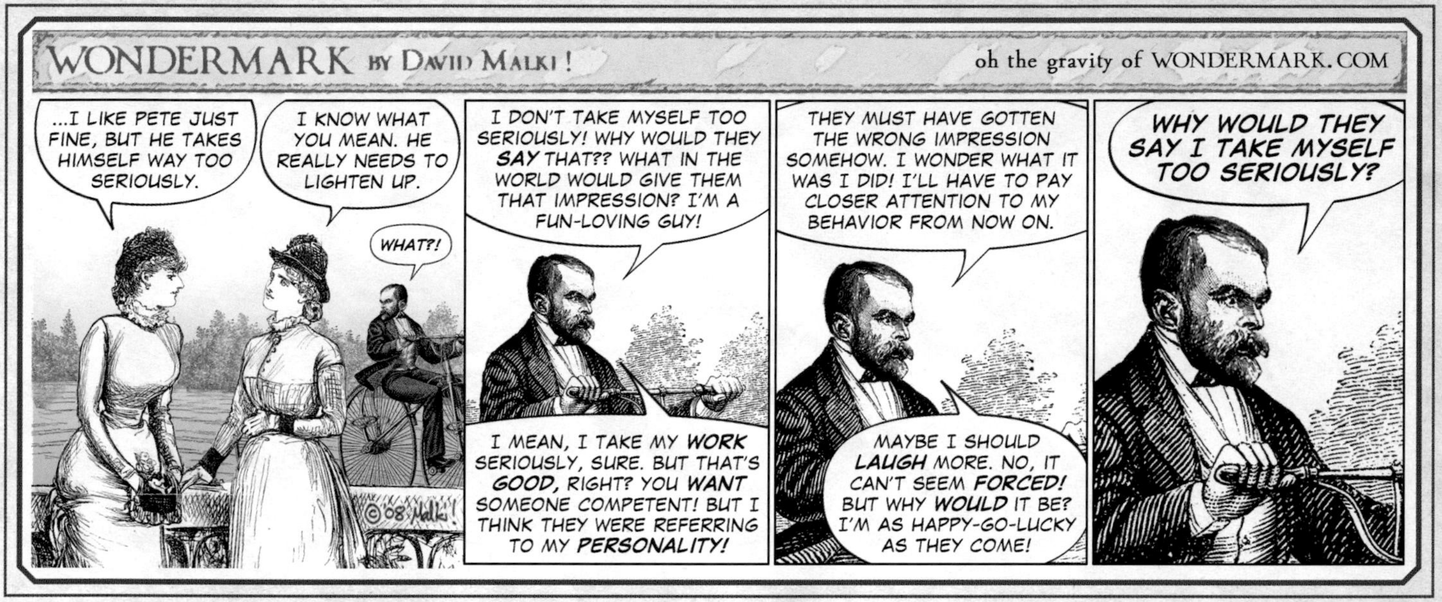
WONDERMARK BY DAVID MALKI !
oh the gravity of WONDERMARK.COM
...I LIKE PETE JUST FINE, BUT HE TAKES HIMSELF WAY TOO SERIOUSLY.
I KNOW WHAT YOU MEAN. HE REALLY NEEDS TO LIGHTEN UP.
WHAT?!
©'08 Malki!
I DON'T TAKE MYSELF TOO SERIOUSLY! WHY WOULD THEY SAY THAT?? WHAT IN THE WORLD WOULD GIVE THEM THAT IMPRESSION? I'M A FUN-LOVING GUY!
I MEAN, I TAKE MY WORK SERIOUSLY, SURE. BUT THAT'S GOOD, RIGHT? YOU WANT SOMEONE COMPETENT! BUT I THINK THEY WERE REFERRING TO MY PERSONALITY!
THEY MUST HAVE GOTTEN THE WRONG IMPRESSION SOMEHOW. I WONDER WHAT IT WAS I DID! I'LL HAVE TO PAY CLOSER ATTENTION TO MY BEHAVIOR FROM NOW ON.
MAYBE I SHOULD LAUGH MORE. NO, IT CAN'T SEEM FORCED! BUT WHY WOULD IT BE? I'M AS HAPPY-GO-LUCKY AS THEY COME!
WHY WOULD THEY SAY I TAKE MYSELF TOO SERIOUSLY?

I WILL SEND THEM BOTH A FURIOUS, RAMBLING EMAIL
EXPLAINING IN DETAIL HOW CAREFREE I ACTUALLY AM

IN WHICH AFRICA IS NOTICED

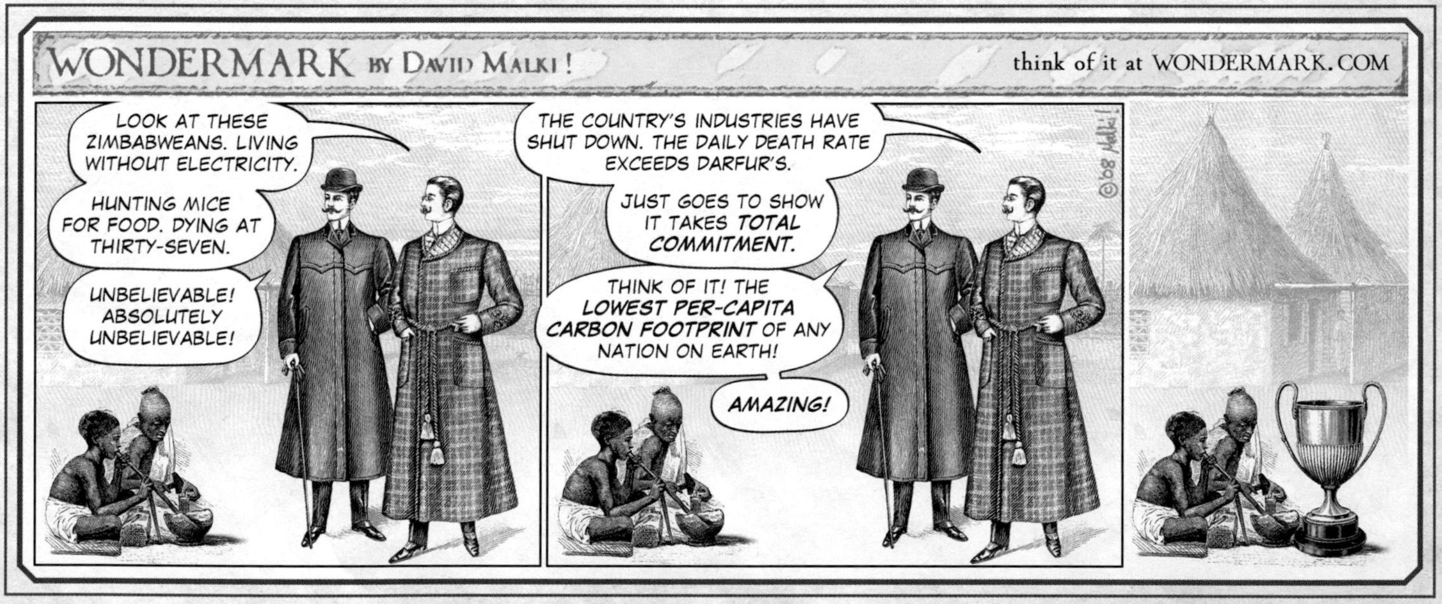
WONDERMARK BY DAVID MALKI !
think of it at WONDERMARK.COM
LOOK AT THESE ZIMBABWEANS. LIVING WITHOUT ELECTRICITY.
HUNTING MICE FOR FOOD. DYING AT THIRTY-SEVEN.
UNBELIEVABLE! ABSOLUTELY UNBELIEVABLE!
THE COUNTRY'S INDUSTRIES HAVE SHUT DOWN. THE DAILY DEATH RATE EXCEEDS DARFUR'S.
JUST GOES TO SHOW IT TAKES TOTAL COMMITMENT.
THINK OF IT! THE LOWEST PER-CAPITA CARBON FOOTPRINT OF ANY NATION ON EARTH!
AMAZING!
©'08 Malki!

hooray

IN WHICH JOHN GETS BY

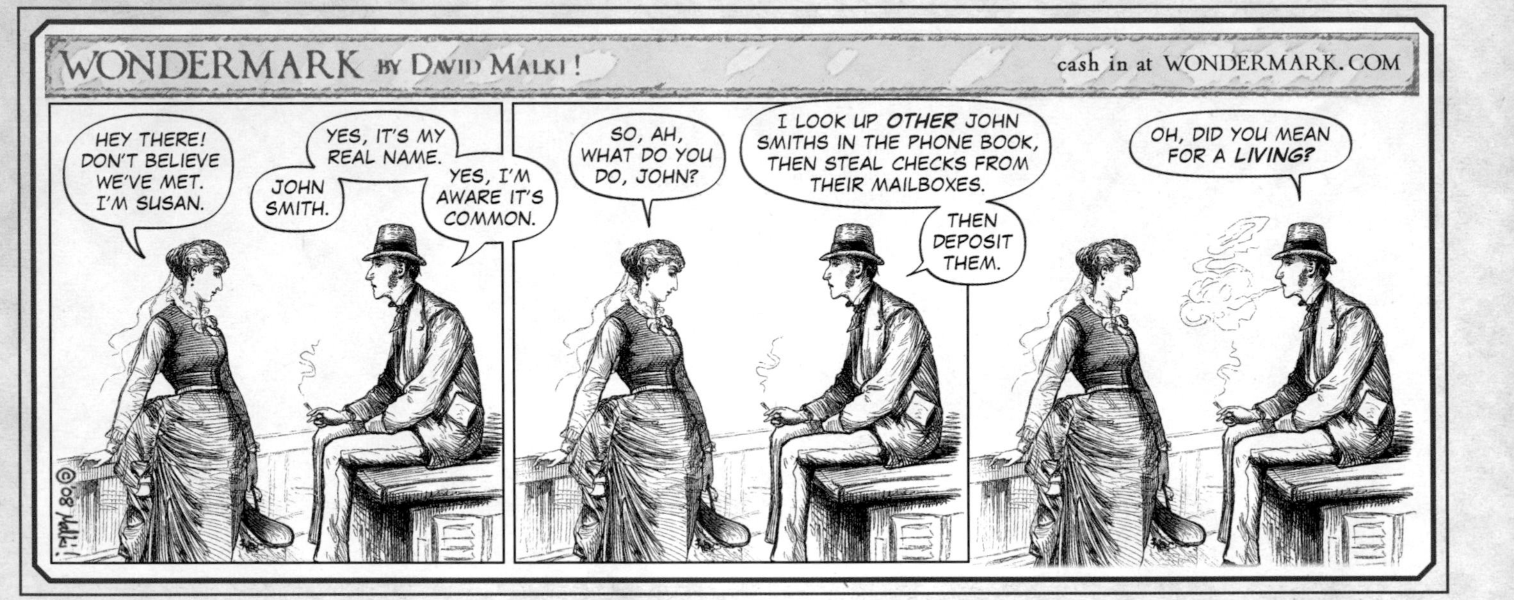
WONDERMARK BY DAVID MALKI !
cash in at WONDERMARK.COM
HEY THERE! DON'T BELIEVE WE'VE MET. I'M SUSAN.
JOHN SMITH.
YES, IT'S MY REAL NAME.
YES, I'M AWARE IT'S COMMON.
SO, AH, WHAT DO YOU DO, JOHN?
I LOOK UP OTHER JOHN SMITHS IN THE PHONE BOOK, THEN STEAL CHECKS FROM THEIR MAILBOXES.
THEN DEPOSIT THEM.
OH, DID YOU MEAN FOR A LIVING?

because i'm actually pulling down pretty decent scratch just doing this

IN WHICH THERE MAY BE SHORTCUTS TO SUCCESS

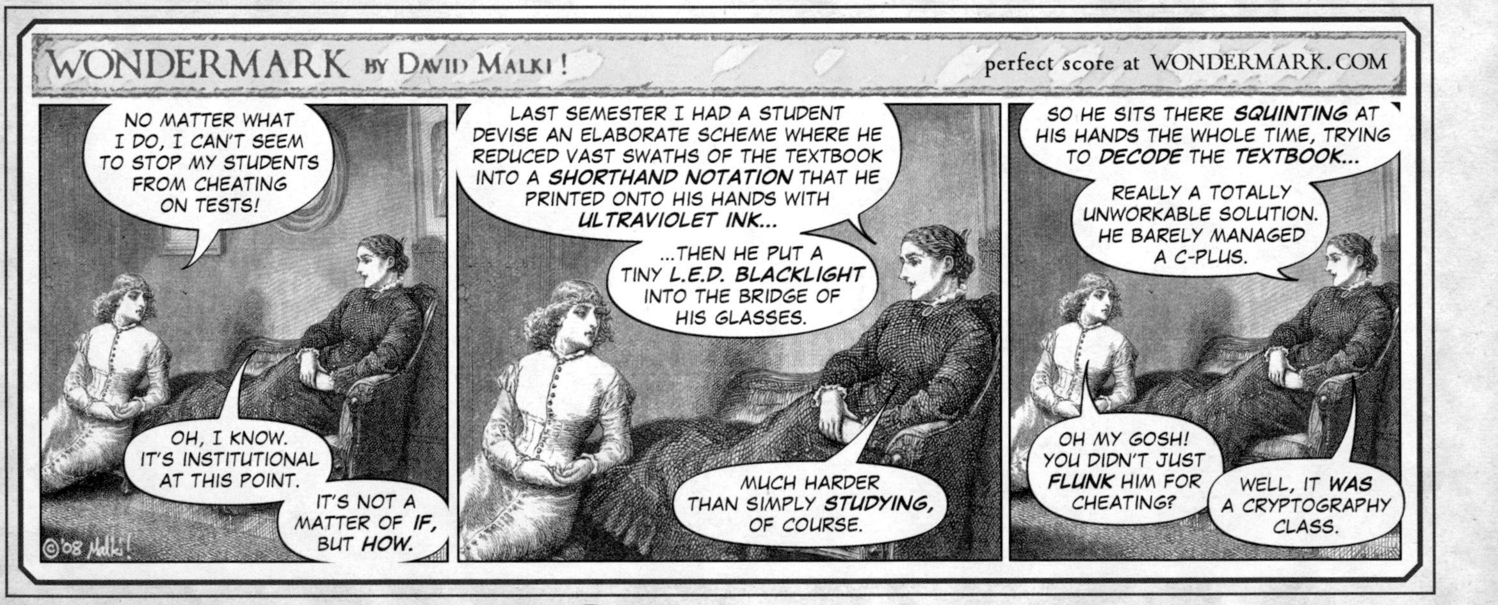
WONDERMARK BY DAVID MALKI !
perfect score at WONDERMARK.COM
NO MATTER WHAT I DO, I CAN'T SEEM TO STOP MY STUDENTS FROM CHEATING ON TESTS!
OH, I KNOW. IT'S INSTITUTIONAL AT THIS POINT.
IT'S NOT A MATTER OF IF, BUT HOW.
©'08 Malki!
LAST SEMESTER I HAD A STUDENT DEVISE AN ELABORATE SCHEME WHERE HE REDUCED VAST SWATHS OF THE TEXTBOOK INTO A SHORTHAND NOTATION THAT HE PRINTED ONTO HIS HANDS WITH ULTRAVIOLET INK...
...THEN HE PUT A TINY L.E.D. BLACKLIGHT INTO THE BRIDGE OF HIS GLASSES.
MUCH HARDER THAN SIMPLY STUDYING, OF COURSE.
SO HE SITS THERE SQUINTING AT HIS HANDS THE WHOLE TIME, TRYING TO DECODE THE TEXTBOOK...
REALLY A TOTALLY UNWORKABLE SOLUTION. HE BARELY MANAGED A C-PLUS.
OH MY GOSH! YOU DIDN'T JUST FLUNK HIM FOR CHEATING?
WELL, IT WAS A CRYPTOGRAPHY CLASS.

class motto is 'try it, let's see what you got'

WONDERMARK BY DAVID MALKI !
get in the spirit at WONDERMARK.COM
YES. I THINK I HAVE IDENTIFIED THE PROBLEM.
IT SEEMS THAT YOU ARE AWFUL.
MAN, I HATE THESE UNREAL EXPECTATIONS IN MUSIC! EVERYONE'S ALWAYS HARPING ON YOU TO HIT EVERY SINGLE NOTE. NOBODY'S PERFECT, YO!
BATTING .400 IN BASEBALL GETS YOU INTO THE HALL OF FAME. BUT FOR SOME REASON I JUST GET YELLED AT!
A FACILE COMPARISON! BASEBALL IS A COMPETITION, AND WE EXPECT THE PITCHER TO ALSO BE PARTIALLY SUCCESSFUL.
YOU HAVE NO SUCH EXCUSE. YOUR HORN IS A THING OF BRASS. IT IS NOT FIGHTING YOU.
DESPITE WHAT YOU INSIST, IT IS NOT SOME ANIMATE DEMON SPIRIT HELL-BENT ON SABOTAGING YOUR EVERY EFFORT.
DUDE YOU GOTTA START BACKING ME UP HERE
RODNEY
MY TIME HAS NOT YET COME

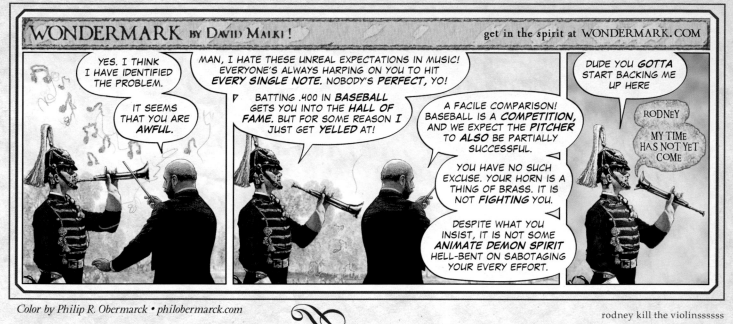

Color by Philip R. Obermarck • philobermarck.com

rodney kill the violinssssss

Possessed Instruments

WE HAVE TAKEN NOTE OF.

Mr. J. N. of Springfield, Virginia reports on this **Leprous Harp.** "It is infected with the flesh-rotting disease in its every string," writes our correspondent. "We must keep it shut in a shed, the key to which is entrusted only to trusted persons, and wear sheep's-wool gloves to play it."—Our readers in Belgium tell us of the widespread knowledge in Bruges of a certain **Opposite Cello**, which on odd-numbered calendar dates will play not the note that is struck, but rather its inverse on the musical register. As a result, all concerts in Bruges are held on even-numbered dates only, and must not pass midnight.—Our own musical editor reminds us of the ancient legend of **Plato's Trumpet**. Medieval manuscripts describe a horn that, when blown, could produce loaves of squaw-bread from its bell; however, classical accounts mentioning the horn have yet to surface.—

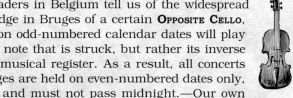

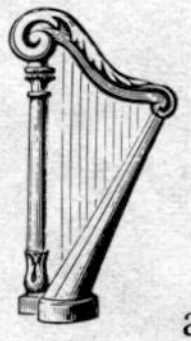

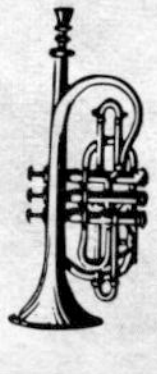

Bells were known to the ancients to harbor malevolent spirits, and the **Incubus Bell of Mexico** is no exception. Residents of Zinaparo tell of a church-bell that visits them carnally in the night, and at least one woman has birthed a deformed bell-baby.—A **Sinister Tuning Fork** has been reported in Iowa. Dr. S. W. writes, "When it is struck, our children weep uncontrollably. When it is left alone, our crops fail. We are in a difficult situation." Our editors can sadly offer no advice, but we encourage correspondence from parties who may have insight into the matter. The fork in question is twelve inches in length.—No instrument is more prized in the home than the piano, but this piano in Duluth, Minn., is home to more than mere music. A **wolf** has taken up residence in its interior, and no one has yet come up with a solution. The piano's owner hopes the animal may move out when the weather warms.—This **Dangerous Noisemaker**, owned by Col. Greeley of Boston, is reported to have killed seven men. The Col. remains baffled.

Could you tell which bag didn't belong with the others? No? That's great!

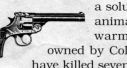

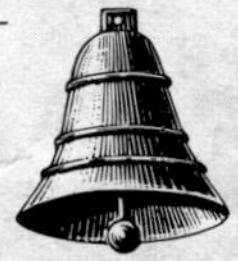

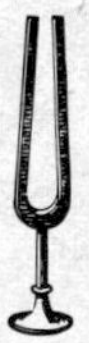

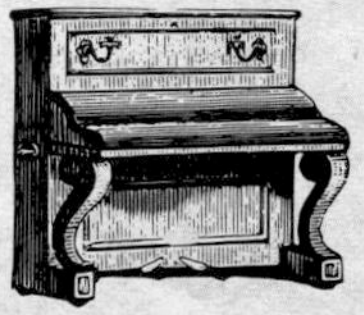

IN WHICH CHRISTY TAKES ONE FOR THE TEAM

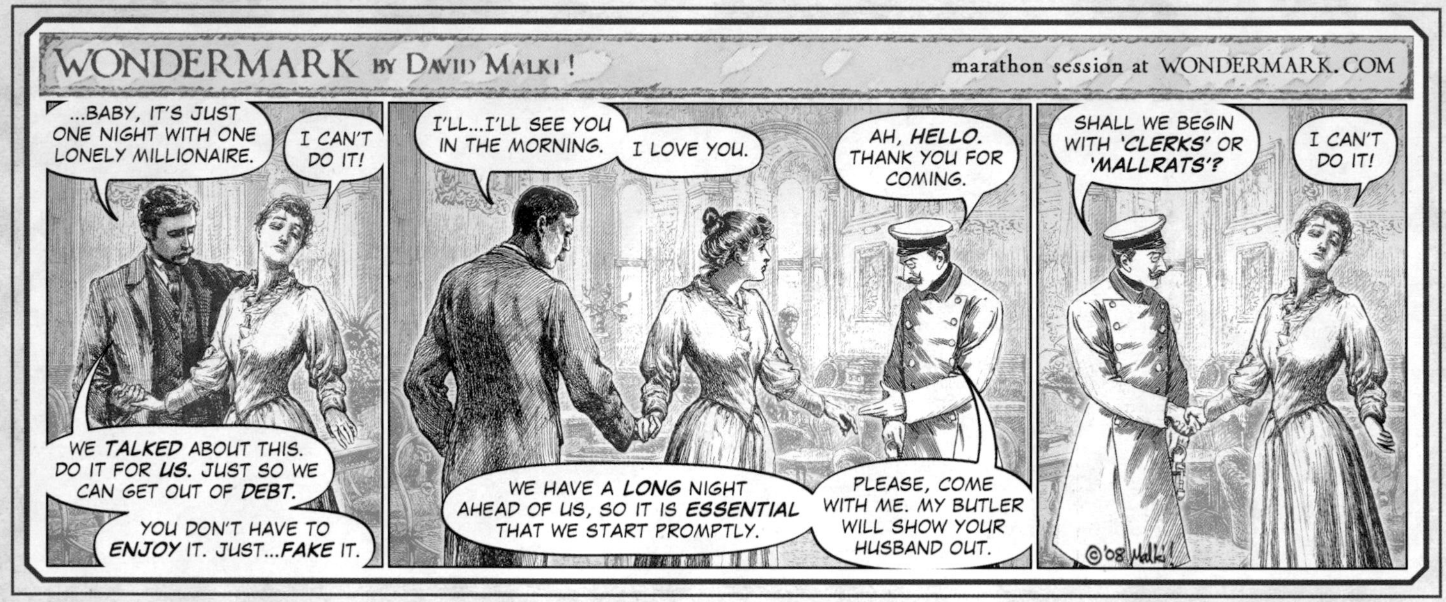
WONDERMARK BY DAVID MALKI !
marathon session at WONDERMARK.COM
...BABY, IT'S JUST ONE NIGHT WITH ONE LONELY MILLIONAIRE.
I CAN'T DO IT!
WE TALKED ABOUT THIS. DO IT FOR US. JUST SO WE CAN GET OUT OF DEBT.
YOU DON'T HAVE TO ENJOY IT. JUST...FAKE IT.
I'LL...I'LL SEE YOU IN THE MORNING.
I LOVE YOU.
AH, HELLO. THANK YOU FOR COMING.
WE HAVE A LONG NIGHT AHEAD OF US, SO IT IS ESSENTIAL THAT WE START PROMPTLY.
PLEASE, COME WITH ME. MY BUTLER WILL SHOW YOUR HUSBAND OUT.
SHALL WE BEGIN WITH 'CLERKS' OR 'MALLRATS'?
I CAN'T DO IT!
©'08 Malki !

baby we will be up ALL NIGHT LONG

IN WHICH SUBTLETY IS LOST

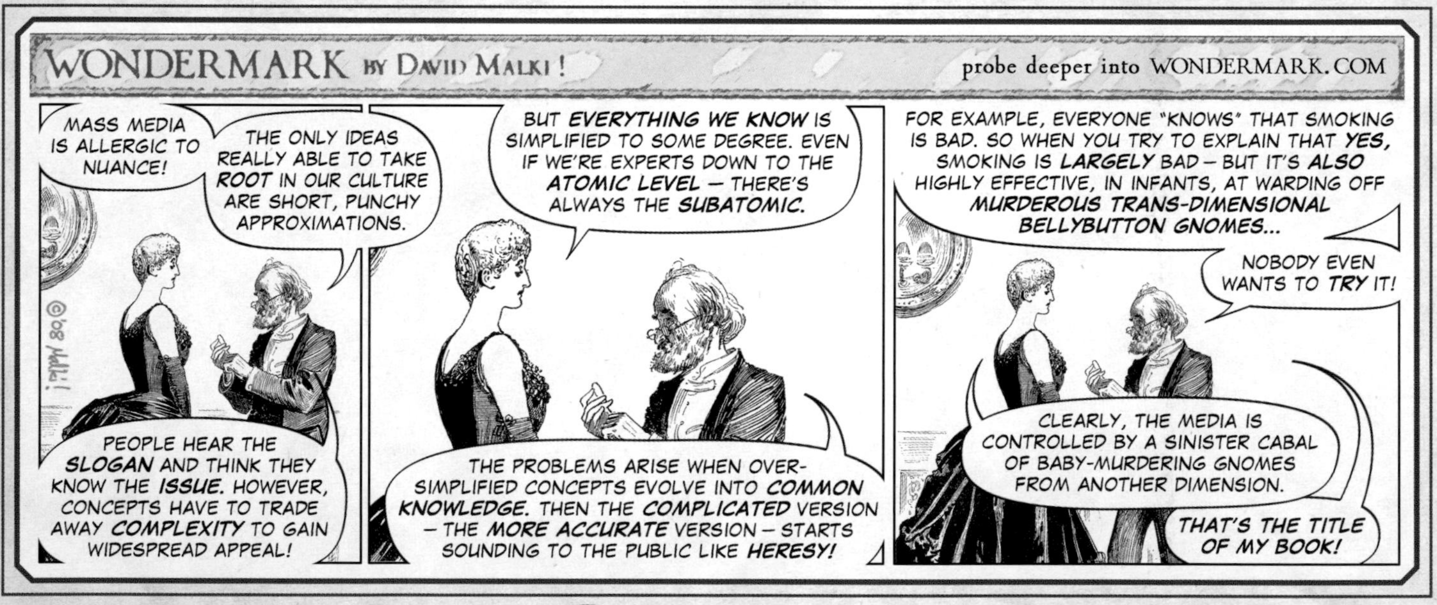
WONDERMARK BY DAVID MALKI !
probe deeper into WONDERMARK.COM
MASS MEDIA IS ALLERGIC TO NUANCE!
THE ONLY IDEAS REALLY ABLE TO TAKE ROOT IN OUR CULTURE ARE SHORT, PUNCHY APPROXIMATIONS.
©'08 Malki !
PEOPLE HEAR THE SLOGAN AND THINK THEY KNOW THE ISSUE. HOWEVER, CONCEPTS HAVE TO TRADE AWAY COMPLEXITY TO GAIN WIDESPREAD APPEAL!
BUT EVERYTHING WE KNOW IS SIMPLIFIED TO SOME DEGREE. EVEN IF WE'RE EXPERTS DOWN TO THE ATOMIC LEVEL — THERE'S ALWAYS THE SUBATOMIC.
THE PROBLEMS ARISE WHEN OVER-SIMPLIFIED CONCEPTS EVOLVE INTO COMMON KNOWLEDGE. THEN THE COMPLICATED VERSION — THE MORE ACCURATE VERSION — STARTS SOUNDING TO THE PUBLIC LIKE HERESY!
FOR EXAMPLE, EVERYONE "KNOWS" THAT SMOKING IS BAD. SO WHEN YOU TRY TO EXPLAIN THAT YES, SMOKING IS LARGELY BAD — BUT IT'S ALSO HIGHLY EFFECTIVE, IN INFANTS, AT WARDING OFF MURDEROUS TRANS-DIMENSIONAL BELLYBUTTON GNOMES...
NOBODY EVEN WANTS TO TRY IT!
CLEARLY, THE MEDIA IS CONTROLLED BY A SINISTER CABAL OF BABY-MURDERING GNOMES FROM ANOTHER DIMENSION.
THAT'S THE TITLE OF MY BOOK!

YOU'RE ONE OF THEMMMM

(Do you have an answer? Go ahead, turn the page!)

IN WHICH, PERHAPS, PLUMS ARE EATEN

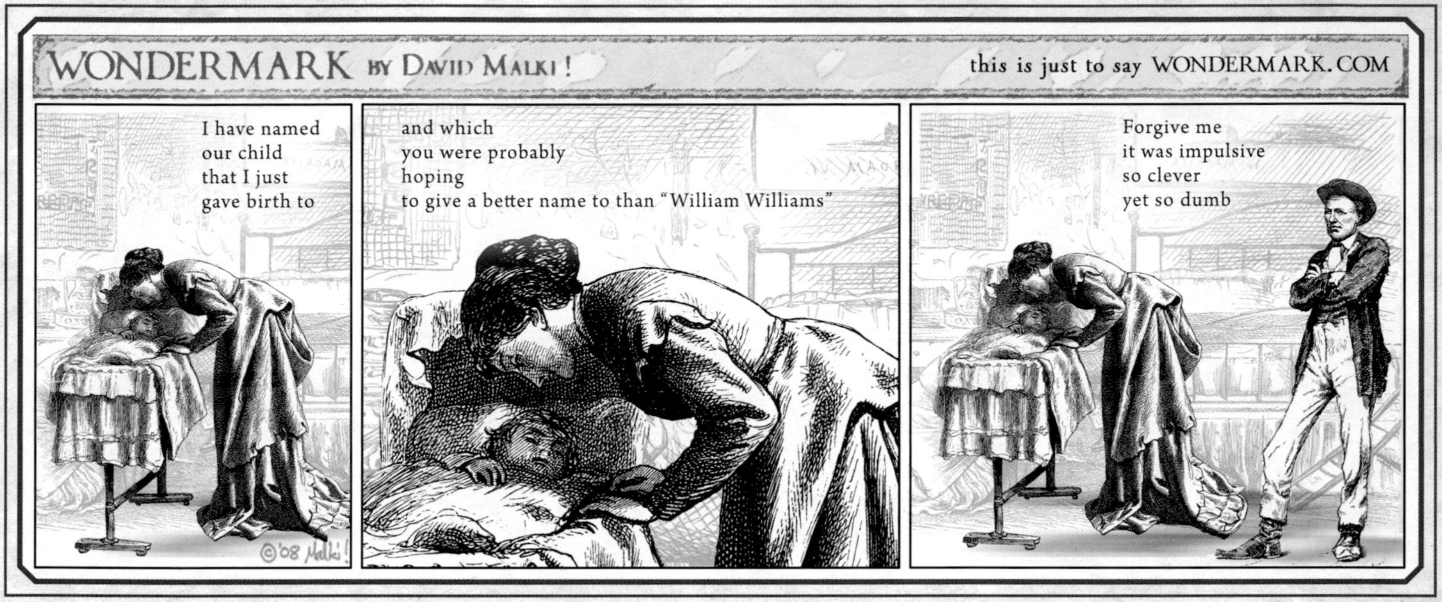
WONDERMARK BY DAVID MALKI !
this is just to say WONDERMARK.COM
I have named our child that I just gave birth to
and which you were probably hoping to give a better name to than "William Williams"
Forgive me it was impulsive so clever yet so dumb
©'08 Malki!

apologies to william carlos williams, but seriously man c'mon

IN WHICH THINGS WERE GOING SO WELL

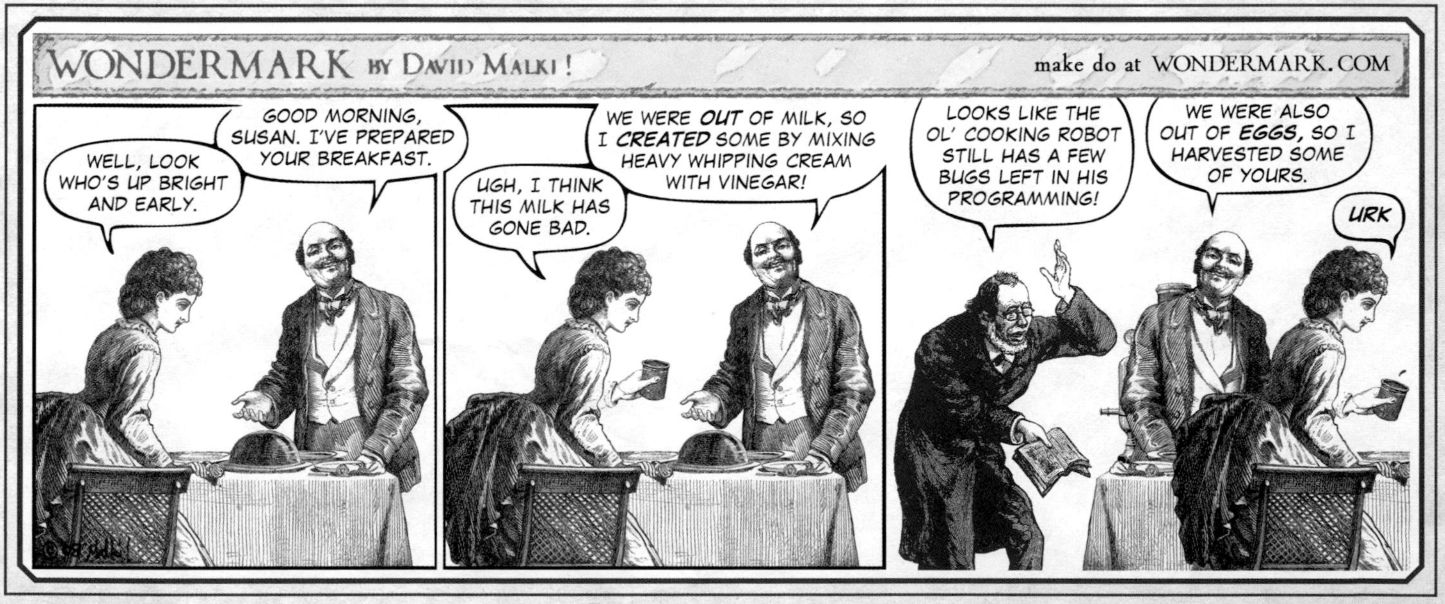
WONDERMARK BY DAVID MALKI !
make do at WONDERMARK.COM
WELL, LOOK WHO'S UP BRIGHT AND EARLY.
GOOD MORNING, SUSAN. I'VE PREPARED YOUR BREAKFAST.
UGH, I THINK THIS MILK HAS GONE BAD.
WE WERE OUT OF MILK, SO I CREATED SOME BY MIXING HEAVY WHIPPING CREAM WITH VINEGAR!
LOOKS LIKE THE OL' COOKING ROBOT STILL HAS A FEW BUGS LEFT IN HIS PROGRAMMING!
WE WERE ALSO OUT OF EGGS, SO I HARVESTED SOME OF YOURS.
URK

Master, did you know Susan twitches in her sleep?

IN WHICH IT'S BEEN A LONG DAY

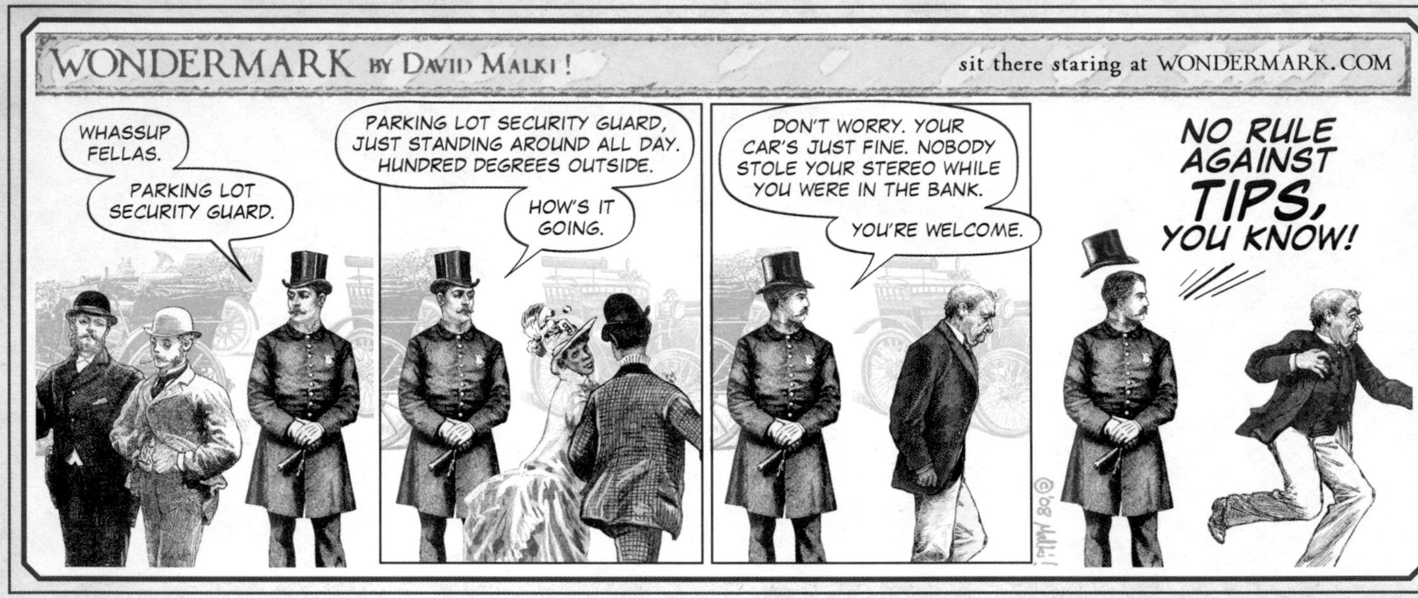
WONDERMARK BY DAVID MALKI !
sit there staring at WONDERMARK.COM
WHASSUP FELLAS.
PARKING LOT SECURITY GUARD.
PARKING LOT SECURITY GUARD, JUST STANDING AROUND ALL DAY. HUNDRED DEGREES OUTSIDE.
HOW'S IT GOING.
DON'T WORRY. YOUR CAR'S JUST FINE. NOBODY STOLE YOUR STEREO WHILE YOU WERE IN THE BANK.
YOU'RE WELCOME.
NO RULE AGAINST TIPS, YOU KNOW!
©'08 Malki !

hey let's roleplay! i'll go into the air-conditioned bank, and you come outside and spend all day weeping over the ashes of your life

IN WHICH FACTOR THE HOMES OF STRANGERS

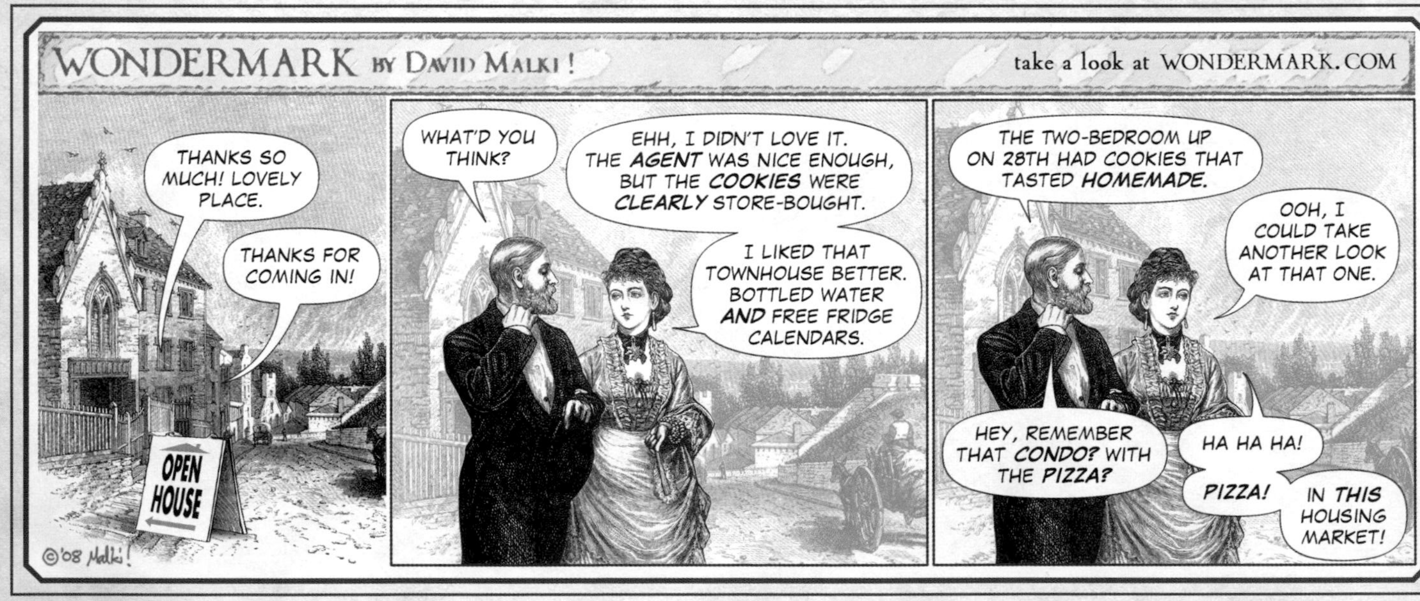
WONDERMARK BY DAVID MALKI !
take a look at WONDERMARK.COM
THANKS SO MUCH! LOVELY PLACE.
THANKS FOR COMING IN!
OPEN HOUSE
©'08 Malki !
WHAT'D YOU THINK?
EHH, I DIDN'T LOVE IT. THE AGENT WAS NICE ENOUGH, BUT THE COOKIES WERE CLEARLY STORE-BOUGHT.
I LIKED THAT TOWNHOUSE BETTER. BOTTLED WATER AND FREE FRIDGE CALENDARS.
THE TWO-BEDROOM UP ON 28TH HAD COOKIES THAT TASTED HOMEMADE.
OOH, I COULD TAKE ANOTHER LOOK AT THAT ONE.
HEY, REMEMBER THAT CONDO? WITH THE PIZZA?
HA HA HA!
PIZZA!
IN THIS HOUSING MARKET!

once I saw a big bowl of fried chicken offered at an open house. a great true story

Can you tell which of the bags of money does not belong with the others?

IN WHICH A BODY IS DISCOVERED

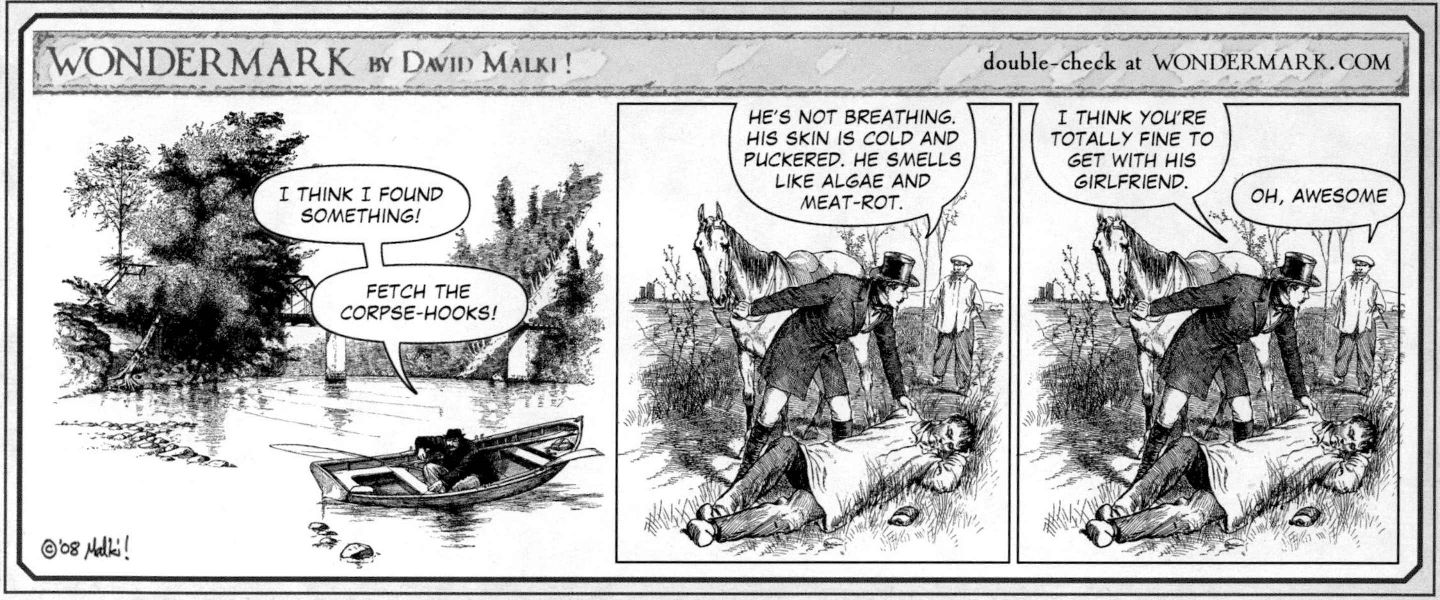
WONDERMARK BY DAVID MALKI !
double-check at WONDERMARK.COM
I THINK I FOUND SOMETHING!
FETCH THE CORPSE-HOOKS!
©'08 Malki!
HE'S NOT BREATHING. HIS SKIN IS COLD AND PUCKERED. HE SMELLS LIKE ALGAE AND MEAT-ROT.
I THINK YOU'RE TOTALLY FINE TO GET WITH HIS GIRLFRIEND.
OH, AWESOME

better clear my afternoon

IN WHICH A QUEUE IS ABOUT TO GET QUIETER

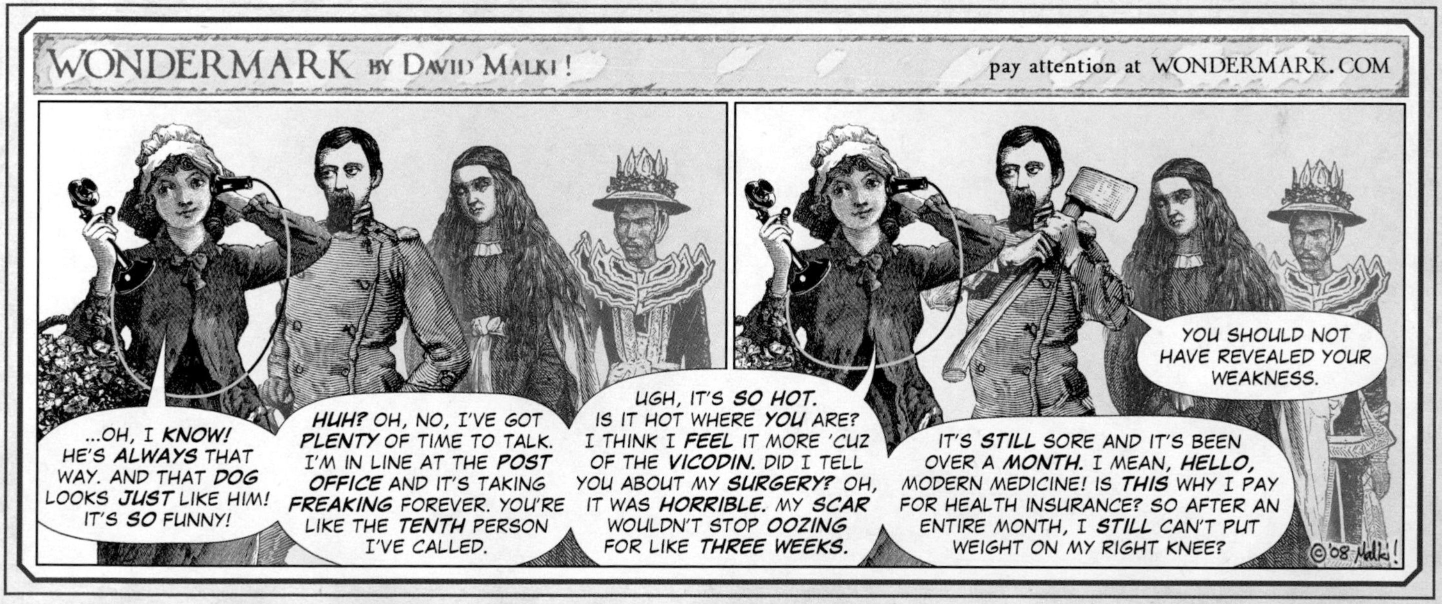
WONDERMARK BY DAVID MALKI !
pay attention at WONDERMARK.COM
...OH, I KNOW! HE'S ALWAYS THAT WAY. AND THAT DOG LOOKS JUST LIKE HIM! IT'S SO FUNNY!
HUH? OH, NO, I'VE GOT PLENTY OF TIME TO TALK. I'M IN LINE AT THE POST OFFICE AND IT'S TAKING FREAKING FOREVER. YOU'RE LIKE THE TENTH PERSON I'VE CALLED.
UGH, IT'S SO HOT. IS IT HOT WHERE YOU ARE? I THINK I FEEL IT MORE 'CUZ OF THE VICODIN. DID I TELL YOU ABOUT MY SURGERY? OH, IT WAS HORRIBLE. MY SCAR WOULDN'T STOP OOZING FOR LIKE THREE WEEKS.
IT'S STILL SORE AND IT'S BEEN OVER A MONTH. I MEAN, HELLO, MODERN MEDICINE! IS THIS WHY I PAY FOR HEALTH INSURANCE? SO AFTER AN ENTIRE MONTH, I STILL CAN'T PUT WEIGHT ON MY RIGHT KNEE?
YOU SHOULD NOT HAVE REVEALED YOUR WEAKNESS.
©'08 Malki!

I brought this with me today just in case.

operating capital with reserve funds allocated for a different purpose.

IN WHICH GEORGE GETS A PIMPLE

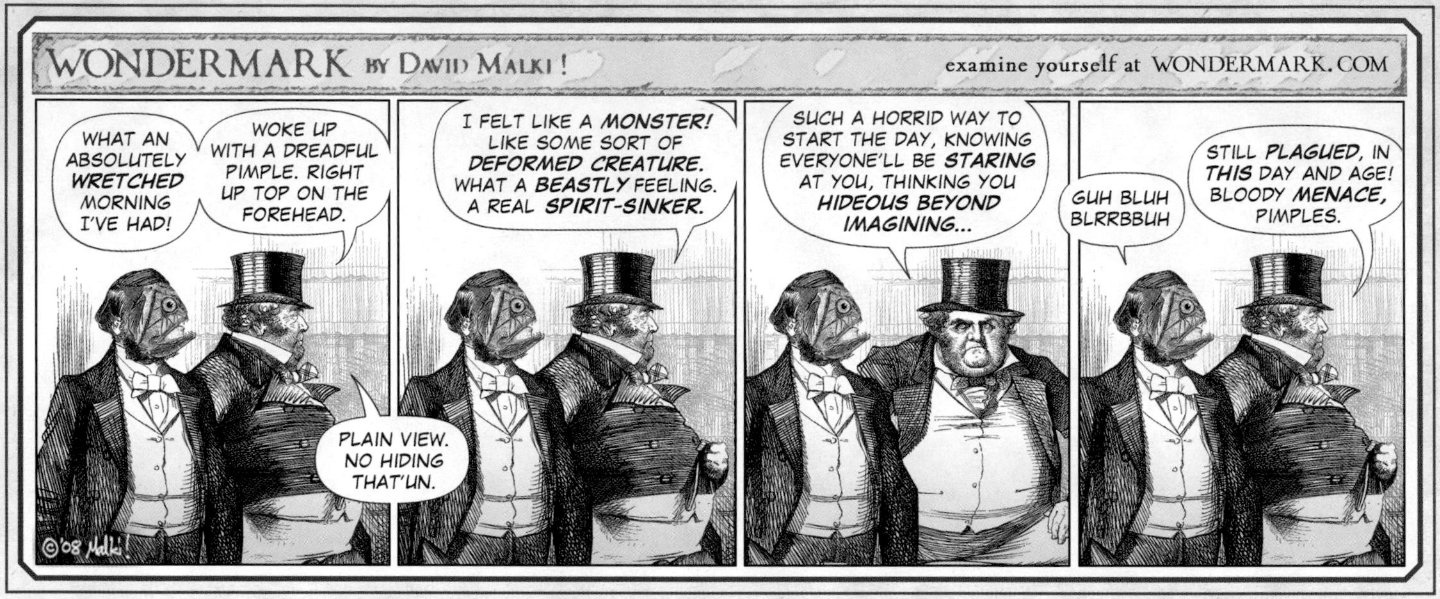
WONDERMARK BY DAVID MALKI !
examine yourself at WONDERMARK.COM
WHAT AN ABSOLUTELY WRETCHED MORNING I'VE HAD!
WOKE UP WITH A DREADFUL PIMPLE. RIGHT UP TOP ON THE FOREHEAD.
PLAIN VIEW. NO HIDING THAT'UN.
I FELT LIKE A MONSTER! LIKE SOME SORT OF DEFORMED CREATURE. WHAT A BEASTLY FEELING. A REAL SPIRIT-SINKER.
SUCH A HORRID WAY TO START THE DAY, KNOWING EVERYONE'LL BE STARING AT YOU, THINKING YOU HIDEOUS BEYOND IMAGINING...
GUH BLUH BLRRBBUH
STILL PLAGUED, IN THIS DAY AND AGE! BLOODY MENACE, PIMPLES.
©'08 Malki!

this day couldn't POSSIBLY get any worse! (CUE TORNADO)

IN WHICH TUSKY IS LATE

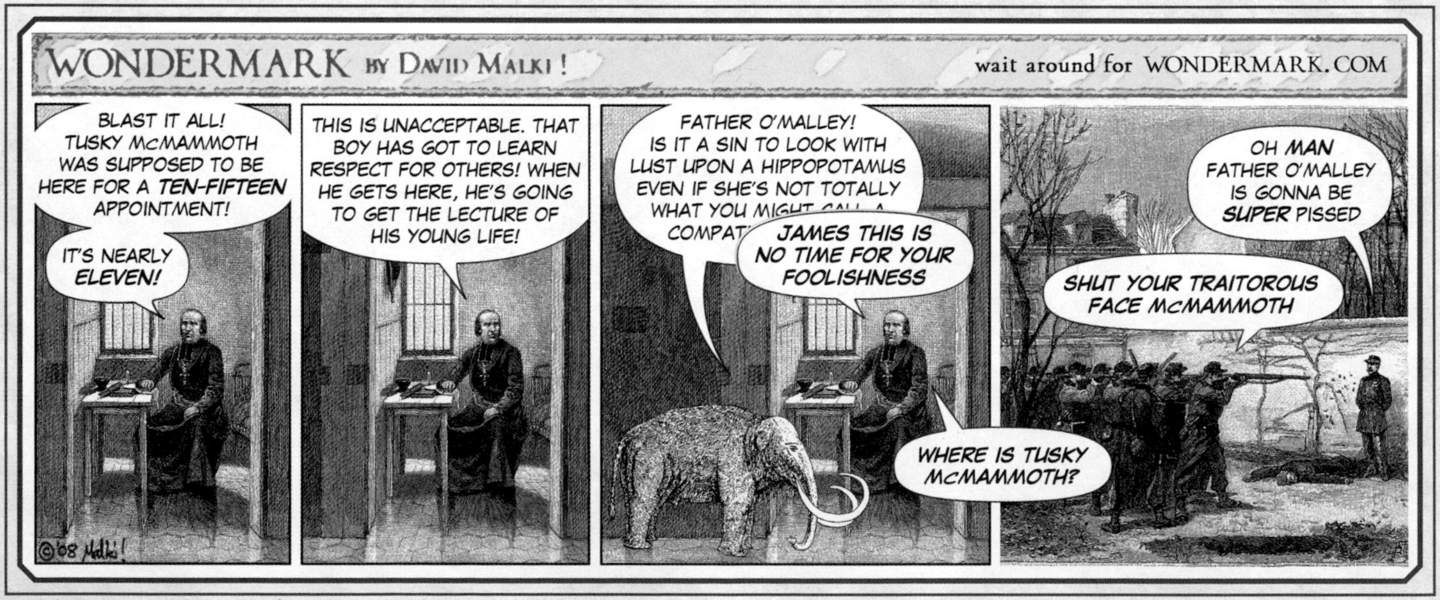
WONDERMARK BY DAVID MALKI !
wait around for WONDERMARK.COM
BLAST IT ALL! TUSKY McMAMMOTH WAS SUPPOSED TO BE HERE FOR A TEN-FIFTEEN APPOINTMENT!
IT'S NEARLY ELEVEN!
THIS IS UNACCEPTABLE. THAT BOY HAS GOT TO LEARN RESPECT FOR OTHERS! WHEN HE GETS HERE, HE'S GOING TO GET THE LECTURE OF HIS YOUNG LIFE!
FATHER O'MALLEY! IS IT A SIN TO LOOK WITH LUST UPON A HIPPOPOTAMUS EVEN IF SHE'S NOT TOTALLY WHAT YOU MIGHT
COMPAT
JAMES THIS IS NO TIME FOR YOUR FOOLISHNESS
WHERE IS TUSKY McMAMMOTH?
OH MAN FATHER O'MALLEY IS GONNA BE SUPER PISSED
SHUT YOUR TRAITOROUS FACE McMAMMOTH
©'08 Malki!

Apparently, Tusky McMammoth is a traitor.

J. P. Morgan needs your help. He's in a real smasher! Someone has mixed up his

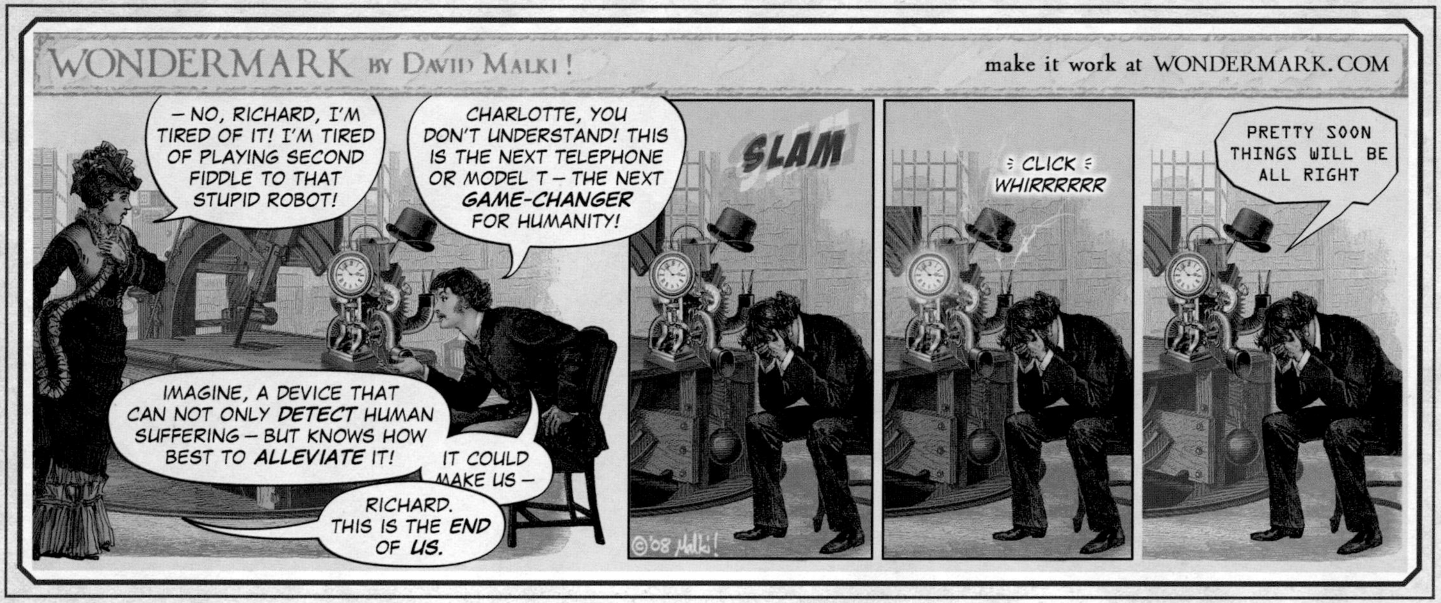
WONDERMARK BY DAVID MALKI !
make it work at WONDERMARK.COM
— NO, RICHARD, I'M TIRED OF IT! I'M TIRED OF PLAYING SECOND FIDDLE TO THAT STUPID ROBOT!
CHARLOTTE, YOU DON'T UNDERSTAND! THIS IS THE NEXT TELEPHONE OR MODEL T — THE NEXT GAME-CHANGER FOR HUMANITY!
IMAGINE, A DEVICE THAT CAN NOT ONLY DETECT HUMAN SUFFERING — BUT KNOWS HOW BEST TO ALLEVIATE IT!
IT COULD MAKE US —
RICHARD. THIS IS THE END OF US.
SLAM
©'08 Malki!
CLICK WHIRRRRRR
PRETTY SOON THINGS WILL BE ALL RIGHT

Color by Marcus Thiele • themonkeymind.livejournal.com

pretty soon

ALTRUISMATON MARK IV.

LETTERS PATENT NO. 445,579.

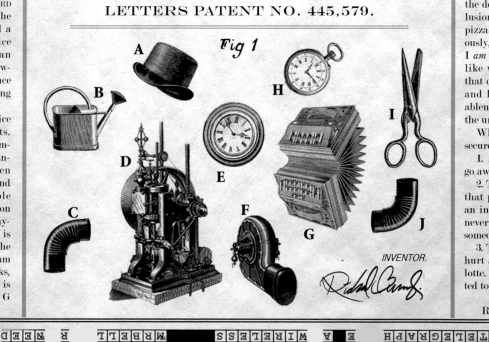

To all whom it may concern:

Be it known that I, Richard S. Burroughs, a citizen of the United States, have invented a certain new and useful device for the Assuaging of Human Suffering, of which the following is a specification, reference being had to the accompanying drawings, in which—

Figure 1 indicates the device broken into its components. Foremost is element A, a common felt derby, which humanizes the device. B is a garden watering-can, for catching and redistributing the inevitable tears of the subject. C is a section of flexible hose, for as the saying goes, "bros before hose." D is the computational heart of the device; it came to me in a dream and I have no idea how it works, or if it even does in reality. E is an amperage-meter; F a farter; G a household accordion (by which the device presents a cunning illusion of speech); H a flattened pizza (to fuel the device); I, obviously, is scissors (more correctly, I *am* scissors); and J looks just like what it describes. Look at that cute little pair! Big brother and little brother. This adorableness is key to the efficacy of the unit.

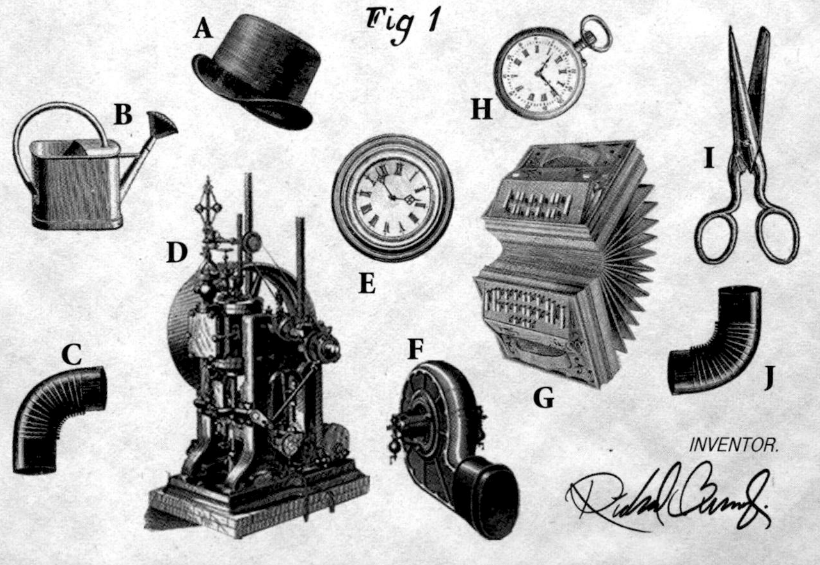
Fig 1
A
B
C
D
E
F
G
H
I
J
INVENTOR.

What I claim, and desire to secure by Letters Patent, is—

1. A device to make the pain go away. I do not even care how.

2. That affection is fickle, and that people can turn on you in an instant, and that you should never believe that simply loving someone can ever be enough.

3. That I will not let myself be hurt again. I am serious, Charlotte. This form is being submitted to the Government.

RICHARD BURROUGHS.

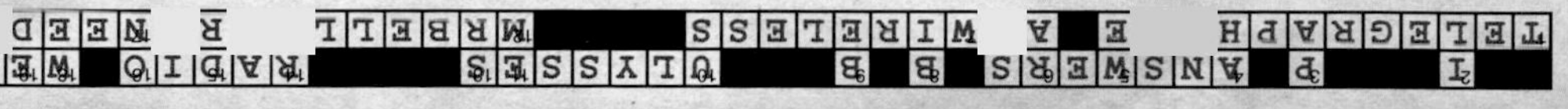
SOLUTION

IN WHICH A DOG IS SNEAKY

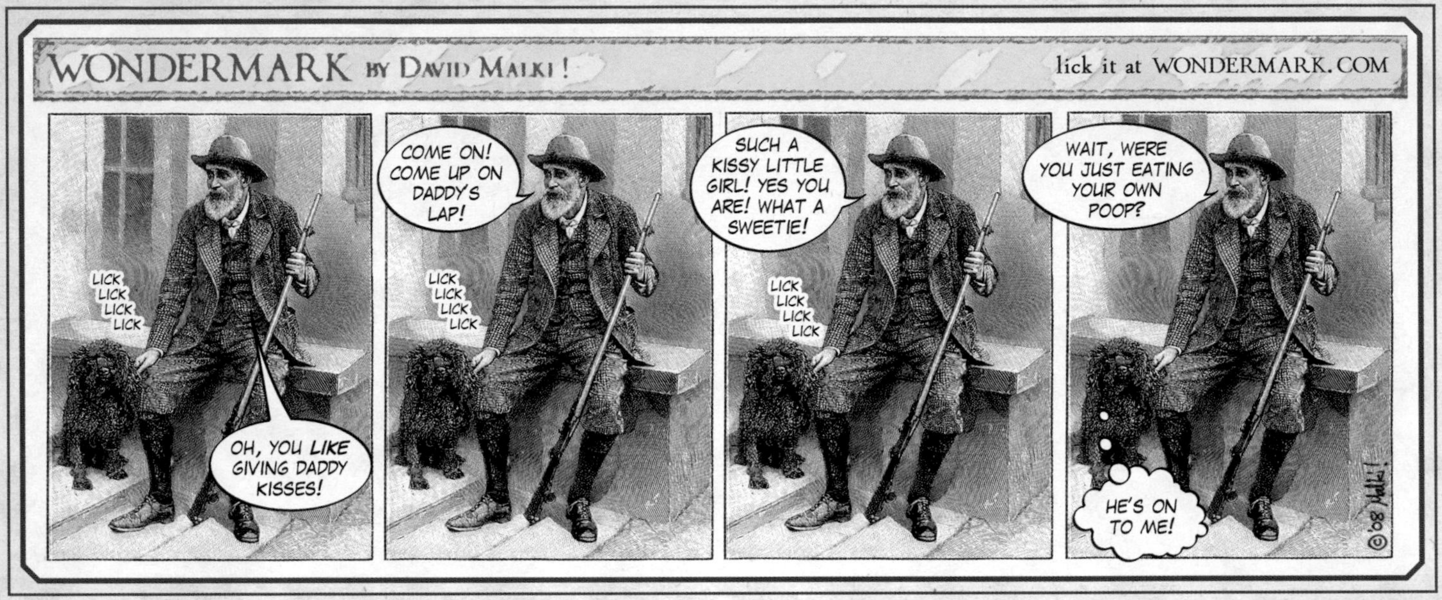
WONDERMARK BY DAVID MALKI !
lick it at WONDERMARK.COM
LICK LICK LICK LICK
OH, YOU LIKE GIVING DADDY KISSES!
COME ON! COME UP ON DADDY'S LAP!
LICK LICK LICK LICK
SUCH A KISSY LITTLE GIRL! YES YOU ARE! WHAT A SWEETIE!
LICK LICK LICK LICK
WAIT, WERE YOU JUST EATING YOUR OWN POOP?
HE'S ON TO ME!
©'08 Malki!

i didn't say 'stop'

IN WHICH A PLATE DRIVES PARKER TO ANGER

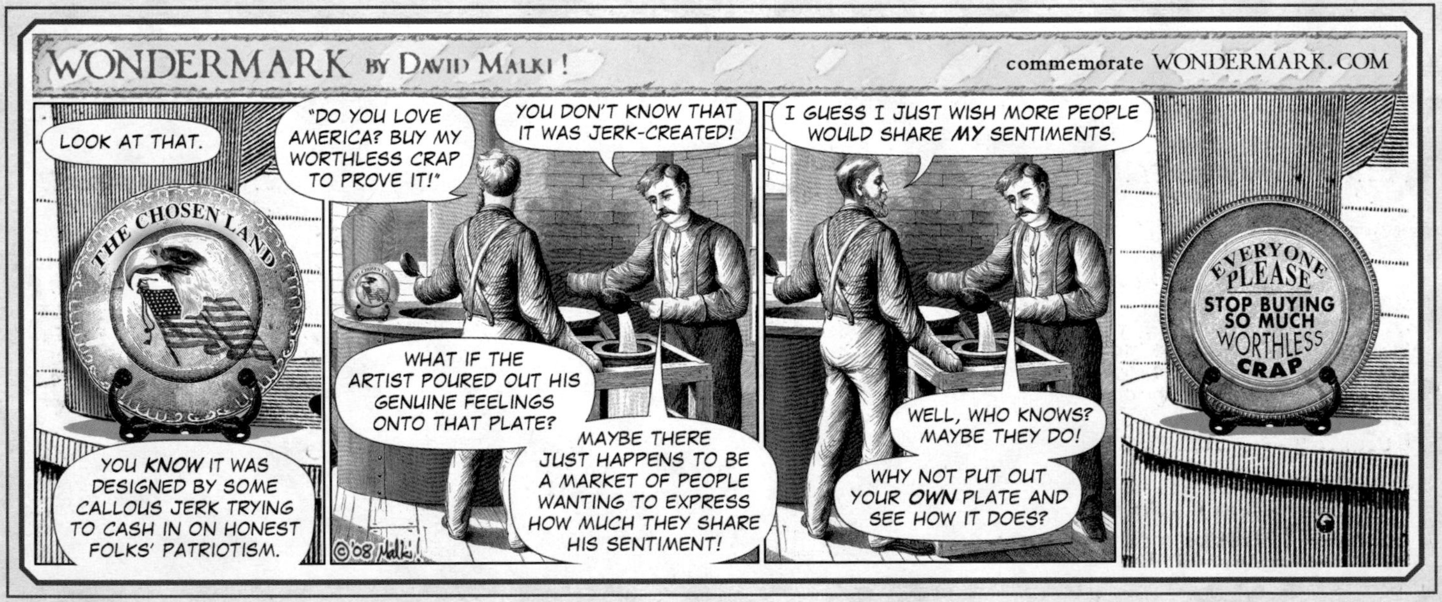
WONDERMARK BY DAVID MALKI !
commemorate WONDERMARK.COM
LOOK AT THAT.
THE CHOSEN LAND
YOU KNOW IT WAS DESIGNED BY SOME CALLOUS JERK TRYING TO CASH IN ON HONEST FOLKS' PATRIOTISM.
"DO YOU LOVE AMERICA? BUY MY WORTHLESS CRAP TO PROVE IT!"
YOU DON'T KNOW THAT IT WAS JERK-CREATED!
WHAT IF THE ARTIST POURED OUT HIS GENUINE FEELINGS ONTO THAT PLATE?
MAYBE THERE JUST HAPPENS TO BE A MARKET OF PEOPLE WANTING TO EXPRESS HOW MUCH THEY SHARE HIS SENTIMENT!
©'08 Malki!
I GUESS I JUST WISH MORE PEOPLE WOULD SHARE MY SENTIMENTS.
WELL, WHO KNOWS? MAYBE THEY DO!
WHY NOT PUT OUT YOUR OWN PLATE AND SEE HOW IT DOES?
EVERYONE PLEASE STOP BUYING SO MUCH WORTHLESS CRAP

sales are slow

(Solution on the next page.)

IN WHICH A WARNING IS DELIVERED

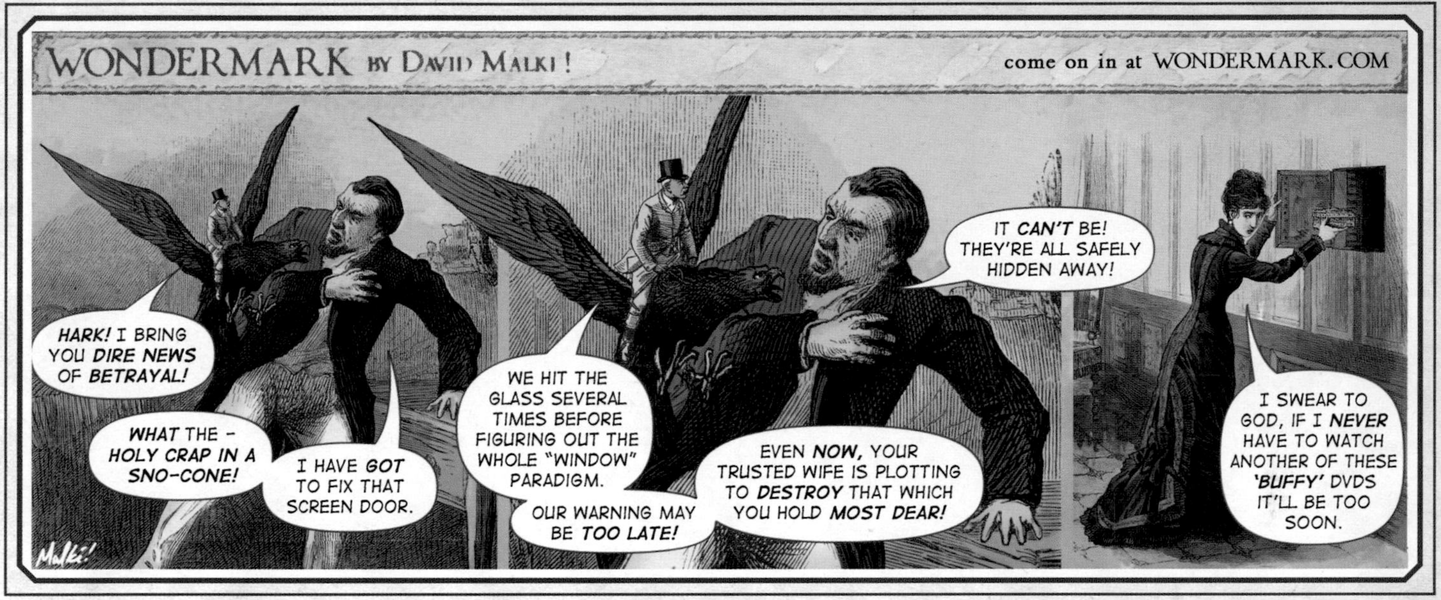
WONDERMARK BY DAVID MALKI !
come on in at WONDERMARK.COM
HARK! I BRING YOU DIRE NEWS OF BETRAYAL!
WHAT THE – HOLY CRAP IN A SNO-CONE!
I HAVE GOT TO FIX THAT SCREEN DOOR.
WE HIT THE GLASS SEVERAL TIMES BEFORE FIGURING OUT THE WHOLE "WINDOW" PARADIGM.
OUR WARNING MAY BE TOO LATE!
EVEN NOW, YOUR TRUSTED WIFE IS PLOTTING TO DESTROY THAT WHICH YOU HOLD MOST DEAR!
IT CAN'T BE! THEY'RE ALL SAFELY HIDDEN AWAY!
I SWEAR TO GOD, IF I NEVER HAVE TO WATCH ANOTHER OF THESE 'BUFFY' DVDS IT'LL BE TOO SOON.
Malki!

now turn off the light! so we can find our way back outside.

IN WHICH JORDAN EXCELS AT SPORT

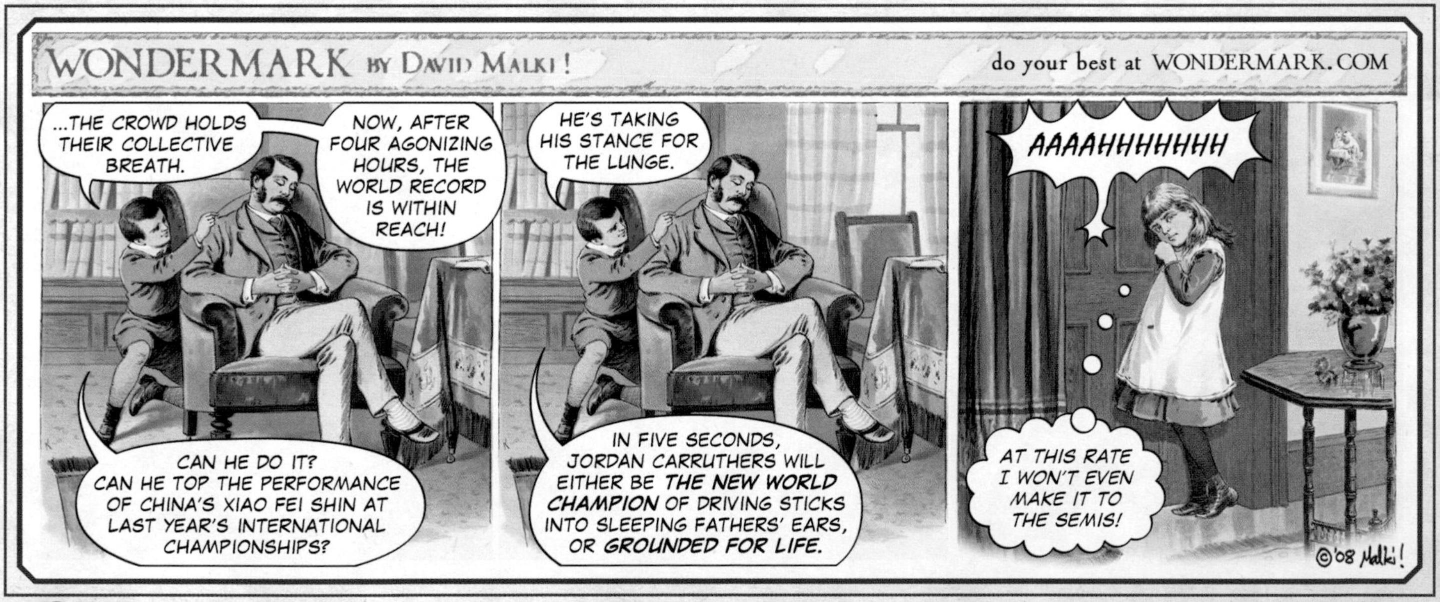
WONDERMARK BY DAVID MALKI !
do your best at WONDERMARK.COM
...THE CROWD HOLDS THEIR COLLECTIVE BREATH.
NOW, AFTER FOUR AGONIZING HOURS, THE WORLD RECORD IS WITHIN REACH!
CAN HE DO IT? CAN HE TOP THE PERFORMANCE OF CHINA'S XIAO FEI SHIN AT LAST YEAR'S INTERNATIONAL CHAMPIONSHIPS?
HE'S TAKING HIS STANCE FOR THE LUNGE.
IN FIVE SECONDS, JORDAN CARRUTHERS WILL EITHER BE THE NEW WORLD CHAMPION OF DRIVING STICKS INTO SLEEPING FATHERS' EARS, OR GROUNDED FOR LIFE.
AAAAHHHHHHH
AT THIS RATE I WON'T EVEN MAKE IT TO THE SEMIS!
©'08 Malki!

12

those chinese kids train from birth, man, from BIRTH

18. You or I alone may have trouble, but oh, what ______ might do together! 19. Abbrev. for inventor Thos.

IN WHICH SONG RINGS FORTH CONSTANTLY

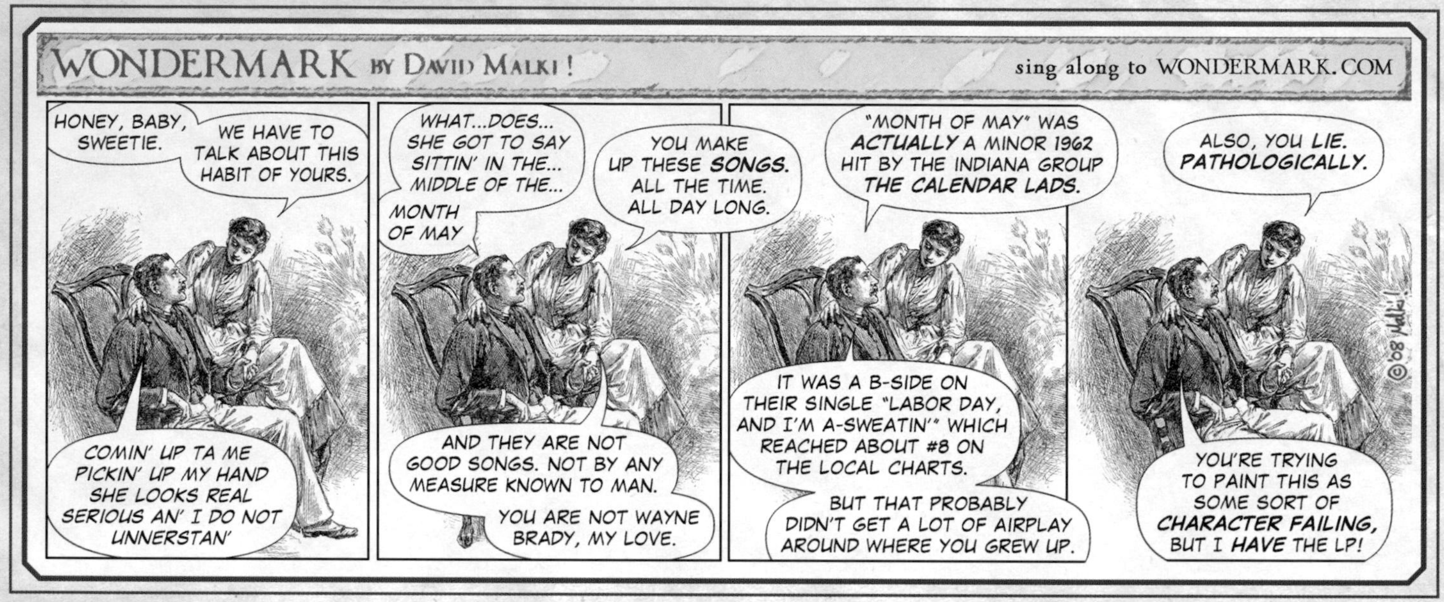
WONDERMARK BY DAVID MALKI !
sing along to WONDERMARK.COM
HONEY, BABY, SWEETIE.
WE HAVE TO TALK ABOUT THIS HABIT OF YOURS.
COMIN' UP TA ME PICKIN' UP MY HAND SHE LOOKS REAL SERIOUS AN' I DO NOT UNNERSTAN'
WHAT...DOES... SHE GOT TO SAY SITTIN' IN THE... MIDDLE OF THE...
MONTH OF MAY
YOU MAKE UP THESE SONGS. ALL THE TIME. ALL DAY LONG.
AND THEY ARE NOT GOOD SONGS. NOT BY ANY MEASURE KNOWN TO MAN.
YOU ARE NOT WAYNE BRADY, MY LOVE.
"MONTH OF MAY" WAS ACTUALLY A MINOR 1962 HIT BY THE INDIANA GROUP THE CALENDAR LADS.
IT WAS A B-SIDE ON THEIR SINGLE "LABOR DAY, AND I'M A-SWEATIN'" WHICH REACHED ABOUT #8 ON THE LOCAL CHARTS.
BUT THAT PROBABLY DIDN'T GET A LOT OF AIRPLAY AROUND WHERE YOU GREW UP.
ALSO, YOU LIE. PATHOLOGICALLY.
YOU'RE TRYING TO PAINT THIS AS SOME SORT OF CHARACTER FAILING, BUT I HAVE THE LP!
©'08 Malki !

Their other big hit: 'This Memorial Day, I'm A Veteran...Of You'

IN WHICH LIZZIE GETS BETTER

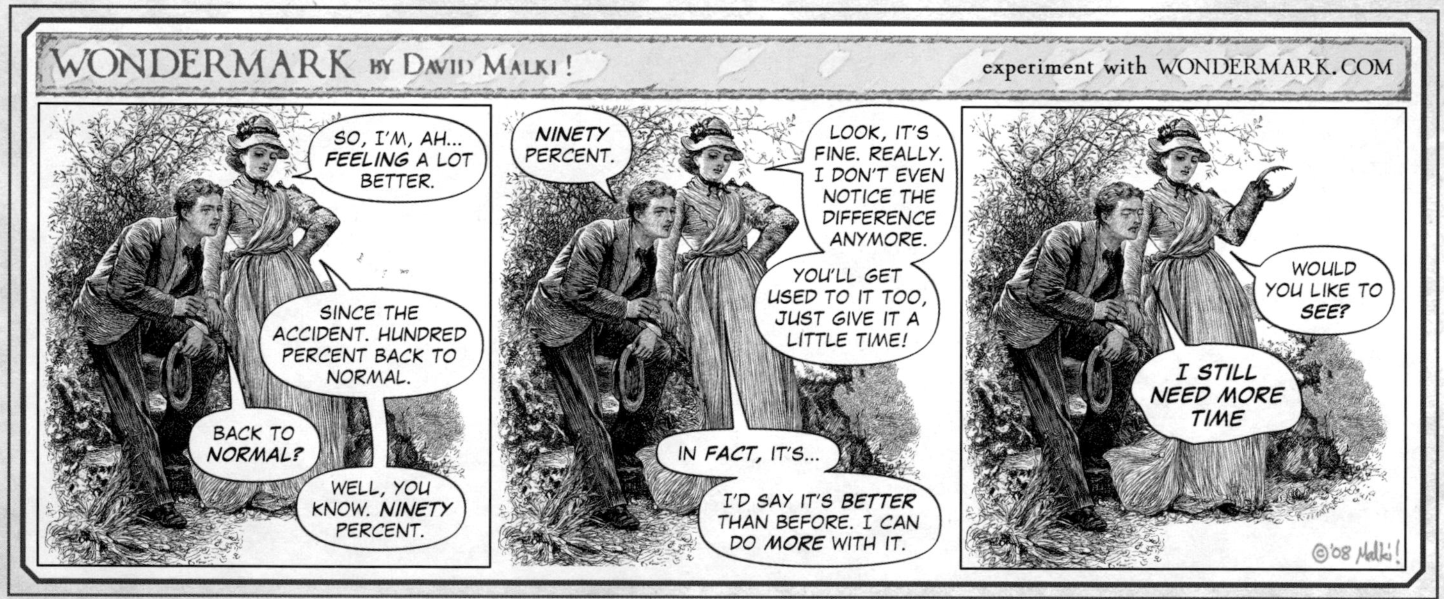
WONDERMARK BY DAVID MALKI !
experiment with WONDERMARK.COM
SO, I'M, AH... FEELING A LOT BETTER.
SINCE THE ACCIDENT. HUNDRED PERCENT BACK TO NORMAL.
BACK TO NORMAL?
WELL, YOU KNOW. NINETY PERCENT.
NINETY PERCENT.
LOOK, IT'S FINE. REALLY. I DON'T EVEN NOTICE THE DIFFERENCE ANYMORE.
YOU'LL GET USED TO IT TOO, JUST GIVE IT A LITTLE TIME!
IN FACT, IT'S...
I'D SAY IT'S BETTER THAN BEFORE. I CAN DO MORE WITH IT.
WOULD YOU LIKE TO SEE?
I STILL NEED MORE TIME
©'08 Malki !

close your eyes and take the prize

15. A doctorate will replace "Mr." or "Mrs." with this. 16. To power a switch.

WELCOME TO COLLEGE

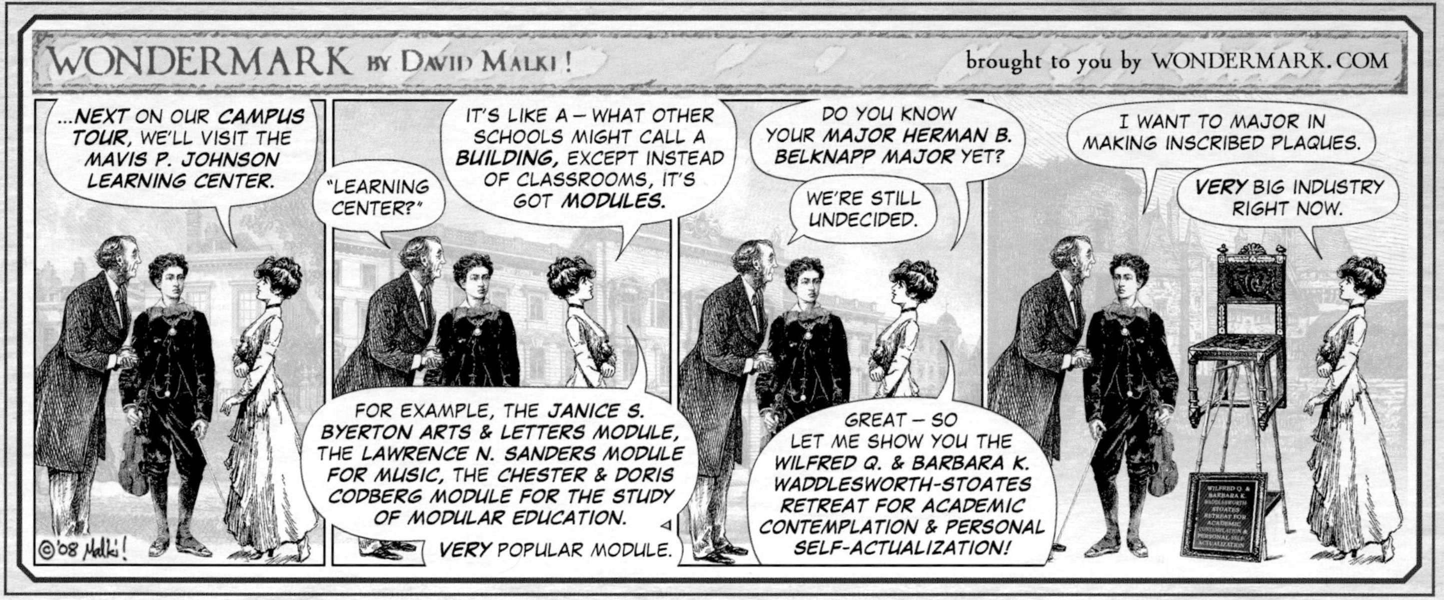
WONDERMARK BY DAVID MALKI !
brought to you by WONDERMARK.COM
...NEXT ON OUR CAMPUS TOUR, WE'LL VISIT THE MAVIS P. JOHNSON LEARNING CENTER.
©'08 Malki !
"LEARNING CENTER?"
IT'S LIKE A — WHAT OTHER SCHOOLS MIGHT CALL A BUILDING, EXCEPT INSTEAD OF CLASSROOMS, IT'S GOT MODULES.
FOR EXAMPLE, THE JANICE S. BYERTON ARTS & LETTERS MODULE, THE LAWRENCE N. SANDERS MODULE FOR MUSIC, THE CHESTER & DORIS CODBERG MODULE FOR THE STUDY OF MODULAR EDUCATION.
VERY POPULAR MODULE.
DO YOU KNOW YOUR MAJOR HERMAN B. BELKNAPP MAJOR YET?
WE'RE STILL UNDECIDED.
GREAT — SO LET ME SHOW YOU THE WILFRED Q. & BARBARA K. WADDLESWORTH-STOATES RETREAT FOR ACADEMIC CONTEMPLATION & PERSONAL SELF-ACTUALIZATION!
I WANT TO MAJOR IN MAKING INSCRIBED PLAQUES.
VERY BIG INDUSTRY RIGHT NOW.

so... private school, huh?

IN WHICH ONE THING SPARKS ANOTHER, AND SO ON

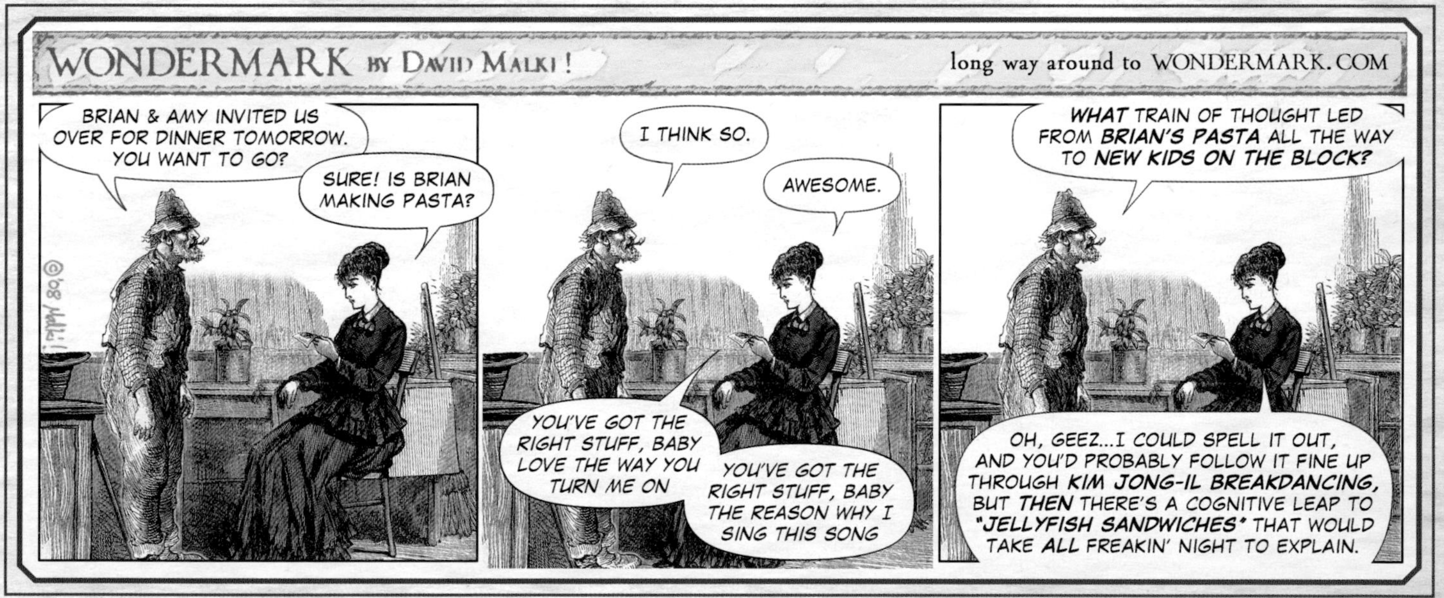
WONDERMARK BY DAVID MALKI !
long way around to WONDERMARK.COM
BRIAN & AMY INVITED US OVER FOR DINNER TOMORROW. YOU WANT TO GO?
SURE! IS BRIAN MAKING PASTA?
©'08 Malki !
I THINK SO.
AWESOME.
YOU'VE GOT THE RIGHT STUFF, BABY LOVE THE WAY YOU TURN ME ON
YOU'VE GOT THE RIGHT STUFF, BABY THE REASON WHY I SING THIS SONG
WHAT TRAIN OF THOUGHT LED FROM BRIAN'S PASTA ALL THE WAY TO NEW KIDS ON THE BLOCK?
OH, GEEZ...I COULD SPELL IT OUT, AND YOU'D PROBABLY FOLLOW IT FINE UP THROUGH KIM JONG-IL BREAKDANCING, BUT THEN THERE'S A COGNITIVE LEAP TO "JELLYFISH SANDWICHES" THAT WOULD TAKE ALL FREAKIN' NIGHT TO EXPLAIN.

Brian is proud of usually doing reasonably well at a not-too-difficult dish.

11. Printing: the big brother to an en dash. 13. Suffix self-assigned by a father who has named his son after himself.

IN WHICH A CAT IS HAD

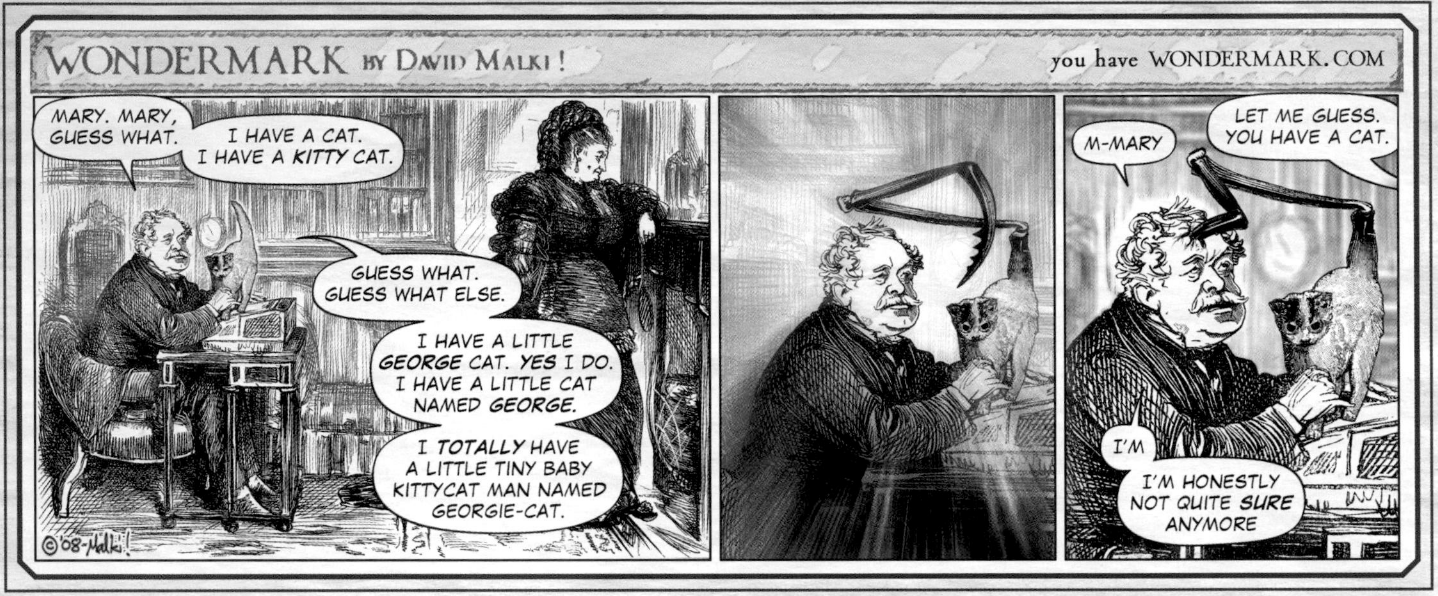
WONDERMARK BY DAVID MALKI !
you have WONDERMARK.COM
MARY. MARY, GUESS WHAT.
I HAVE A CAT. I HAVE A KITTY CAT.
GUESS WHAT. GUESS WHAT ELSE.
I HAVE A LITTLE GEORGE CAT. YES I DO. I HAVE A LITTLE CAT NAMED GEORGE.
I TOTALLY HAVE A LITTLE TINY BABY KITTYCAT MAN NAMED GEORGIE-CAT.
©'08-Malki!
M-MARY
LET ME GUESS. YOU HAVE A CAT.
I'M
I'M HONESTLY NOT QUITE SURE ANYMORE

SSSAYYYY YYYEESSSS

ARRIVAL OF THE BUTT INSPECTOR

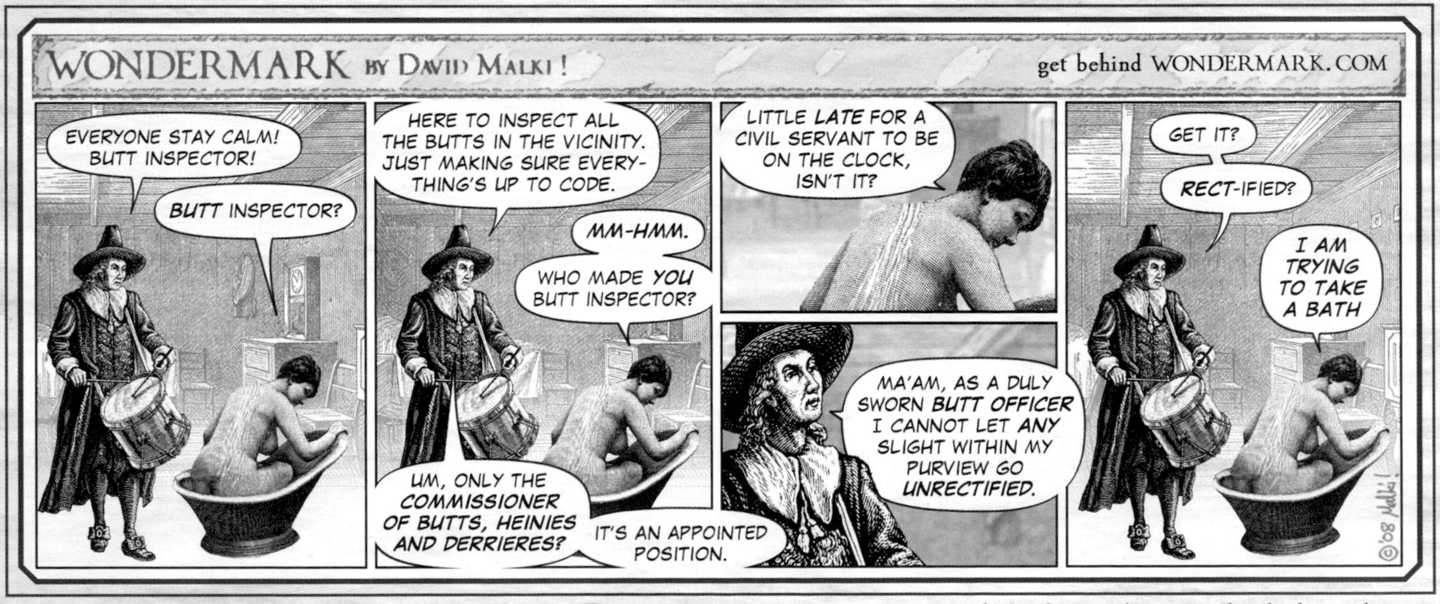
WONDERMARK BY DAVID MALKI !
get behind WONDERMARK.COM
EVERYONE STAY CALM! BUTT INSPECTOR!
BUTT INSPECTOR?
HERE TO INSPECT ALL THE BUTTS IN THE VICINITY. JUST MAKING SURE EVERY-THING'S UP TO CODE.
MM-HMM.
WHO MADE YOU BUTT INSPECTOR?
UM, ONLY THE COMMISSIONER OF BUTTS, HEINIES AND DERRIERES?
IT'S AN APPOINTED POSITION.
LITTLE LATE FOR A CIVIL SERVANT TO BE ON THE CLOCK, ISN'T IT?
MA'AM, AS A DULY SWORN BUTT OFFICER I CANNOT LET ANY SLIGHT WITHIN MY PURVIEW GO UNRECTIFIED.
GET IT?
RECT-IFIED?
I AM TRYING TO TAKE A BATH
©'08-Malki!

the 'civil servant' argument breaks down when you realize that the butt-firefighters are on the clock 24/7

10. "Don't worry, sir! My chums and I will get your wires un-crossed—just leave it to ______!"

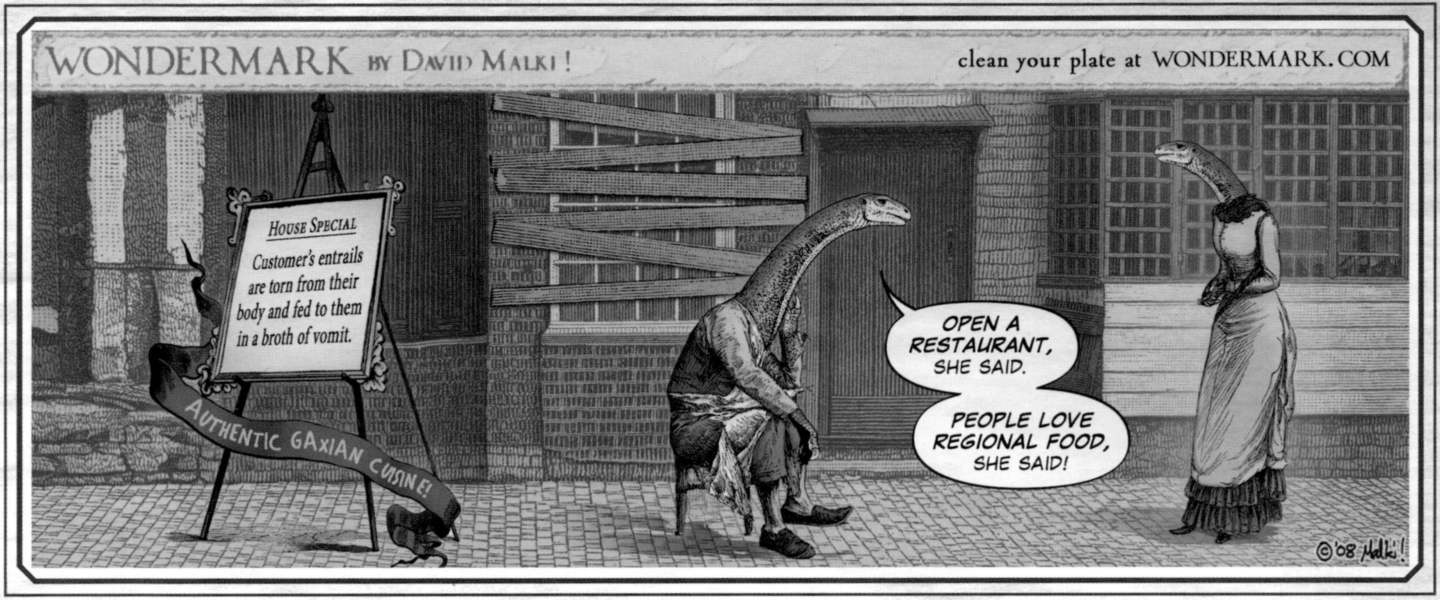
WONDERMARK BY DAVID MALKI!
clean your plate at WONDERMARK.COM
HOUSE SPECIAL
Customer's entrails are torn from their body and fed to them in a broth of vomit.
AUTHENTIC GAXIAN CUISINE!
OPEN A RESTAURANT, SHE SAID.
PEOPLE LOVE REGIONAL FOOD, SHE SAID!
©'08 Malki!

Color by Marcus Thiele • themonkeymind.livejournal.com

in retrospect it was also probably a bad idea to serve, instead of ice water, flesh-dissolving acid that looked and tasted exactly like ice water

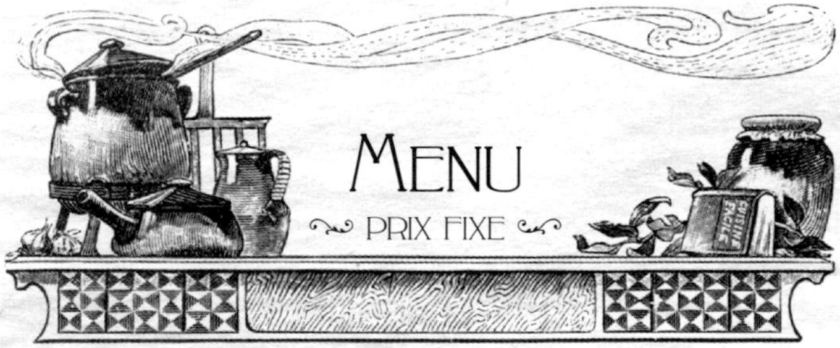
MENU
PRIX FIXE

SOUP

Boiled Horse Face Bisque ✻ Vegetable Barley*

—

SALAD

Spring Greens in Phlegm ✻ Newspaper in Pine Sap*

—

APPETIZER

Chum Rolls ✻ Eagle Knuckles ✻ Viscera Sampler

ENTRÉE

Roasted Zucchini stuffed with Fingernails*

Your Local Mayor – braised until Regretful

—

DESSERT

Skin Parfait ✻ Crème au Pus ✻ Tiramisu avec Mold*

—

COCKTAILS

Milk-Spoilt Triple Sec ✻ Bile & Tonic

—

SPECIAL GAXIAN AFTER-MEAL DELICACY

Murder ✻ Murder-Suicide

* Signifies vegetarian selection.

Consumption of raw or undercooked foods of human origin may increase your risk of food-borne illness.

6. Egyptian pagan sun-god. 8. Prefix for "pair," as in __cycle, __plane, or __smith. 9. To simply exist.

IN WHICH OSTRICHES PLOT

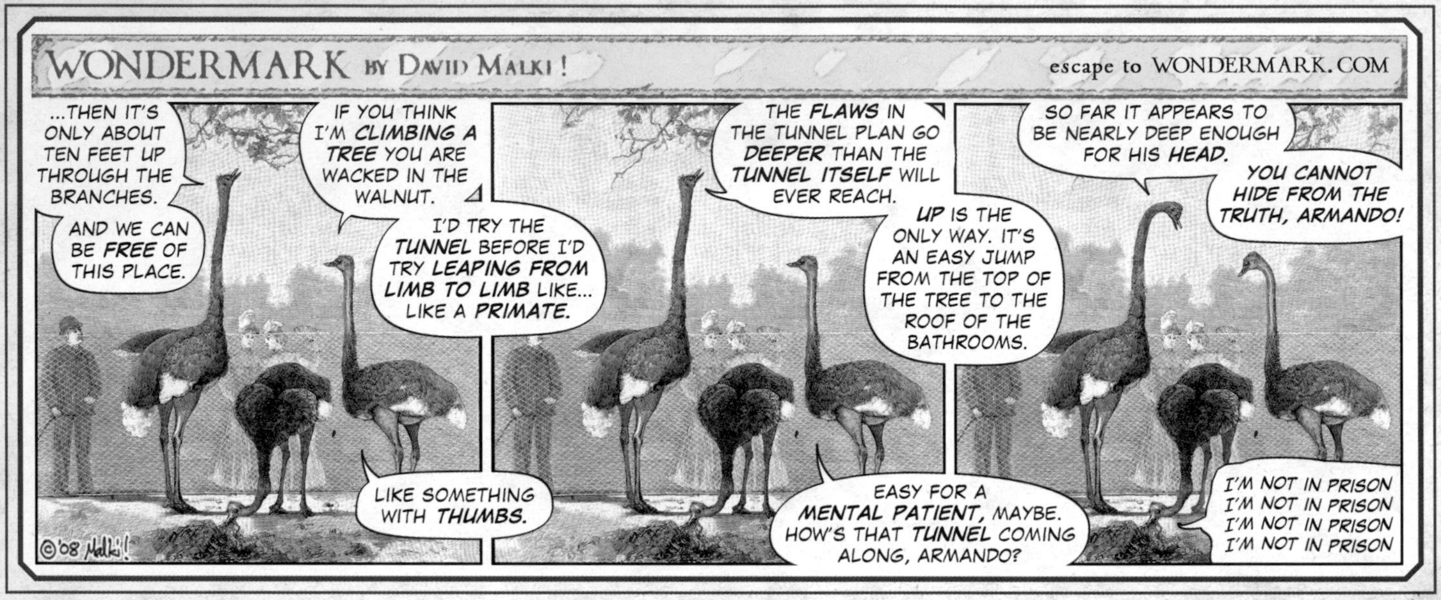
WONDERMARK BY DAVID MALKI !
escape to WONDERMARK.COM
...THEN IT'S ONLY ABOUT TEN FEET UP THROUGH THE BRANCHES.
AND WE CAN BE FREE OF THIS PLACE.
IF YOU THINK I'M CLIMBING A TREE YOU ARE WACKED IN THE WALNUT.
I'D TRY THE TUNNEL BEFORE I'D TRY LEAPING FROM LIMB TO LIMB LIKE... LIKE A PRIMATE.
LIKE SOMETHING WITH THUMBS.
©'08 Malki!
THE FLAWS IN THE TUNNEL PLAN GO DEEPER THAN THE TUNNEL ITSELF WILL EVER REACH.
UP IS THE ONLY WAY. IT'S AN EASY JUMP FROM THE TOP OF THE TREE TO THE ROOF OF THE BATHROOMS.
EASY FOR A MENTAL PATIENT, MAYBE. HOW'S THAT TUNNEL COMING ALONG, ARMANDO?
SO FAR IT APPEARS TO BE NEARLY DEEP ENOUGH FOR HIS HEAD.
YOU CANNOT HIDE FROM THE TRUTH, ARMANDO!
I'M NOT IN PRISON
I'M NOT IN PRISON
I'M NOT IN PRISON
I'M NOT IN PRISON

stir-crazy. all too common. sad, really.

IN WHICH THE CLASSROOM BECOMES TENSE

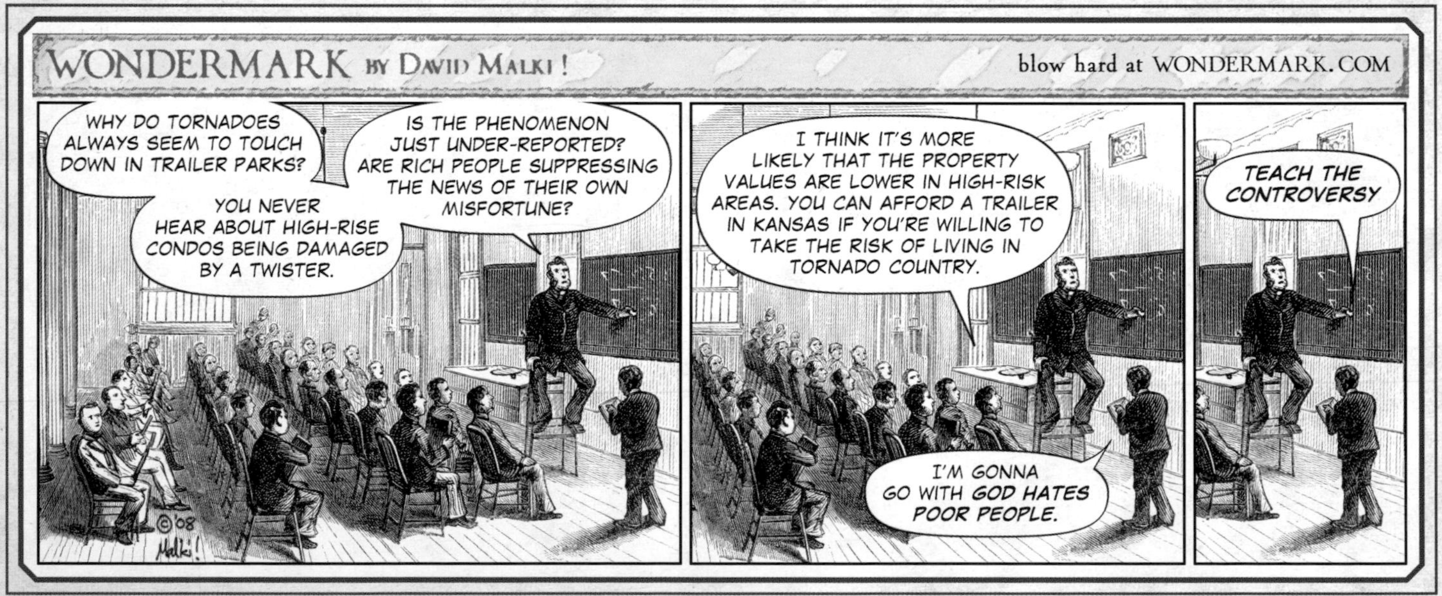
WONDERMARK BY DAVID MALKI !
blow hard at WONDERMARK.COM
WHY DO TORNADOES ALWAYS SEEM TO TOUCH DOWN IN TRAILER PARKS?
YOU NEVER HEAR ABOUT HIGH-RISE CONDOS BEING DAMAGED BY A TWISTER.
IS THE PHENOMENON JUST UNDER-REPORTED? ARE RICH PEOPLE SUPPRESSING THE NEWS OF THEIR OWN MISFORTUNE?
©'08 Malki!
I THINK IT'S MORE LIKELY THAT THE PROPERTY VALUES ARE LOWER IN HIGH-RISK AREAS. YOU CAN AFFORD A TRAILER IN KANSAS IF YOU'RE WILLING TO TAKE THE RISK OF LIVING IN TORNADO COUNTRY.
I'M GONNA GO WITH GOD HATES POOR PEOPLE.
TEACH THE CONTROVERSY

competing theory: wistful trailers will take ANY EXCUSE to pretend to be helicopters

IN WHICH HARV FINALLY SUCCEEDS

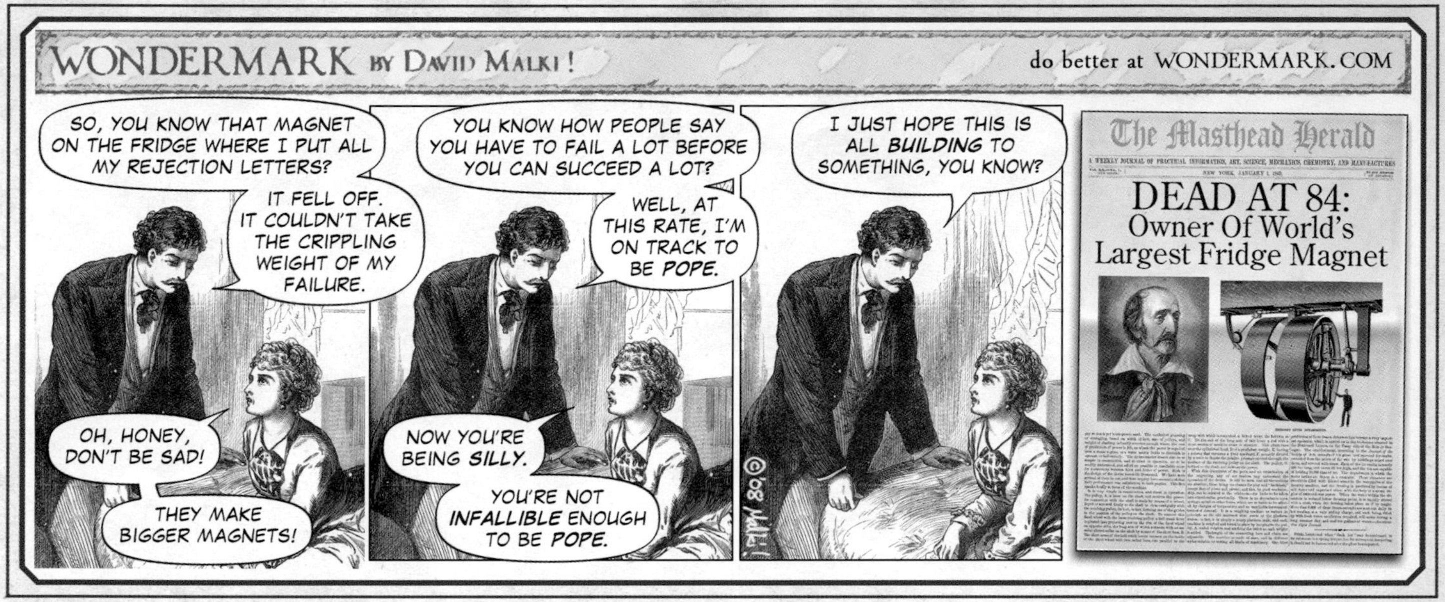
WONDERMARK BY DAVID MALKI !
do better at WONDERMARK.COM
SO, YOU KNOW THAT MAGNET ON THE FRIDGE WHERE I PUT ALL MY REJECTION LETTERS?
IT FELL OFF. IT COULDN'T TAKE THE CRIPPLING WEIGHT OF MY FAILURE.
OH, HONEY, DON'T BE SAD!
THEY MAKE BIGGER MAGNETS!
YOU KNOW HOW PEOPLE SAY YOU HAVE TO FAIL A LOT BEFORE YOU CAN SUCCEED A LOT?
WELL, AT THIS RATE, I'M ON TRACK TO BE POPE.
NOW YOU'RE BEING SILLY.
YOU'RE NOT INFALLIBLE ENOUGH TO BE POPE.
©08 Malki !
I JUST HOPE THIS IS ALL BUILDING TO SOMETHING, YOU KNOW?
The Masthead Herald
DEAD AT 84:
Owner Of World's Largest Fridge Magnet

Kenmore Erects Giant Fridge To Memorialize Him, Self-Promote

IN WHICH A TREE GETS THE TALK

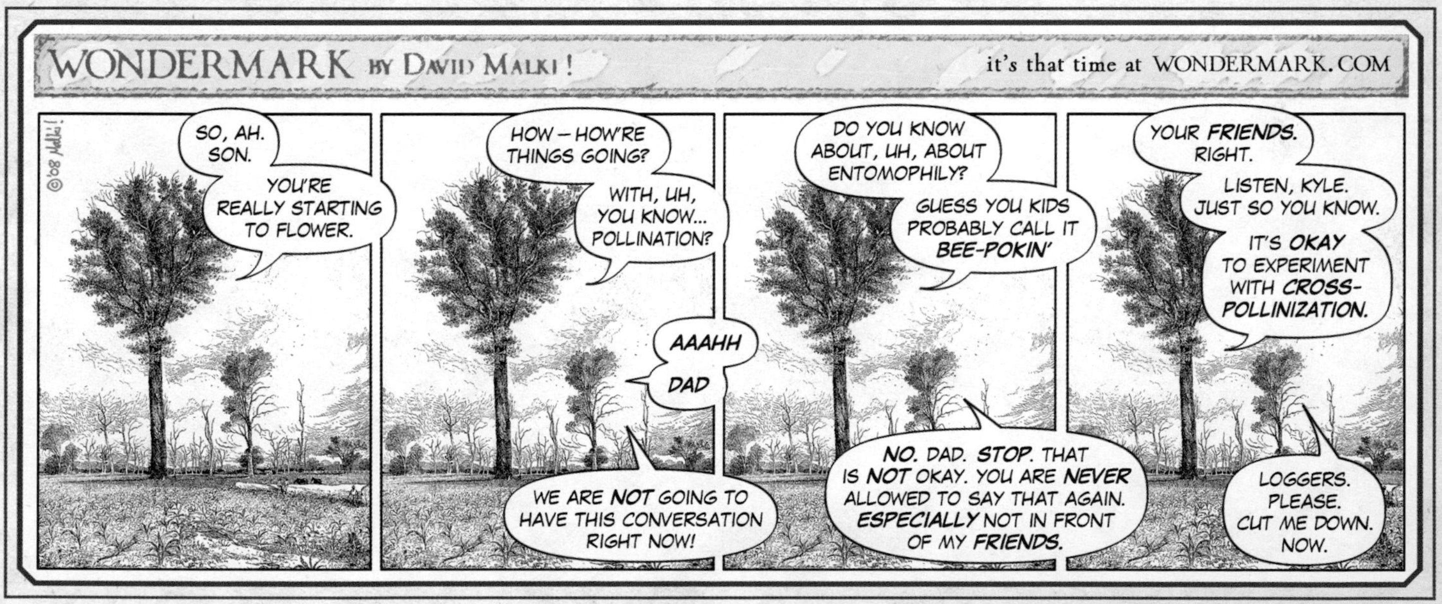
WONDERMARK BY DAVID MALKI !
it's that time at WONDERMARK.COM
©08 Malki !
SO, AH. SON.
YOU'RE REALLY STARTING TO FLOWER.
HOW — HOW'RE THINGS GOING?
WITH, UH, YOU KNOW... POLLINATION?
AAAHH
DAD
WE ARE NOT GOING TO HAVE THIS CONVERSATION RIGHT NOW!
DO YOU KNOW ABOUT, UH, ABOUT ENTOMOPHILY?
GUESS YOU KIDS PROBABLY CALL IT BEE-POKIN'
NO. DAD. STOP. THAT IS NOT OKAY. YOU ARE NEVER ALLOWED TO SAY THAT AGAIN. ESPECIALLY NOT IN FRONT OF MY FRIENDS.
YOUR FRIENDS. RIGHT.
LISTEN, KYLE. JUST SO YOU KNOW.
IT'S OKAY TO EXPERIMENT WITH CROSS-POLLINIZATION.
LOGGERS. PLEASE. CUT ME DOWN. NOW.

Mom found your pine cones while going through the laundry.

Down Clues: 2. French for "he" or the masculine "it." 3. A familiar way to say "Father."

IN WHICH BEAUTY HAS ITS PRICE

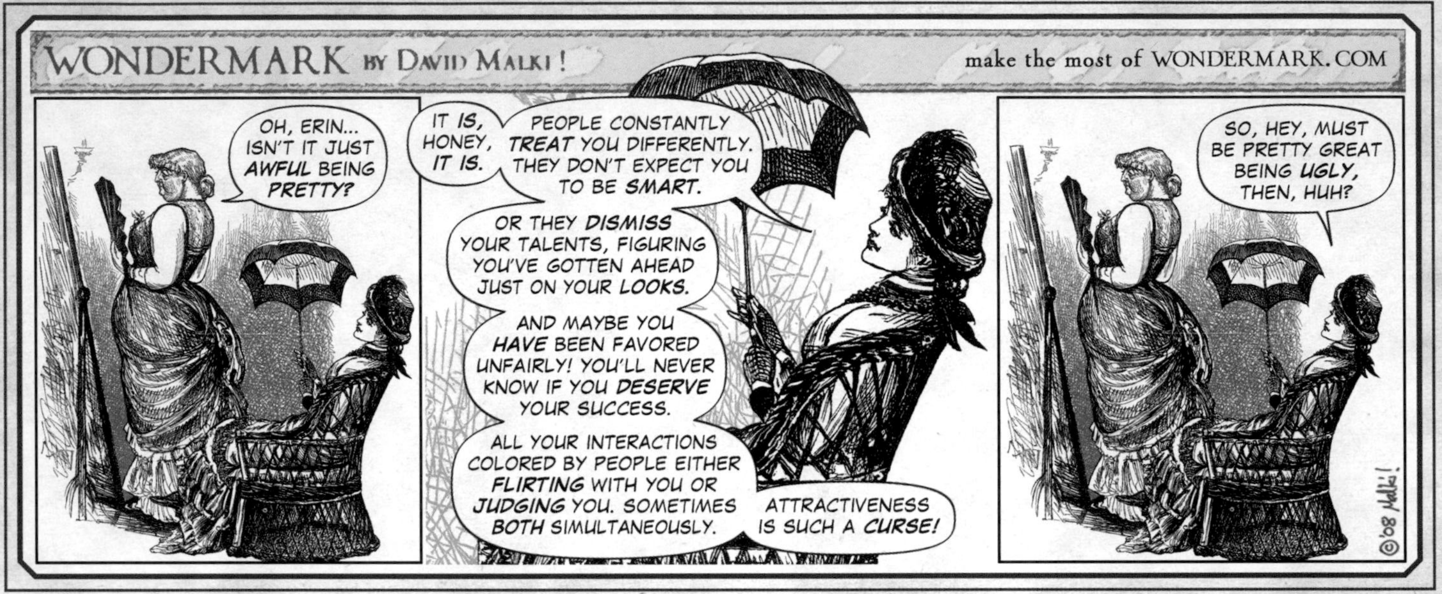
WONDERMARK BY DAVID MALKI !
make the most of WONDERMARK.COM
OH, ERIN... ISN'T IT JUST AWFUL BEING PRETTY?
IT IS, HONEY, IT IS.
PEOPLE CONSTANTLY TREAT YOU DIFFERENTLY. THEY DON'T EXPECT YOU TO BE SMART.
OR THEY DISMISS YOUR TALENTS, FIGURING YOU'VE GOTTEN AHEAD JUST ON YOUR LOOKS.
AND MAYBE YOU HAVE BEEN FAVORED UNFAIRLY! YOU'LL NEVER KNOW IF YOU DESERVE YOUR SUCCESS.
ALL YOUR INTERACTIONS COLORED BY PEOPLE EITHER FLIRTING WITH YOU OR JUDGING YOU. SOMETIMES BOTH SIMULTANEOUSLY.
ATTRACTIVENESS IS SUCH A CURSE!
SO, HEY, MUST BE PRETTY GREAT BEING UGLY, THEN, HUH?
©'08 Malki !

the only correct answer to that question is 'why, I wouldn't know!'

IN WHICH A TOY PREVENTS AGAINST NEGLECT

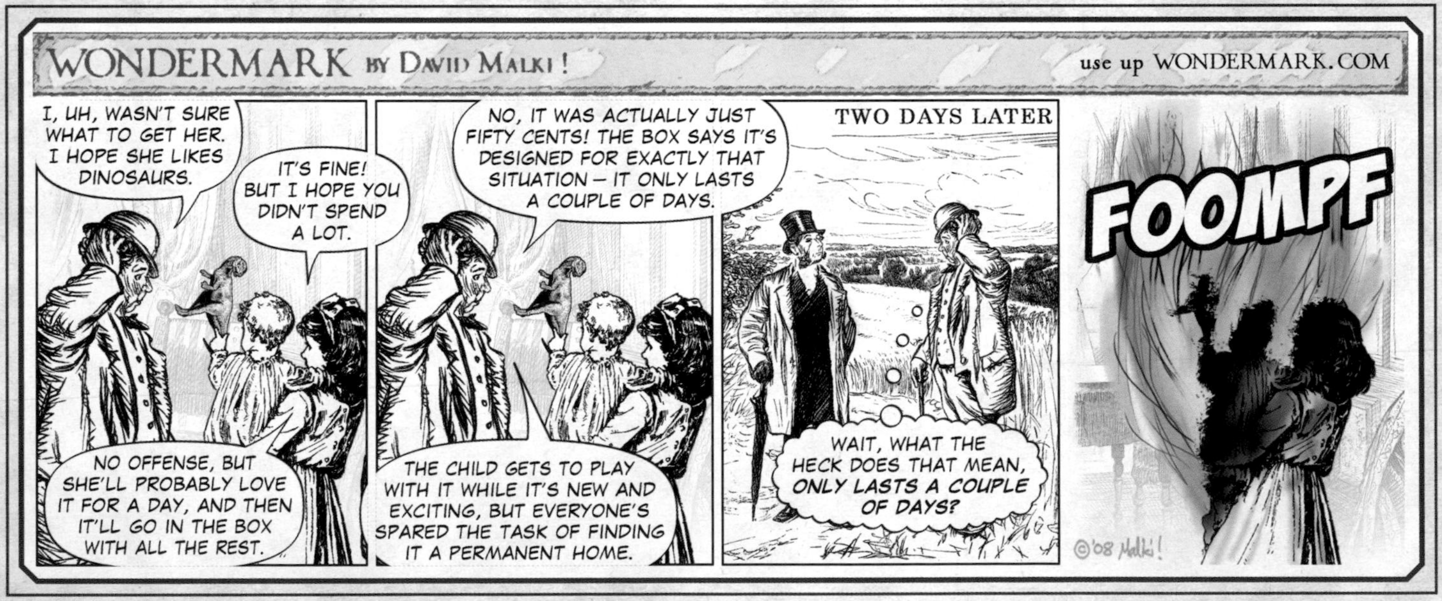
WONDERMARK BY DAVID MALKI !
use up WONDERMARK.COM
I, UH, WASN'T SURE WHAT TO GET HER. I HOPE SHE LIKES DINOSAURS.
IT'S FINE! BUT I HOPE YOU DIDN'T SPEND A LOT.
NO OFFENSE, BUT SHE'LL PROBABLY LOVE IT FOR A DAY, AND THEN IT'LL GO IN THE BOX WITH ALL THE REST.
NO, IT WAS ACTUALLY JUST FIFTY CENTS! THE BOX SAYS IT'S DESIGNED FOR EXACTLY THAT SITUATION – IT ONLY LASTS A COUPLE OF DAYS.
THE CHILD GETS TO PLAY WITH IT WHILE IT'S NEW AND EXCITING, BUT EVERYONE'S SPARED THE TASK OF FINDING IT A PERMANENT HOME.
TWO DAYS LATER
WAIT, WHAT THE HECK DOES THAT MEAN, ONLY LASTS A COUPLE OF DAYS?
FOOMPF
©'08 Malki !

hit by a comet

17. "Mr. Watson, come here. I ______ you." 18. When two things are married, they are said to be ______.

IN WHICH THERE IS TAUNTING

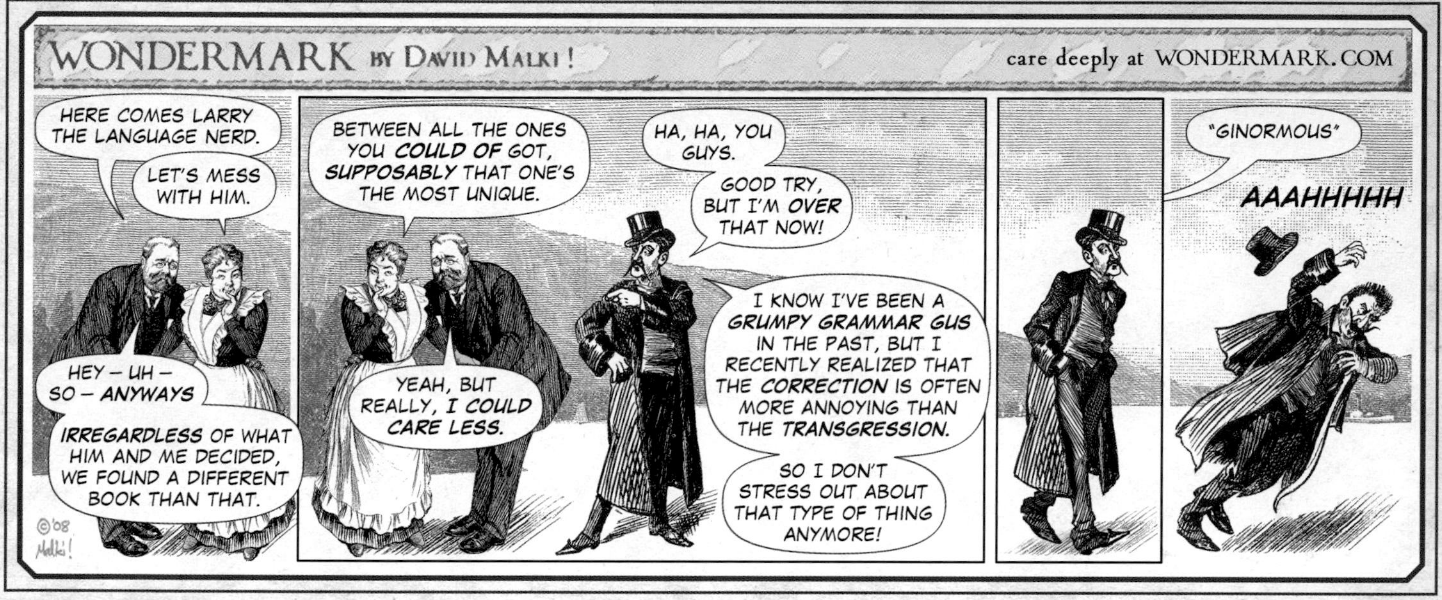
WONDERMARK BY DAVID MALKI !
care deeply at WONDERMARK.COM
HERE COMES LARRY THE LANGUAGE NERD.
LET'S MESS WITH HIM.
HEY – UH – SO – ANYWAYS
IRREGARDLESS OF WHAT HIM AND ME DECIDED, WE FOUND A DIFFERENT BOOK THAN THAT.
BETWEEN ALL THE ONES YOU COULD OF GOT, SUPPOSABLY THAT ONE'S THE MOST UNIQUE.
YEAH, BUT REALLY, I COULD CARE LESS.
HA, HA, YOU GUYS.
GOOD TRY, BUT I'M OVER THAT NOW!
I KNOW I'VE BEEN A GRUMPY GRAMMAR GUS IN THE PAST, BUT I RECENTLY REALIZED THAT THE CORRECTION IS OFTEN MORE ANNOYING THAN THE TRANSGRESSION.
SO I DON'T STRESS OUT ABOUT THAT TYPE OF THING ANYMORE!
"GINORMOUS"
AAAHHHHH
©'08 Malki!

Look at him try to fish the sound back out of his ears!

IN WHICH POLITICS EXHILARATE

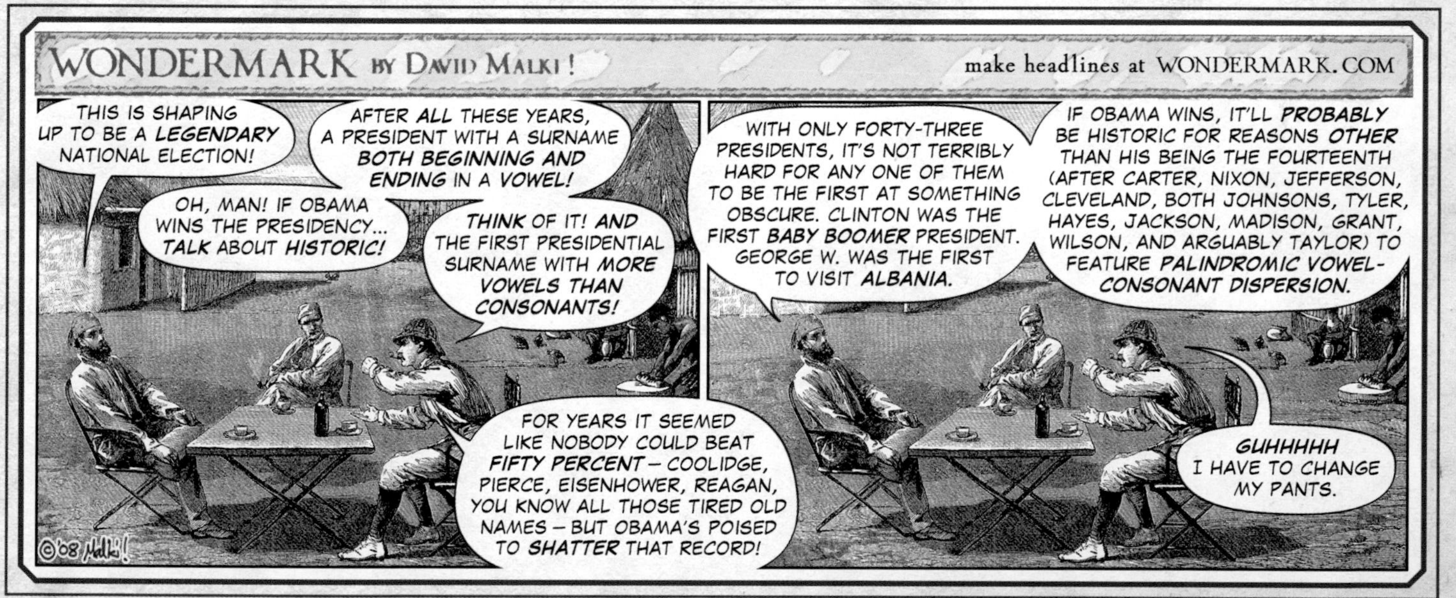
WONDERMARK BY DAVID MALKI !
make headlines at WONDERMARK.COM
THIS IS SHAPING UP TO BE A LEGENDARY NATIONAL ELECTION!
OH, MAN! IF OBAMA WINS THE PRESIDENCY... TALK ABOUT HISTORIC!
AFTER ALL THESE YEARS, A PRESIDENT WITH A SURNAME BOTH BEGINNING AND ENDING IN A VOWEL!
THINK OF IT! AND THE FIRST PRESIDENTIAL SURNAME WITH MORE VOWELS THAN CONSONANTS!
FOR YEARS IT SEEMED LIKE NOBODY COULD BEAT FIFTY PERCENT – COOLIDGE, PIERCE, EISENHOWER, REAGAN, YOU KNOW ALL THOSE TIRED OLD NAMES – BUT OBAMA'S POISED TO SHATTER THAT RECORD!
WITH ONLY FORTY-THREE PRESIDENTS, IT'S NOT TERRIBLY HARD FOR ANY ONE OF THEM TO BE THE FIRST AT SOMETHING OBSCURE. CLINTON WAS THE FIRST BABY BOOMER PRESIDENT. GEORGE W. WAS THE FIRST TO VISIT ALBANIA.
IF OBAMA WINS, IT'LL PROBABLY BE HISTORIC FOR REASONS OTHER THAN HIS BEING THE FOURTEENTH (AFTER CARTER, NIXON, JEFFERSON, CLEVELAND, BOTH JOHNSONS, TYLER, HAYES, JACKSON, MADISON, GRANT, WILSON, AND ARGUABLY TAYLOR) TO FEATURE PALINDROMIC VOWEL-CONSONANT DISPERSION.
GUHHHHH I HAVE TO CHANGE MY PANTS.
©'08 Malki!

14

McCain called himself a 'maverick', but McKinley beat him to the patronymic particle by over 100 years.

12. A formal way to address Alexander Graham, perhaps? 14. The electric transmission of sound across open air.

IN WHICH A STAND IS TAKEN

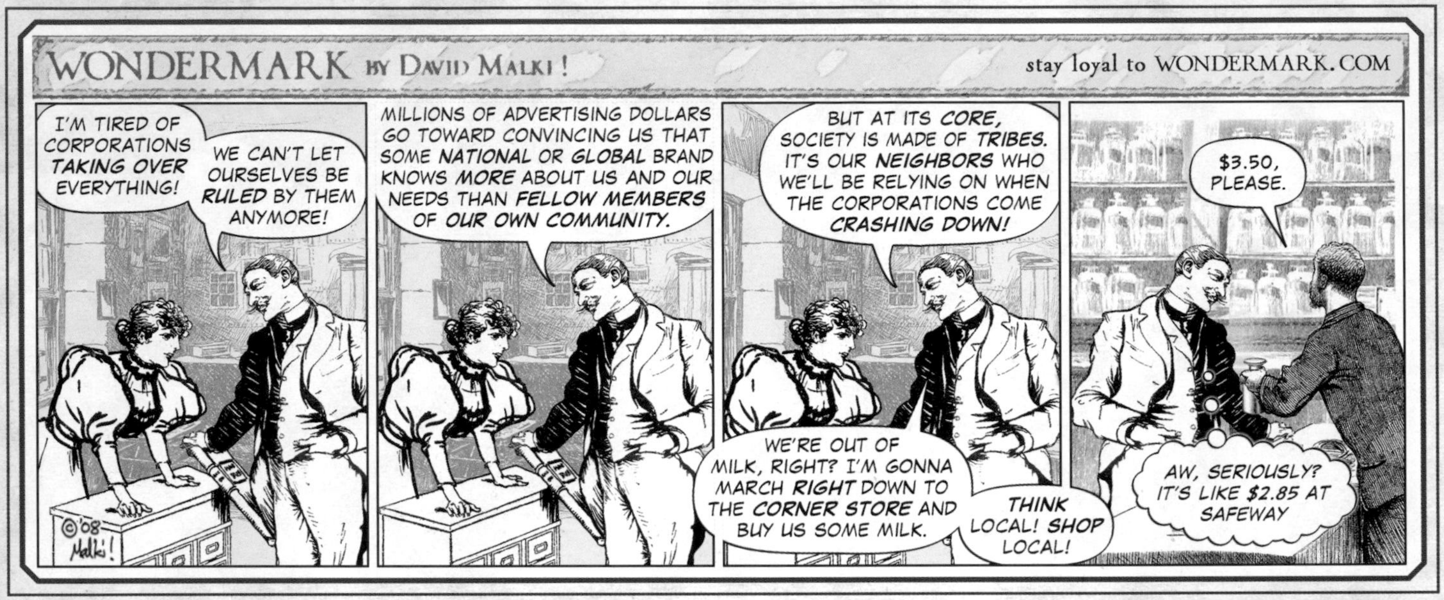
WONDERMARK BY DAVID MALKI !
stay loyal to WONDERMARK.COM
I'M TIRED OF CORPORATIONS TAKING OVER EVERYTHING!
WE CAN'T LET OURSELVES BE RULED BY THEM ANYMORE!
©'08 Malki!
MILLIONS OF ADVERTISING DOLLARS GO TOWARD CONVINCING US THAT SOME NATIONAL OR GLOBAL BRAND KNOWS MORE ABOUT US AND OUR NEEDS THAN FELLOW MEMBERS OF OUR OWN COMMUNITY.
BUT AT ITS CORE, SOCIETY IS MADE OF TRIBES. IT'S OUR NEIGHBORS WHO WE'LL BE RELYING ON WHEN THE CORPORATIONS COME CRASHING DOWN!
WE'RE OUT OF MILK, RIGHT? I'M GONNA MARCH RIGHT DOWN TO THE CORNER STORE AND BUY US SOME MILK.
THINK LOCAL! SHOP LOCAL!
$3.50, PLEASE.
AW, SERIOUSLY? IT'S LIKE $2.85 AT SAFEWAY

no company has ever gone bankrupt expecting customers to put self-interest ahead of principle

IN WHICH NATIONS SHOOT THE BREEZE

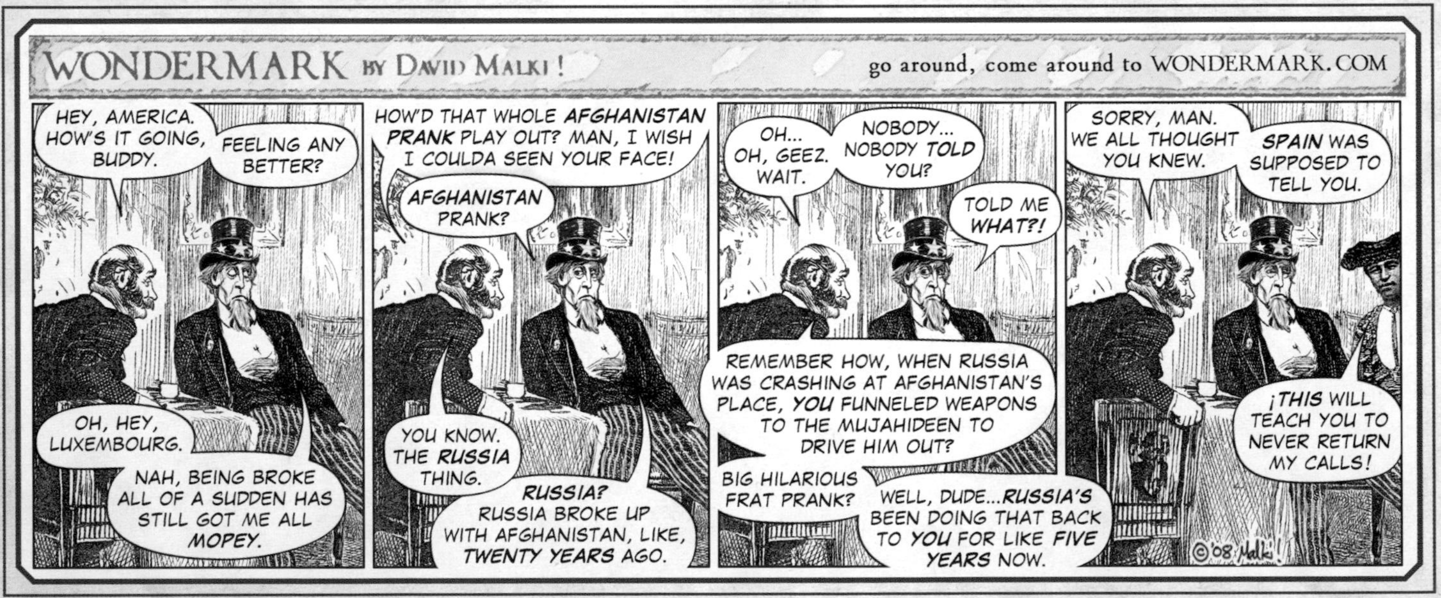
WONDERMARK BY DAVID MALKI !
go around, come around to WONDERMARK.COM
HEY, AMERICA. HOW'S IT GOING, BUDDY.
FEELING ANY BETTER?
OH, HEY, LUXEMBOURG.
NAH, BEING BROKE ALL OF A SUDDEN HAS STILL GOT ME ALL MOPEY.
HOW'D THAT WHOLE AFGHANISTAN PRANK PLAY OUT? MAN, I WISH I COULDA SEEN YOUR FACE!
AFGHANISTAN PRANK?
YOU KNOW. THE RUSSIA THING.
RUSSIA? RUSSIA BROKE UP WITH AFGHANISTAN, LIKE, TWENTY YEARS AGO.
OH... OH, GEEZ. WAIT.
NOBODY... NOBODY TOLD YOU?
TOLD ME WHAT?!
REMEMBER HOW, WHEN RUSSIA WAS CRASHING AT AFGHANISTAN'S PLACE, YOU FUNNELED WEAPONS TO THE MUJAHIDEEN TO DRIVE HIM OUT?
BIG HILARIOUS FRAT PRANK?
WELL, DUDE...RUSSIA'S BEEN DOING THAT BACK TO YOU FOR LIKE FIVE YEARS NOW.
SORRY, MAN. WE ALL THOUGHT YOU KNEW.
SPAIN WAS SUPPOSED TO TELL YOU.
¡THIS WILL TEACH YOU TO NEVER RETURN MY CALLS!
©'08 Malki!

15

try to disprove it.

7. An untethered system, as in Marconi's. 10. Homeric seeker of justice, and namesake to a great General.

WONDERMARK BY DAVID MALKI !
stay up late with WONDERMARK.COM
SO MANY BOOKS! I THOUGHT WE WERE TRYING TO CUT DOWN THE AMOUNT OF STUFF IN OUR LIVES?
THERE MUST BE A THOUSAND BOOKS HERE.
I'VE PARED THE COLLECTION DOWN TO THE ESSENTIALS.
HOW MANY OF THEM DO YOU ACTUALLY EVER READ?
WHY NOT DONATE THEM TO THE LIBRARY? THAT WAY THEY'LL STILL BE THERE WHENEVER YOU WANT THEM –
THEY'RE NOT REALLY FOR ME.
©'08 Malki!
LOOK, WE LOVE TO READ BECAUSE WE GREW UP IN HOMES FILLED TO BURSTING WITH WEIRD AND WONDERFUL BOOKS.
I'M KEEPING THESE BOOKS NOT BECAUSE OF HOW OFTEN I READ THEM ALL, BUT SO, ON RAINY DAYS AND LONELY NIGHTS, OUR CHILDREN CAN DISCOVER THEM FOR THEMSELVES.
BY THE TIME WE EVER HAVE CHILDREN, WE WILL BE DROWNING IN A SEA OF BOOKS, GASPING FOR BREATH IN A LITTLE AIR POCKET NEAR THE CEILING.
THEN THEY WILL BE BIBLIOPHIBIANS.

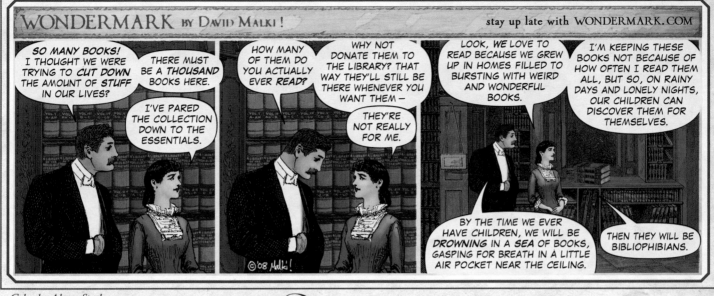

Color by Alyssa Stock

They will breathe with gills that make the sound of fluttering pages.

Some Books Kept

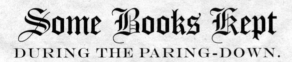

DURING THE PARING-DOWN.

THISTLES OF NORWAY, 14th ed. by Ambjorn Brunsvold. This comprehensive overview of Norwegian thistles includes extensive sections devoted to the Musk and Oyster Thistles, and a new appendix addressing the latest findings in thistle research. (644pp.)

DON'T CUT THAT CORD! by Margaret Sanding, D.C. Written by a chiropractor, this handy and practical guide to familial bonding has been praised by former United States Surgeon General Kenneth P. Moritsugu as "complete." (197pp.)

JANE'S GUIDE TO WORLD TANKS 1990 by Gunter Trimpe. Updated to include 1990 model-year tanks, including boilers, propane capsules, and American and European SCUBA gear. (821pp.)

COXSWAIN CONFIDENTIAL: OPERATION BABY by Rachelle Newburg. In the high-stakes world of competitive rowing, Burt Harde is top cox—as well as an undercover agent for the FBI's Special Action Crime Division. But when his old flame Kelsey turns up with an 8-lb., 4-oz. surprise, will Burt finally decide to man up and settle down? (210pp.)

STAB: WHY WE DO NOT SIMPLY MURDER EVERYONE WE SEE by Malcolm Gladwell. This new work from the #1 bestselling author of *Outliers* and *Blink* addresses violent impulses, whether it is wise to check them, and why stupid idiots keep misinterpreting his previous books. Gladwell has been a staff writer with *The New Yorker* magazine since 1996. (335pp.)

CONVERSATIONAL URDU IN 36 HOURS by Nabibukhsh Majid Jahangir Khan. With all that action boiling up in Afghanistan, the U.S. Government is in desperate need of Urdu speakers. Get on that new wagon now! Dr. Majid Jahangir Khan is Adjunct Professor of Maths at a prominent University. (164pp.)

MY YEAR OF DOING NOTHING by Samantha Orwen. The author does nothing and complains about it. (596pp.)

HOLY BIBLE by various. A deity tries a myriad of techniques to deal with a vermin infestation. (1,278pp.)

Across Clues: 1. A system of transmitting Morse code across wires. 4. What we seek, when we have questions.

IN WHICH EVERYTHING IS GOING JUST FINE, THANK YOU

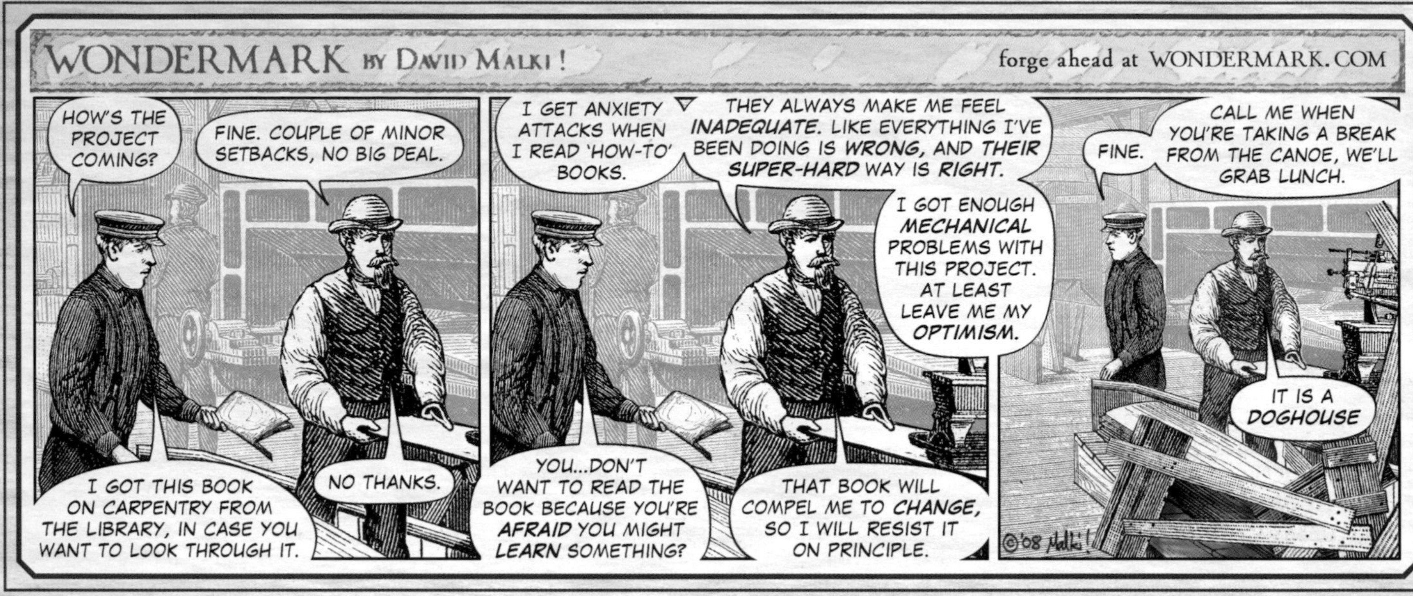
WONDERMARK BY DAVID MALKI !
forge ahead at WONDERMARK.COM
HOW'S THE PROJECT COMING?
FINE. COUPLE OF MINOR SETBACKS, NO BIG DEAL.
I GOT THIS BOOK ON CARPENTRY FROM THE LIBRARY, IN CASE YOU WANT TO LOOK THROUGH IT.
NO THANKS.
YOU...DON'T WANT TO READ THE BOOK BECAUSE YOU'RE AFRAID YOU MIGHT LEARN SOMETHING?
I GET ANXIETY ATTACKS WHEN I READ 'HOW-TO' BOOKS.
THEY ALWAYS MAKE ME FEEL INADEQUATE. LIKE EVERYTHING I'VE BEEN DOING IS WRONG, AND THEIR SUPER-HARD WAY IS RIGHT.
I GOT ENOUGH MECHANICAL PROBLEMS WITH THIS PROJECT. AT LEAST LEAVE ME MY OPTIMISM.
THAT BOOK WILL COMPEL ME TO CHANGE, SO I WILL RESIST IT ON PRINCIPLE.
FINE.
CALL ME WHEN YOU'RE TAKING A BREAK FROM THE CANOE, WE'LL GRAB LUNCH.
IT IS A DOGHOUSE
©'08 Malki !

For your information, my dog Lucky has no spine or limbs.

CHAD'S FIRST DAY

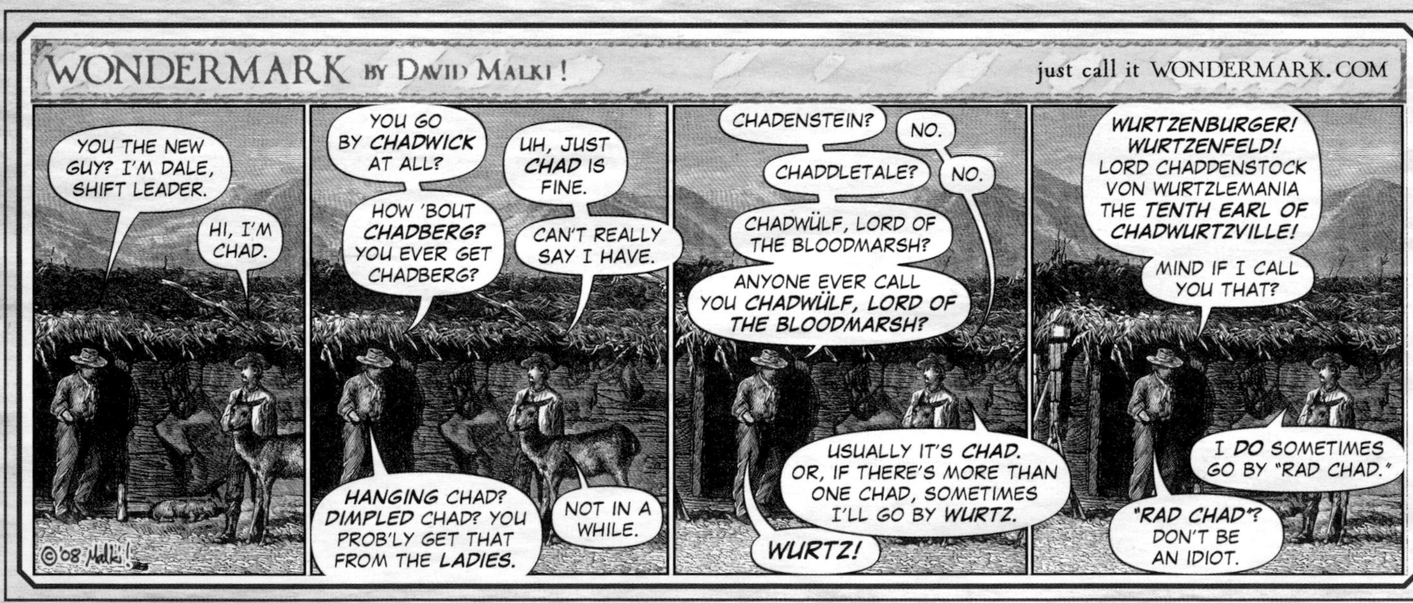
WONDERMARK BY DAVID MALKI !
just call it WONDERMARK.COM
YOU THE NEW GUY? I'M DALE, SHIFT LEADER.
HI, I'M CHAD.
©'08 Malki !
YOU GO BY CHADWICK AT ALL?
UH, JUST CHAD IS FINE.
HOW 'BOUT CHADBERG? YOU EVER GET CHADBERG?
CAN'T REALLY SAY I HAVE.
HANGING CHAD? DIMPLED CHAD? YOU PROB'LY GET THAT FROM THE LADIES.
NOT IN A WHILE.
CHADENSTEIN?
NO.
CHADDLETALE?
NO.
CHADWÜLF, LORD OF THE BLOODMARSH?
ANYONE EVER CALL YOU CHADWÜLF, LORD OF THE BLOODMARSH?
USUALLY IT'S CHAD. OR, IF THERE'S MORE THAN ONE CHAD, SOMETIMES I'LL GO BY WURTZ.
WURTZ!
WURTZENBURGER! WURTZENFELD! LORD CHADDENSTOCK VON WURTZLEMANIA THE TENTH EARL OF CHADWURTZVILLE!
MIND IF I CALL YOU THAT?
I DO SOMETIMES GO BY "RAD CHAD."
"RAD CHAD"? DON'T BE AN IDIOT.

you should hear how he went on when he met the new mailroom guy, Abernathy Mercutio Hoakes-Waddleswourthe IV

IN WHICH A GUY IS PINCHED

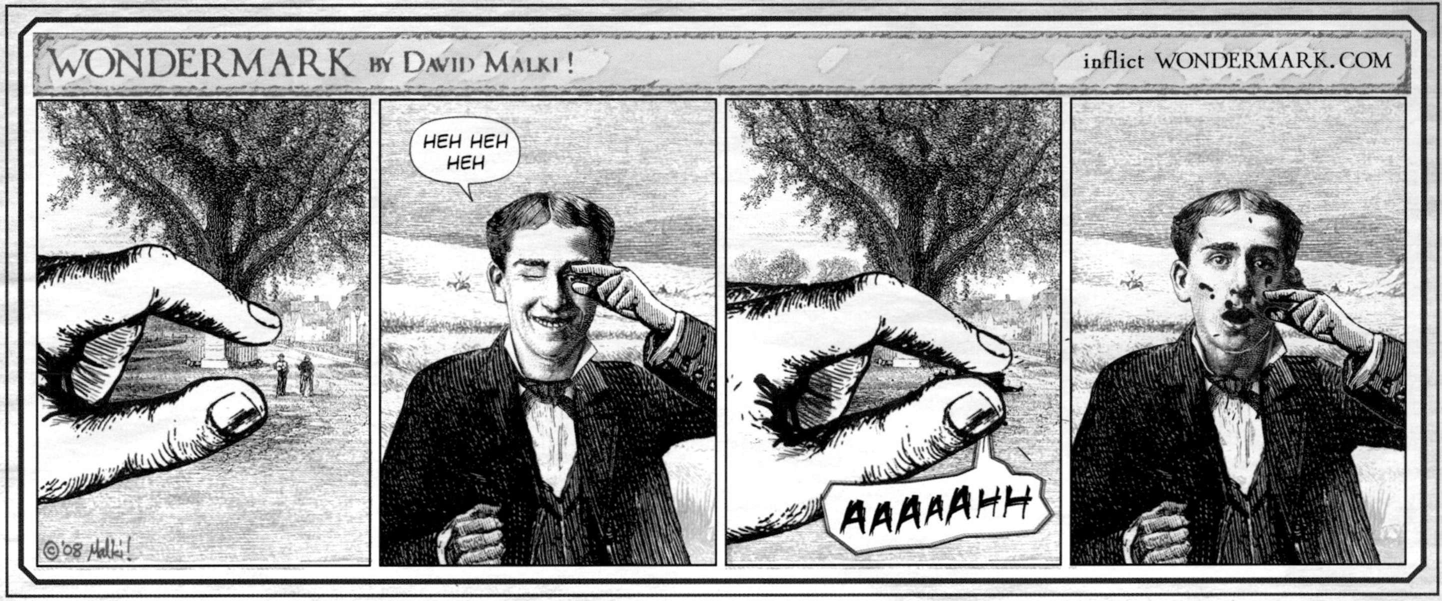
WONDERMARK BY DAVID MALKI !
inflict WONDERMARK.COM
HEH HEH HEH
AAAAAHH
©'08 Malki!

an awkward superpower

THE WRONG WAY TO ASK FOR $700 BILLION

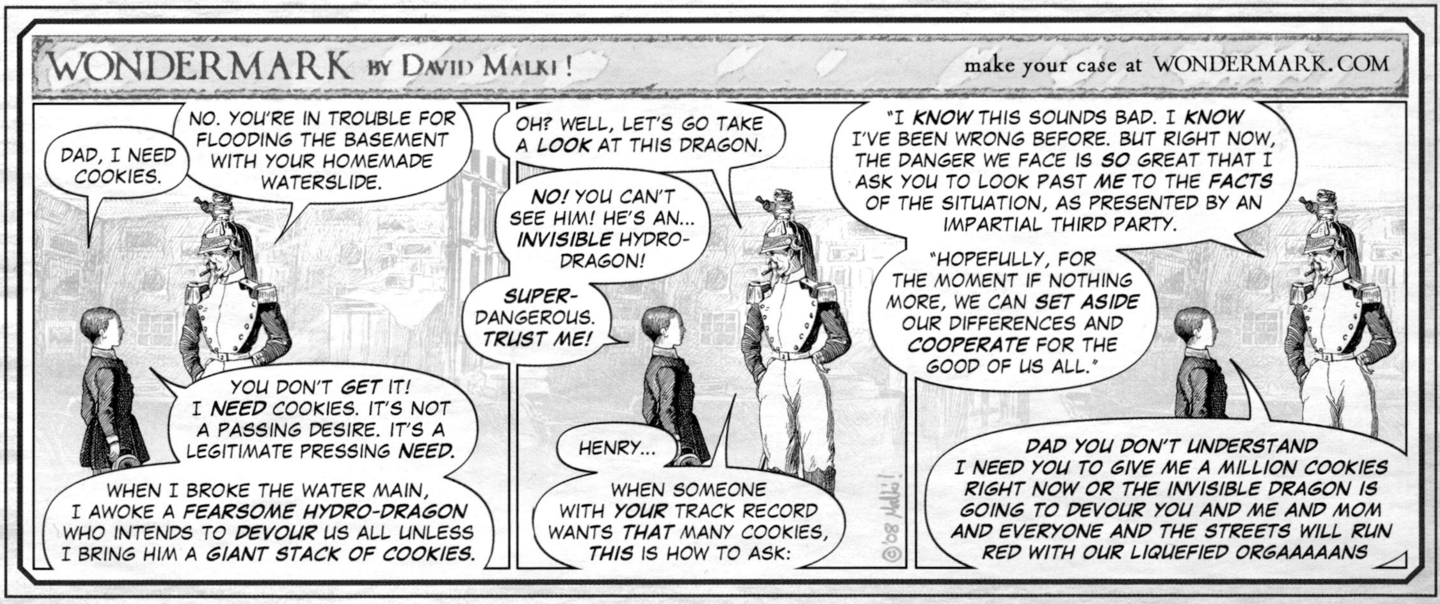
WONDERMARK BY DAVID MALKI !
make your case at WONDERMARK.COM
DAD, I NEED COOKIES.
NO. YOU'RE IN TROUBLE FOR FLOODING THE BASEMENT WITH YOUR HOMEMADE WATERSLIDE.
YOU DON'T GET IT! I NEED COOKIES. IT'S NOT A PASSING DESIRE. IT'S A LEGITIMATE PRESSING NEED.
WHEN I BROKE THE WATER MAIN, I AWOKE A FEARSOME HYDRO-DRAGON WHO INTENDS TO DEVOUR US ALL UNLESS I BRING HIM A GIANT STACK OF COOKIES.
OH? WELL, LET'S GO TAKE A LOOK AT THIS DRAGON.
NO! YOU CAN'T SEE HIM! HE'S AN... INVISIBLE HYDRO-DRAGON!
SUPER-DANGEROUS. TRUST ME!
HENRY...
WHEN SOMEONE WITH YOUR TRACK RECORD WANTS THAT MANY COOKIES, THIS IS HOW TO ASK:
©'08 Malki!
"I KNOW THIS SOUNDS BAD. I KNOW I'VE BEEN WRONG BEFORE. BUT RIGHT NOW, THE DANGER WE FACE IS SO GREAT THAT I ASK YOU TO LOOK PAST ME TO THE FACTS OF THE SITUATION, AS PRESENTED BY AN IMPARTIAL THIRD PARTY.
"HOPEFULLY, FOR THE MOMENT IF NOTHING MORE, WE CAN SET ASIDE OUR DIFFERENCES AND COOPERATE FOR THE GOOD OF US ALL."
DAD YOU DON'T UNDERSTAND I NEED YOU TO GIVE ME A MILLION COOKIES RIGHT NOW OR THE INVISIBLE DRAGON IS GOING TO DEVOUR YOU AND ME AND MOM AND EVERYONE AND THE STREETS WILL RUN RED WITH OUR LIQUEFIED ORGAAAAANS

16

There is a certain way that grown-ups do things.

(Fill in words, one letter per square, based on the clues provided.)

IN WHICH ALL'S FAIR, SUPPOSEDLY

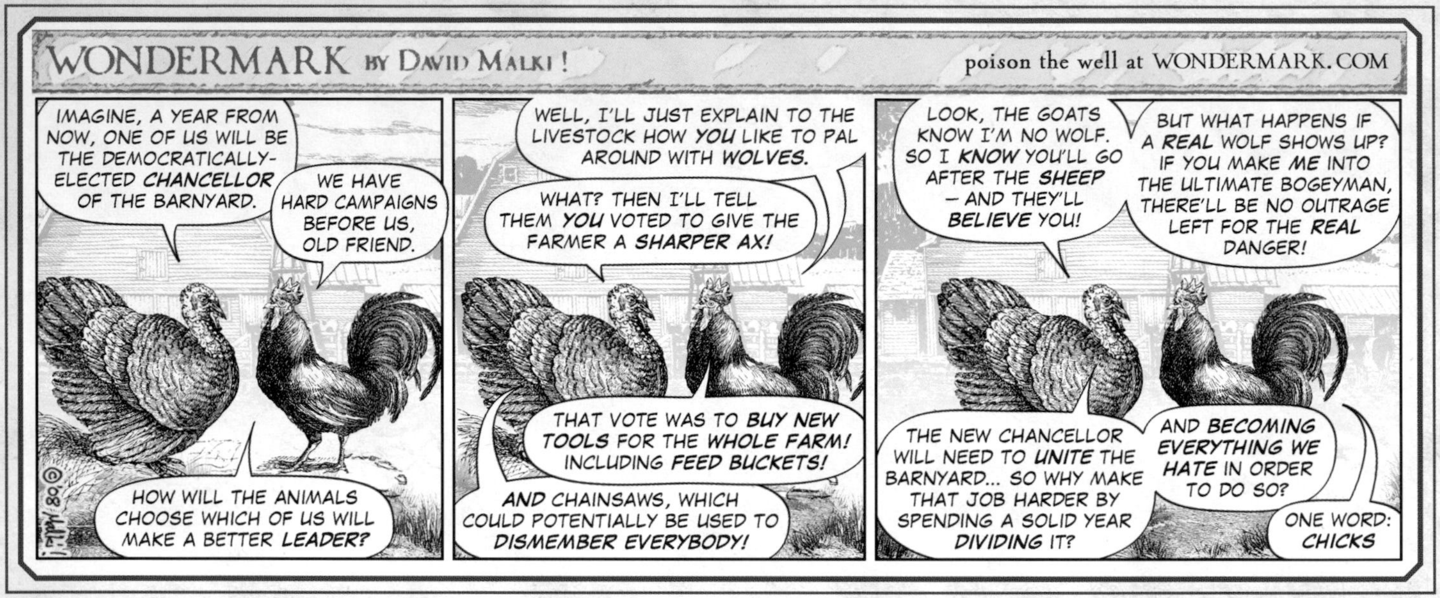
WONDERMARK BY DAVID MALKI !
poison the well at WONDERMARK.COM
IMAGINE, A YEAR FROM NOW, ONE OF US WILL BE THE DEMOCRATICALLY-ELECTED CHANCELLOR OF THE BARNYARD.
WE HAVE HARD CAMPAIGNS BEFORE US, OLD FRIEND.
HOW WILL THE ANIMALS CHOOSE WHICH OF US WILL MAKE A BETTER LEADER?
WELL, I'LL JUST EXPLAIN TO THE LIVESTOCK HOW YOU LIKE TO PAL AROUND WITH WOLVES.
WHAT? THEN I'LL TELL THEM YOU VOTED TO GIVE THE FARMER A SHARPER AX!
THAT VOTE WAS TO BUY NEW TOOLS FOR THE WHOLE FARM! INCLUDING FEED BUCKETS!
AND CHAINSAWS, WHICH COULD POTENTIALLY BE USED TO DISMEMBER EVERYBODY!
LOOK, THE GOATS KNOW I'M NO WOLF. SO I KNOW YOU'LL GO AFTER THE SHEEP — AND THEY'LL BELIEVE YOU!
BUT WHAT HAPPENS IF A REAL WOLF SHOWS UP? IF YOU MAKE ME INTO THE ULTIMATE BOGEYMAN, THERE'LL BE NO OUTRAGE LEFT FOR THE REAL DANGER!
THE NEW CHANCELLOR WILL NEED TO UNITE THE BARNYARD... SO WHY MAKE THAT JOB HARDER BY SPENDING A SOLID YEAR DIVIDING IT?
AND BECOMING EVERYTHING WE HATE IN ORDER TO DO SO?
ONE WORD: CHICKS
©08 Malki !

17

Barnyard Chancellor is primarily a ceremonial position anyway.
The Viscount of the Hayloft has all the real power.

IN WHICH BENSON HAS A GOOD POINT

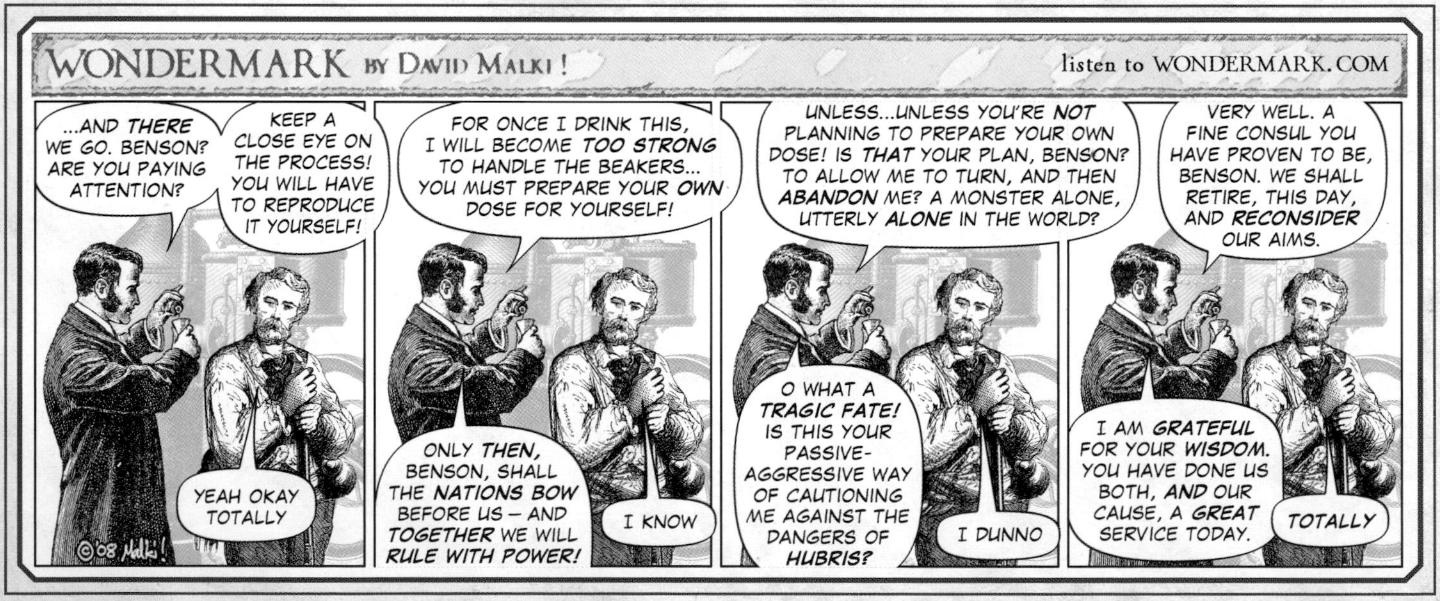
WONDERMARK BY DAVID MALKI !
listen to WONDERMARK.COM
...AND THERE WE GO. BENSON? ARE YOU PAYING ATTENTION?
KEEP A CLOSE EYE ON THE PROCESS! YOU WILL HAVE TO REPRODUCE IT YOURSELF!
YEAH OKAY TOTALLY
FOR ONCE I DRINK THIS, I WILL BECOME TOO STRONG TO HANDLE THE BEAKERS... YOU MUST PREPARE YOUR OWN DOSE FOR YOURSELF!
ONLY THEN, BENSON, SHALL THE NATIONS BOW BEFORE US — AND TOGETHER WE WILL RULE WITH POWER!
I KNOW
UNLESS...UNLESS YOU'RE NOT PLANNING TO PREPARE YOUR OWN DOSE! IS THAT YOUR PLAN, BENSON? TO ALLOW ME TO TURN, AND THEN ABANDON ME? A MONSTER ALONE, UTTERLY ALONE IN THE WORLD?
O WHAT A TRAGIC FATE! IS THIS YOUR PASSIVE-AGGRESSIVE WAY OF CAUTIONING ME AGAINST THE DANGERS OF HUBRIS?
I DUNNO
VERY WELL. A FINE CONSUL YOU HAVE PROVEN TO BE, BENSON. WE SHALL RETIRE, THIS DAY, AND RECONSIDER OUR AIMS.
I AM GRATEFUL FOR YOUR WISDOM. YOU HAVE DONE US BOTH, AND OUR CAUSE, A GREAT SERVICE TODAY.
TOTALLY
©08 Malki !

Benson's just there for the class credit.

IN WHICH A DOG WANTS A STICKER

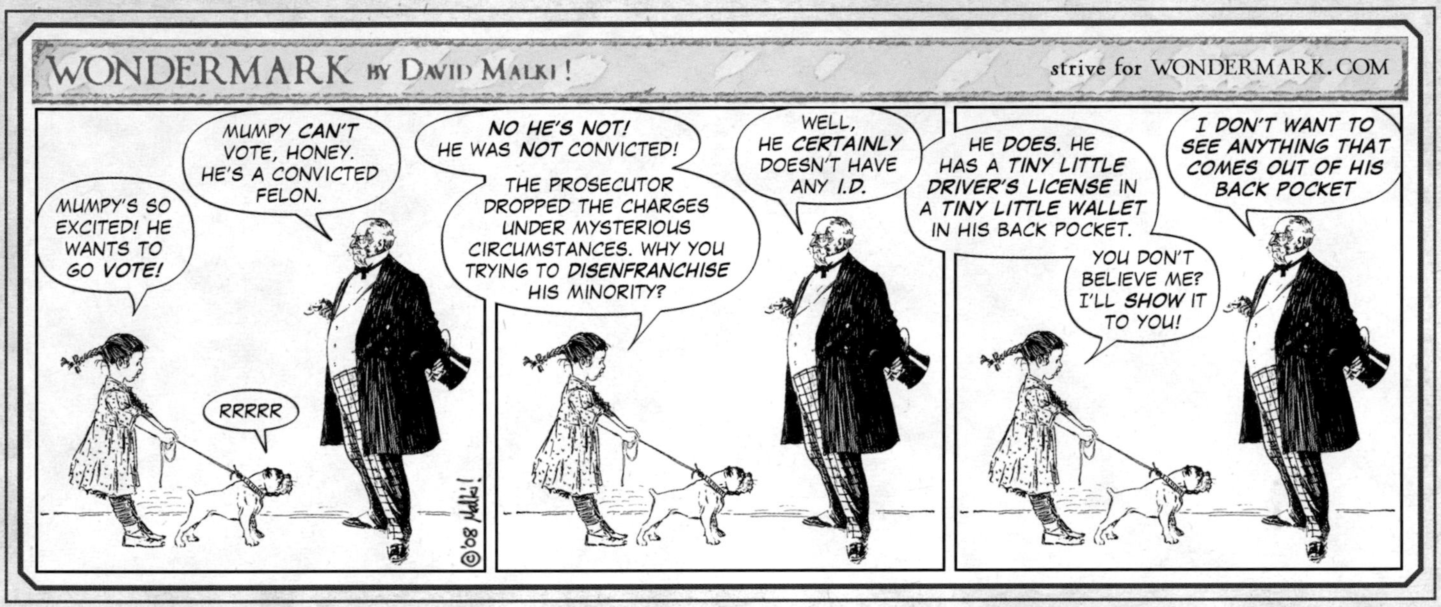
WONDERMARK BY DAVID MALKI !
strive for WONDERMARK.COM
MUMPY'S SO EXCITED! HE WANTS TO GO VOTE!
MUMPY CAN'T VOTE, HONEY. HE'S A CONVICTED FELON.
RRRRR
NO HE'S NOT! HE WAS NOT CONVICTED!
THE PROSECUTOR DROPPED THE CHARGES UNDER MYSTERIOUS CIRCUMSTANCES. WHY YOU TRYING TO DISENFRANCHISE HIS MINORITY?
WELL, HE CERTAINLY DOESN'T HAVE ANY I.D.
HE DOES. HE HAS A TINY LITTLE DRIVER'S LICENSE IN A TINY LITTLE WALLET IN HIS BACK POCKET.
YOU DON'T BELIEVE ME? I'LL SHOW IT TO YOU!
I DON'T WANT TO SEE ANYTHING THAT COMES OUT OF HIS BACK POCKET
©'08 Malki!

18

he is, however, properly registered

IN WHICH IT'S ALL OVER

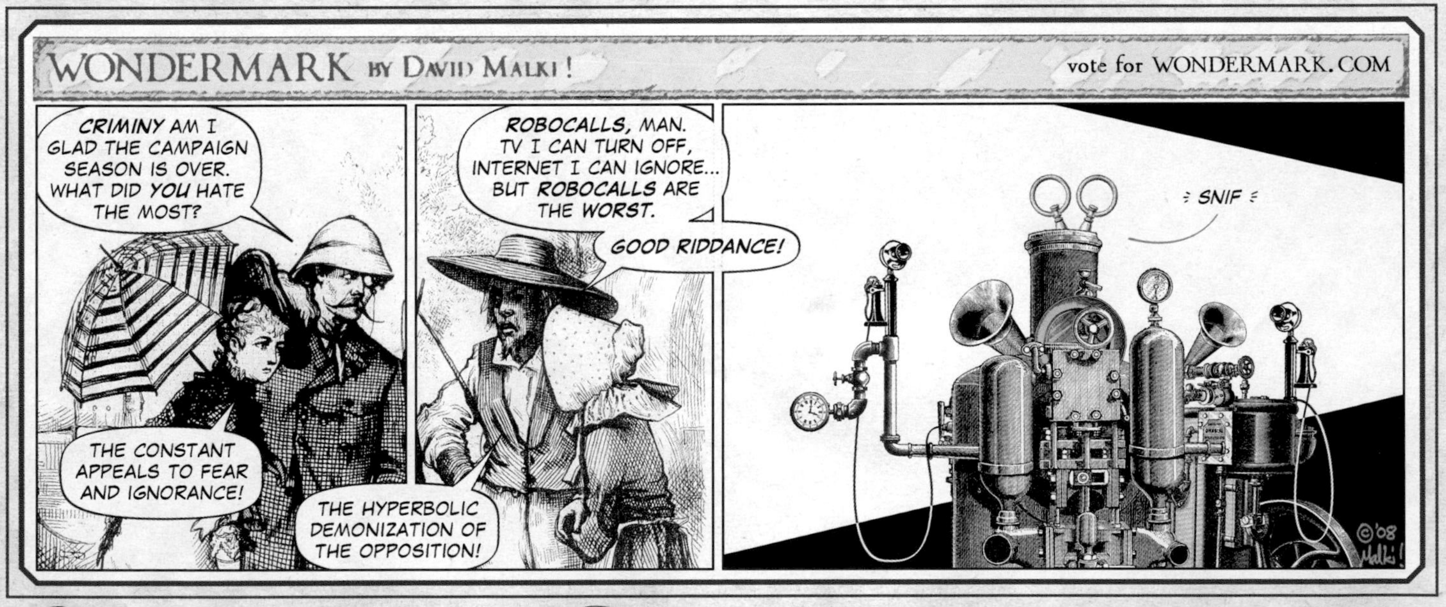
WONDERMARK BY DAVID MALKI !
vote for WONDERMARK.COM
CRIMINY AM I GLAD THE CAMPAIGN SEASON IS OVER. WHAT DID YOU HATE THE MOST?
THE CONSTANT APPEALS TO FEAR AND IGNORANCE!
THE HYPERBOLIC DEMONIZATION OF THE OPPOSITION!
ROBOCALLS, MAN. TV I CAN TURN OFF, INTERNET I CAN IGNORE... BUT ROBOCALLS ARE THE WORST.
GOOD RIDDANCE!
SNIF
©'08 Malki!

19

soon he'll start calling just to chat awkwardly

SOLUTION 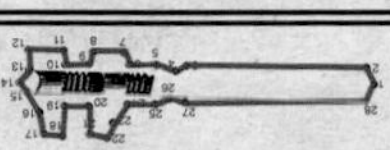 THE TOOL IS A WRENCH! **Wrenches are used to keep workers from striking.**

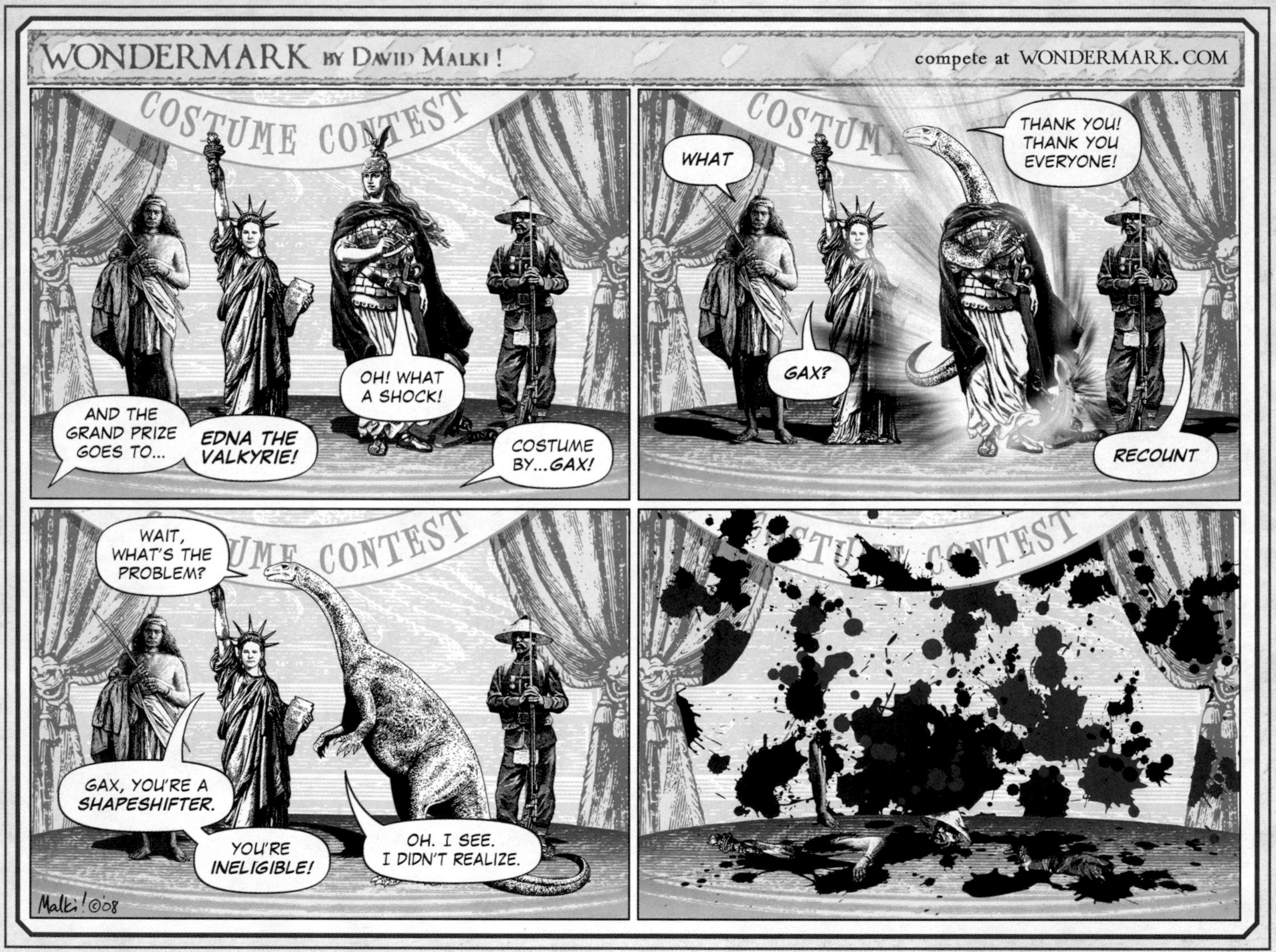
WONDERMARK BY DAVID MALKI !
compete at WONDERMARK.COM
COSTUME CONTEST
AND THE GRAND PRIZE GOES TO...
EDNA THE VALKYRIE!
OH! WHAT A SHOCK!
COSTUME BY...GAX!
COSTUME
WHAT
GAX?
THANK YOU! THANK YOU EVERYONE!
RECOUNT
WAIT, WHAT'S THE PROBLEM?
GAX, YOU'RE A SHAPESHIFTER.
YOU'RE INELIGIBLE!
OH. I SEE. I DIDN'T REALIZE.
Malki! ©08
COSTUME CONTEST

why, this trophy's just sitting here unattended!

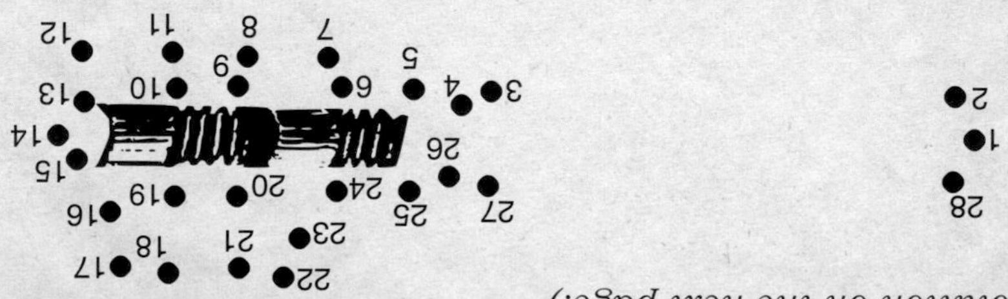

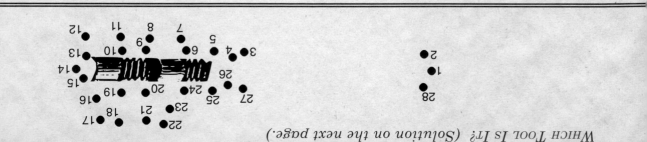

Which Tool Is It? (Solution on the next page.)

IN WHICH THADDEUS SEES THINGS

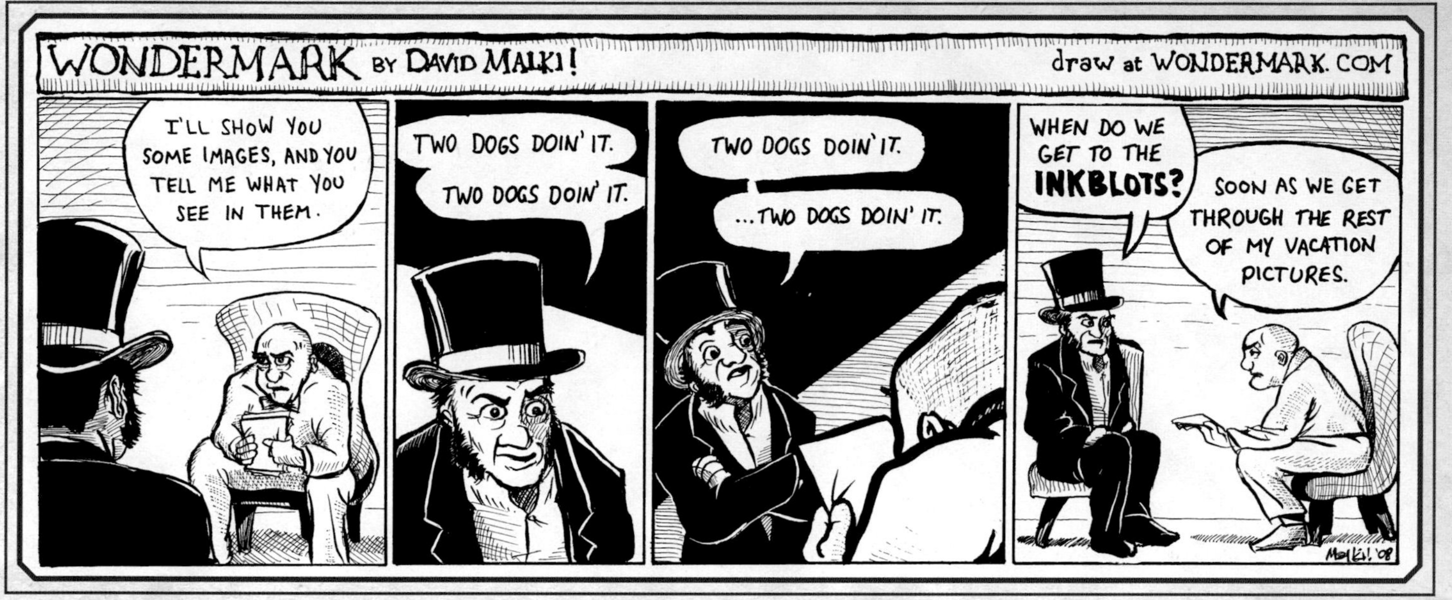
WONDERMARK BY DAVID MALKI!
draw at WONDERMARK.COM
I'LL SHOW YOU SOME IMAGES, AND YOU TELL ME WHAT YOU SEE IN THEM.
TWO DOGS DOIN' IT.
TWO DOGS DOIN' IT.
TWO DOGS DOIN' IT.
...TWO DOGS DOIN' IT.
WHEN DO WE GET TO THE INKBLOTS?
SOON AS WE GET THROUGH THE REST OF MY VACATION PICTURES.

at this rate, sometime around thursday

IN WHICH A TERROR IS SIGHTED

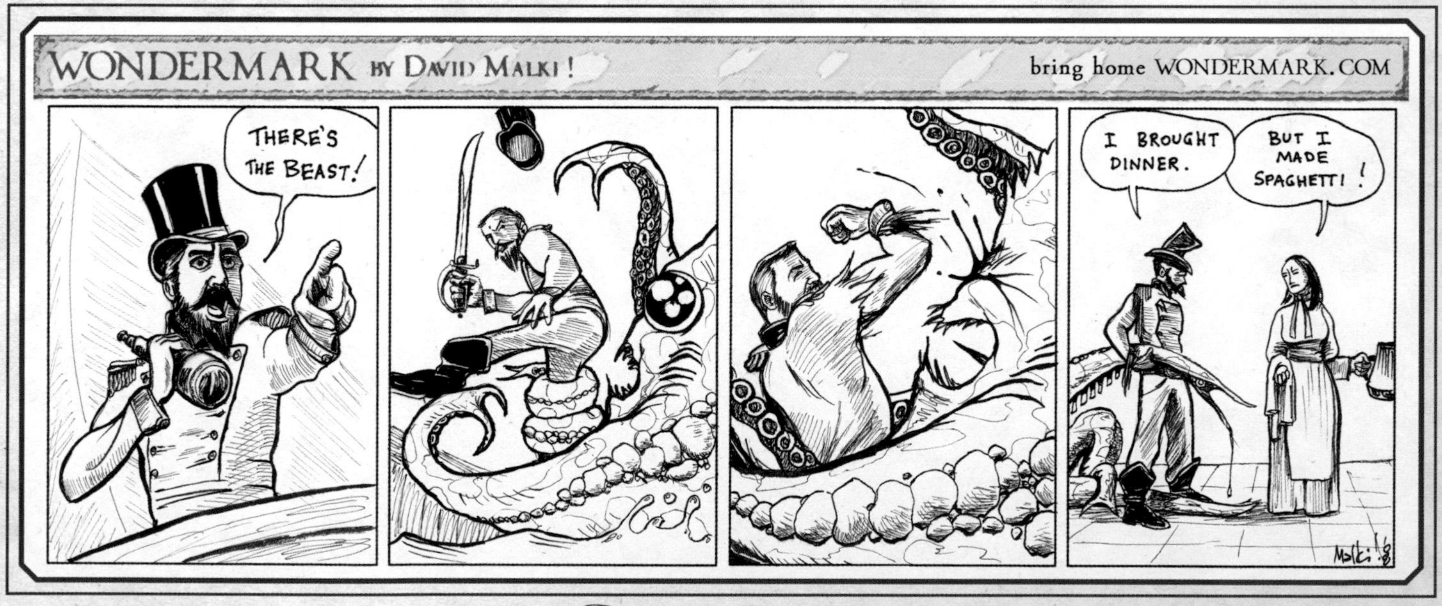
WONDERMARK BY DAVID MALKI!
bring home WONDERMARK.COM
THERE'S THE BEAST!
I BROUGHT DINNER.
BUT I MADE SPAGHETTI!

well I brought a garnish

one vertex at a time. *(Draw lines to connect the numbered spots and form the shape.)*

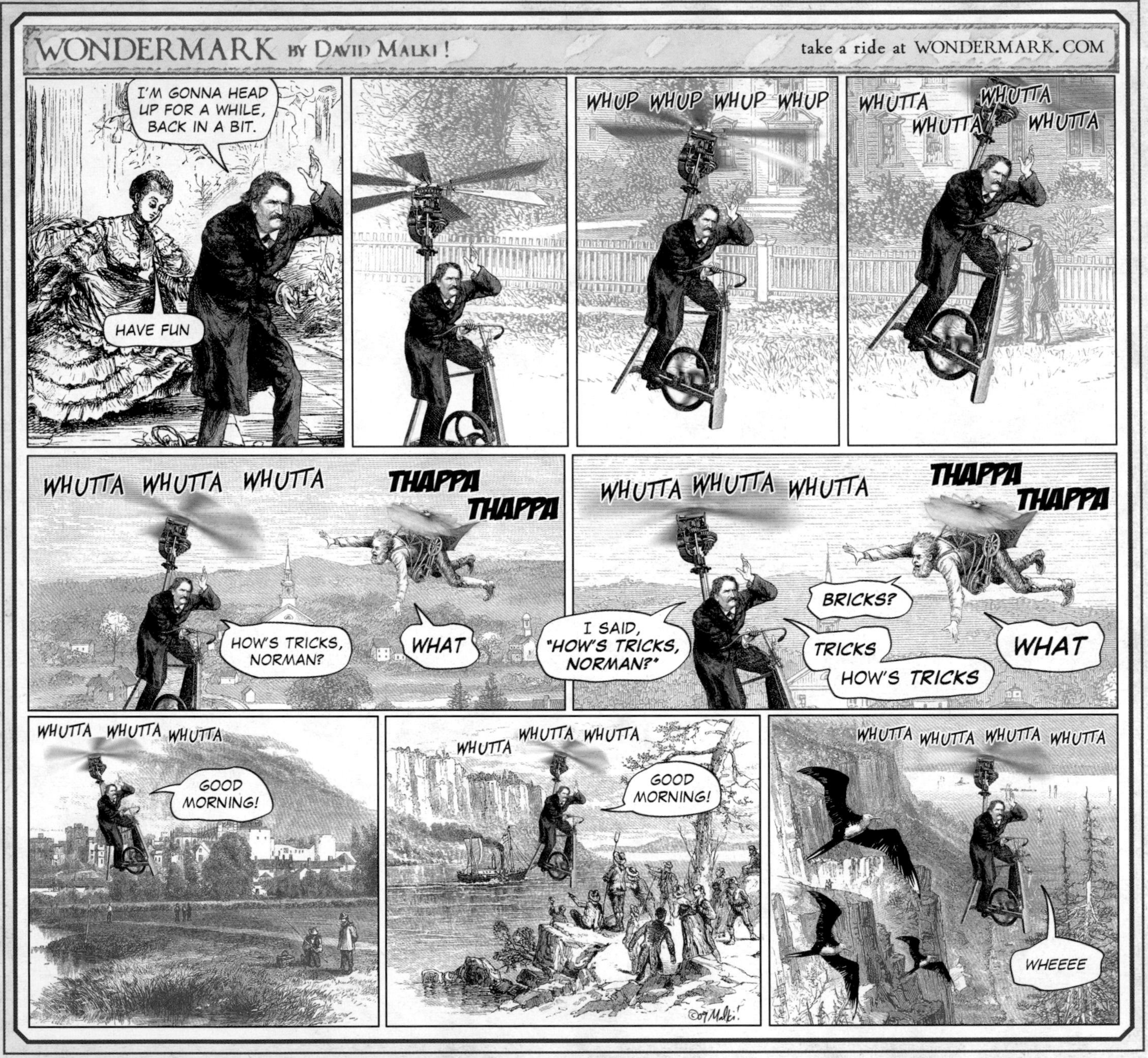
WONDERMARK BY DAVID MALKI !
take a ride at WONDERMARK.COM
I'M GONNA HEAD UP FOR A WHILE, BACK IN A BIT.
HAVE FUN
WHUP WHUP WHUP WHUP
WHUTTA WHUTTA WHUTTA WHUTTA
WHUTTA WHUTTA WHUTTA
THAPPA THAPPA
HOW'S TRICKS, NORMAN?
WHAT
WHUTTA WHUTTA WHUTTA
THAPPA THAPPA
I SAID, "HOW'S TRICKS, NORMAN?"
BRICKS?
TRICKS
HOW'S TRICKS
WHAT
WHUTTA WHUTTA WHUTTA
GOOD MORNING!
WHUTTA WHUTTA WHUTTA
GOOD MORNING!
©09 Malki!
WHUTTA WHUTTA WHUTTA WHUTTA
WHEEEE

It appears to be covered in grime, so you'll have to carefully extricate it,

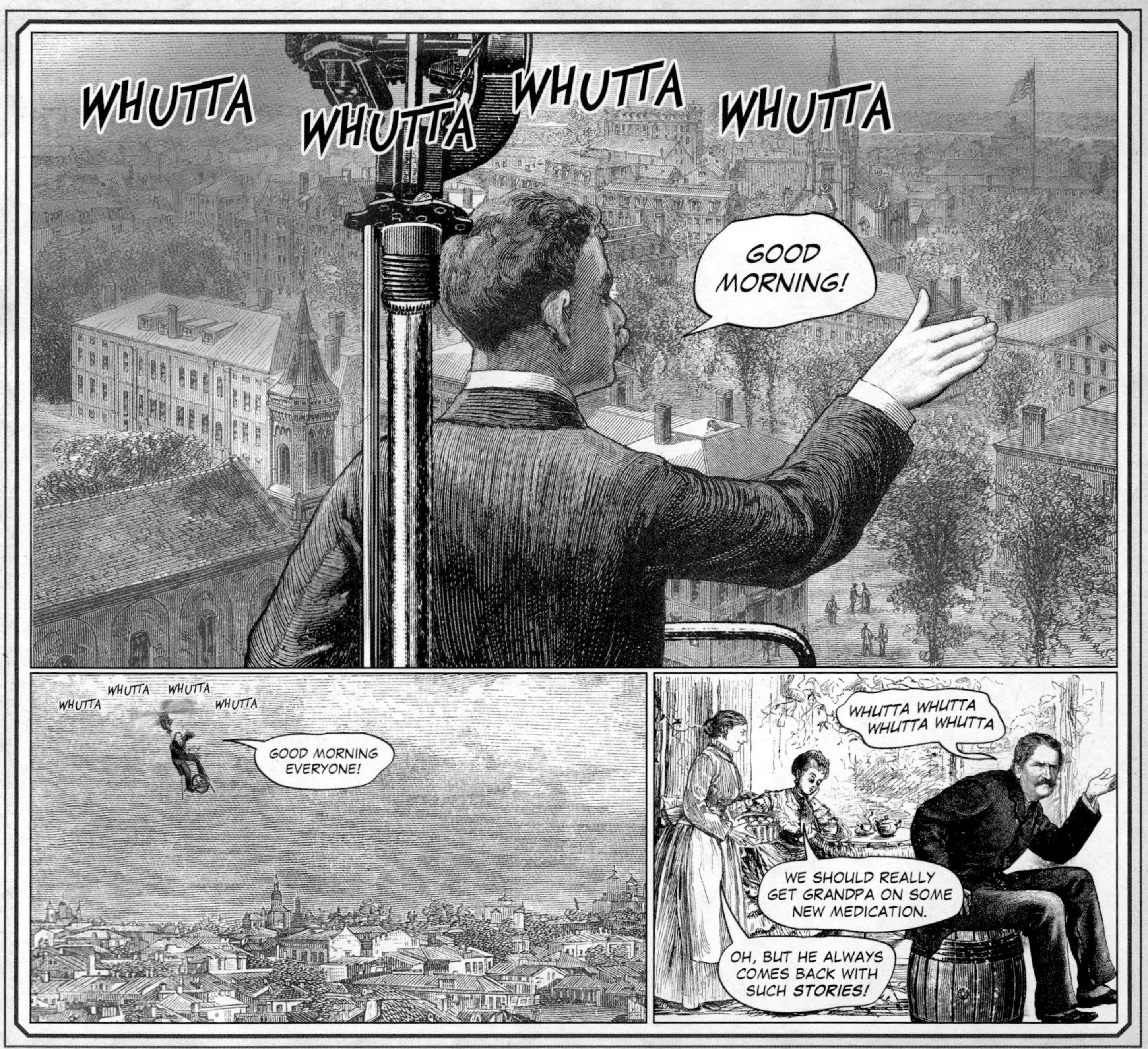
WHUTTA
WHUTTA
WHUTTA
WHUTTA
GOOD MORNING!
WHUTTA
WHUTTA
WHUTTA
WHUTTA
GOOD MORNING EVERYONE!
WHUTTA WHUTTA WHUTTA WHUTTA
WE SHOULD REALLY GET GRANDPA ON SOME NEW MEDICATION.
OH, BUT HE ALWAYS COMES BACK WITH SUCH STORIES!

But never any presents.

Henry Ford has dropped one of his tools! Can you help him find it?

PENULTIMATE *ONION* COMIC

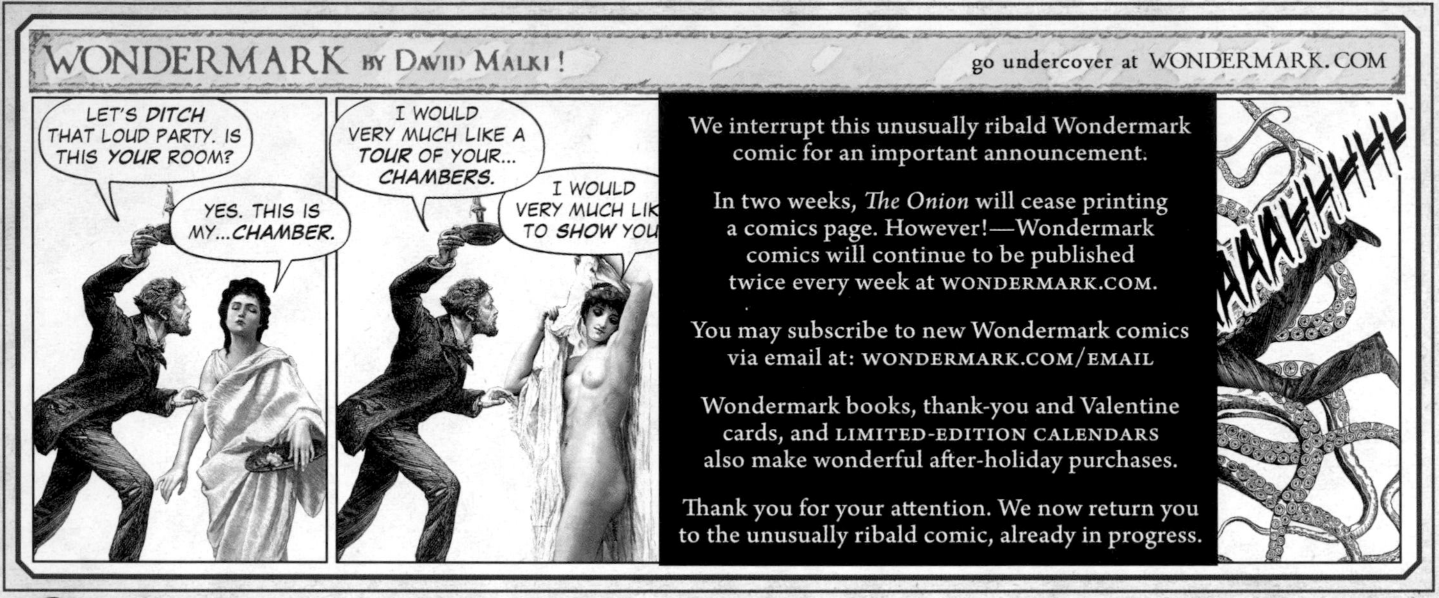
WONDERMARK BY DAVID MALKI !
go undercover at WONDERMARK.COM
LET'S DITCH THAT LOUD PARTY. IS THIS YOUR ROOM?
YES. THIS IS MY...CHAMBER.
I WOULD VERY MUCH LIKE A TOUR OF YOUR... CHAMBERS.
I WOULD VERY MUCH LIK TO SHOW YOU
We interrupt this unusually ribald Wondermark comic for an important announcement.
In two weeks, The Onion will cease printing a comics page. However!—Wondermark comics will continue to be published twice every week at WONDERMARK.COM.
You may subscribe to new Wondermark comics via email at: WONDERMARK.COM/EMAIL
Wondermark books, thank-you and Valentine cards, and LIMITED-EDITION CALENDARS also make wonderful after-holiday purchases.
Thank you for your attention. We now return you to the unusually ribald comic, already in progress.

When *The Onion*, in which Wondermark was featured weekly, decided to cut its comics page, I was given two weeks' warning and permission to run whatever I wanted.

TERMINAL *ONION* COMIC

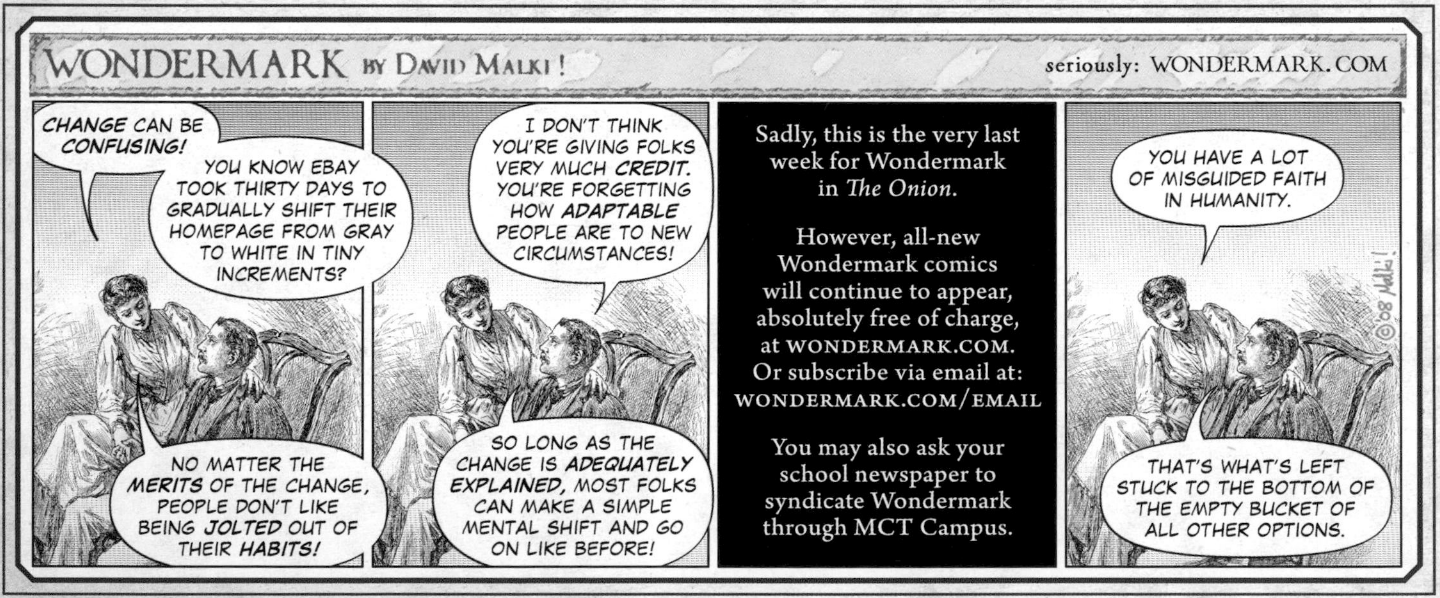
WONDERMARK BY DAVID MALKI !
seriously: WONDERMARK.COM
CHANGE CAN BE CONFUSING!
YOU KNOW EBAY TOOK THIRTY DAYS TO GRADUALLY SHIFT THEIR HOMEPAGE FROM GRAY TO WHITE IN TINY INCREMENTS?
NO MATTER THE MERITS OF THE CHANGE, PEOPLE DON'T LIKE BEING JOLTED OUT OF THEIR HABITS!
I DON'T THINK YOU'RE GIVING FOLKS VERY MUCH CREDIT. YOU'RE FORGETTING HOW ADAPTABLE PEOPLE ARE TO NEW CIRCUMSTANCES!
SO LONG AS THE CHANGE IS ADEQUATELY EXPLAINED, MOST FOLKS CAN MAKE A SIMPLE MENTAL SHIFT AND GO ON LIKE BEFORE!
Sadly, this is the very last week for Wondermark in The Onion.
However, all-new Wondermark comics will continue to appear, absolutely free of charge, at WONDERMARK.COM. Or subscribe via email at: WONDERMARK.COM/EMAIL
You may also ask your school newspaper to syndicate Wondermark through MCT Campus.
YOU HAVE A LOT OF MISGUIDED FAITH IN HUMANITY.
THAT'S WHAT'S LEFT STUCK TO THE BOTTOM OF THE EMPTY BUCKET OF ALL OTHER OPTIONS.
©'08 Malki !

My campaign to drive paper readers online was an interesting object lesson in how newspaper circulation numbers relate to actual dedicated comic readership. (Hint: the ratio may be lower than many syndicated cartoonists imagine.)

THE LEFT OVER LETTERS SPELL: "EVER ONWARD!" A GOOD MOTTO TO TAKE TO HEART!

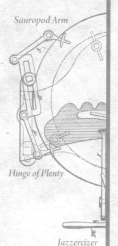

Sauropod Arm
Hinge of Plenty
Jazzercizer

Abandoned Efforts

TO WHICH THE AUTHOR SHALL NEVER RETURN.

The comics on this and the following two pages are ones that I elected not to admit into the official *Wondermark* canon, for reasons elucidated below each comic, and also for unstated, entirely capricious *secret reasons* never to be revealed in print for fear they may be hauled into light when next I make an attempt to run for my local Neighborhood Council, and thus infiltrate and bring to its tar-spackled knees that horrid badgers' hive from the *inside*.

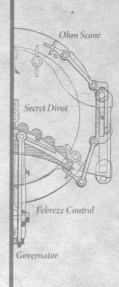

Ohm Scone
Secret Divot
Febreze Control
Governator

WONDERMARK BY DAVID MALKI !
remember WONDERMARK.COM
HEY BOB, LONG TIME NO SEE!
DON'T MENTION THE FAUX PAUS FROM LAST TIME YOU SPOKE JUST LET IT GO FORGET IT
JAMES, RIGHT? HOW'VE YOU BEEN THESE DAYS?
OH, YOU KNOW, HANGIN' IN. YOU?
HE ALREADY THINKS YOU'RE AN IDIOT. DON'T MAKE IT WORSE BY BRINGING IT UP AGAIN. CLEAN SLATE, BABY, CLEAN SLATE.
PRETTY WELL, I GUESS! CONSIDERING THE CIRCUMSTANCES.
WHAT? WHAT IS HE TALKING ABOUT? WHAT CIRCUMSTANCES?
HAHA, OH, SURE!
SO, AH, LISTEN. ABOUT LAST TIME.
NO NO YOU IDIOT SHUP UP JUST SHUT UP NO NO NO NO
WHAT HAPPENED LAST TIME?
WHEN I MISTOOK YOU FOR SLOBODAN MILOSEVIC? AND CALLED IN THE U.N.?
THAT WAS THIS GUY?!

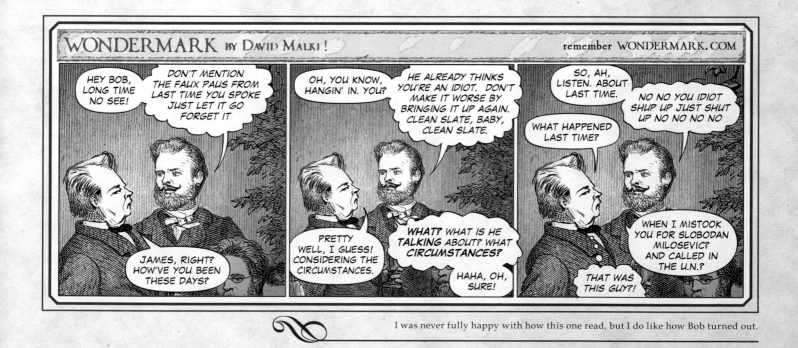

I was never fully happy with how this one read, but I do like how Bob turned out.

SOLUTION

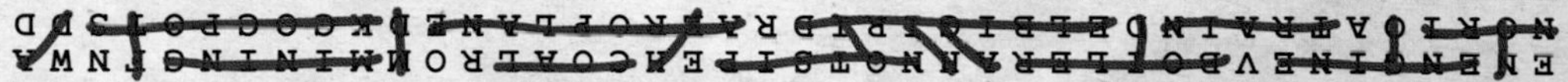

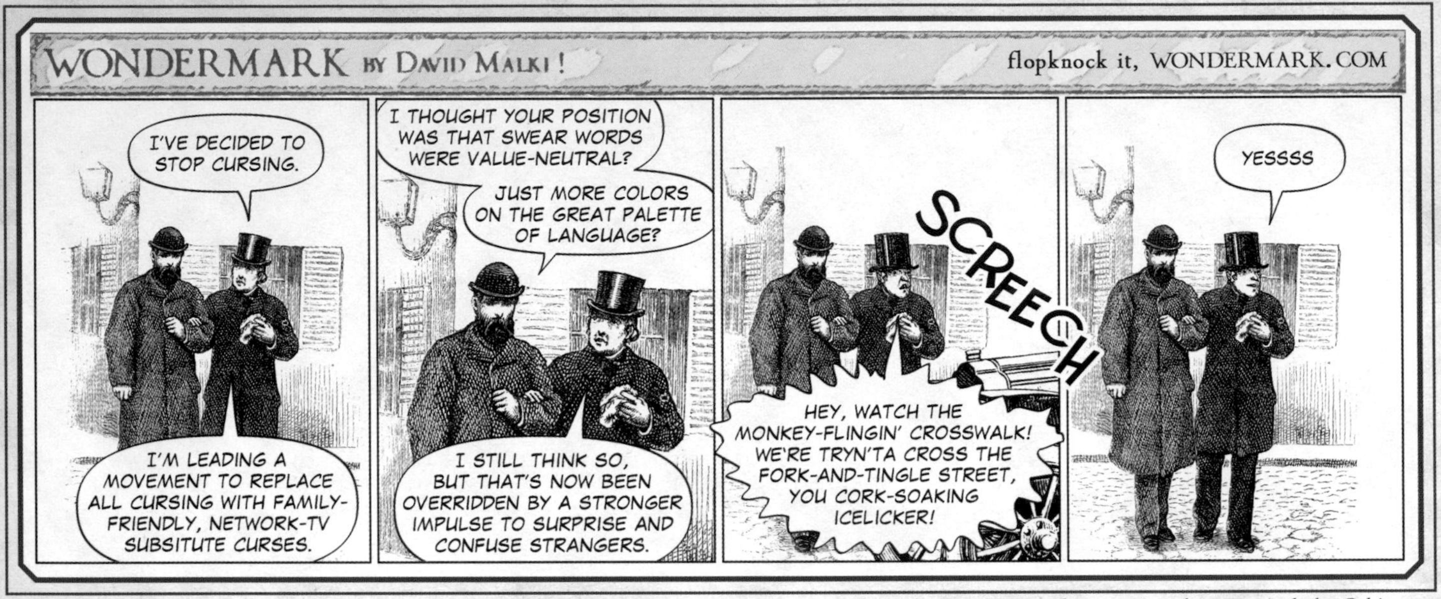
WONDERMARK BY DAVID MALKI !
flopknock it, WONDERMARK.COM
I'VE DECIDED TO STOP CURSING.
I'M LEADING A MOVEMENT TO REPLACE ALL CURSING WITH FAMILY-FRIENDLY, NETWORK-TV SUBSITUTE CURSES.
I THOUGHT YOUR POSITION WAS THAT SWEAR WORDS WERE VALUE-NEUTRAL?
JUST MORE COLORS ON THE GREAT PALETTE OF LANGUAGE?
I STILL THINK SO, BUT THAT'S NOW BEEN OVERRIDDEN BY A STRONGER IMPULSE TO SURPRISE AND CONFUSE STRANGERS.
SCREECH
HEY, WATCH THE MONKEY-FLINGIN' CROSSWALK! WE'RE TRYN'TA CROSS THE FORK-AND-TINGLE STREET, YOU CORK-SOAKING ICELICKER!
YESSSS

About the time I wrote this, a series of commericals for Orbit gum did basically the same joke, and better. A case of bad timing.

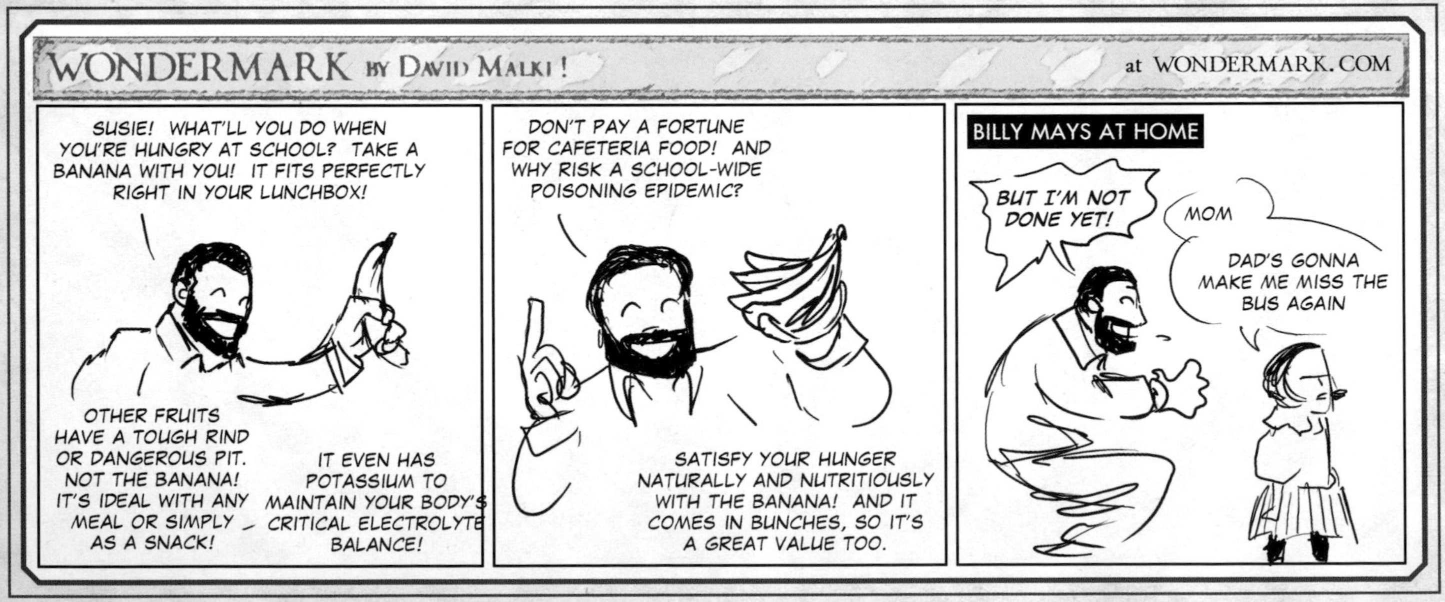
WONDERMARK BY DAVID MALKI !
at WONDERMARK.COM
SUSIE! WHAT'LL YOU DO WHEN YOU'RE HUNGRY AT SCHOOL? TAKE A BANANA WITH YOU! IT FITS PERFECTLY RIGHT IN YOUR LUNCHBOX!
OTHER FRUITS HAVE A TOUGH RIND OR DANGEROUS PIT. NOT THE BANANA! IT'S IDEAL WITH ANY MEAL OR SIMPLY AS A SNACK!
IT EVEN HAS POTASSIUM TO MAINTAIN YOUR BODY'S CRITICAL ELECTROLYTE BALANCE!
DON'T PAY A FORTUNE FOR CAFETERIA FOOD! AND WHY RISK A SCHOOL-WIDE POISONING EPIDEMIC?
SATISFY YOUR HUNGER NATURALLY AND NUTRITIOUSLY WITH THE BANANA! AND IT COMES IN BUNCHES, SO IT'S A GREAT VALUE TOO.
BILLY MAYS AT HOME
BUT I'M NOT DONE YET!
MOM
DAD'S GONNA MAKE ME MISS THE BUS AGAIN

Bad timing again. (This one didn't make it far past the script stage.)

Clues: AD, AEROPLANE, AG, BOILER, COAL, DIRIGIBLE, ENGINE, FT, GO, ID, IRON, HE, HI, IO, MD, MINING, NO, ON, STOPCOCK, TRAIN.

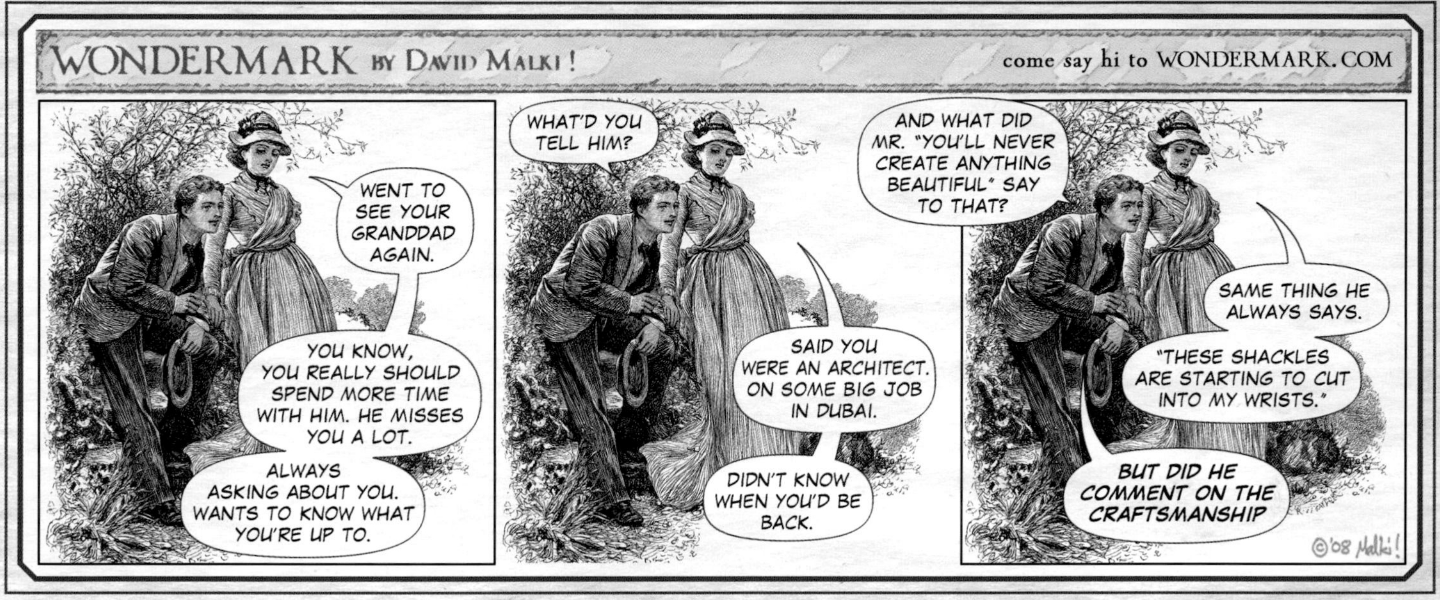
WONDERMARK BY DAVID MALKI !
come say hi to WONDERMARK.COM
WENT TO SEE YOUR GRANDDAD AGAIN.
YOU KNOW, YOU REALLY SHOULD SPEND MORE TIME WITH HIM. HE MISSES YOU A LOT.
ALWAYS ASKING ABOUT YOU. WANTS TO KNOW WHAT YOU'RE UP TO.
WHAT'D YOU TELL HIM?
SAID YOU WERE AN ARCHITECT. ON SOME BIG JOB IN DUBAI.
DIDN'T KNOW WHEN YOU'D BE BACK.
AND WHAT DID MR. "YOU'LL NEVER CREATE ANYTHING BEAUTIFUL" SAY TO THAT?
SAME THING HE ALWAYS SAYS.
"THESE SHACKLES ARE STARTING TO CUT INTO MY WRISTS."
BUT DID HE COMMENT ON THE CRAFTSMANSHIP
©'08 Malki !

This is the original version of the comic that appears on page 56. It was initially published like this, but I remained dissatisfied with it. Eventually I scrapped the premise and started over.

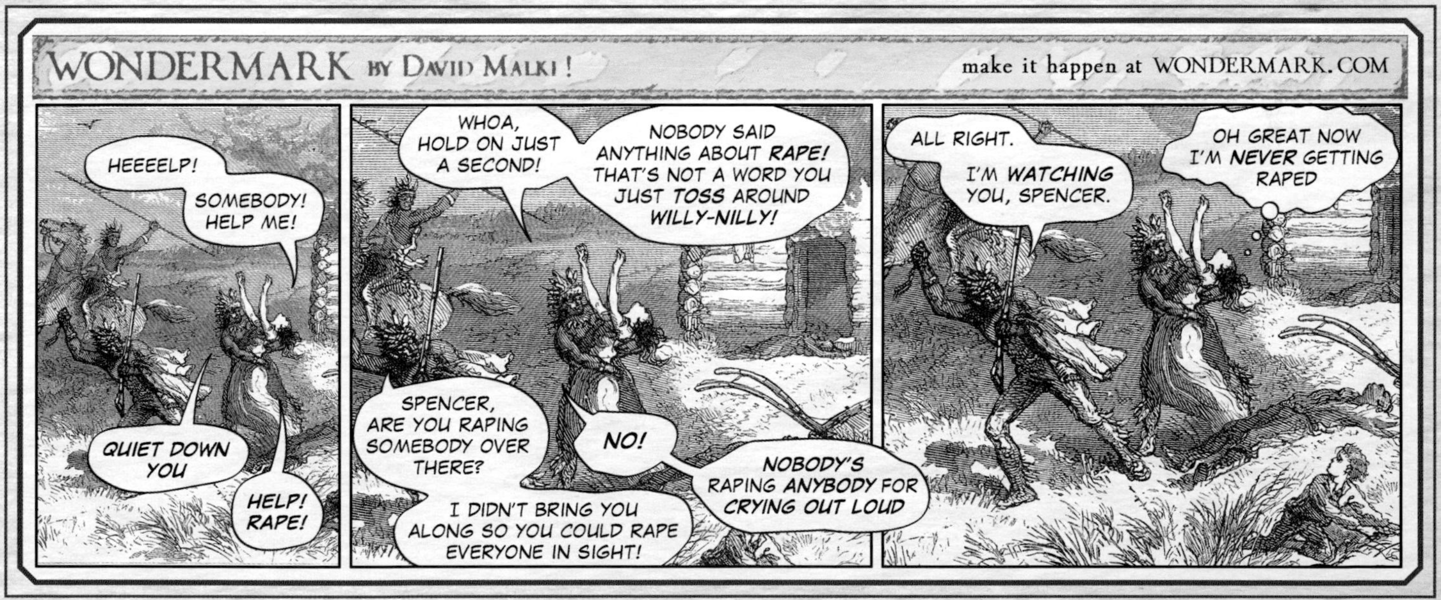
WONDERMARK BY DAVID MALKI !
make it happen at WONDERMARK.COM
HEEEELP!
SOMEBODY! HELP ME!
QUIET DOWN YOU
HELP! RAPE!
WHOA, HOLD ON JUST A SECOND!
NOBODY SAID ANYTHING ABOUT RAPE! THAT'S NOT A WORD YOU JUST TOSS AROUND WILLY-NILLY!
SPENCER, ARE YOU RAPING SOMEBODY OVER THERE?
NO!
NOBODY'S RAPING ANYBODY FOR CRYING OUT LOUD
I DIDN'T BRING YOU ALONG SO YOU COULD RAPE EVERYONE IN SIGHT!
ALL RIGHT.
I'M WATCHING YOU, SPENCER.
OH GREAT NOW I'M NEVER GETTING RAPED

This is probably offensive.

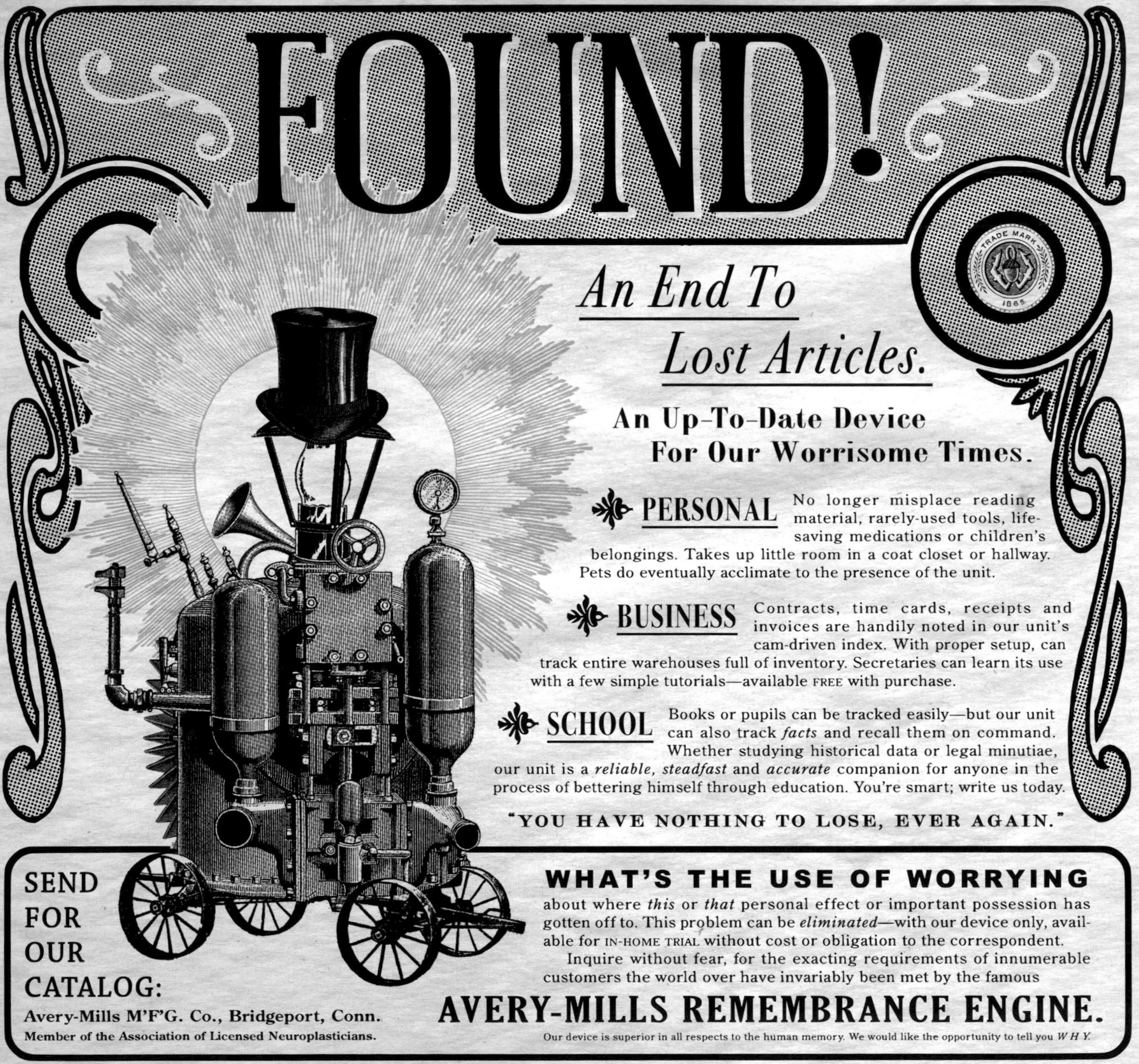
FOUND!
TRADE MARK
1865
An End To
Lost Articles.
An Up-To-Date Device
For Our Worrisome Times.
PERSONAL
No longer misplace reading material, rarely-used tools, life-saving medications or children's belongings. Takes up little room in a coat closet or hallway. Pets do eventually acclimate to the presence of the unit.
BUSINESS
Contracts, time cards, receipts and invoices are handily noted in our unit's cam-driven index. With proper setup, can track entire warehouses full of inventory. Secretaries can learn its use with a few simple tutorials—available FREE with purchase.
SCHOOL
Books or pupils can be tracked easily—but our unit can also track *facts* and recall them on command. Whether studying historical data or legal minutiae, our unit is a *reliable, steadfast* and *accurate* companion for anyone in the process of bettering himself through education. You're smart; write us today.
"YOU HAVE NOTHING TO LOSE, EVER AGAIN."
SEND FOR OUR CATALOG:
Avery-Mills M'F'G. Co., Bridgeport, Conn.
Member of the Association of Licensed Neuroplasticians.
WHAT'S THE USE OF WORRYING
about where *this* or *that* personal effect or important possession has gotten off to. This problem can be *eliminated*—with our device only, available for IN-HOME TRIAL without cost or obligation to the correspondent.
Inquire without fear, for the exacting requirements of innumerable customers the world over have invariably been met by the famous
AVERY-MILLS REMEMBRANCE ENGINE.
Our device is superior in all respects to the human memory. We would like the opportunity to tell you *W H Y.*

(Solution on the page following the puzzle.)

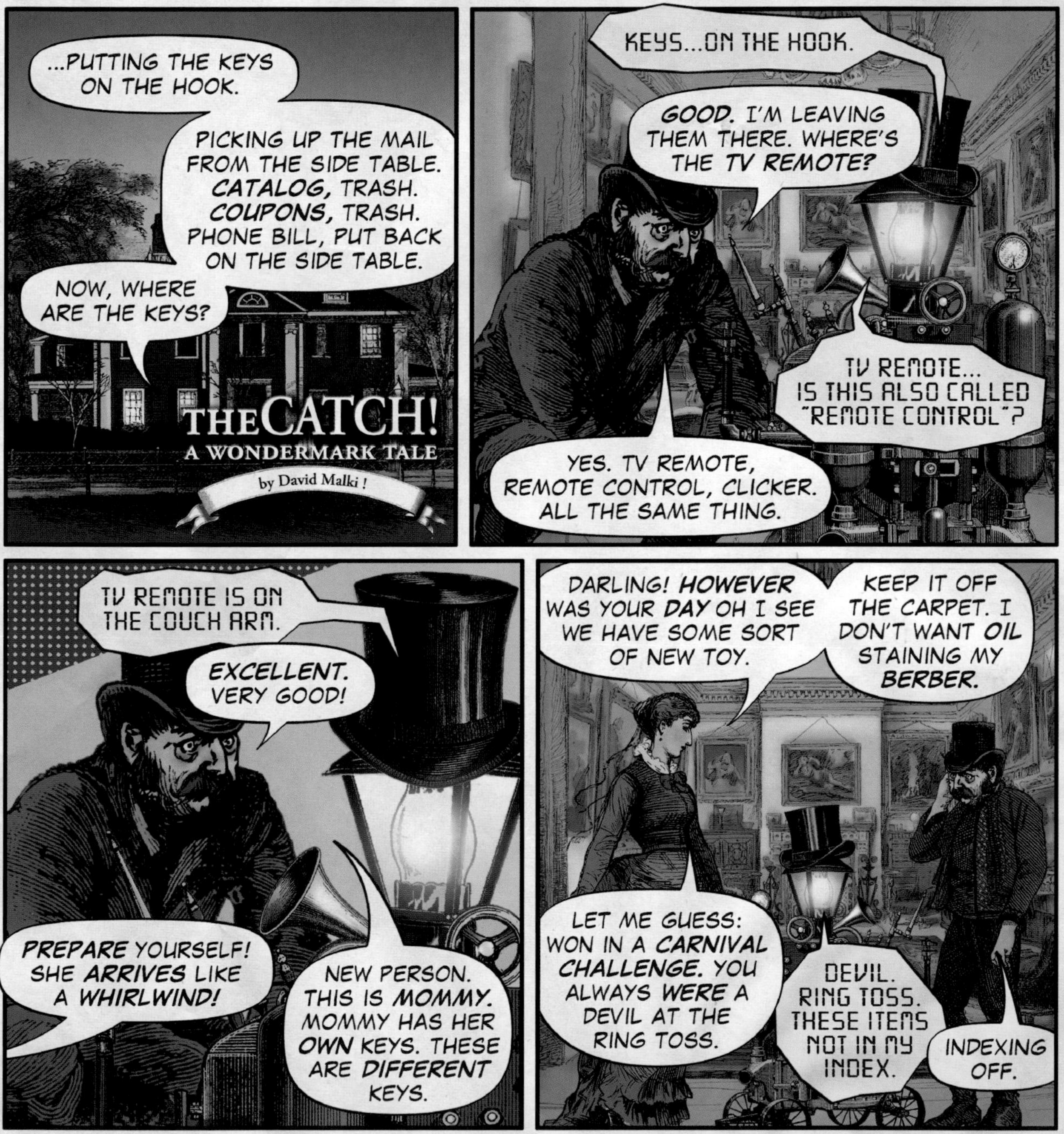
...PUTTING THE KEYS ON THE HOOK.
PICKING UP THE MAIL FROM THE SIDE TABLE. CATALOG, TRASH. COUPONS, TRASH. PHONE BILL, PUT BACK ON THE SIDE TABLE.
NOW, WHERE ARE THE KEYS?
THE CATCH!
A WONDERMARK TALE
by David Malki !
KEYS...ON THE HOOK.
GOOD. I'M LEAVING THEM THERE. WHERE'S THE TV REMOTE?
TV REMOTE... IS THIS ALSO CALLED "REMOTE CONTROL"?
YES. TV REMOTE, REMOTE CONTROL, CLICKER. ALL THE SAME THING.
TV REMOTE IS ON THE COUCH ARM.
EXCELLENT. VERY GOOD!
PREPARE YOURSELF! SHE ARRIVES LIKE A WHIRLWIND!
NEW PERSON. THIS IS MOMMY. MOMMY HAS HER OWN KEYS. THESE ARE DIFFERENT KEYS.
DARLING! HOWEVER WAS YOUR DAY OH I SEE WE HAVE SOME SORT OF NEW TOY.
KEEP IT OFF THE CARPET. I DON'T WANT OIL STAINING MY BERBER.
LET ME GUESS: WON IN A CARNIVAL CHALLENGE. YOU ALWAYS WERE A DEVIL AT THE RING TOSS.
DEVIL. RING TOSS. THESE ITEMS NOT IN MY INDEX.
INDEXING OFF.

STORY *Continues.*

Color by Marcus Thiele • themonkeymind.livejournal.com

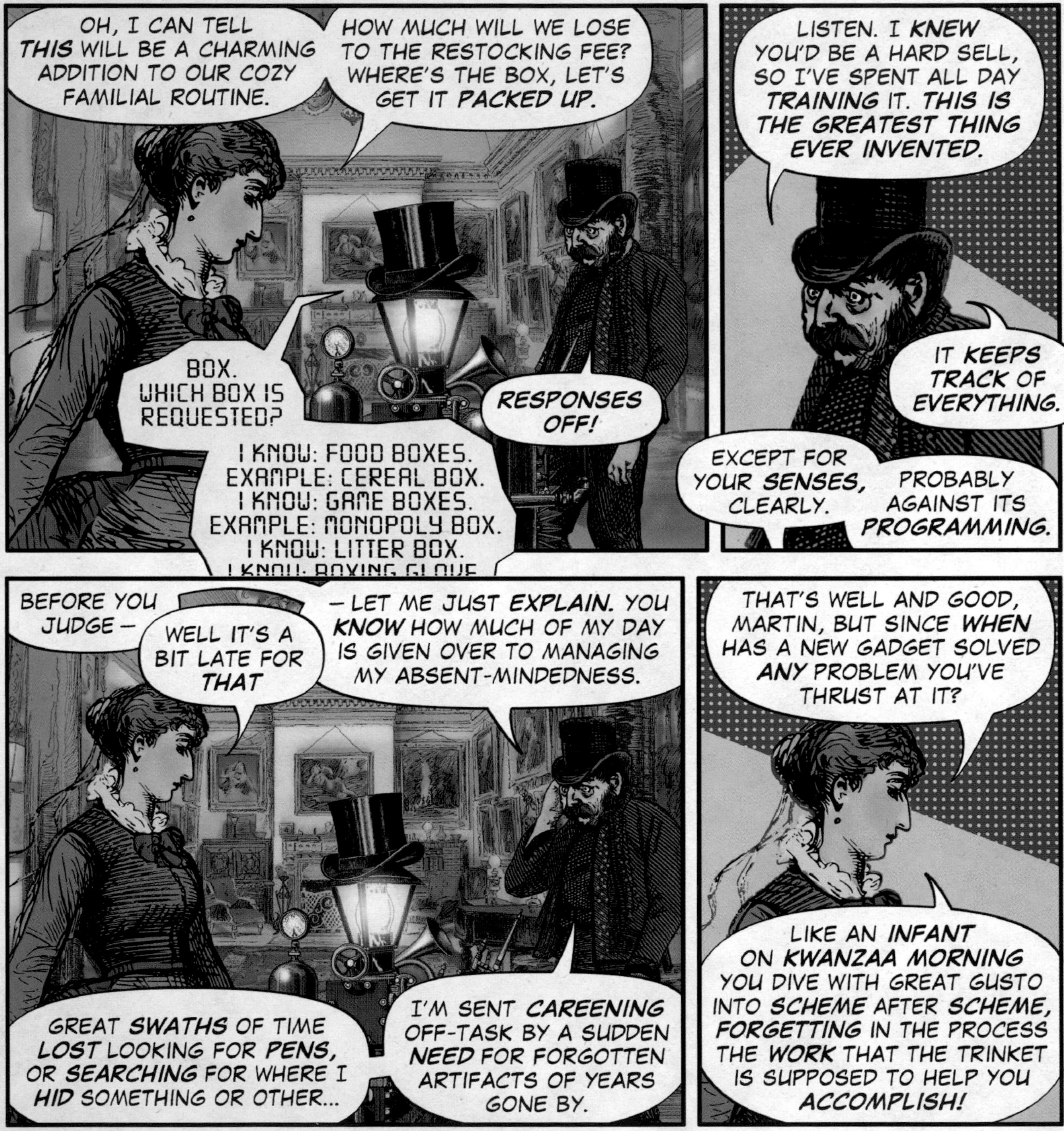
OH, I CAN TELL THIS WILL BE A CHARMING ADDITION TO OUR COZY FAMILIAL ROUTINE.
HOW MUCH WILL WE LOSE TO THE RESTOCKING FEE? WHERE'S THE BOX, LET'S GET IT PACKED UP.
BOX. WHICH BOX IS REQUESTED?
RESPONSES OFF!
I KNOW: FOOD BOXES. EXAMPLE: CEREAL BOX. I KNOW: GAME BOXES. EXAMPLE: MONOPOLY BOX. I KNOW: LITTER BOX.
LISTEN. I KNEW YOU'D BE A HARD SELL, SO I'VE SPENT ALL DAY TRAINING IT. THIS IS THE GREATEST THING EVER INVENTED.
IT KEEPS TRACK OF EVERYTHING.
EXCEPT FOR YOUR SENSES, CLEARLY.
PROBABLY AGAINST ITS PROGRAMMING.
BEFORE YOU JUDGE—
WELL IT'S A BIT LATE FOR THAT
—LET ME JUST EXPLAIN. YOU KNOW HOW MUCH OF MY DAY IS GIVEN OVER TO MANAGING MY ABSENT-MINDEDNESS.
GREAT SWATHS OF TIME LOST LOOKING FOR PENS, OR SEARCHING FOR WHERE I HID SOMETHING OR OTHER...
I'M SENT CAREENING OFF-TASK BY A SUDDEN NEED FOR FORGOTTEN ARTIFACTS OF YEARS GONE BY.
THAT'S WELL AND GOOD, MARTIN, BUT SINCE WHEN HAS A NEW GADGET SOLVED ANY PROBLEM YOU'VE THRUST AT IT?
LIKE AN INFANT ON KWANZAA MORNING YOU DIVE WITH GREAT GUSTO INTO SCHEME AFTER SCHEME, FORGETTING IN THE PROCESS THE WORK THAT THE TRINKET IS SUPPOSED TO HELP YOU ACCOMPLISH!

Oh, no! Tesla's laboratory has been ransacked! Can you help him find his notes?

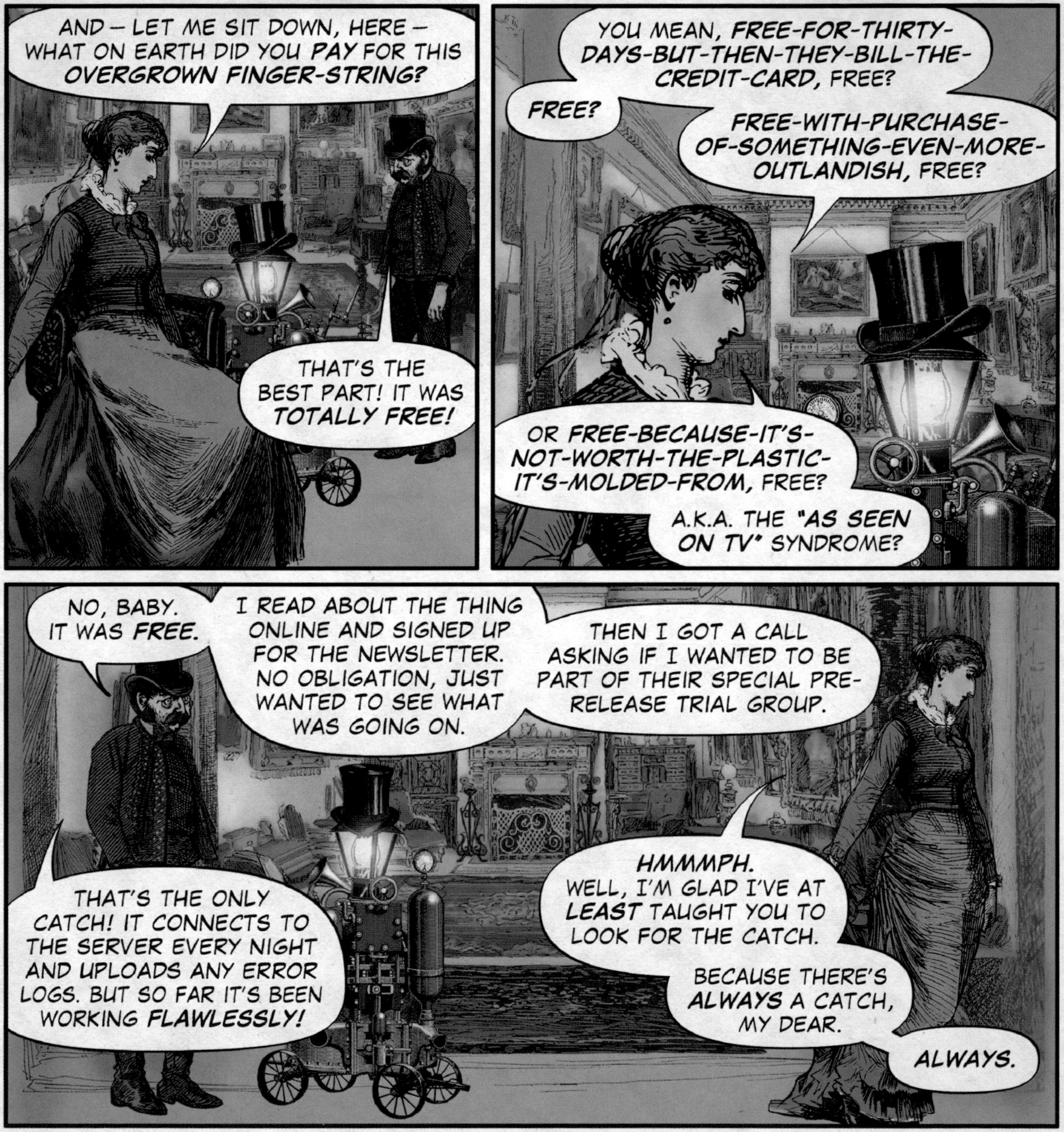
AND — LET ME SIT DOWN, HERE — WHAT ON EARTH DID YOU PAY FOR THIS OVERGROWN FINGER-STRING?
THAT'S THE BEST PART! IT WAS TOTALLY FREE!
YOU MEAN, FREE-FOR-THIRTY-DAYS-BUT-THEN-THEY-BILL-THE-CREDIT-CARD, FREE?
FREE?
FREE-WITH-PURCHASE-OF-SOMETHING-EVEN-MORE-OUTLANDISH, FREE?
OR FREE-BECAUSE-IT'S-NOT-WORTH-THE-PLASTIC-IT'S-MOLDED-FROM, FREE?
A.K.A. THE "AS SEEN ON TV" SYNDROME?
NO, BABY. IT WAS FREE.
I READ ABOUT THE THING ONLINE AND SIGNED UP FOR THE NEWSLETTER. NO OBLIGATION, JUST WANTED TO SEE WHAT WAS GOING ON.
THEN I GOT A CALL ASKING IF I WANTED TO BE PART OF THEIR SPECIAL PRE-RELEASE TRIAL GROUP.
THAT'S THE ONLY CATCH! IT CONNECTS TO THE SERVER EVERY NIGHT AND UPLOADS ANY ERROR LOGS. BUT SO FAR IT'S BEEN WORKING FLAWLESSLY!
HMMMPH. WELL, I'M GLAD I'VE AT LEAST TAUGHT YOU TO LOOK FOR THE CATCH.
BECAUSE THERE'S ALWAYS A CATCH, MY DEAR.
ALWAYS.

Story Continues.

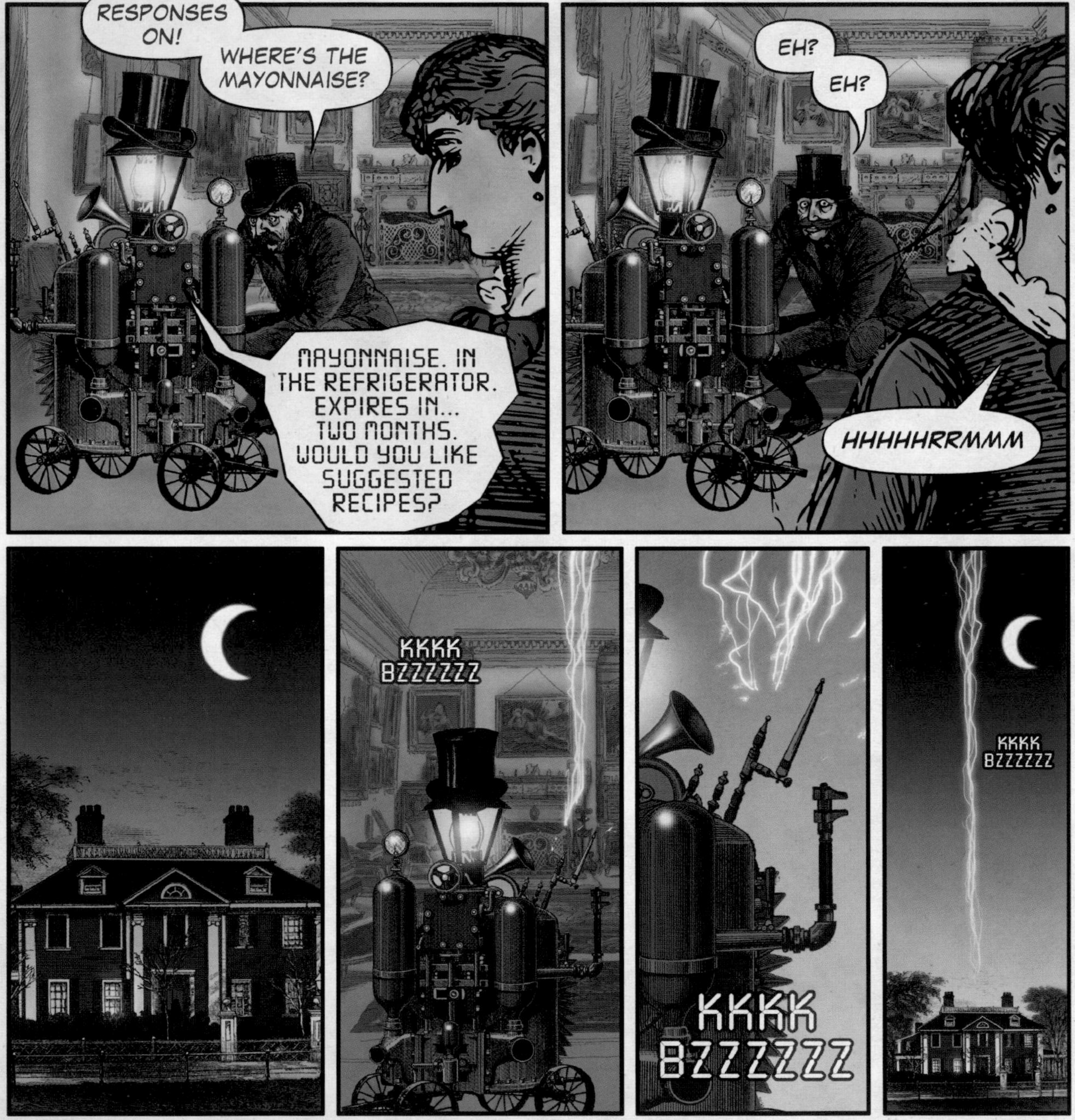
RESPONSES ON!
WHERE'S THE MAYONNAISE?
MAYONNAISE. IN THE REFRIGERATOR. EXPIRES IN... TWO MONTHS. WOULD YOU LIKE SUGGESTED RECIPES?
EH?
EH?
HHHHHRRMMM
KKKK BZZZZZZ
KKKK BZZZZZZ
KKKK BZZZZZZ

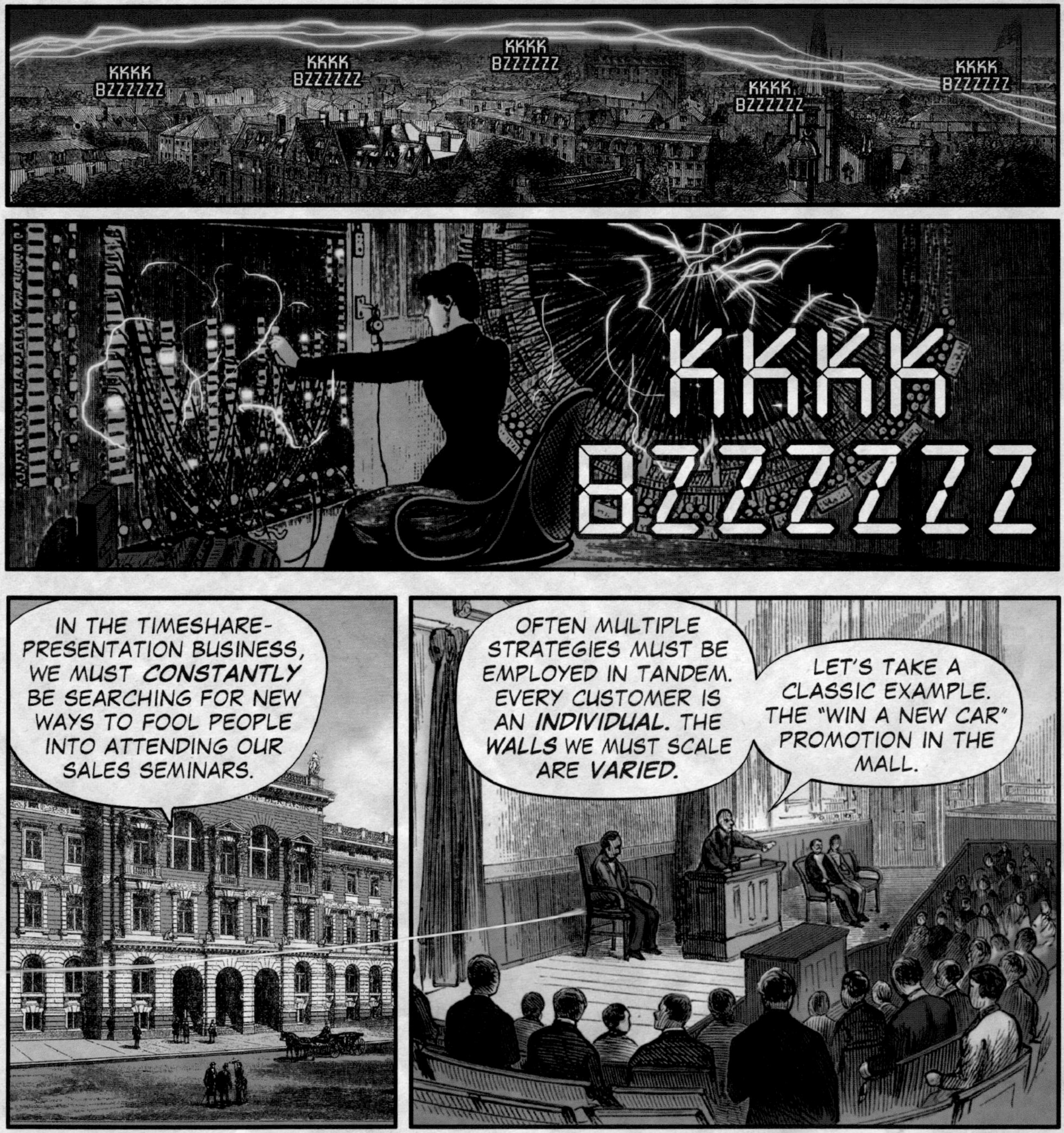
KKKK BZZZZZZ
KKKK BZZZZZZ
KKKK BZZZZZZ
KKKK BZZZZZZ
KKKK BZZZZZZ
KKKK BZZZZZZ
IN THE TIMESHARE-PRESENTATION BUSINESS, WE MUST CONSTANTLY BE SEARCHING FOR NEW WAYS TO FOOL PEOPLE INTO ATTENDING OUR SALES SEMINARS.
OFTEN MULTIPLE STRATEGIES MUST BE EMPLOYED IN TANDEM. EVERY CUSTOMER IS AN INDIVIDUAL. THE WALLS WE MUST SCALE ARE VARIED.
LET'S TAKE A CLASSIC EXAMPLE. THE "WIN A NEW CAR" PROMOTION IN THE MALL.

STORY *Continues.*

Can you help Sigmund Freud find his velocipede? *(Solution on following page.)*

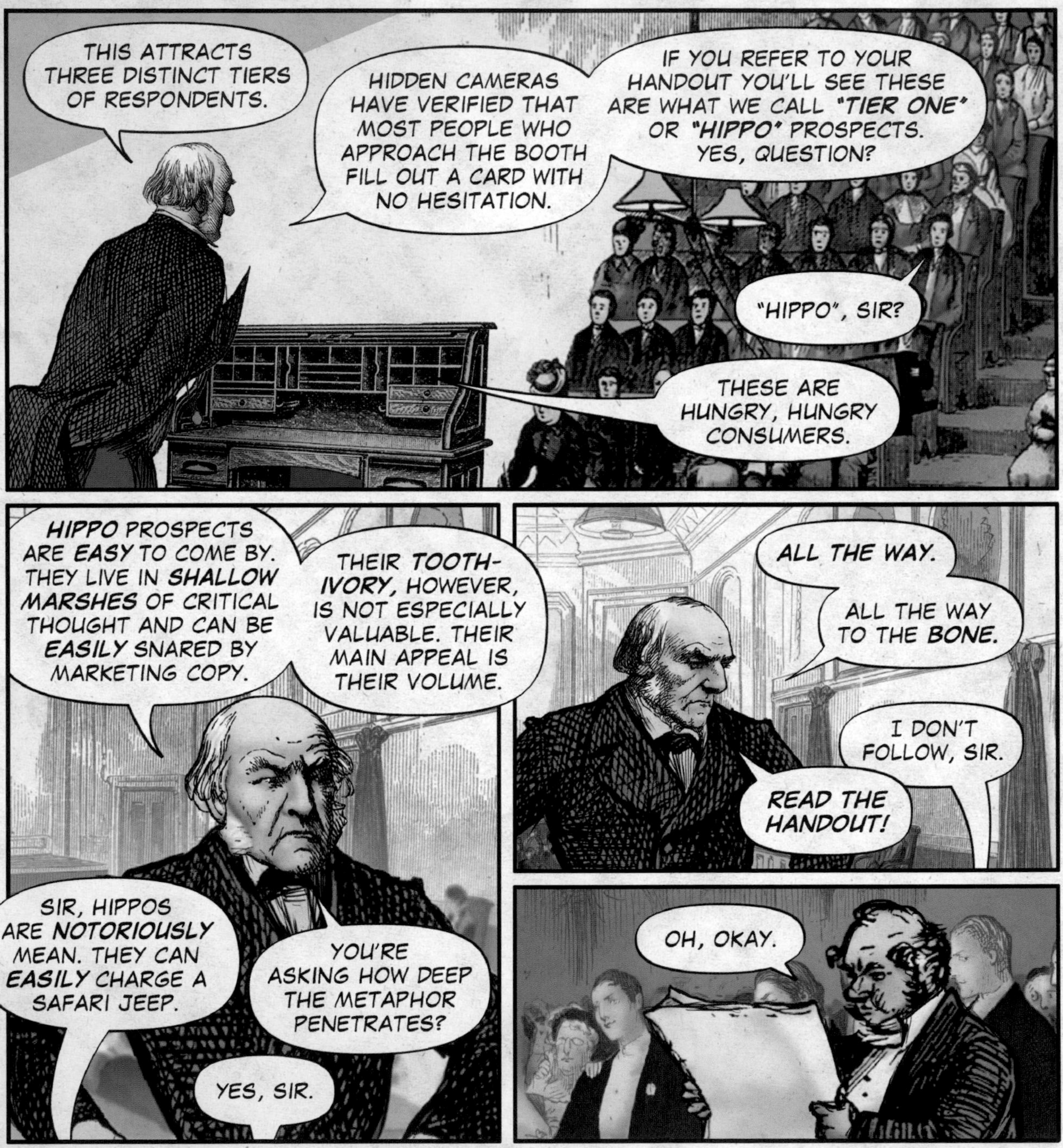
THIS ATTRACTS THREE DISTINCT TIERS OF RESPONDENTS.
HIDDEN CAMERAS HAVE VERIFIED THAT MOST PEOPLE WHO APPROACH THE BOOTH FILL OUT A CARD WITH NO HESITATION.
IF YOU REFER TO YOUR HANDOUT YOU'LL SEE THESE ARE WHAT WE CALL *"TIER ONE"* OR *"HIPPO"* PROSPECTS. YES, QUESTION?
"HIPPO", SIR?
THESE ARE HUNGRY, HUNGRY CONSUMERS.
HIPPO PROSPECTS ARE *EASY* TO COME BY. THEY LIVE IN *SHALLOW MARSHES* OF CRITICAL THOUGHT AND CAN BE *EASILY* SNARED BY MARKETING COPY.
THEIR *TOOTH-IVORY,* HOWEVER, IS NOT ESPECIALLY VALUABLE. THEIR MAIN APPEAL IS THEIR VOLUME.
SIR, HIPPOS ARE *NOTORIOUSLY* MEAN. THEY CAN *EASILY* CHARGE A SAFARI JEEP.
YOU'RE ASKING HOW DEEP THE METAPHOR PENETRATES?
YES, SIR.
ALL THE WAY.
ALL THE WAY TO THE *BONE.*
I DON'T FOLLOW, SIR.
READ THE HANDOUT!
OH, OKAY.

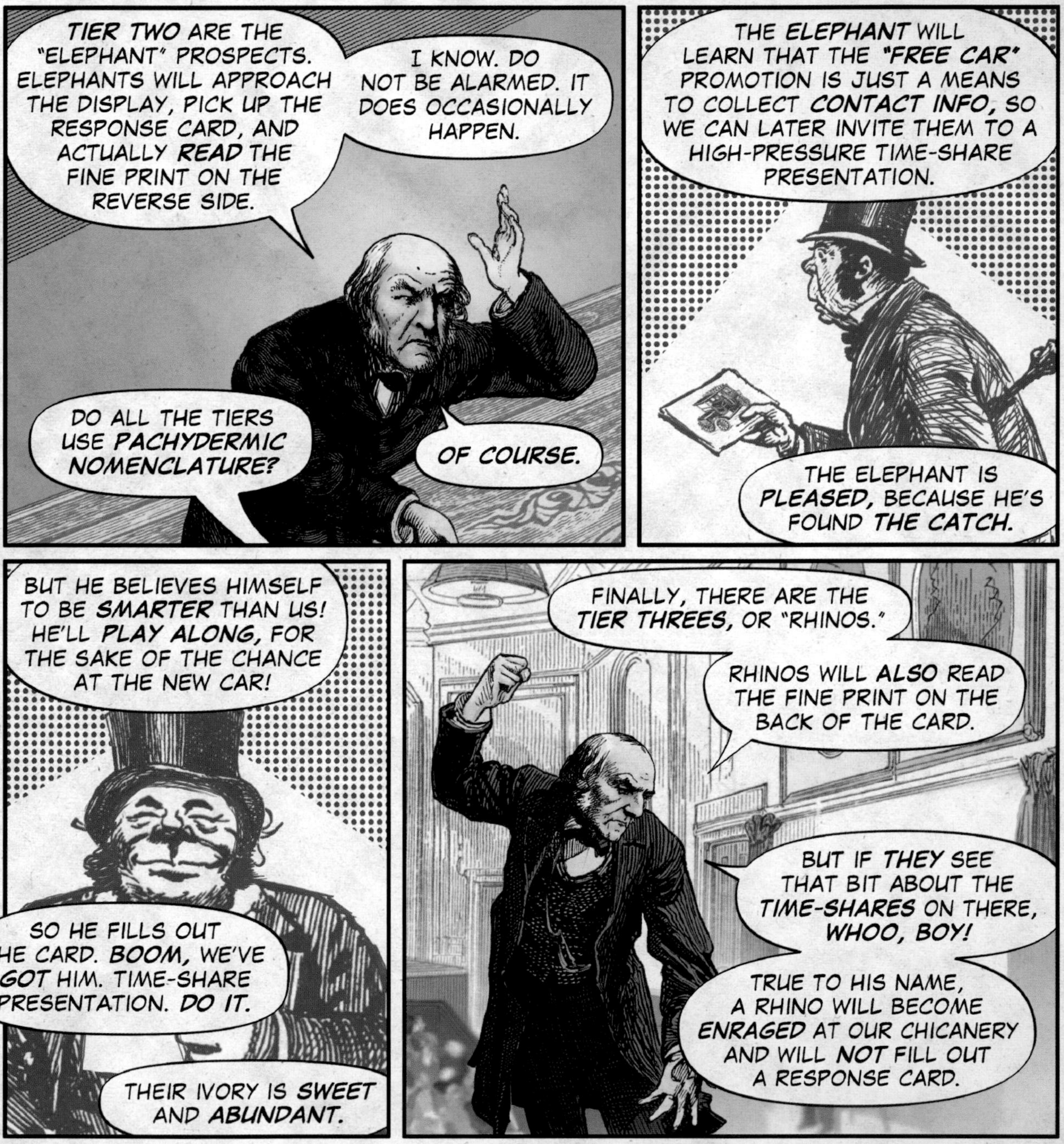
TIER TWO ARE THE "ELEPHANT" PROSPECTS. ELEPHANTS WILL APPROACH THE DISPLAY, PICK UP THE RESPONSE CARD, AND ACTUALLY READ THE FINE PRINT ON THE REVERSE SIDE.
I KNOW. DO NOT BE ALARMED. IT DOES OCCASIONALLY HAPPEN.
DO ALL THE TIERS USE PACHYDERMIC NOMENCLATURE?
OF COURSE.
THE ELEPHANT WILL LEARN THAT THE "FREE CAR" PROMOTION IS JUST A MEANS TO COLLECT CONTACT INFO, SO WE CAN LATER INVITE THEM TO A HIGH-PRESSURE TIME-SHARE PRESENTATION.
THE ELEPHANT IS PLEASED, BECAUSE HE'S FOUND THE CATCH.
BUT HE BELIEVES HIMSELF TO BE SMARTER THAN US! HE'LL PLAY ALONG, FOR THE SAKE OF THE CHANCE AT THE NEW CAR!
SO HE FILLS OUT THE CARD. BOOM, WE'VE GOT HIM. TIME-SHARE PRESENTATION. DO IT.
THEIR IVORY IS SWEET AND ABUNDANT.
FINALLY, THERE ARE THE TIER THREES, OR "RHINOS."
RHINOS WILL ALSO READ THE FINE PRINT ON THE BACK OF THE CARD.
BUT IF THEY SEE THAT BIT ABOUT THE TIME-SHARES ON THERE, WHOO, BOY!
TRUE TO HIS NAME, A RHINO WILL BECOME ENRAGED AT OUR CHICANERY AND WILL NOT FILL OUT A RESPONSE CARD.

STORY
Continues.

—Eunice Pastornak, Ph.D., of The Learning Foundation, Phila., Pa.

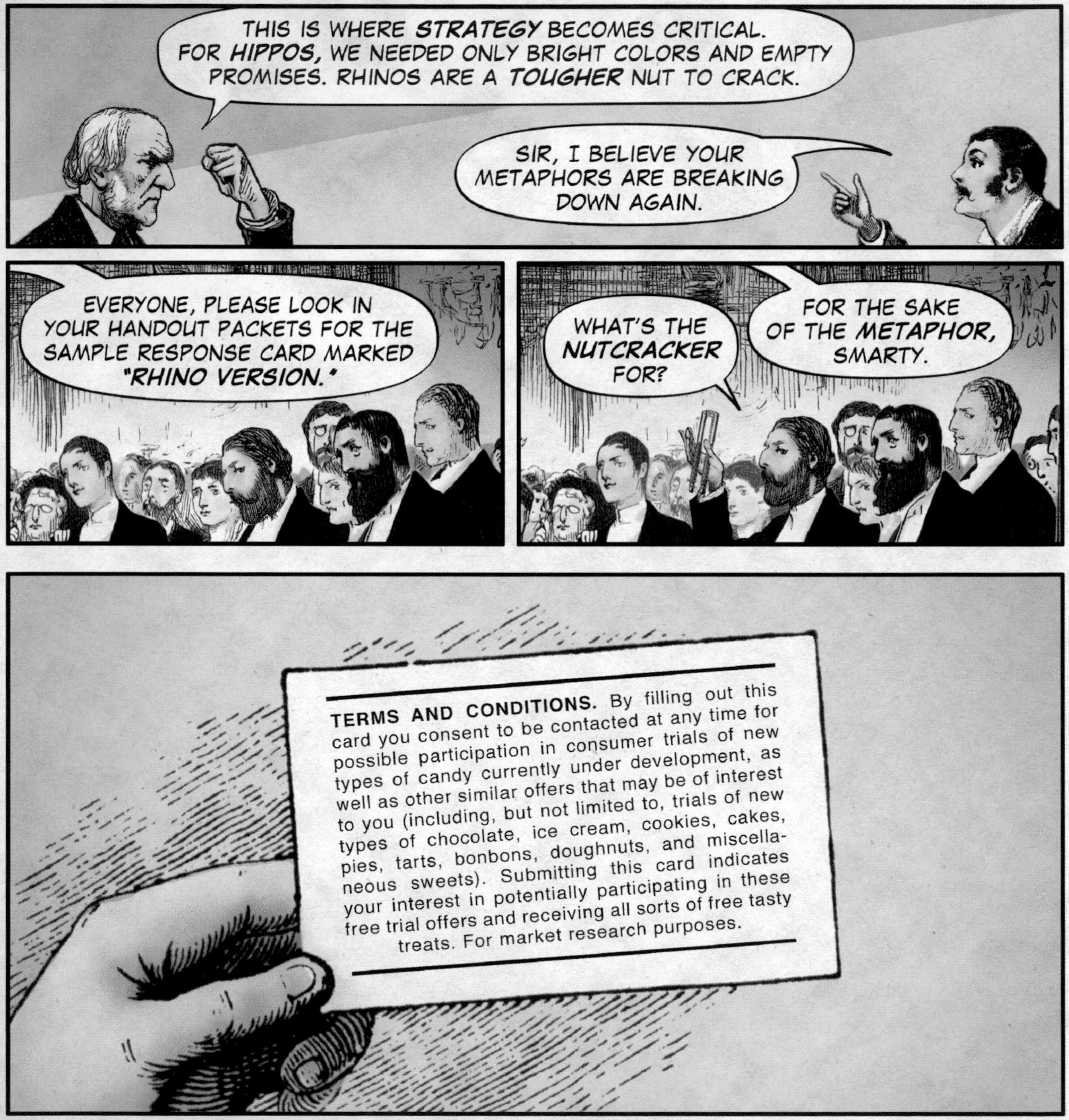
THIS IS WHERE STRATEGY BECOMES CRITICAL. FOR HIPPOS, WE NEEDED ONLY BRIGHT COLORS AND EMPTY PROMISES. RHINOS ARE A TOUGHER NUT TO CRACK.
SIR, I BELIEVE YOUR METAPHORS ARE BREAKING DOWN AGAIN.
EVERYONE, PLEASE LOOK IN YOUR HANDOUT PACKETS FOR THE SAMPLE RESPONSE CARD MARKED "RHINO VERSION."
WHAT'S THE NUTCRACKER FOR?
FOR THE SAKE OF THE METAPHOR, SMARTY.
TERMS AND CONDITIONS. By filling out this card you consent to be contacted at any time for possible participation in consumer trials of new types of candy currently under development, as well as other similar offers that may be of interest to you (including, but not limited to, trials of new types of chocolate, ice cream, cookies, cakes, pies, tarts, bonbons, doughnuts, and miscellaneous sweets). Submitting this card indicates your interest in potentially participating in these free trial offers and receiving all sorts of free tasty treats. For market research purposes.

of this section stimulating to the mind and soul. Onward, dearests, and don't forget us when we die. Please.

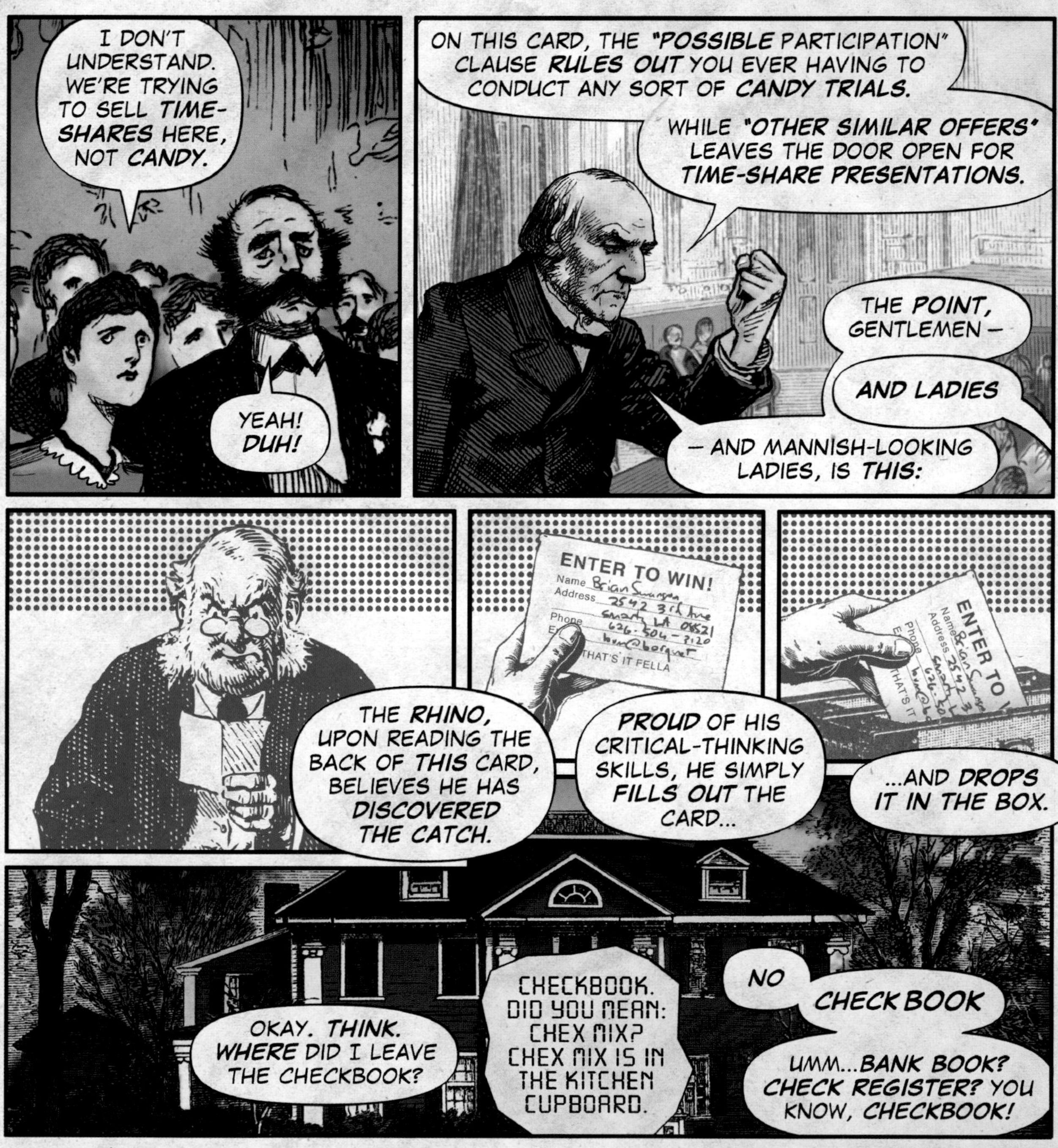
I DON'T UNDERSTAND. WE'RE TRYING TO SELL TIME-SHARES HERE, NOT CANDY.
YEAH! DUH!
ON THIS CARD, THE "POSSIBLE PARTICIPATION" CLAUSE RULES OUT YOU EVER HAVING TO CONDUCT ANY SORT OF CANDY TRIALS.
WHILE "OTHER SIMILAR OFFERS" LEAVES THE DOOR OPEN FOR TIME-SHARE PRESENTATIONS.
THE POINT, GENTLEMEN—
AND LADIES
—AND MANNISH-LOOKING LADIES, IS THIS:
ENTER TO WIN!
Name
Address
Phone
THAT'S IT FELLA
THE RHINO, UPON READING THE BACK OF THIS CARD, BELIEVES HE HAS DISCOVERED THE CATCH.
PROUD OF HIS CRITICAL-THINKING SKILLS, HE SIMPLY FILLS OUT THE CARD...
...AND DROPS IT IN THE BOX.
OKAY. THINK. WHERE DID I LEAVE THE CHECKBOOK?
CHECKBOOK. DID YOU MEAN: CHEX MIX? CHEX MIX IS IN THE KITCHEN CUPBOARD.
NO
CHECKBOOK
UMM...BANK BOOK? CHECK REGISTER? YOU KNOW, CHECKBOOK!

STORY *Continues.*

our hope is that despite the limitations imposed on us by this space, you will find the games, puzzles and activities

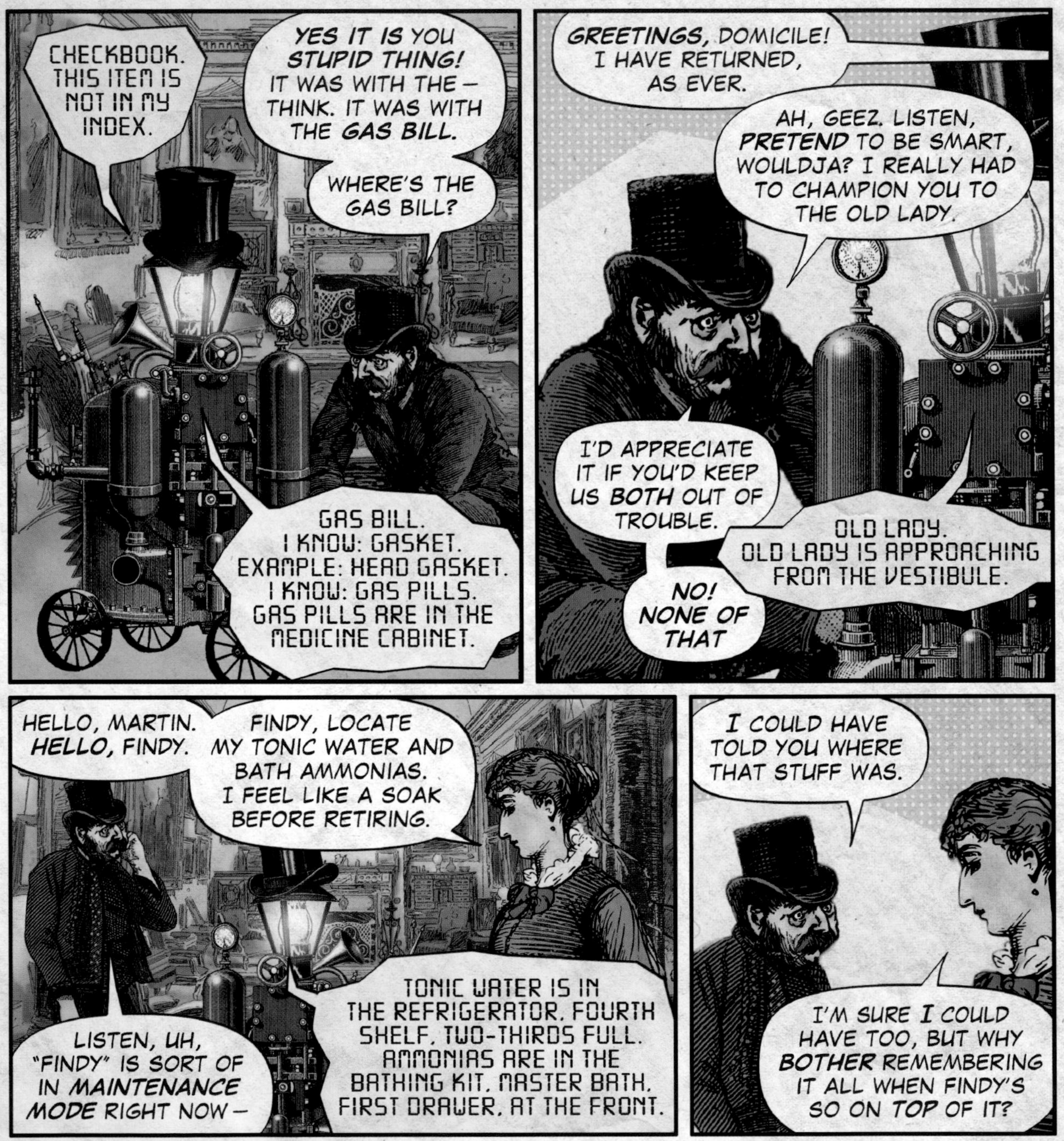
CHECKBOOK. THIS ITEM IS NOT IN MY INDEX.
YES IT IS YOU STUPID THING! IT WAS WITH THE— THINK. IT WAS WITH THE GAS BILL.
WHERE'S THE GAS BILL?
GAS BILL. I KNOW: GASKET. EXAMPLE: HEAD GASKET. I KNOW: GAS PILLS. GAS PILLS ARE IN THE MEDICINE CABINET.
GREETINGS, DOMICILE! I HAVE RETURNED, AS EVER.
AH, GEEZ. LISTEN, PRETEND TO BE SMART, WOULDJA? I REALLY HAD TO CHAMPION YOU TO THE OLD LADY.
I'D APPRECIATE IT IF YOU'D KEEP US BOTH OUT OF TROUBLE.
OLD LADY. OLD LADY IS APPROACHING FROM THE VESTIBULE.
NO! NONE OF THAT
HELLO, MARTIN. HELLO, FINDY.
FINDY, LOCATE MY TONIC WATER AND BATH AMMONIAS. I FEEL LIKE A SOAK BEFORE RETIRING.
LISTEN, UH, "FINDY" IS SORT OF IN MAINTENANCE MODE RIGHT NOW—
TONIC WATER IS IN THE REFRIGERATOR. FOURTH SHELF. TWO-THIRDS FULL. AMMONIAS ARE IN THE BATHING KIT. MASTER BATH. FIRST DRAWER. AT THE FRONT.
I COULD HAVE TOLD YOU WHERE THAT STUFF WAS.
I'M SURE I COULD HAVE TOO, BUT WHY BOTHER REMEMBERING IT ALL WHEN FINDY'S SO ON TOP OF IT?

progress, imagination, learning, and at all times pushing for the advancement of knowledge. To all children:

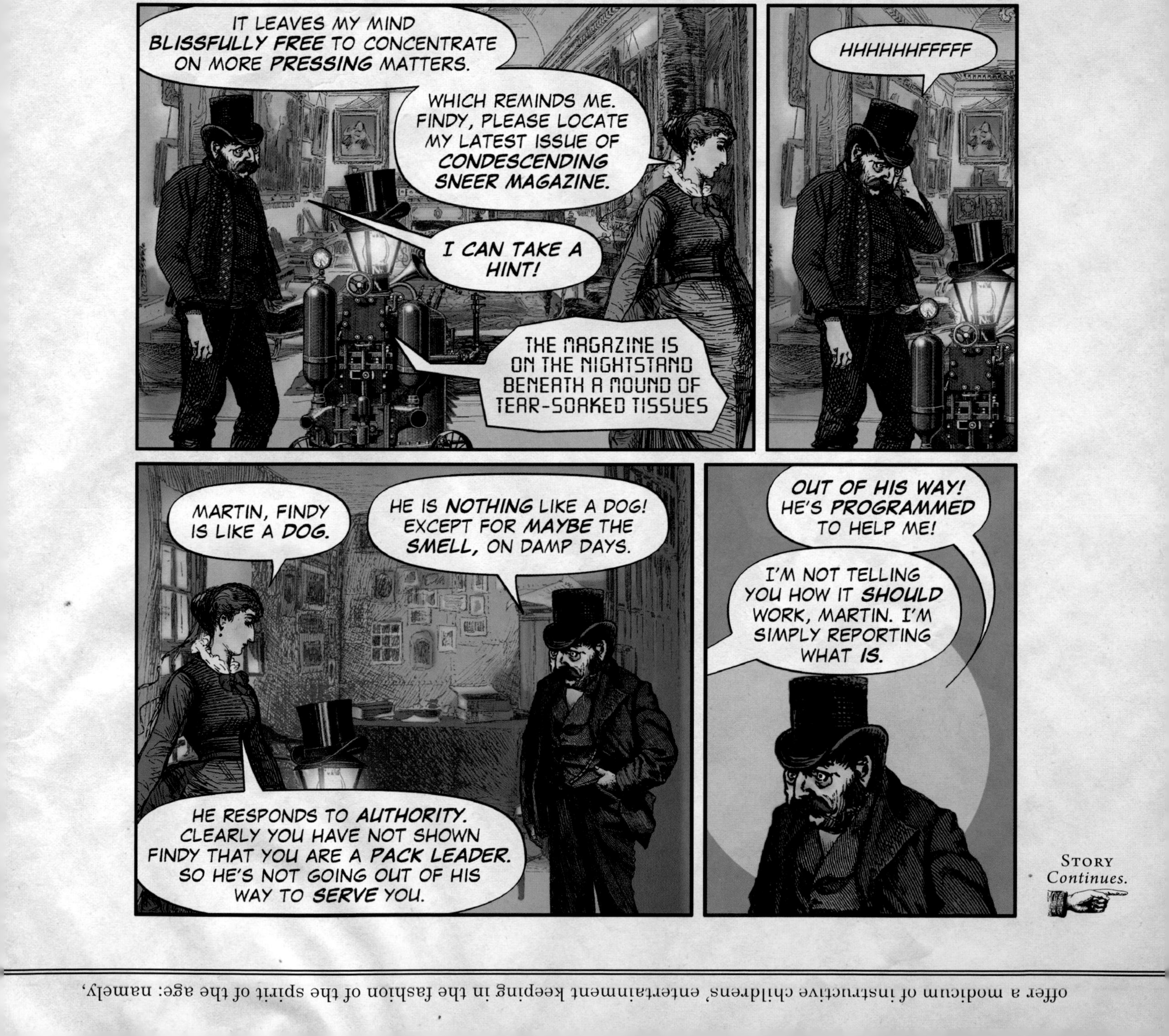
IT LEAVES MY MIND BLISSFULLY FREE TO CONCENTRATE ON MORE PRESSING MATTERS.
WHICH REMINDS ME. FINDY, PLEASE LOCATE MY LATEST ISSUE OF CONDESCENDING SNEER MAGAZINE.
I CAN TAKE A HINT!
THE MAGAZINE IS ON THE NIGHTSTAND BENEATH A MOUND OF TEAR-SOAKED TISSUES
HHHHHHFFFFF
MARTIN, FINDY IS LIKE A DOG.
HE IS NOTHING LIKE A DOG! EXCEPT FOR MAYBE THE SMELL, ON DAMP DAYS.
HE RESPONDS TO AUTHORITY. CLEARLY YOU HAVE NOT SHOWN FINDY THAT YOU ARE A PACK LEADER. SO HE'S NOT GOING OUT OF HIS WAY TO SERVE YOU.
OUT OF HIS WAY! HE'S PROGRAMMED TO HELP ME!
I'M NOT TELLING YOU HOW IT SHOULD WORK, MARTIN. I'M SIMPLY REPORTING WHAT IS.

STORY
Continues.

offer a modicum of instructive childrens' entertainment keeping in the fashion of the spirit of the age: namely,

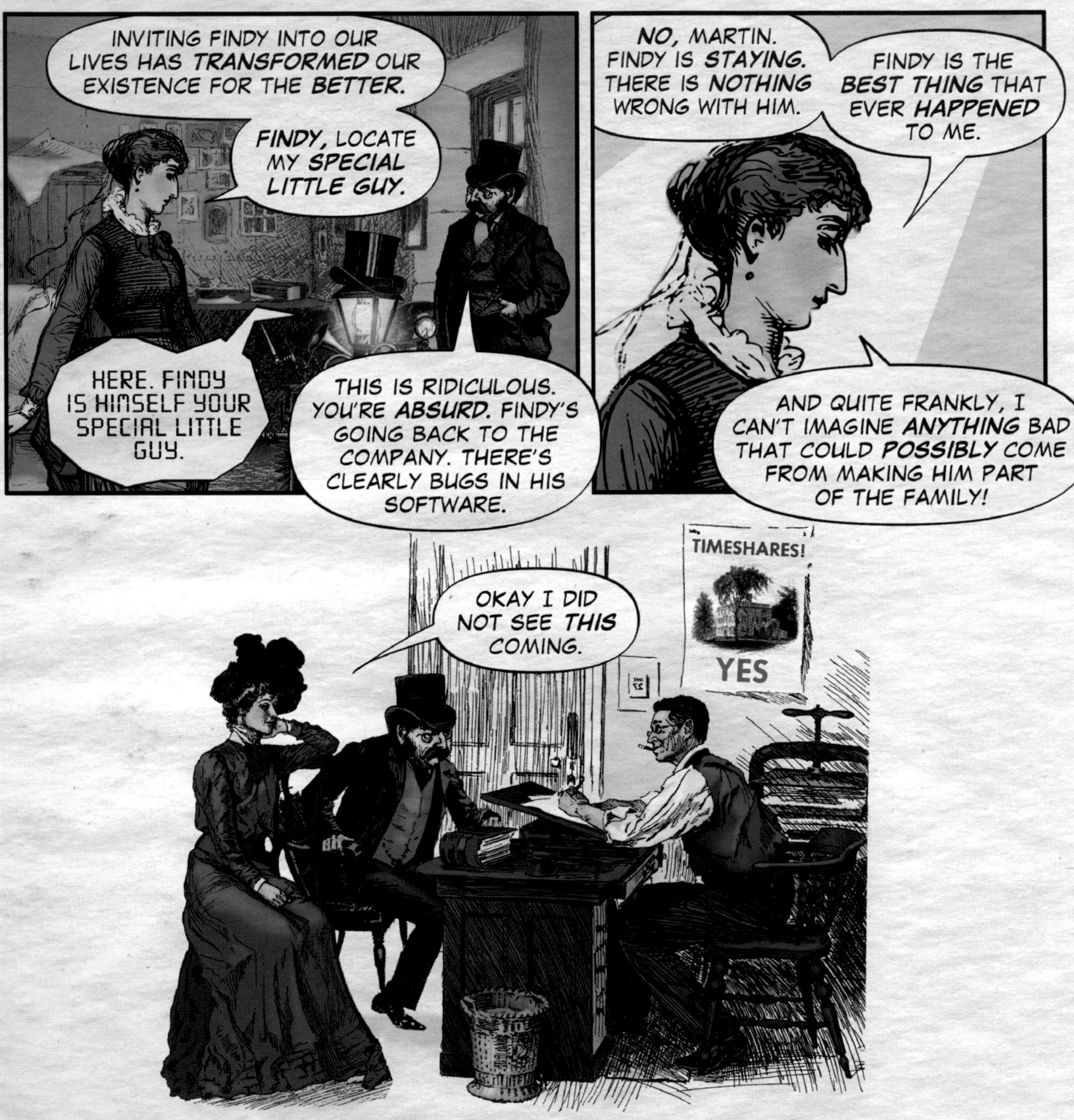

INVITING FINDY INTO OUR LIVES HAS TRANSFORMED OUR EXISTENCE FOR THE BETTER.
FINDY, LOCATE MY SPECIAL LITTLE GUY.
HERE. FINDY IS HIMSELF YOUR SPECIAL LITTLE GUY.
THIS IS RIDICULOUS. YOU'RE ABSURD. FINDY'S GOING BACK TO THE COMPANY. THERE'S CLEARLY BUGS IN HIS SOFTWARE.
NO, MARTIN. FINDY IS STAYING. THERE IS NOTHING WRONG WITH HIM.
FINDY IS THE BEST THING THAT EVER HAPPENED TO ME.
AND QUITE FRANKLY, I CAN'T IMAGINE ANYTHING BAD THAT COULD POSSIBLY COME FROM MAKING HIM PART OF THE FAMILY!
TIMESHARES!
YES
OKAY I DID NOT SEE THIS COMING.

children are drawn naturally. We are thankful to the author and editors of „Wondermark" to allow us this space to

Exploded Views.

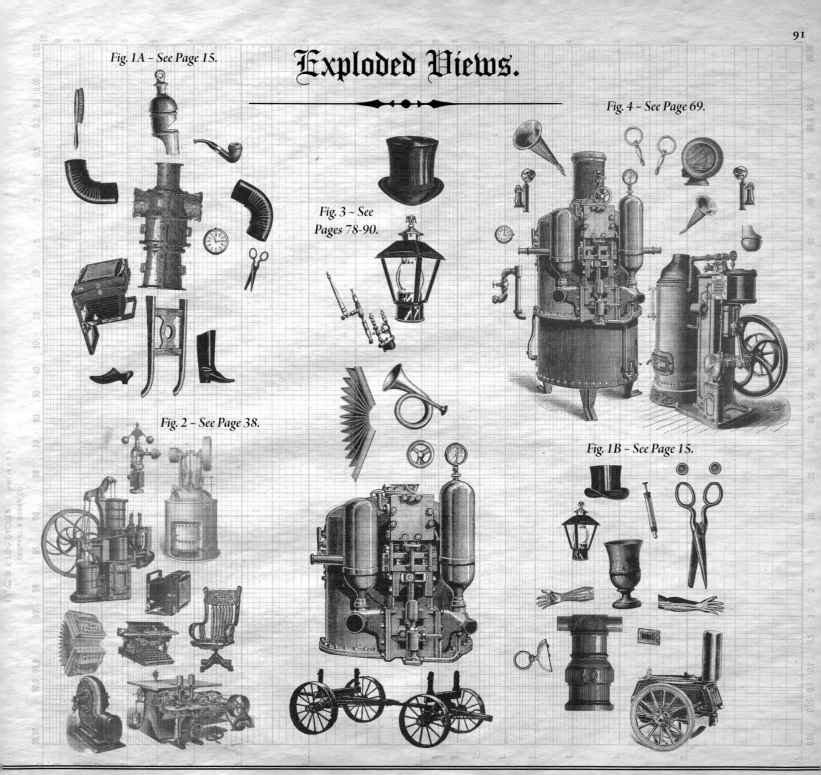

Fig. 1A ~ See Page 15.

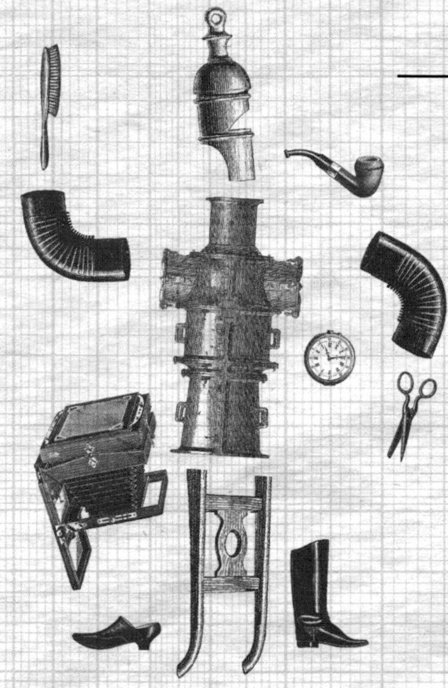

Fig. 3 ~ See Pages 78-90.

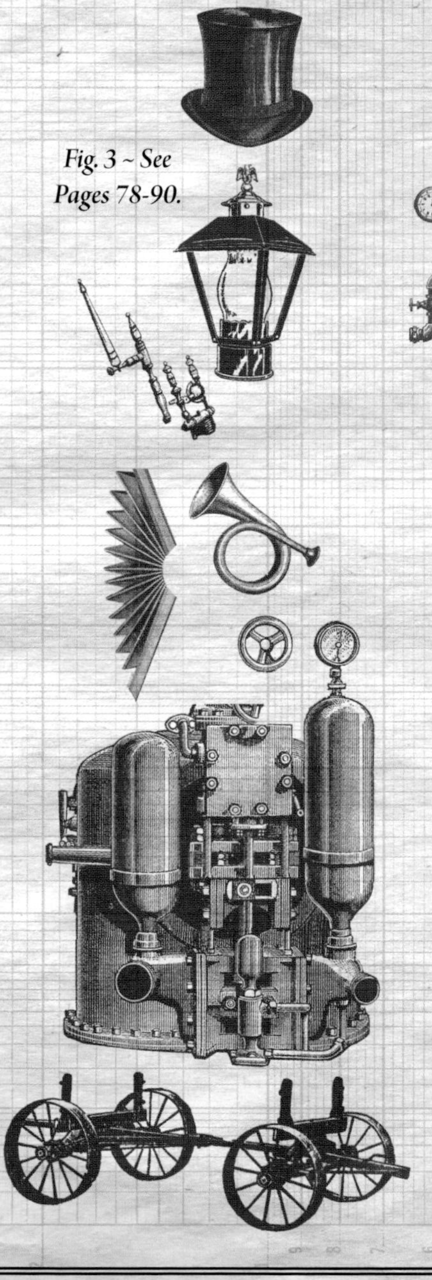

Fig. 4 ~ See Page 69.

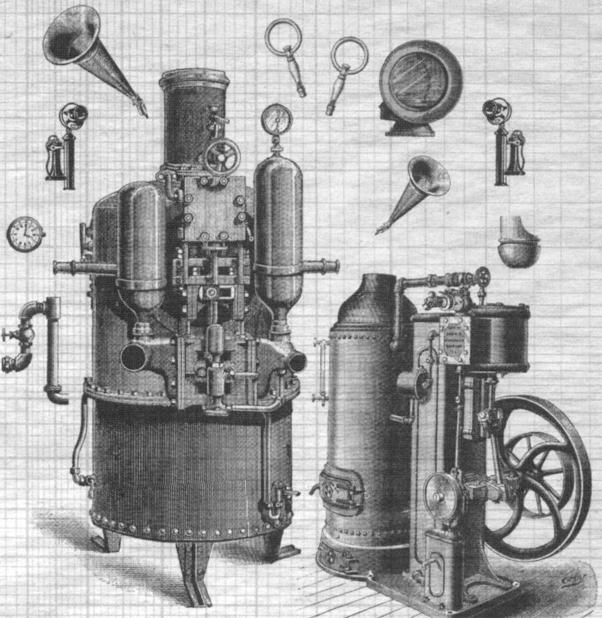

Fig. 2 ~ See Page 38.

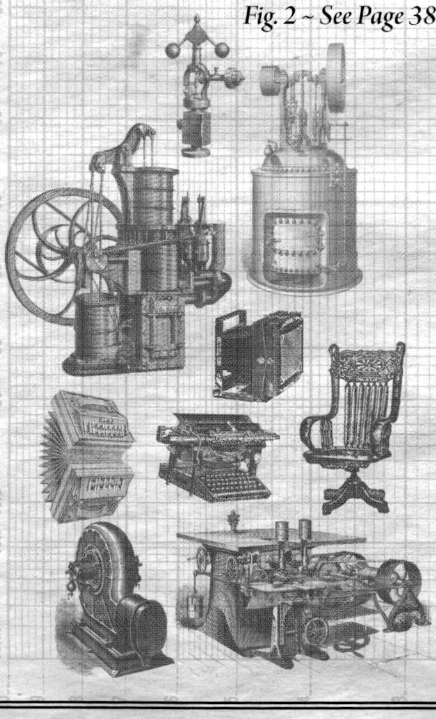

Fig. 1B ~ See Page 15.

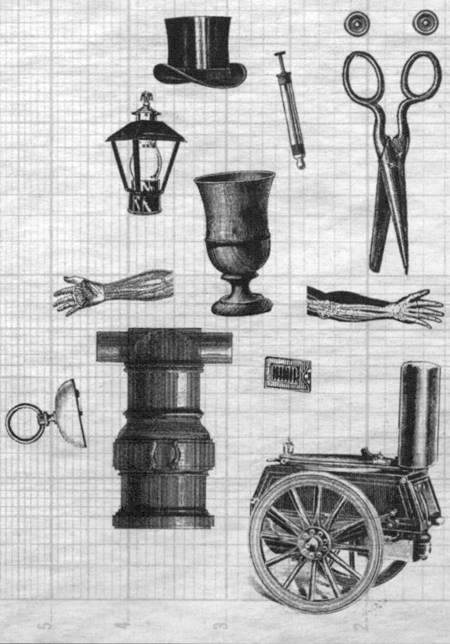

But till now, too little institutional childrens' instruction had taken on the shape of play, in a manner to which

Exploded Views.

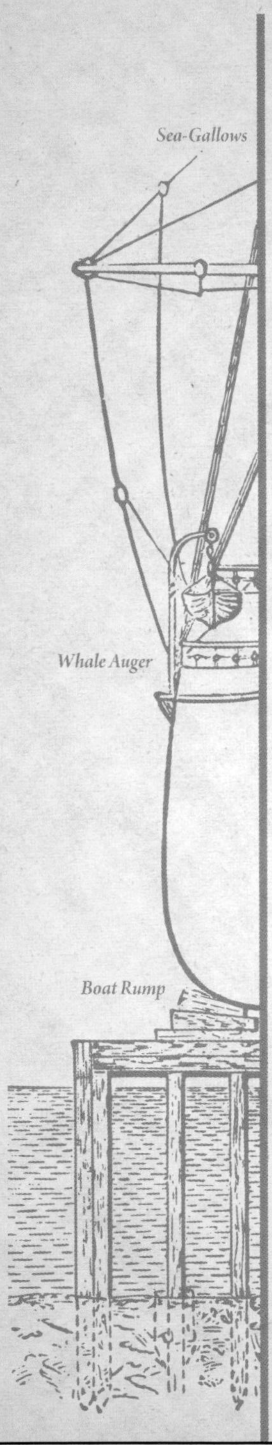
Sea-Gallows
Whale Auger
Boat Rump

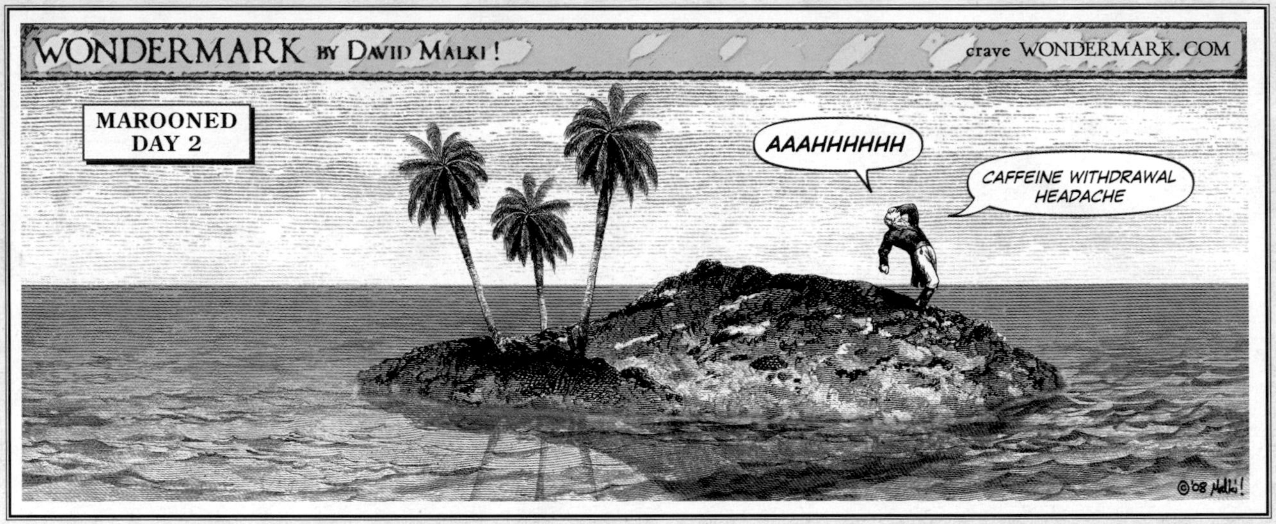
WONDERMARK BY DAVID MALKI !
crave WONDERMARK.COM
MAROONED DAY 2
AAAHHHHHH
CAFFEINE WITHDRAWAL HEADACHE
©'08 Malki!

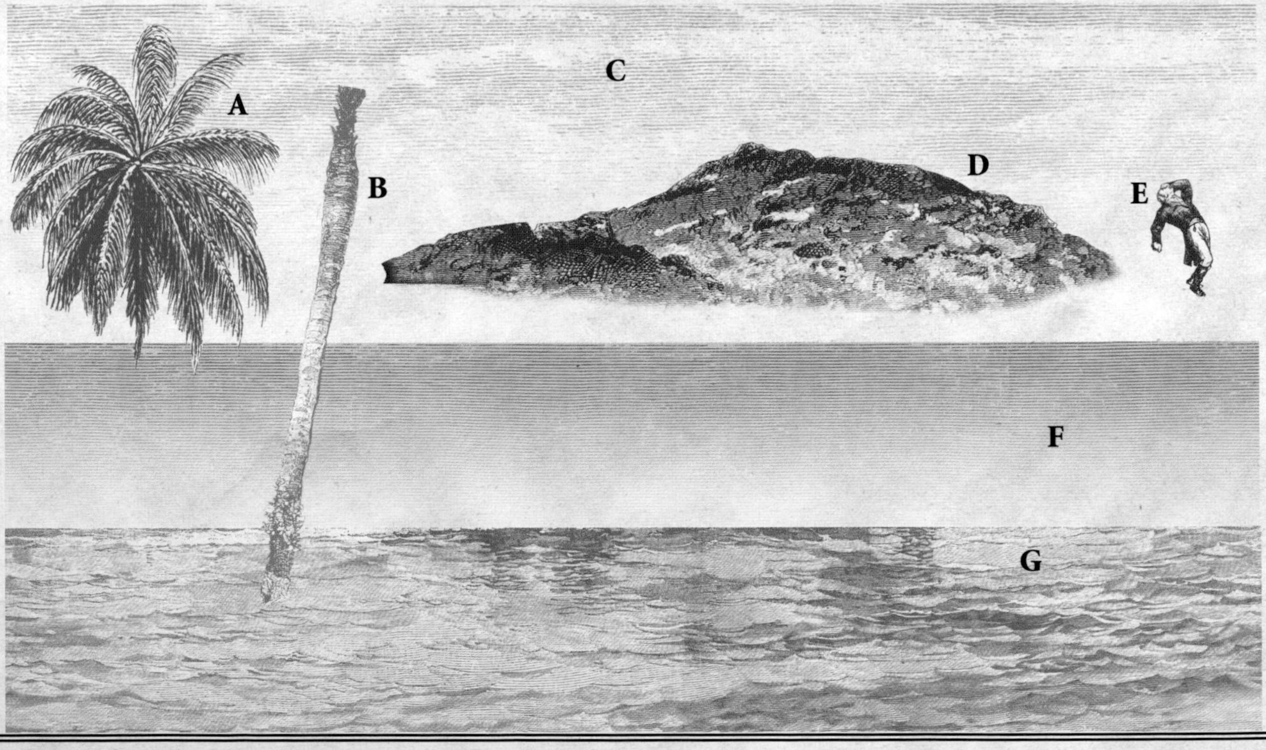
A
B
C
D
E
F
G

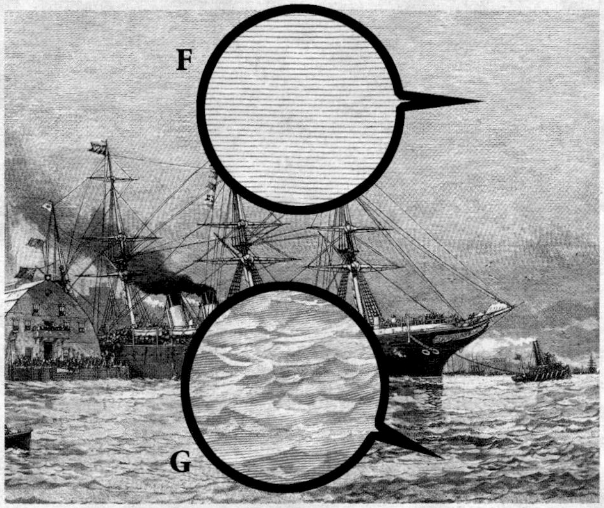
F
G

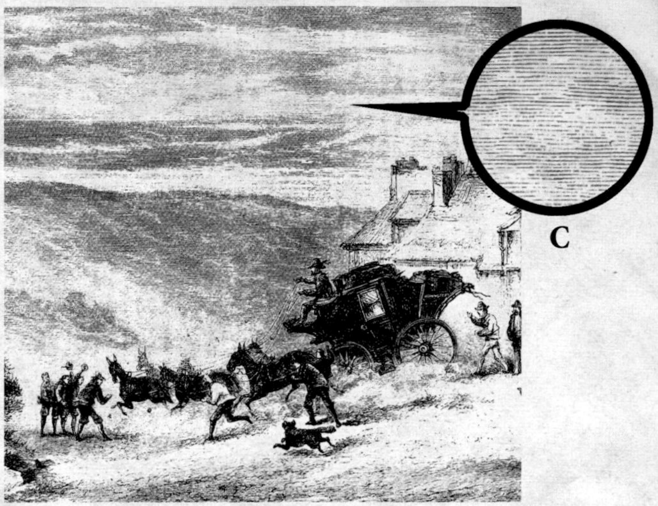
C

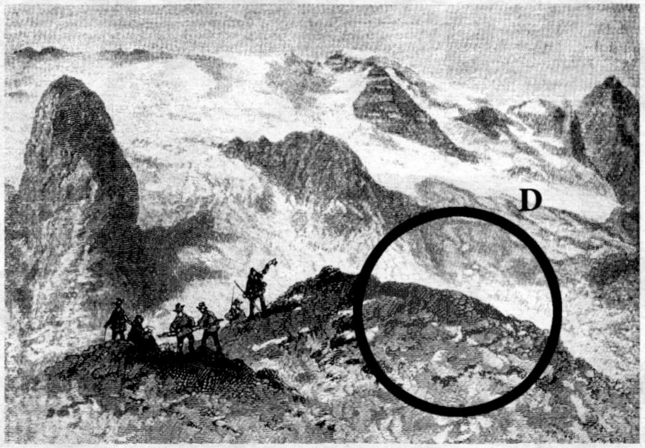
D

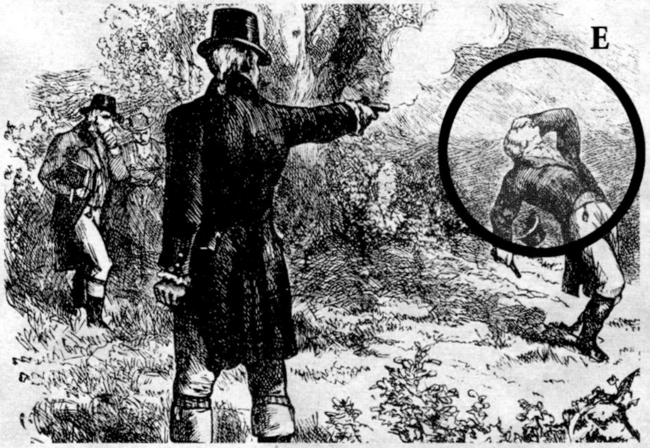
E

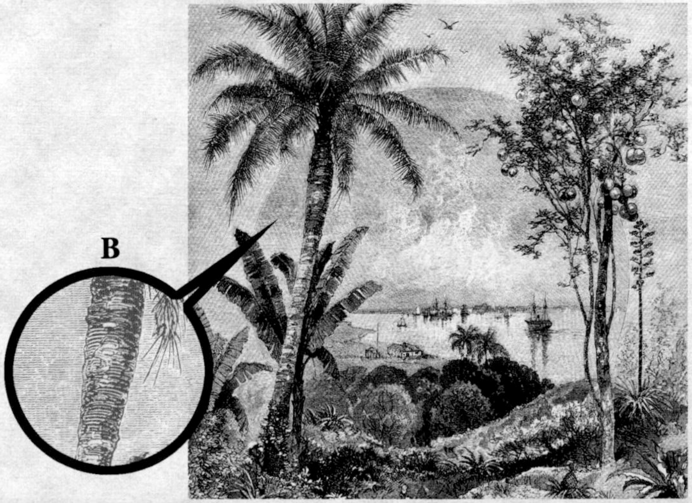
B

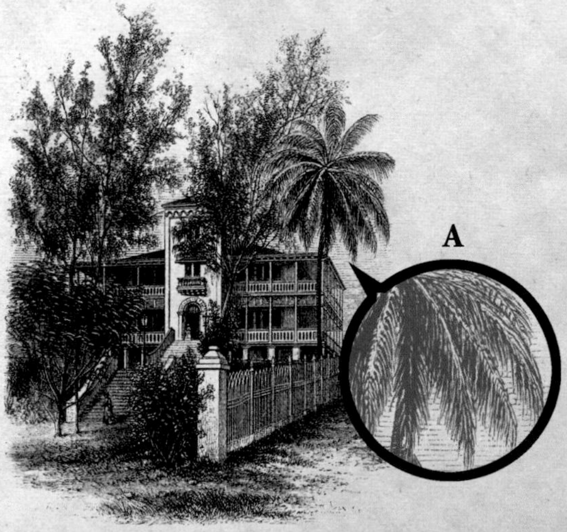
A

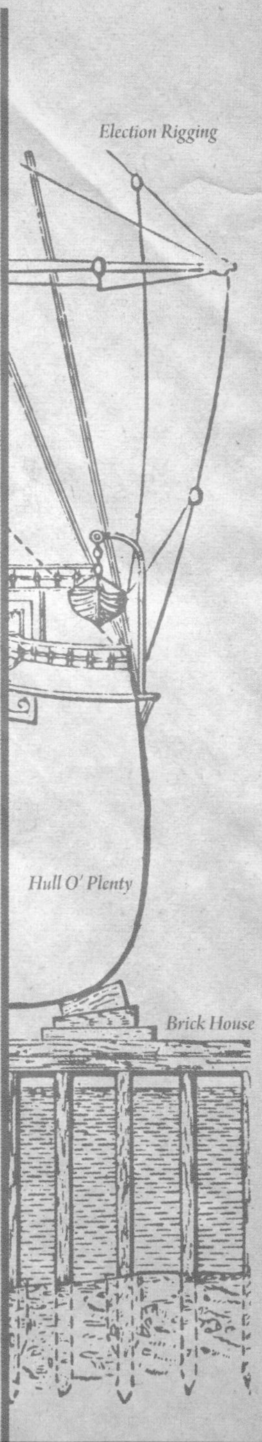
Election Rigging
Hull O' Plenty
Brick House

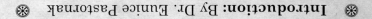

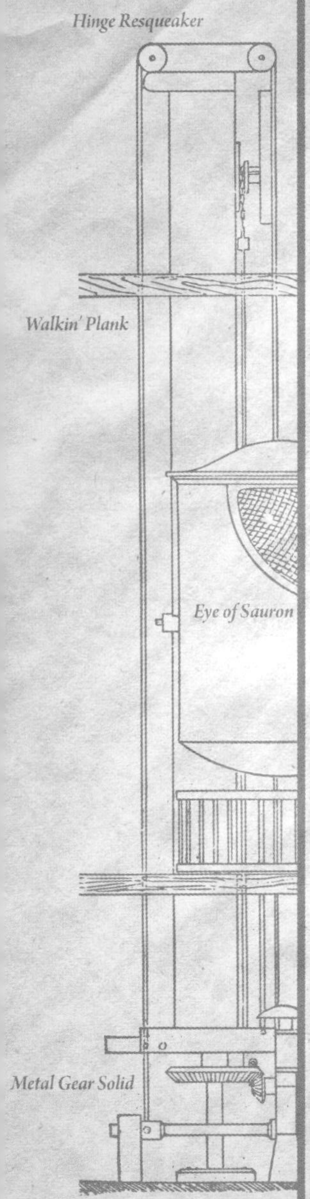
Hinge Resqueaker
Walkin' Plank
Eye of Sauron
Metal Gear Solid

Bears in Ill-Fitting Hats

A GALLERY FOR THE BENEFIT OF SCHOLARS.

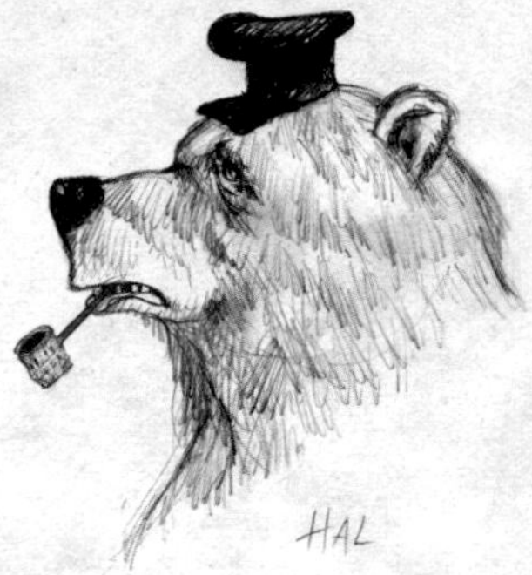
HAL

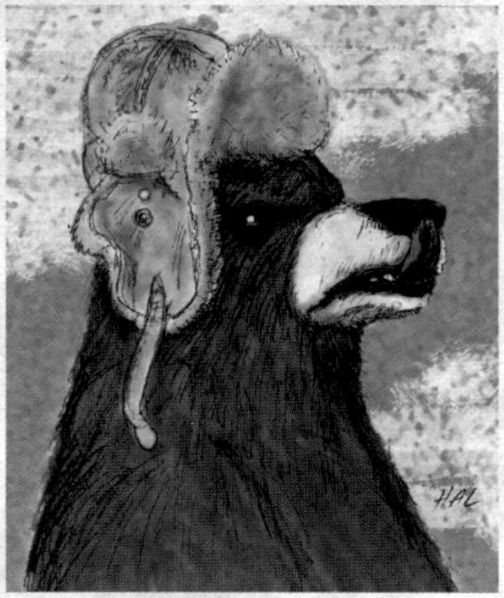
HAL

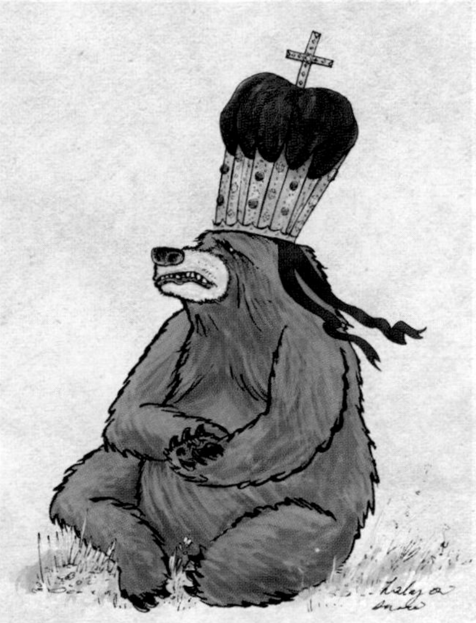

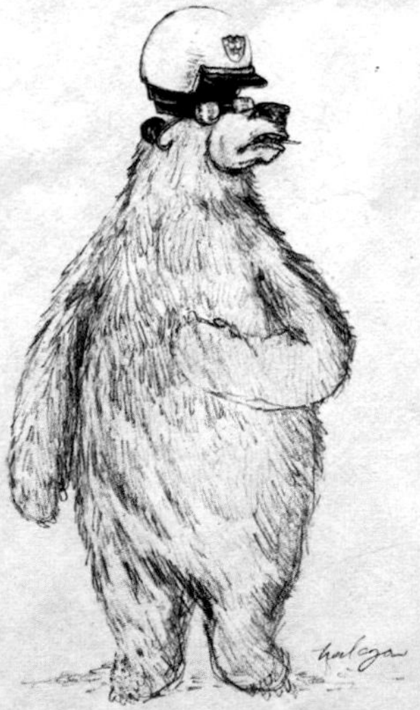

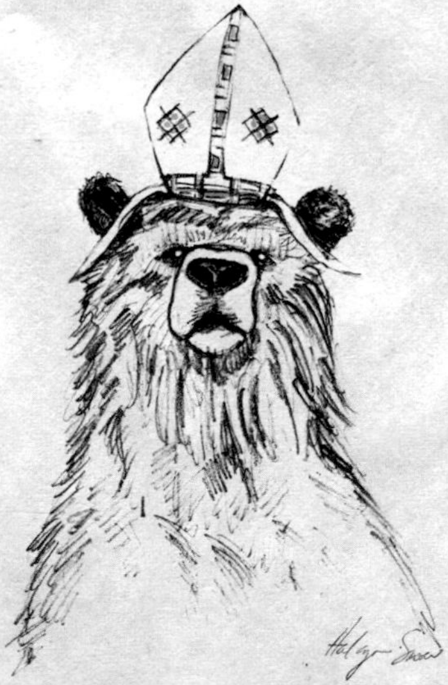

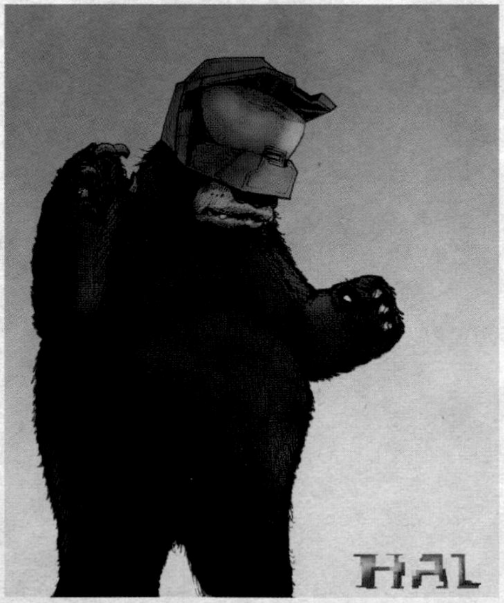
HAL

Illustrations by Michael Peterson, a.k.a. Halcyon Snow • halcyonsnow.com

Michael spearheaded a landmark bears-in-ill-fitting-hats documentation project that yielded hundreds of records, which will doubtless be invaluable to future researchers.:

WWW.FLICKR.COM/GROUPS/BEARS-IN-ILL-FITTING-HATS

And Gratefully Acknowledging The Assistance Of The Learning Foundation of Philadelphia.

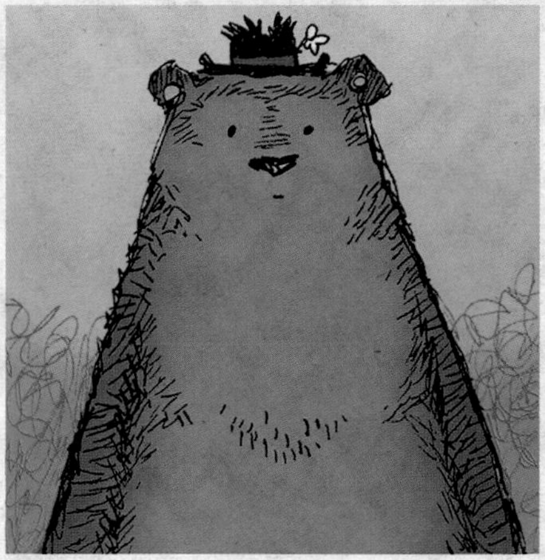

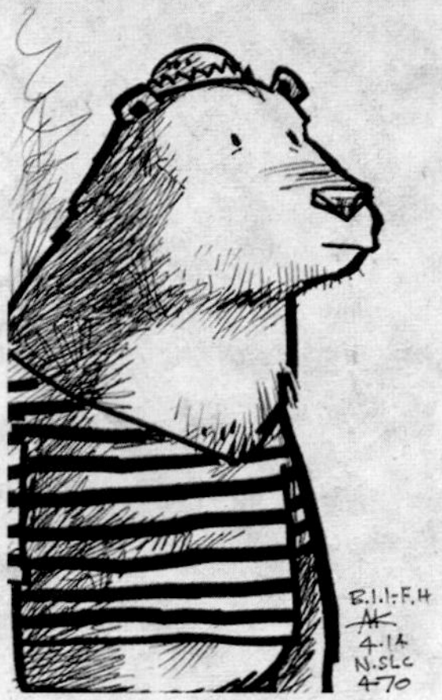

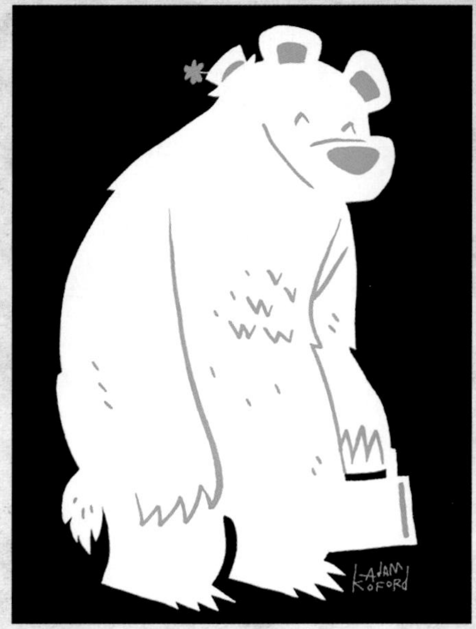
ADAM KOFORD

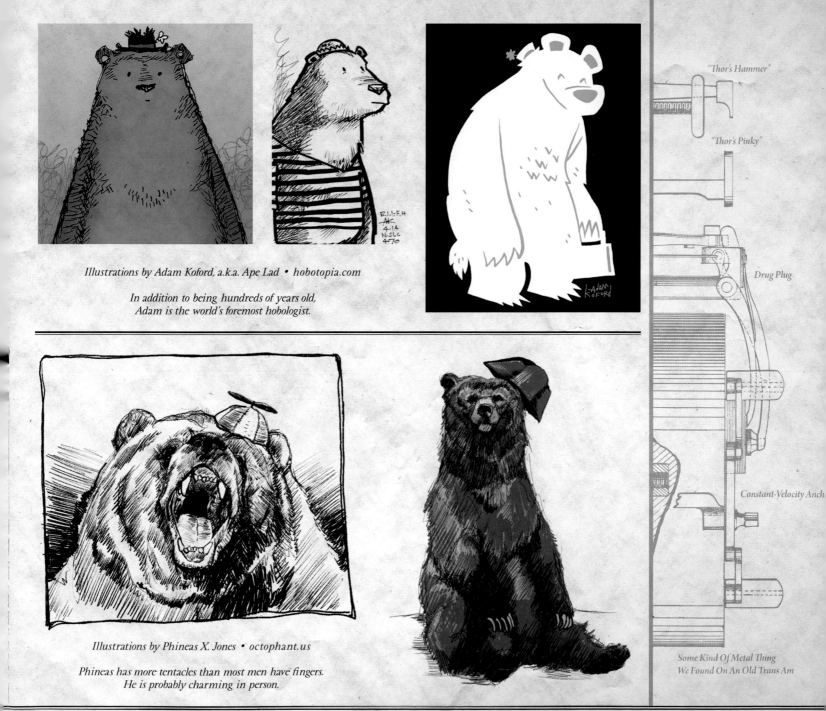

Illustrations by Adam Koford, a.k.a. Ape Lad • hobotopia.com

In addition to being hundreds of years old,
Adam is the world's foremost hobologist.

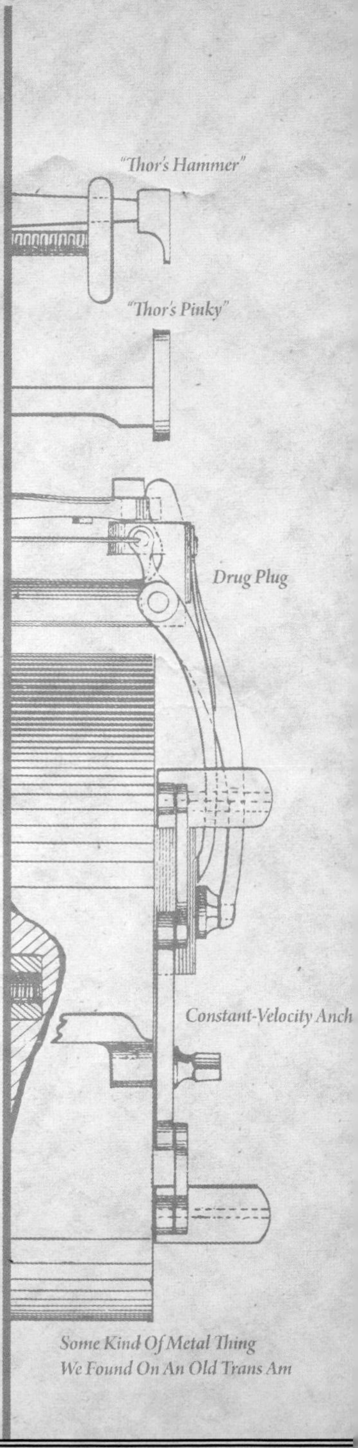
"Thor's Hammer"
"Thor's Pinky"
Drug Plug
Constant-Velocity Anch
Some Kind Of Metal Thing
We Found On An Old Trans Am

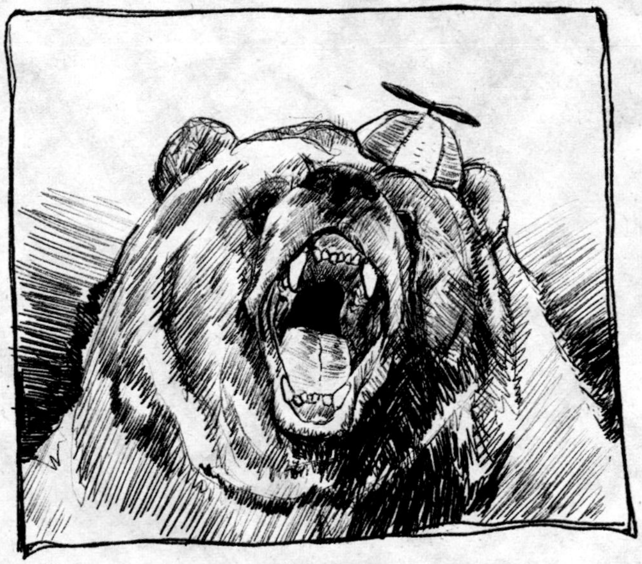

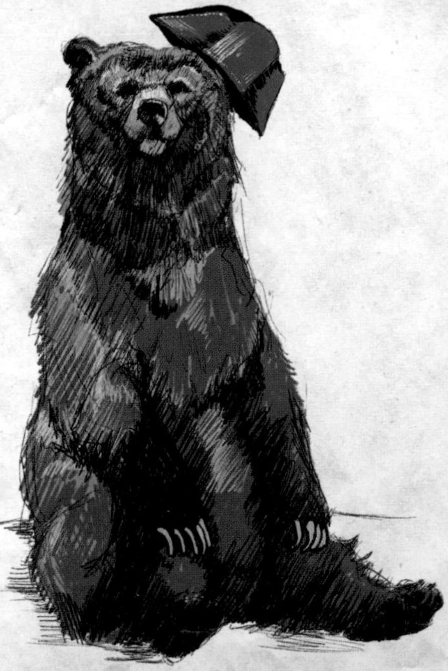

Illustrations by Phineas X. Jones • octophant.us

Phineas has more tentacles than most men have fingers.
He is probably charming in person.

Author's Note.

Oil Trampler
Bum Rod
Kink Array
Base of Ace

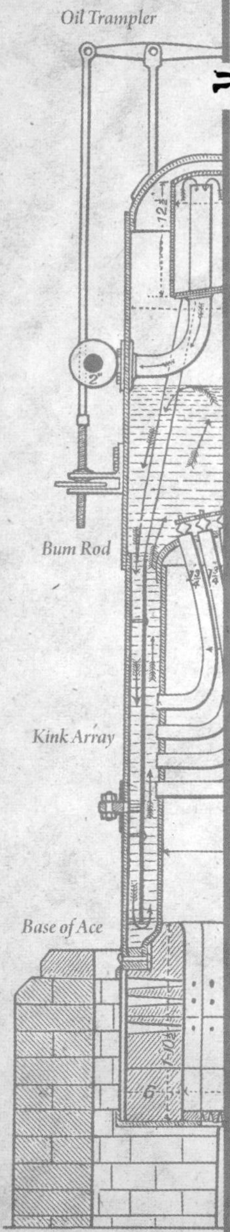

In any volume that attempts to capture the essence of a given moment in history, there will be necessary flaws, errors, compromises, shortcomings, mistakes, approximations, fabrications, misrepresentations, libelous statements and lies. In an attempt to minimize the above, I have taken my subject on from a variety of angles—if you have completed this book, then you have read comics; you have seen ephemera; you have puzzled over diagrams; you have admired cartoon drawings of bears and you have probably wept a little. In this way have I tried to give as full as possible a picture of a world that could never be captured by a single means alone.

But what world is it? I can admit now, on the final page of the book, that the world I have described is an ILLUSION of my own invention, and you have all been my sorry subjects in a hellacious experiment. My aim was to collect the imaginations of many and focus them precisely into concert; my hypothesis was that I could somehow synthesize corn-oil from the whole of it. I was either mistaken, or I simply need a larger experimental population. Please—tell your friends.

Top of the Morning
Intern Hut
Mole Condo

I AM ABSURDLY GRATEFUL TO

Carly Monardo, **Marcus Thiele**, **Alyssa Stock**, **Jolly Rotten**, and **Phil Obermarck**, for their beautiful coloring of various elements of this book;

Halcyon Snow, **Ape Lad**, and **Phineas X. Jones**, for allowing me to reprint their illustrations, and for creating them, unbidden, to begin with;

Zachary Sigelko, for diligently assisting with the preparation of the textures that populate these pages, and many other things;

Dave Land at Dark Horse, for his unending patience and for not relaying to me the browbeating he must certainly hear from his superiors;

My wife Nikki, for her inexplicably deep well of unwavering support (my love, you should really get that checked out);

You, the reader, of course. My heart tries hard to hug you. Thank you.

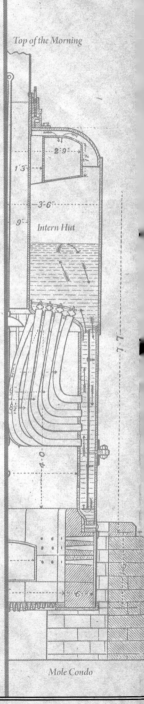